Latin American Prospects for the 1970s

edited by
David H. Pollock
Arch R. M. Ritter

Latin American Prospects for the 1970s
What Kinds of Revolutions?

PRAEGER SPECIAL STUDIES IN INTERNATIONAL POLITICS AND GOVERNMENT

Praeger Publishers   New York   Washington   London

PRAEGER PUBLISHERS
111 Fourth Avenue, New York, N.Y. 10003, U.S.A.
5, Cromwell Place, London S.W.7, England

Published in the United States of America in 1973
by Praeger Publishers, Inc.

Library of Congress Catalog Card Number: 72-86841

Printed in the United States of America

With the entry of Great Britain into the European Common
Market and the consequent uncertainty as to the future role of the
Commonwealth, Canada is in the process of redefining its basic
relationships with the rest of the world. As the Preface of this book
notes, one aspect of that redefinition is a more formal, if still tentative,
relationship with the Latin American countries. Canada has just
become a member of the Inter-American Development Bank and only
recently has been accorded Permanent Observer status at the Organization of American States. Moreover, increasing concern over preserving its national identity has led to substantial intellectual ferment
in Canada, most sharply evidenced by a vivid debate over the role of
the multinational (i.e., U.S.) corporations. These concerns are of
course paralleled in Latin America, although perhaps in more dramatic
ways. It is not surprising then that in Canada there should be an
increasing interest in Latin American developmental issues, an interest
evidenced by the convening of a conference on these issues at Carlton
University, Ottawa, in the autumn of 1970.

The individual studies in this work are a provocative introduction
to the intellectual ferment that now prevails with respect to development
questions in Latin America. As noted in the Preface they do not pretend to provide a comprehensive thesis about Latin American development. This is just as well, for if there is one characteristic that
stands out in the early years of this decade, in contrast to the previous
decade, it is the degree to which cherished concepts about Latin
American development—political, economic, and social—are open to
challenge. The intellectual moorings of the past have been cut loose
without any clear guidelines as to what is to be substituted. The studies
presented here evidence this fluid situation. Their tone is less one
of certainty than of tentative hypotheses, still to be tested as to their
basic validity.

The Alliance for Progress was premised on the theme that
political democracy, economic growth, and social reform were in the
short run not only complementary but mutually reinforcing. There
is now a greater awareness that for the immediate future these
objectives may be more nearly conflicting than complementary.
Paul Rosenstein-Rodan, in his chapter on "Planning for Full Employment in Latin America," evidences this awareness in his emphasis
on the need for clear choices among economic policy objectives. He
candidly acknowledges that there is a tradeoff between a growth.

oriented economic strategy and one with a more immediate income-redistribution objective. He opts for the growth strategy, restating the traditional view that it is easier to distribute the increment of income more equitably than to distribute poverty. Rosenstein-Rodan's study is noteworthy for its frank skepticism about the limited possibilities of improving the tradeoff by use of labor-intensive technology, a theory much in vogue among contemporary developmental thinkers. David Pollock is less pessimistic than his colleague about the possibility of reconciling the two objectives. Both studies reflect the professional economic discipline of the authors, in that they view the problem primarily from a technical point of view. Neither deals with the social and political aspects of emphasizing one or the other strategy, growth or redistribution.

A growth-oriented strategy, for example, by its very nature may maximize the income potential of the capital-accumulating middle- and upper-income classes, who are likely to save and invest, thus reinforcing their relative political power vis-à-vis the lower-income "consuming" sectors of the population. How willing are these more advanced sectors to see a significant part of their economic gains siphoned off to benefit the poorest (and therefore least powerful) segment of society? This is the central question that must be addressed in any discussion of the tradeoff between growth and redistribution. The stereotype of the wicked oligarch rudely standing in the way of economic progress of the more disadvantaged sectors of society has given way to a more sophisticated differentiation of interests within the "core" society in Latin America. The new middle class, defending its hard-won and often still precarious economic status, may now be the most serious obstacle preventing the rapid incorporation of the marginal elements of Latin American society into the economy and social fabric of those nations.

A strategy that maximizes the economic status and political power of the middle and upper strata of society thus may in practice not permit obtaining a significant percentage of the increment in income for the benefit of the lower strata. This is the lesson of Brazil, as Brady Tyson graphically shows in his chapter, "The Emerging Role of the Military as National Modernizers and Managers in Latin America: The Cases of Brazil and Peru." In Brazil it is the middle class as much as any other element of the society that supports the economic strategy of the military leaders who have ruled Brazil since the 1964 coup that overthrew President João Goulart. That strategy is based on impressively high economic growth rates, but as Robert McNamara, president of the World Bank, pointed out in his address to the Third UN Conference on Trade and Development (UNCTAD) in Santiago, Chile, in April 1972, that growth has been accompanied by an increasingly regressive distribution of income.

The alternative strategy is the one followed by Cuba in the 1960s. The Cuban revolutionaries, who came to power with Fidel Castro in 1959, concluded that the middle and upper classes would never permit a rapid redistribution of income and relative shift in political power in favor of the lowest-income strata of Cuban society. They therefore made the clear but cold-blooded choice of destroying the economic base and political power of the middle- and upper-income strata. The massive migration of Cubans into the United States via the Cuban "Freedom Flights" in the decade of the 1960s is a graphic manifestation of this policy decision. Arch Ritter's chapter on "Institutional Strategy and Economic Performance in Revolutionary Cuba" analyzes the high price paid by Cuba for the loss of managerial competence in the aftermath of the revolution. This loss of managerial capacity was one of the decisive factors in the poor economic growth performance of the Cuban economy in the 1960s. Critics of Cuba's economic growth performance, however, are often reluctant to face the fundamental question posed by the Cuban experience: would it have been possible to achieve the dramatic and sudden redistribution of income and change in social status of Cuba's lower class, manifested in nearly total adult literacy and improved standards of public health, without the destruction of the political power of the middle- and upper-income strata?

The Alliance for Progress was an attempt to provide a positive answer to that question. The post-Alliance period is marked by a search for a formula that will avoid the Cuban or Brazilian "extremes." Perhaps the most interesting attempt to devise a middle ground is that of Peru. The military regime that came to power in October 1968 has initiated an ambitious program of social reform. For the first time in Peruvian history a government through a far-reaching agrarian reform has struck at the roots of power of landed interests that have played such a dominant role in the history of that country. It has also initiated fundamental changes in the educational system, providing for the teaching of Indian children in their native Quechua tongue as well as the Spanish idiom.

The Peruvian regime now faces fundamental questions. On what terms should it permit foreign investment in mineral resources development? How far and how fast should it push agrarian reform? What should be the extent of worker participation in industry and agriculture? Should it implement the revolution primarily by military means or by creating a mass political base? As time goes on, and the military retains control of the governmental apparatus and political decision making, the military establishment risks assuming the characteristics of a political party, a process that already may be occurring.

Nevertheless it is a measure of the distance we have travelled in the past decade that, in this most conservative society in Latin

America, the process of change in the conditions of life of the great mass of Peruvian people has been initiated under the leadership of the two institutions, the military and the Catholic church, that at the beginning of the decade were viewed as major obstacles to achieving the goals of the Alliance for Progress. Carlos Astiz in two studies in this volume, "The Military Establishment as a Political Elite: The Peruvian Case" and "The Catholic Church in Latin American Politics: A Case Study of Peru" illuminates many of the factors that have made this possible.

The past decade however has also been marked by more radical attempts to achieve revolutionary change. Two Canadian authors, J. C. M. Ogelsby and G. S. Smith, in their respective chapters, "Some Observations on Latin American Guerrilla Movements" and "The Diplomat as Hostage: Reflections on Power and Violence in Latin America," analyze these more radical attempts through organized guerrilla movements and urban terrorist activities. Both conclude that these movements have received more notoriety than they have effected significant change. The authors are probably right in assessing the marginal impact of the guerrillas upon Latin American society. Their role may well have been, however, that of catalytic agents, embodying the specter of revolution rather than the reality, and consequently galvanizing such traditional institutions as the church and the military to reassess their fundamental roles in society.

In short, the contents of this book are designed more to whet the appetite, by introducing the reader to some of the more provocative themes now current in Latin American development thinking, than to provide definitive answers. As such, the volume should be particularly welcome in Canada, but more generally as well, providing a thoughtful reader with much to think about.

During the autumn of 1970 a conference entitled "Latin American Prospects for the 1970s: What Kinds of Revolutions?" was held at Carleton University in Ottawa under the joint auspices of the School of International Affairs and the Canadian Institute of International Affairs with assistance from the Canada Council. Approximately 200 persons, from Canada, Latin America, and the United States, took part in the working sessions of the conference. This book is a direct product of that conference.

In a certain sense the timing of the meeting coincided with the beginning of a new type of Canadian relationship with Latin America: a relationship that has subsequently become institutionalized in a variety of ways, such as membership in the Inter-American Development Bank, the Pan American Health Organization, and the establishment of a Permanent Observer Mission of Canada to the Organization of American States (OAS). Consequently one of the prime objectives of the conference was to acquaint Canadians in the academic community and in the governmental and business worlds with some of the diversity and complexity that is encapsuled in the words "Latin America."

Often, a conference held in North America dealing with Latin American development tends to be devoted to one or a few highly specialized issues, for instance, "Latin American development and exports," or "agrarian reform," or "the church and military," or "art and literature," or the like. Typically moreover such a theme is then followed by the name of a country "as a case history in point." The Carleton conference however did not follow this "single theme" approach. On the contrary, it deliberately sought to cast its net very widely, the guiding intention being to provide basic background information on and venture some future assessments about a wide number of functional problems that range throughout the length and breadth of Latin America.

This was done because Latin America is clearly not a homogeneous whole. It is quite the reverse in fact. Not only are there tremendous quantitative economic and geographic disparities between the different countries of the region (think merely of Brazil versus Bolivia, or Mexico versus Barbados) but perhaps even more important are the equally diverse qualitative differences characterizing the social, political, cultural, and ethical systems of the various countries. The need to throw some light on these myriad differences and yet not lose all sense of regional cohesiveness—for despite its heterogeneity

Latin America still possesses a distinctive sense of organic unity—provided both the challenge and the reason for bringing together such a large number of participants and themes at the Carleton conference.

The Appendix a lists the panorama of topics and gives the names of all those who presented formal papers or who otherwise participated in seminars, round tables, and discussion groups. The resulting dialogue proved to be very provocative and aroused much give-and-take. As a result it was decided to edit various of the more interesting papers and tapes. From this process finally emerged the texts that appear as chapters in the compendium that follows.

The editors ask in particular that the reader keep three additional explanatory comments in mind. The first is that the contents of this book reflect the structure of the Carleton conference that engendered the papers. Thus it is essential to remember that the book is not intended to provide a comprehensive or even a balanced survey of Latin American problems and solutions. Omitted for instance are detailed examinations of the present regimes in Chile, Argentina, Venezuela, and Colombia, whereas Brazil, Peru, and Cuba are given considerable coverage. Omitted moreover are final recommendations as to particular overall sets of policies that could for instance bring out (or avoid) certain types of structural sociopolitical and economic transformations. Similarly some important issues (such as employment) are given considerable attention whereas others (such as income distribution) are not accorded the priority they merit in a compendium that seeks to provide a panoramic survey of Latin American problems and prospects. Second, in the title of this book as in that of the conference, the words "Kinds of Revolutions" were deliberately written in plural. This was done, as Chapter 1 describes in more detail, to probe the complexity and diversity of the manifold "revolutionary" transformations that seem likely to dominate the Latin American scene during the rest of the 1970s, and even beyond. The word "revolutions" in sum was employed in its most pluralistic sense, encompassing anything from "The Green Revolution" to "The Revolution of Rising Expectations" to "The Fidelista Revolution." The third and final comment is that although some internationally known personages took part in the conference most of the participants were not so widely known. Thus it is hoped that the following chapters may add some new names and new ideas to the ever-growing postwar literature concerned with Latin American development. As "Latinists"—both within the region and outside of it—look back over the postwar era and seek to set out some milestones that could serve as guideposts to the 1970s, perhaps this volume can help to facilitate that process. The authors hope so.

CONTENTS

    integrates   33
World War II: A Period of Hiatus   35
The 1950s: The Emergence of an In-
    digenous Ideology   36
The Alliance for Progress: Its Origin
    and Aftermath   38
The 1970s and Beyond: The Past as a
    Guide to the Future   41

PART II: KEY POLICY AREAS FOR THE 1970s

3   OBSTACLES TO DEVELOPMENT IN LATIN
    AMERICA: AN EVALUATION OF THE PLAN-
    NING PROCESS   47
    Harold A. Wood

4   REGIONAL ALLOCATION OF INDUSTRIAL
    CAPACITY IN THE LATIN AMERICAN FREE
    TRADE ASSOCIATION   58
    Jaleel Ahmad

    Industrial Policy in LAFTA   61
    Problems of Scale and External Effects   63
    Structural Disabilities   64
    Equitable Distribution of Regional
        Activities   66

5   THE PEARSON AND PREBISCH REPORTS:
    THE CRUCIAL ISSUE OF UNEMPLOYMENT   70
    David H. Pollock

    Introduction   70
    Three Points of Fundamental Identities   71
        The "Partnership" and "Convergence"
            Principles   71
        Mutual Reinforcement Politically   72
        Intellectual Agreement on Specific
            Measures of International Eco-
            nomic Collaboration   73
    Four Points of Divergence   76
        An Inventory of Recommendations Versus
            an Organic Ideological Framework   76

LIST OF TABLES

LIST OF FIGURES

INTRODUCTION

**REVOLUTION
IN LATIN AMERICA:
AN OVERVIEW**
Arch R. M. Ritter
David H. Pollock

For many decades but in particular since the 1930s Latin
America has been in the throes of economic, social, and political
changes of "revolutionary" dimension. During the 1970s these forces
for change will continue to grip Latin America. Indeed, due to the
stability or resiliency (or perhaps merely the obstinacy and inertia)
of many established institutions and attitudes, it is likely that such
changes will be increasingly accompanied by "revolutionary" and
"counterrevolutionary" violence and political upheaval.

Must violence be an inexorable prerequisite for the types of
political changes required to bring about the varied development
objectives of the countries of Latin America? That question is both
provocative and debatable. But, clearly, if violent upheaval and blood-
shed are to be minimized let alone avoided in the 1970s vigorous
actions of a "revolutionary" nature are required in a great many
areas such as employment creation, income redistribution, economic
integration, regional development planning, choice of technology,
foreign investment policy, population policy, social planning, and
economic and political democratization. Indeed, vigorous actions in
these policy areas will have to be taken by all prospective political
regimes in Latin America, whether "reformist" or "revolutionary,"
if basic developmental problems are to be squarely faced and overcome, and if the covert violence done to people through malnutrition,
bad health, and poverty as well as overt repressive violence are to
be eliminated.

Because of the uniqueness of different national historical traditions, economic bases, social structures, and power configurations;
because of the unpredictability of the behavior of some groups and
classes; because of ideological heterogeneity of the Latin American
countries; and because of the complexities of socioeconomic and
political change; simple generalizations can rarely be made without

distorting and deforming the realities of Latin America. Therefore
the studies comprising this book do not pretend to provide a general
prescription for making or avoiding "revolution," nor do they try to
sketch any forecasts of prospective change in Latin America. Rather,
the purpose of this book, as of the conference from which these chapters were generated (see Appendix a), is to probe and sample the
types of change that are likely to occur in the 1970s. The coverage
of the book is thus broad, since the universe from which the "sample"
of probes is drawn is very large indeed. The sample is necessarily
restricted by space limitations. One set of studies in Part II of the
book examines some of the types of radical and imaginative policies
required to deal with the problems currently confronting Latin America.
Another set examines certain groups, including the church, guerrillas,
and in particular military elites that are playing and will continue to
play important roles in reform mongering or revolution making. In
Part IV recent experiences of a number of countries and regions of
Latin America pertaining to the continuance of political, social, and
economic change are examined.

The purpose of this chapter is to provide a brief initial exploration into the prospects for revolution in Latin America. After an
examination of the word "revolution"—a most overused and misused
term—the general problems confronting many Latin American nations
are outlined, together with the types of policies that will be required
if the problems are to be tackled effectively. Following this is an
outline and critique of a currently popular theory which concludes
that violent political upheaval is the only means by which meaningful
economic and social changes can be introduced. The unpredictability
of the future behavior of Latin America's military and the middle
classes is stressed in the final section.

THE SEMANTICS OF "REVOLUTION"

Before we discuss the "prospects of revolution in Latin America
in the 1970s" a semantic digression is necessary on that most promis-
cuously employed term "revolution."

Revolution as "Change"

In recent decades the term "revolution" has become progressively debased at the hands of social scientists, journalists, and
practical politicians, in that it has been used so freely and loosely
as to no longer have any single or even generally accepted definition.
In its broadest sense it has been used to label almost any qualitative

structural change in the polity, economy, or society. In this sense
for instance the process of industrialization is revolutionary if the
new industrial technology significantly alters the roles of individuals
caught up in the process—their work habits, their places of residence,
their life styles, and in time their consciousness, political and otherwise.

Historians, social scientists, and futurologists have used the
word "revolution" to label certain technological and economic changes
that have social and political ramifications. They speak, for example,
of "Industrial Revolution," "Commercial Revolution," "Agricultural
Revolution," "Computer Revolution," and more recently of "Green
Revolution" and "Technetronic Revolution." Politicians, pundits, and
political scientists, among others, have used the term to label various
political phenomena that have economic and social ramifications.
Thus we have "Quiet Revolution" (as in Quebec under Premier Jean
Lesage), "Guerrilla Revolution," "Puritan Revolution," "Nasserite
Revolution," "Revolution with Liberty," the "New American Revolution"
(once proposed by President Nixon as well as various "new left" groups),
and finally unqualified "Revolution" (as in Cuba). The term has also
been used in a social context as in "Social Revolution," "Cultural
Revolution," and "Revolution of Rising Expectations." It would not be
surprising to see many of these types of revolution occurring in Latin
America (and elsewhere) in the decade of the 1970s. Indeed it would
be surprising if they did not occur. But this in itself merely highlights
the generally loose manner in which the word "revolution" has been
increasingly used.

Revolution as Coercive Overthrowal of Governments

The term "revolution" has also been used in a second sense to
refer to any situation in which "physical force (or the convincing
threat of it) has actually been used successfully to overthrow a government or regime."[1]

According to this definition political violence and revolution in
Latin America (excluding a few countries such as those in the Commonwealth Caribbean) have been fairly recurrent phenomena. Between
the achievement of independence from Spain and 1965, for instance,
some 213 such revolutions had occurred, with at least 40 taking place
from 1950 to the end of 1964.[2] Using this second definition it is
rather safe to predict that there will be more of the same, with respect
to the "prospects for revolution in the 1970s". Moreover, in view of
the sacrosanct nature of the term "revolution" in Latin America,
many future coups or barracks putsches (cuartelazos) will likely
attempt to legitimize themselves through the use of this label.

Revolution as Changing the Rules of the
Political Game

In a third and more restrictive sense the word "revolution" is often used to refer specifically to a large-scale change in the power structure of a society, accompanied by a reformulation of the rules of the political game and inspired by "grand designs" or utopian visions of improved if not perfect future societies. A similar definition was made by Luis Ratinoff, "There are certain changes which affect the mechanics and the dynamics of the society to produce changes. When you have a change or replacement of the mechanism that itself produces change, then you have a revolution."[3] Usually, but not always, such changes in the distribution of power between groups, sectors, or classes are related to the redistribution of property rights. This is so because political power typically flows from the ownership or control of natural and capital resources. Thus the "Green Revolution" would not be revolutionary in this sense if it merely reinforced the power of landlords vis-à-vis sharecroppers or landless laborers and if there were no redistribution of property rights, income flows, and political power. Revolution in this narrower sense would undoubtedly be accompanied by some of the first-mentioned types of economic and social revolution. But contrary to popular thought, violence in the form of bloodletting is neither a precondition nor a necessary concommitant of deep-rooted structural change. In fact both the Cuban revolution that commenced after the battle against Batista (now officially labelled "The Rebellion") and the structural changes in Chile under Frei and Allende have been surprisingly non-violent so far. On the other hand, it seems to have often been the case historically that the rules of the political game have been re-written most rapidly when governments were able and willing to use coercion or the threat of coercion to enforce their designs for social reconstruction. The reason why Premier Castro was able to push through changes more rapidly than President Allende is clearly that Premier Castro was not only himself the government but was also in absolute control of the military and the police. Allende neither possesses a majority in the houses of the congress nor is in personal control of the military (which gives allegiance to the constitution).

"Reform" and "Revolution"

Generalizations concerning the political mechanics of stage-managing change are often couched in terms of the alleged dichotomy between "reform" and "revolution". "Reform" (that is, the making of changes within the existing rules of the political game) is held

to be either impossible or insufficiently radical when the rules of
the game are biased in favor of the oligarchical landholding and business groups in alliance with the military—and foreign interests as
well. Such privileged groups presumably would not undertake any
reforms that would hurt their material interests. Moreover, these
groups may employ violence through the established organs of internal
security and the military to enforce the status quo. Under such circumstances only a replacement of the existing elite and the installation
of a new set of political rules of the game by revolutionary insurrection
would permit the implementation of radical social and economic
changes to benefit the bulk of the populace.[4] However, while this
discription undoubtedly has been and is still applicable to a number
of Latin American countries, the situation in other Latin nations in
the early 1970s is certainly much less rigid. A number of countries
have been making important changes in their fiscal systems, patterns
of land tenure, policies pertaining to foreign investment, and other
areas.

Gradual, piecemeal reforms have often had the cumulative "revolutionary" effect of altering the distribution of economic and political
power as well as modifying the political rules of the game. On the
other hand, ostensibly revolutionary regimes (such as Cuba under
Premier Castro) must, after the seizure of power, also embark on
the arduous process of undertaking economic, social, and perhaps
further radical political change. Thus reform and revolution should
be considered not as dichotomous, polar opposites but as phenomena
that may merge, one into the other, over time.

However, the use of higher levels of coercion is seen by many
as an intrinsic ingredient of revolution. Regimes are judged to be
"revolutionary" if, after taking power, the political regime is not only
capable of rewriting the rules of the political game but can also use
its monopoly of the instruments of coercion (the military and the
police), and perhaps a monopoly of the media and the dissemination
of information, to overcome opposition and implement the desired
changes. Regis Debray, for example, is concerned about the constitutional constraints accepted by Allende's government in Chile in the
face of powerful opposition that is currently stalemating his reforms.
Debray states: "In the last analysis and until further notice, power
grows out of the barrel of a gun and (Allende's) government does not
have its own apparatus, its own institutions of defense on a national
scale".[5] Implied in Debray's view is that despite the lack of clear
majority support at the polls and in the congress the Allende government's main obstacle is its lack of unquestioned control of the military
and the police. In fact the main obstacle to the Unidad Popular is its
minority position in Congress—assuming continued neutrality of the
military. Thus Debray's position on Chile's unique and highly democratic situation turns out to be elitist and undemocratic.

DEVELOPMENTAL PROBLEMS AND POLICIES:
A RESUME OF ENDS AND MEANS

Objectives

Different individuals, groups, classes, and nations often disagree about ultimate values and hence about a vision or image of a future society toward which they should strive. Thus there is not and perhaps never can be complete agreement about priorities among developmental objectives, and consequently on phenomena accepted as problems. Most observers of the Latin American political scene however would include the following among their objectives:
  1. the reduction of unemployment and "marginality";
  2. greater equity in the distribution of income and the allocation of basic social services;
  3. more rapid economic growth and the general reduction of poverty; and
  4. reduced "dependence" on uncontrollable external decision makers.
Assigning priorities to these objectives in a manner acceptable to all nations or to individuals within nations in Latin America would obviously be impossible. Additionally it should be noted that some of these goals may in certain respects be complementary (e.g., accelerated growth and reduced unemployment) whereas some objectives may sometimes conflict (e.g., accelerated growth and reduced "dependence").
In any event, beginning with the objectives mentioned above, the commonality, heterogeneity, and dimensions of the developmental problems confronting Latin America can be reviewed quickly.
The "marginality" problem is difficult to pin down because the term is employed in a bewildering variety of ways. One useful definition, however, is that of the UN Economic Commission for Latin America (ECLA):

Marginality . . . is a structural situation . . . characterized by non-participation in the prevailing social structures combined with the impossibility of acting without reference to all or some of them: a non-participation accompanied by the aspiration to secure at least a minimum share of the assets of a given society.[6]

"Marginal" individuals have typically been ejected from and (or) attracted out of their traditional employment and life style in rural

TABLE 1.1

Demographic and Social Information on Latin America

	Population Mid-1970 (millions)	Population Growth Rate, 1960-70 (percentage)	Percentage of Population in Cities, 1970	Rate of Urbanization, 1960-69 (percentage)	Percentage of Labor Force in Agriculture, 1968	Literacy Rate	Unemployment Rates (overt only), 1965	Number of Dependents Per 100 Persons of Working Age	Life Expectancy at Birth
Argentina	24.3	1.6	78.9	2.3	15.8	91.5	2.6	57.3	67.4
Barbados	0.3	1.0	40.3	N/A	22.0	97.4	N/A	N/A	
Bolivia	4.5	2.6	29.3	4.1	57.1	39.8	N/A	82.7	45.3
Brazil	90.6	2.8	47.6	4.6	46.4	71.0	11.6	84.3	60.6
Chile	9.6	1.3	74.2	3.5	25.5	89.6	6.4	80.6	60.9
Colombia	21.4	3.2	57.7	5.5	45.1	72.9	10.5	98.6	58.5
Costa Rica	1.7	3.5	49.0	4.6	46.7	84.4	N/A	104.7	66.8
Cuba	8.2	2.8	53.7	0.2	33.	96.1	N/A	66.4	66.8
Dominican Republic	4.2	2.8	40.0	5.9	60.4	53.1	15.0	101.0	52.1
Ecuador	5.8	3.4	45.7	5.9	53.7	69.1	5.6	97.1	57.2
El Salvador	3.3	3.7	38.8	5.1	57.6	49.0	N/A	98.3	54.9
Guatemala	2.0	3.1	30.8	4.2	64.1	37.9	N/A	97.9	51.1
Guyana	0.7	3.3	26.0	N/A	N/A	N/A	20.9	N/A	N/A
Haiti	5.1	2.0	17.3	5.8	83.2	22.0	15.0	82.0	44.5
Honduras	2.5	3.4	32.2	6.4	65.5	47.3	N/A	100.0	48.9
Jamaica	1.8	2.0	N/A	N/A	22.4	81.9	N/A	N/A	N/A
Mexico	49.0	3.3	58.7	5.0	46.1	83.71	2.7	97.8	62.4
Nicaragua	2.0	3.5	39.7	4.8	56.0	49.8	N/A	102.9	49.9
Panama	1.4	2.8	47.1	5.0	42.3	76.7	10.9	90.9	63.4
Paraguay	2.4	3.1	36.0	5.3	54.5	74.4	5.3	99.9	59.3
Peru	13.2	3.1	51.9	5.6	44.6	61.1	2.8	93.1	58.0
Trinidad - Tobago	1.1	2.5	40.0	N/A	20.9	88.6	N/A	N/A	N/A
Uruguay	2.9	1.3	79.9	2.0	19.9	90.5	12.3	57.0	69.2
Venezuela	10.4	3.5	74.9	4.7	24.5	73.9	10.0	94.0	63.7
Latin America	270.0			4.4	42.9			85.6	

N/A = not available

Sources: Inter-American Development Bank, Socio-Economic Progress in Latin America, pp. 91-360 (for first, second, third, and sixth columns); p. 7 (for fifth column). UN Economic Commission for Latin America (ECLA), Trends and Structures of the Latin American Economy, 1970, p. 19 (for fourth column); p. 113 (for seventh column). UN ECLA, Social Change and Social Development Policy in Latin America, 1969, p. 16 (for eighth column). Raul Prebisch, Change and Development: Latin America's Great Task, Report submitted to the Inter-American Development Bank, 1970, p. 25 (for ninth column).

TABLE 1.2

Economic Information on Latin America

	Gross National Product Per Capita, 1969 (U.S. $ at 1960 prices)	Growth Rate of Per Capita (Real) GNP, 1960-69	Employment Structure: Percentage of Employment, 1969			Changes in Shares of Sectors in Total Employment, 1960-69			Invest-ment Co-efficient, 1969	Aid Per Capita Per Year, 1966-67
			Agri-culture	Industry & Basic Serv.	Ser-vices	Manuf. & Basic Serv.	Ser-vices	Agri-culture		
Argentina	980	2.3	15.6	36.9	47.5	- 2.9	10.7	-18.3	20.9	1.41
Barbados	400	N/A	22.0	N/A	N/A	N/A	N/A	N/A	N/A	N/A
Bolivia	203	3.0	55.0	21.1	23.9	5.0	18.3	- 7.9	15.1	8.03
Brazil	390	3.1	46.6	23.3	30.1	1.3	21.4	-10.7	19.6	N/A
Chile	650	2.3	22.5	31.6	45.9	- 4.3	14.5	-16.4	17.1	14.45
Colombia	381	1.5	42.3	23.0	34.7	- 6.1	27.1	-12.3	18.6	6.03
Costa Rica	580	3.3	49.3	19.6	31.1	- 4.4	15.2	- 6.1	20.3	12.63
Cuba	(455)*	(0.0)	N/A	N/A	N/A	N/A	N/A	N/A	(31.0)	(29.5)
Dominican R	237	0.2	59.8	14.2	26.0	- 0.7	24.4	- 7.7	18.8	15.59
Ecuador	316	1.2	52.5	20.4	27.1	N/A	22.0	- 5.9	15.2	5.45
El Salvador	340	2.2	56.1	19.1	24.8	3.8	6.4	- 3.8	14.1	5.89
Guatemala	359	1.9	64.7	15.5	19.8	1.3	18.6	- 4.9	12.5	3.06
Guyana	276	N/A	N/A	N/A	N/A	N/A	N/A	N/A	N/A	15.04
Haiti	98	-0.3							5.0	0.76
Honduras	253	1.5	66.9	12.3	20.8	5.1	23.1	- 6.3	20.7	5.04
Jamaica	548	N/A	N/A	N/A	N/A	N/A	N/A	N/A	N/A	9.55
Mexico	680	3.4	47.2	22.3	29.5	8.4	21.9	-13.1	20.7	2.66
Nicaragua	339	2.9	56.0	17.4	26.6	- 4.4	33.0	- 9.4	18.8	9.89
Panama	710	4.8	43.9	17.0	39.1	15.6	2.1	- 6.0	23.7	16.87
Paraguay	284	1.0	51.1	20.1	28.8	5.8	15.7	- 8.9	16.9	7.71
Peru	408	2.5	N/A	N/A	N/A	4.0	21.7	-11.5	18.4	5.33
Trinidad	768	N/A	20.9	N/A	N/A	N/A	N/A	N/A	N/A	5.56
Uruguay	720	-0.2	16.6	31.7	51.7	-6.5	11.9	-16.6	15.6	3.80
Venezuela	790	1.0	26.6	27.2	46.2	14.3	10.0	-22.2	20.3	9.24
Latin America	514	2.5	N/A	N/A	N/A	N/A	N/A	N/A	19.4	N/A

*Figures in parentheses are estimates.
N/A = not available

Sources: UN Economic Commission for Latin America, Trends and Structures in the Latin American Economy, April 1971. pp. 25, 42, and 71 (for first through fifth columns). Organization for Economic Co-operation and Development, The Flow of Financial Resources to Developing Countries, 1969 (for sixth column).

areas, and into the favelas, callampas, or shanty-towns surrounding major cities. Here they participate only "marginally" in the modern sector of society, usually in insecure labor-intensive, "low-status" service activities, notably street-vending. Though statistics on unemployment, overt or covert, are fragmentary, certain other types of information provide clues to the roots of the marginality phenomena. Rapid population growth has been accompanied by very high rates of urbanization (see Table 1.1) and relatively slow expansion in employment opportunities in industry and basic services (see Table 1.2). The consequence has been what Raul Prebisch has termed the "spurious absorption" of labor in some areas of the service sector (see Table 1.2) concurrent with increasing overt unemployment (see Table 1.1).

The overall rate of growth of per capita real gross national product (GNP) in the 1960s was a fairly respectable 2.5 percent per year, with quite rapid growth in industry though not in agriculture. (See Table 1.2.)

Despite the good intentions of the Alliance for Progress, relatively little of the gains from the growth in GNP trickled down to the lower-income groups. Income distribution continues to be highly inequitable in Latin America considered as a whole, with the highest 20 percent of the income-receivers obtaining over 60 percent of the total pretax personal income and the highest 5 percent receiving about 33 percent. (See Table 1.3). In Mexico the share of pretax income of the lowest 40 percent of the income-receivers decreased between 1950 and 1963.[7] (See Table 1.3). It is unlikely that the incidence of the tax system and of governmental expenditures has become sufficiently progressive to improve the distribution of income significantly in most Latin American countries. Indeed, it is likely that both governmental income and expenditure patterns have typically been regressive, at least until quite recently.

There are a number of possible indicators of "dependence." Foreign ownership of large proportions of national economies is perceived by Latin Americans as a serious constraint on national economic policy and on the emergence of domestic entrepreneurship, and as an excessively costly means of obtaining the use of foreign technology, managerial expertise, and financial capital. Many Latin Americans consider such foreign investment undesirable if it creates a permanent "dependence" on foreign decision makers whose prime allegiance is to the internationally oriented parent corporation rather than to the national entities concerned. Finally, as seems to have been the case with International Telephone and Telegraph in Chile recently, foreign corporations are quite capable of interfering in the internal affairs of host countries, by operating their own independent foreign policies designed to further their own interests. Foreign investment has been growing in all but a few Latin countries and is

TABLE 1.3

Personal (Pretax) Income Distribution, Selected Countries
(in percentage of total income by quintiles
of families)

Country	Year	Lowest 20% 0-20	21-40	41-60	61-80	Highest 20% 80-100	Highest 10% 90-100	Highest 5% 95-100	Ratio of Highest 20% to Lowest 20%
Argentina	1953	7.5		41.4		50.0	36.8	27.2	6.7
	1961	7.0	10.0	13.0	18.0	52.0	39.0	29.0	7.0
Brazil	1960	6.0	8.0	12.0	18.0	56.0	41.0	31.0	9.0
Colombia	1962		26.0		17.0	57.0	43.0	30.0	N/A
Costa Rica		5.5		24.5		60.0	N/A	35.0	11.0
El Salvador		5.5		33.1		61.3	N/A	32.9	11.0
Mexico	1950	6.1	8.2	10.3	15.6	59.8	49.0	32.3*	10.0
	1957	4.4	6.9	9.9	17.4	61.4	46.7	24.0*	14.0
	1963	4.0	7.0	10.5	19.5	59.0	41.5	16.0*	15.0
Panama City, Panama	1962	6.0	11.0	13.0	22.0	48.0	31.0	N/A	8.0
Puerto Rico	1953	5.6		44.6		49.8	32.9	23.4	9.0
	1963	5.0	9.0	14.0	22.0	51.0	34.0	22.0	10.0
Caracas, Venezuela	1962	6.0	11.0	13.0	22.0	48.0	31.0	N/A	8.0
Latin America		3.1		34.4		62.6	N/A	33.4	20.0
United Kingdom	1964	5.0	10.0	17.0	24.0	44.0	29.0	19.0	9.0
United States	1968	4.0	11.0	17.0	25.0	43.0	27.0	17.0	11.0
Czechoslavakia	1965	6.3	14.0	19.7	25.6	34.4	21.2		5.0
Norway		4.5		55.0		40.3	N/A	N/A	9.0
Canada	1967	6.8	13.3	17.9	23.5	38.5	N/A	N/A	6.0

*Highest 2.4% of the income receivers.

N/A = not available.

Sources: D. J. Turnham, Income Distribution: Measurement and Problems, SID Conference, Ottawa, May 1971, p. 4; R. Hansen, The Politics of Mexican Development (Baltimore: Johns Hopkins Press, 1971 for Mexican data. UN Economic Commission for Latin America, Economics Survey of Latin America, 1969. pp. 364-417. Senate Committee, Poverty in Canada (Queen's Printer, 1971) for Canadian data.

becoming increasingly concentrated in the most dynamic sectors of the economy, including mineral extraction and petroleum. (See Table 1.4.)

Many Latin American countries are also very reliant on one or a few export products and on a few markets for these products (see Table 1.4). This type of dependence can lead to undue short-term instability superimposed on only a modestly rising long-run trend in export earnings, with consequent difficulties for national planning.

During the post-World War II period, because of the gap between export earnings and import requirements, there was a rather heavy recourse by many Latin American countries to developmental foreign loans and export credits. Much of the so-called aid took the form of loans on only mildly concessional terms. The consequence of this has been an "explosive increase in development debt," as the Pearson Commission put it. The debt load both on a per capita basis and in relation to export earnings has reached very high levels in most Latin countries. (See Table 1.4.)

One final indicator of "dependence" is the geographical pattern of trade of Latin America. Historically there has been little intra-area trade; the historical ties of trade of individual countries have been with Spain and then with Europe and the United States. In the decade of the 1960s, however, intraarea trade increased, from 6.1 percent to 11.2 percent of Latin America's total trade.[8]

Policies

Vigorous, radical, and imaginative policies will be required on the part of both "reformers" and "revolutionaries" if the key developmental problems facing Latin America in the decade of the 1970s are to be successfully tackled. Some of the policies required to redistribute income, reduce unemployment, and eliminate the marginality phenomenon on the one hand and to reduce external "dependence" on the other are suggested below. We emphasize that these are only suggestions of general policy areas that require exploration and that they are not intended as specific prescriptions for any given country.

Income Redistribution, Unemployment, and "Marginality"

The current maldistribution of income in Latin America—closely related to the problems of unemployment and "marginality"—cannot be justified on either economic or ideological grounds. Some income redistribution is essential, not only from an ethical but also from an economic standpoint. Broadened markets (resulting from such redistribution as well as other changes) are necessary to bring

TABLE 1.4

Possible Indicators of Latin American External Dependence

Country	Major Export Commodity	% of Total Exports, 1966-68	U.S. Direct Investment by Sector, Book Value, 1969 (millions of U.S. dollars)							Average Export Coefficient (Exports as % of GDP[a]), 1967-69	Ratio of External Debt Service to Value of Exports, 1966-69 Average	Total Trade with the U.S. as % of Total, 1970		Total Trade with L. Am as % of Total, 1970	
			Total	Mining	Petroleum	Manufactur.	Utilities & Transport	Trade	Other			Exp.	Imp.	Exp.	Imp.
Argentina	Livestock products	38	1,244	N/A	N/A	789	N/A	68	387	11.7	25.6	8.0	24.0	20.0	21.80
Barbados	Sugar	89(1963)										*20.1	16.0	*0.8	17.00
Bolivia	Tin	56								18.7	5.3	15.0	30.0	*7.6	16.0
Brazil	Coffee	43	1,633	99	100	1,112	25	188	108	6.1	26.5	24.0	32.0	9.0	10.0
Chile	Copper	74	846	452	N/A	65	N/A	41	288	13.6	13.4	*17.0	*30.6	*10.7	*24.0
Colombia	Coffee	64	684	N/A	342	220	29	63	30	14.4	13.7	*39.0	*45.0	*10.1	*11.0
Costa Rica	Coffee	36	630	8	154	113	129	43	182	25.9	11.6	41.0	34.0	23.0	28.0
El Salvador	Coffee	48	(Total for Central America)							25.9	3.0	21.0	33.0	30.0	31.0
Honduras	Bananas	47								24.7	1.8	59.0	59.0	9.0	40.0
Nicaragua	Cotton	42								24.9	6.6	*34.0	*37.0	*21.0	*32.0
Guatemala	Coffee	42								18.7	8.2	29.0	38.0	33.0	27.0
Cuba	Sugar	80	0	0	0	0	0	0	0						—
Dominican Republic	Sugar	56								16.4	8.9	83.0	53.0	0.7	2.6
Ecuador	Bananas	61								18.3	7.9	49.0	49.0	14.0	19.0
Guyana	Bauxite											32.0	20.0	2.0	0.7
Haiti										12.4	11.9	79.7	70.7	0.0	1.9
Jamaica	Alumina	85									4.0	54.6	46.0	2.9	6.7
Mexico	Diversified		1,631	136	35	1,108	28	191	133	9.3	22.6	59.8	63.0	8.0	3.0
Panama	Bananas	54	1,071	19	239	90	56	345	322	38.5	2.3	59.0	35.0	3.0	21.0
Paraguay										14.6	7.6	11.0	18.0	31.0	22.4
Peru	Copper	26	704	443	N/A	97	N/A	59	106	21.0	14.0	33.0	33.0	6.0	17.0
Trinidad	Petroleum	98									1.8	48.0	17.0	3.0	33.0
Uruguay	Livestock products	83								19.2	17.7	8.0	12.0	12.0	32.0
Venezuela	Oil	93	2,668	N/A	1,771	416	18	276	186	28.1	2.0	41.0	*47.0	9.0	*3.0
Latin America			13,811	1,922	3,722	4,347	695	1,406	1,720	10.7	14.5	32.0	41.0	12.0	13.0

[a]GDP = Gross domestic product.

N/A = not available.

Sources: UN Economic Commission for Latin America (ECLA), Economic Survey of Latin American, 1969. (New York, 1970), p. 275 (for second column). U.S. Department of Commerce, Survey of Business, October 1971, p. 28 (for third through ninth columns). Inter-American Development Bank, Socio-Economic Progress in Latin America, 1970, Table 57, p. 74 (for tenth column). UN ECLA, Trends and Structures in the Latin American Economy, Table 25, p. 71 (for eleventh column). International Monetary Fund and International Bank for Reconstruction and Development Direction of Trade (for twelfth through fifteenth columns).

about not only industrial specialization and economies of large-scale
production but also efficient industrialization. To make income distribution more equitable a wide range of policies will be required.
A good proportion of these policies will "take from the rich" as well
as "give to the poor."

Reduction of unemployment is an important means of raising
the incomes of the lower-income groups.[9] To achieve this, employment-oriented developmental strategies must be designed to replace
or at least to complement the growth-oriented strategies that only
too often have failed to expand employment opportunities. Such revised
strategies would attempt to stimulate demand for labor-intensive
commodities (beginning for example with unsophisticated, domestically
produced consumer goods) and certain public works. To increase
demand for labor-intensive commodities with high domestic content
requires a redistribution of income in favor of lower-income groups.
This is so because the propensity to consume labor-intensive commodities is greater among low-income groups than it is among high-
income groups (which have a stronger taste for capital-intensive
durable goods with a high import content). Governments could also
increase their demand for labor-intensive public works such as low-
income housing.

A second general method by which the demand for labor can be
increased is to change the way in which commodities are produced,
that is, to increase the labor-intensity of technology. To change the
environment within which techniques are selected, so that the current
bias toward capital-intensity is corrected, will require such policies
as—

the devaluation of overvalued exchange rates;

the raising of interest rates (which in many cases are far below
the real cost of capital);

the elimination of various indirect subsidies to the employment
of capital (e.g., tariff-free capital imports and accelerated depreciation
allowances);

tax or tariff scales that would bias the choice of technique toward
labor-intensity; and

the untying of aid (tying necessitates the importation of capital-
intensive technology from donor countries).[10]

Perhaps most important of all would be an ambitious research
and development program in the actual engineering of a more labor-
intensive "intermediate technology" carried out on a continental or
perhaps Third World basis. Finally, as Paul Rosenstein-Rodan
argues (in Chapter 6), high "threshold" rates of growth are required
to expand employment opportunities at a sufficiently rapid rate.
Rosenstein-Rodan doubts that labor-intensive technology can expand
employment without sacrificing growth (i.e., he postulates that an

efficient labor-intensive technology not only does not yet exist but perhaps cannot be developed). If he is correct, the effect of using an inefficient intermediate technology would merely be to "redistribute poverty." This does not mean however that the present biases in favor of capital-intensity should not be eliminated, or that research and development in labor-intensive technology are not worthwhile. On the contrary, there is a great need for comprehensive research into the feasibility of evolving indigenous intermediate technologies.

Other policies are necessary to improve income distribution substantially, thereby reducing unemployment. Obviously, progressive taxation systems should have high priority. Governmental expenditure programs that have a regressive impact on income distribution also require restructuring. Although generalizations here are difficult, such restructuring often includes the allocation and financing of primary-through-university education, physical infrastructure including transportation, and social security. Due to serious regional disparities in income distribution, batteries of policies must aim at developing the peripheral regions of particular countries, at the decentralization of industry, and at a labor-absorbing development of the agricultural sector. Large-scale land settlement schemes have some potential in a few countries for increasing productive employment and raising the living standards of lower-income agrarian peoples. (See Chapter 16.) Incomes policies—though they are extremely difficult to implement when they require a high degree of commitment to the commonwealth on the part of the higher-income groups—are especially important if income differentials between marginados and rural peoples on the one hand and the politically articulate and strategically placed middle- and upper-income groups on the other hand are to be diminished.

Finally, direct changes in property rights through land reform and nationalization are in many countries important means of achieving greater equity in income distribution.

Reduction of Dependency

In the decade of the 1970s greater attempts will be made by Latin American countries to reduce their perceived "dependency" on (or the asymmetry of interdependence with) the developed countries, and in particular the United States. This need not necessarily mean that national economies will become more autarkic, but rather that interdependence within Latin America will increase via-à-vis Latin America's interdependence with the rest of the world.

Nationalization of foreign-owned enterprises will probably be a widely used instrument of Latin America's foreign investment policy, even though taken alone this would not eliminate dependence

on imported technology and foreign markets. It is likely that nationalization will be used with greater precision and articulation than
was the case in Cuba and will be directed toward specific industries
(or particular firms within industries) rather than indiscriminately
toward the whole economy. Careful arrangements for the transfer
of ownership and control (such as the transfer of ownership, with
compensation, of Demberara from Alcan to Guyana, and the reversion
of oil properties to the government of Venezuela by 1983) and new
forms of technological and managerial transfer (management contract
arrangements; turn-key arrangements such as those of Fiat in Russia);
and fade-out arrangements (such as those listed in the common foreign
investment policy of the Grupo Andino) will undoubtedly be increasingly
explored and utilized. It is also to be hoped that "internationalization"
or "Latin Americanization" (i.e., the establishment of supranational,
public Latin American corporations) will be employed for enterprises
that require international integration of their activities for efficient
operation (e.g., United Fruit Company, automobile production), to
prevent the disintegration of their operations to nation-state entities.

To reduce extracontinental "dependence" requires structural
diversification of the Latin economies which in turn requires regional
or subregional economic integration. Because most Latin countries
are too small in terms of effective market size, economic integration
is a prerequisite for the establishment of a widely diversified range
of consumer and capital goods industries. More efficient production
for broader Latin American markets and increased international
competition within Latin America should facilitate the cultivation of
markets for manufactured commodities outside Latin America, thereby
further reducing the traditional dependence upon extractive and agricultural primary product exports. It should be emphasized, of course,
that when the Latin American supply side has finally resulted in a
large and competitive volume of manufactured goods exports the
responsibility will then devolve upon the external demand side. In
short, "competitive domestic availabilities" is the key phrase at
present, but "access to world markets" will soon replace it.

Economic integration has long been a most arduous process,
because of the opposition of bureaucrats and business men with vested
interests in inefficient sectors of the economy and because the less-
advanced countries would lose as a result of the imposition of common
external tariffs, if no explicit mechanisms for the redistribution of
the gains from integration were established. However the formation
of subregional groupings—like CARIFTA (see Chapter 17), the Central
American Common Market, and the Grupo Andino—and the future
integration of the subgroupings may be more expeditious than attempting
to integrate 24 independent national entities all at once.

Economic integration would also be facilitated by the establishment of public Latin American corporations operating in an environment of fiscal harmonization, a harmonized Latin American body of corporate laws, and some approach to a common foreign investment policy. This type of organization could achieve integrated planning within industries on a continental basis.

The Need for Dynamic Growth

The various policies required to raise growth rates in developing countries have been at the center of the discussion of practical developmental problems since World War II. They range from trade, fiscal, foreign investment, agricultural, and industrial policies to population, health, educational, and manpower policies. These policies will not be sketched here, since they have been mentioned in Chapters 3 through 6.

It should be stressed, however, that the objectives of reduced unemployment, improved income distribution, and rapid growth are in large part complementary. Moreover rapid growth requires higher-caliber labor that is well-nourished and well-educated. Intelligent investment in the physical and mental fitness of human beings undoubtedly will have a high rate of return from a growth standpoint, as well as be an important component of a more equitable income distribution. Similarly, rapid growth within an employment-oriented developmental strategy is important if job-creation is to accelerate.

"CAPITALIST UNDERDEVELOPMENT" OR "SOCIALIST REVOLUTION?"

An interpretation of underdevelopment and prescription for the achievement of development that is in vogue throughout the Western Hemisphere comes under the "dependency" label. One popular variant of this interpretation, and an explicitly and exultantly Marxist and revolutionary approach, is that of A. G. Frank,[11] though there are other Marxist and non-Marxist variants of the approach that are also persuasive.[12] The theses of Frank on inevitable and increasing underdevelopment under "Capitalist Imperialism" (and the only alternative, "Socialist Revolution") will be summarized in this section, as his views provide an uncompromising and powerful rationale for violent revolution in Latin America.

The essence of Frank's interpretation is that the economic development of Latin America has been misdirected and limited by the "peripheral satellite" or colonial position of "external dependence" on shifting metropoles—the Iberian Peninsula, Western Europe, and finally the United States—during the last four centuries of mercantile and capitalist imperialism. The world capitalist system has been of such a monopolistic nature that the "actual" and "potential economic surplus" (i.e., resources actually saved and invested, and "potentially investible resources" unavailable for investment due to waste and luxury consumption) is drained or "sucked" toward the metropolitan capitalist centers for their own economic development, leaving the satellite countries without an investible "economic surplus." Thus the expansion of world capitalism has led to the "development of underdevelopment" in the satellite countries. By this, Frank presumably does not mean that per capital real gross domestic product has fallen in Latin America (it has not), but rather that the economic structures of Latin American countries have become more externally oriented and more penetrated by foreign enterprise.13

The key mechanism for the "suction" of investible resources from the periphery to the metropolitan center is monopoly.14 It is the monopoly-monopsony power of businesses in the metropolitan centers that for 400 years has permitted the exploitation of consumers and laborers and the appropriation of the "economic surplus" by the center. Presumably as both buyers (of labor, raw material, or food-crop exports) and sellers (of capital equipment, technology, managerial expertise, consumer goods, and the use of financial capital), the metropolitan centers have been able to exercise their monopoly power to maximize their commercial advantage. Frank argues that this was not only the case with the legal monopoly and monopsony granted to the Board of Trade (Casa de Contractión) at Sevilla under Spanish colonialism but that the situation has continued up to the present and will continue until "capitalist imperialism" is overthrown. The much-noted decline in the terms of trade in recent decades is but one facet of this, in Frank's view. Foreign direct private investment is currently a most effective mechanism for the appropriation and channelling of "economic surplus" from the satellite to the metropole. The granting of economic and military aid to bourgeois governments is a means of ensuring the safety of the foreign investment and the support of the local bourgeois elite.

Frank argues that satellite-metropolis relationships not only exist at an international level but also "penetrate and structure the very economic, political and social structure" of the satellite countries. Just as national capitals are satellites of the foreign metropolis, so also are provincial capitals satellites of the national capital, and regional towns satellites of the provincial capitals: "Thus a whole chain of constellations of metropoli and satellites relates all parts of the whole system from its metropolitan centre in Europe or the United States to the farthest outpost in the Latin American country-side."15 There is in consequence a creaming-off of "economic surplus" from the landless laborer, to the peasant or sharecropper, to the landlord, to the local bourgeoisie, to the provincial and national bourgeoisies, and ultimately to the metropolitan capitalist bourgeoisies.

Frank puts forward a number of subsidiary theses. To show that Latin America has been within the capitalist orbit since the colonial period, he takes great pains to support the hypothesis that the latifundium was not a feudal transplant from Spain but instead was, from the start, a capitalist institution producing cash crops for export to the metropolis.* Another corollary is that the economic development of satellite regions is inversely related to the intensity of their ties or degree of integration with the metropolis. Regions whose economic structures have been mostly closely tied through trade patterns (i.e., regions with open economies and export-oriented growth) have achieved historically the least economic development.

Foreign penetration and acquisition of businesses in the peripheral satellites has the effect of weakening the independent national industrial and commercial bourgeoisies and integrating them solidly into the coalition with the imperialist metropolis and the externally oriented landed oligarchy. Both the business and landowning oligarchies rely (in their exploitation of the workers and peasants) on the support of the metropolitan bourgeoisie, according to Frank, and are thereby driven into ever-closer economic and political alliance with them. Thus there is no hope that a domestic industrial bourgeoisie would break the "dependent" relationship with the metropolis.

According to Frank, economic development of the satellite countries is not possible within the existing international system. Nor can the system be modified or patched up. Only violent socialist revolution by the exploited workers and peasants can wrest power from the comprador bourgeois elites, break the bonds of dependence upon the capitalist metropolis, and enable the "authentic development" of the peripheral countries. Thus, "The capitalist system has developed at the cost of their [the peripheral satellite countries']

------

*One could argue then, that inasmuch as the medieval manor (from the tenth to the fourteenth centuries) produced cash crops for sale to the growing towns in order to purchase manufactured goods, some of which were traded internationally, the manorial system was therefore not a "feudal" but a "capitalistic" organization. Presumably in colonial Latin America as well as medieval Europe one would have to examine carefully the degree of openness of the latifundia system before one affixed simplistic labels such as "capitalistic" or "feudal" to the mode of organization.

underdevelopment, and as the price of their development the capitalist system must be destroyed."16

It is unclear, from Frank's analysis, just what would be done by new revolutionary leaderships after the success of "socialist revolutions" in Latin America. Though Frank seems to accept the Cuban revolutionary experience as a model, he does not spell out what makes a revolution "socialist" or what type of growth strategy, integration scheme, industrialization policy, or whatever, would be necessary to achieve "authentic development."

Many criticisms can be levied against Frank's analysis and prescription. Only a few will be mentioned here.

First, despite Frank's appeals for more scientific political and economic analysis of Latin American development, his own theories are fuzzy and difficult to pin down because he fails to define key terms such as "development," "dependence," "underdevelopment," or "socialist revolution" to which he attaches different meanings in different contexts. To use these terms with clarity is of more than purely academic importance. Because each of these terms has many meanings, Frank's failure to define them with some precision makes his analysis nonoperational. "Economic development," for example, has innumerable definitions. Political leaders and social scientists include many different combinations of "developmental" objectives in their definitions, such as growth of real per capita income, equitable income redistribution, structural diversification of the economy, reduced marginality, reduced unemployment, the establishment of minimum consumption levels, and the like. Frank does not make clear which combination of these comes under the label "economic development." Similarly, "dependence" is a complex multidimensional phenomenon which includes all the means by which decisions made outside a nation influence internal policy-making. Some of the primarily economic facets of dependence are:

1. reliance on single export products (Frank's "structural dependence"),
2. reliance on single import sources and export markets,
3. direct private foreign investment,
4. volumes of foreign aid, and
5. financial dependence.

Once again Frank does not indicate which of these he includes in his concept of "dependence." This is a serious weakness, because for particular countries these types of dependence behave in contradictory ways. Brazil, for example, has been rapidly diversifying its economic structure as well as the composition of its exports, while the volume of foreign ownership has been rising. Is Brazil then becoming more or less "dependent"?

In a number of places Frank seems to imply that by "development" he means structural diversification and the reduction of economic dependence on the metropolitan center and on specific export products.[17] If the degree of structural diversification of the economy is indeed his criterion of underdevelopment, then most so-called developed countries in the world are becoming increasingly underdeveloped because they are becoming more economically specialized and more dependent on trade and technological flows with each other (under the impact of technological change, the general reduction of tariff barriers, and economic integration schemes). This increased international specialization is often called interdependence, and is seen by these countries as a normal concomitant of economic evolution. On the other hand it is correct to stress as Frank does that increased agricultural and industrial diversification are appropriate for most developing countries.

Second, Frank's vision of the Western world in terms of an exploitative hierarchy with the metropolitan center at the top, national and provincial capital cities in the intermediate strata, and eventually the laborers, peasants, and landless laborers at the bottom, is probably a fairly accurate picture of the colonial relationship with Spain, and to a lesser extent with Europe and the United States until World War II. It is less appropriate today and hopefully will be increasingly less appropriate in the decade of the 1970s. The United States has become less predominant in Latin America and can be expected, ceteris paribus, to become increasingly less predominant as regional integration schemes progress and as Japan, the enlarged European Economic Community, and the East European countries continue to expand their economic contact with Latin America. Increased trade with these other regions should continue to give rise to greater price competition among these countries in the provision of capital goods and some manufactures (i.e., monopolistic elements in the relationship are decreasing). Moreover, the establishment of effective producers' cartels in the supplying of certain raw materials (following the example of OPEC, the Organization of Petroleum Exporting Countries) could equalize or reverse the traditional bargaining relationship between supplier nations and the oligopolistic corporations that process and/or market the commodities.

Third, Frank's attempt to explain the economic growth of regions and of countries in terms of the closeness of their economic ties with or the intensity of their dependence on the metropolis is unsatisfactory. There is a sizeable literature in economics (e.g., the "staple" theory of economic growth and regional economic science) that examines the technology of the export commodity of each region concerned, the market demand characteristics for the product, and locational factors in attempting to explain why some regions diversify

more readily from their export base into secondary and tertiary
activities than do others. These factors in many cases overshadow
the exploitative hierarchial structure of colonialism in explaining
the relative growth of countries, regions, cities, and towns. Frank
does not seem to be aware of this literature.

There is one particularly serious logical flaw in Frank's work.
The objective of his analysis is to show that the world capitalist
system generates the underdevelopment of Latin American countries
and of regions, localities, and subgroups within these countries. If
one accepts his analysis to be valid, one could conclude logically that
the world capitalist system was inherently "bad." One could not
however conclude in a post-hoc-ergo-propter-hoc fashion that the
bad system should be destroyed until and unless it was demonstrated
that an alternative system was better and would eliminate or reduce
the ills of the old system. Frank makes no attempt to demonstrate
this, accepting on faith that the new system would be superior and
would permit a speedy solution to current problems. Of course Frank
may be correct, but he may also be incorrect. The answer depends
on the exact nature of the new system (which he does not discuss) and
on the weightings that are attached to various developmental objectives
as well as political goals.

To demonstrate persuasively that a new socialist system of
"development-generating" international relations would function better
than a modified version of the present system might be more difficult
than Frank seems to think. For instance:

1. With respect to the objective of reducing "dependency," it
is too facile to state that nationalization of all means of production in
Latin America would by itself eliminate dependence on the foreign
firm. Dependence on imported technology, imported financial capital
(loans or grants), and foreign export markets would undoubtedly
continue. A relatively amicable nationalization of primary economic
activities can be most profitable in those cases where there are strong
barriers to entry into the industry at the extraction stage (e.g., Guyana
possesses a world monopoly on the supply of calcined bauxite till
1973 or 1974 and has benefited from the market power this has given
her). In other cases, where there are low barriers to entry at the
supplier level (e.g., bananas) an acrimonious nationalization without
compensation may have the effect of cutting the supplier out of the
markets serviced by the oligopoly and of eliminating the inflow of
spare parts and new technology.

2. To diversify the individual economies of all Latin American
countries but the largest (i.e., to reduce "structural underdevelopment") obviously requires a considerable degree of international
economic integration. Presumably Frank feels that this diversification
can be readily accomplished through the establishment of 24 autonomous

national central-planning entities in the orthodox East European style. However, given the experience of COMECON (Council for Mutual Economic Assistance) and the vested interests that central planning administrators have in <u>national</u> structural diversification, it may well be that orthodox socialist international economic relations would do little to achieve meaningful economic integration in Latin America. Less-orthodox alternative approaches may be more effective. (See "Developmental Problems and Policies" above).

3. By eliminating the returns to the owners of capital and natural resources, nationalization of the means of production can undoubtedly reduce income inequality to a large degree. However, regional and rural developmental policies and vigorous incomes policies would also be required to reduce disparities between town and country and between different groups in each region.

4. Communist systems seem to possess the ability of rapidly reducing if not eliminating unemployment, though this is in part a semantic vanishing act in which unemployment and underemployment are merely redefined. For instance, it should be noted that Cuba has experienced its own variant of the "spurious absorption" of manpower into the bureaucracies, which attempt to replace many of the functions performed elsewhere by markets. The expansion of the bureaucracies in Cuba, for example, has been a serious problem. As Premier Castro stated, "Bureaucratism . . . causes us much more damage than imperialism itself."[18]

While Frank's thesis can be faulted for a simplistic view of the world (thus explaining his popularity?) there can be no denying that Latin America's asymmetric interdependency vis-à-vis the industrial countries has seriously constrained national economic policy in Latin American countries. Nor can it be denied that the costs of foreign technology and managerial services obtained through private foreign investment have often been exhorbitant, and hence that levels of internal investment might have been higher in the absence of repatriated profits, interest, royalties, and patent fees to foreign corporation headquarters.[19]

It should be stressed that there are undoubtedly too many situations in Latin America where violent overthrowal of governments may be necessary to rapidly overcome the vested interests opposing those changes required for the benefit of the bulk of the populations concerned. It is to the credit of Frank and the <u>dependencia</u> theorists that they do focus on internal political forces and social structures that are at the core of the political mechanics of bringing about socio-economic improvement. On the other hand, one cannot generalize and say that violent overthrowal of governments is necessary in all cases.

However, violent political upheaval has been shown in the last few years to be unnecessary to change the nature of a country's inter-national economic relations or to reduce its "external dependence". Structural diversification of national economies, regional economic integration, and installation of tight foreign investment policies (as well as fiscal reforms, land reforms, and redistribution of income) are policies that can be and are being currently adopted by reformist regimes in Latin America. Indeed even nationalization (Alcan in Guyana, International Petroleum Company (IPC) in Peru, copper in Chile) can take place without recourse to internal violence and with-out causing serious ruptures in international relations. One can only conclude that the possibilities for changing the international economic constraints on domestic policy making are now greater than was thought by Frank to be the case.

Frank has performed a service in focussing attention on the nature of "dependency" relationships though of course many others (e.g., Prebisch, ECLA, Gonzalez-Casanova) have made detailed exami-nations of aspects of internal and external dependence. The accuracy of his analysis and the full consequences of his policy prescription, however, require close examination before taking precipitate action.

UNPREDICTABILITY OF KEY POLITICAL
PARTICIPANTS

It is futile if not impossible to attempt to make brief (and neces-sarily simplistic) generalizations concerning political prerequisites for socioeconomic change, political strategies, and tactics for "reform mongering", or even techniques of guerrilla action in Latin America. Because of the heterogeneity of political regimes, of political power configurations, of historical traditions, and of economic structures, a multiplicity of political strategies for the achievement of different reforms will likely be appropriate. Consequently this section does not succumb to the temptation of formulating a "general theory" or grand synthesis to explain the political mechanics for the achievement of reforms to meet the varying objectives of all Latin American countries. Instead the purpose of this section is to probe some of the complex political issues surrounding the military and the middle classes, since both will deeply influence future events as the countries of Latin America tackle such key problems as income distribution, unemployment, "dependence," growth, and democratization during the 1970s.

It is relevant to note here that even Premier Castro has become less dogmatic and indeed somewhat pluralistic in his conceptions concerning the appropriate path to the good society. In the mid-1960s Castro not only viewed "socialist revolution" as the only road to salvation but also propounded the theory that the Cuban tactics of guerrilla warfare had universal validity. By 1970, however, he was accepting the Peruvian military regime at face value. And in his visit to Chile in 1971 he conceded that a "socialist revolution" was possible without violent armed struggle and within a constitutional democratic framework (in Chile at any rate).

Guerrilla tactics successful in one country at one particular time will not likely serve as a model that can be applied in toto in another location, or even in the same country at a different time.* (See Chapter 10.) Similarly the political tactics most suitable for continuing change will presumably be radically different for different types of political systems such as constitutional democracies (e.g., Chile, Venezuela, Costa Rica, and the Commonwealth Caribbean), military regimes (e.g., Brazil, Bolivia, Paraguay, Ecuador, and Peru), and "one party" systems (e.g., Cuba, Mexico, and Haiti). Within these general types of political systems the technology of reform mongering obviously will vary greatly. Needless to add, the suitability of particular political strategems and maneuverings also depends on the specific nature of the reform measures themselves, for each such measure will have its own unique constellation of supporters and opponents. To make or to obstruct such changes through the forging of (shifting) political alliances is the very stuff of politics.

Unfortunately the political situation in most Latin American countries is much more complex than simple class analyses suggest. Various subclasses and subgroups are not behaving and cannot be expected to behave in accordance with certain more simplistic or naive Marxist schemata.[20] Indeed, the self-interest of various Latin American subgroups may motivate them to act in increasingly surprising ways in the decade of the 1970s.** What follows is a brief discussion of the unpredictability of the future behavior of the military and the middle classes. (See Chapters 8, 9, and 14.) Space limitations prohibit a thorough examination of the past and prospective political

---

*Even had Guevara's reading of the Cuban revolution (or rebellion) been correct (it wasn't) there was little chance that similar tactics and strategy could have worked in the completely different Bolivian setting.

**It is paradoxical that both Richard M. Nixon and Lyndon B. Johnson (as well as John Diefenbaker) were brought up in less affluent circumstances than Fidel Castro, Che Guevara, and Chou en Lai.

behavior of such important subgroups as large landowners, small
landowners, students, the industrial labor force, the "marginal" service and "penny capitalist" sector, and foreign investors.

The Military

Military officer corps, in conceiving of themselves as modernizing managerial elites, may take it upon themselves to make certain
reforms thought to be necessary for nation building and economic
development such as the land reform and the nationalization of IPC
in Peru (see Chapter 14). It is possible that some military regimes
(aside from the Cuban and Peruvian) will undertake fairly deep-cutting
changes designed to benefit the bulk of the population (e.g., income
redistribution via land reform, some nationalization, regional development, an incomes policy) with the major objective of consolidating
popular support for the regime. The Brazilian regime, which imposed
an income tax and improved the tax administration so that the number
of income taxpayers increased 10-fold from 1965 to 1970 presumably
could expropriate the larger land holdings even without compensation,
thereby winning the support of millions of tenants and sharecroppers
while losing only the support of the relatively small group of large
landlords (see Chapter 13).

Indeed, if some military regimes do behave increasingly as
nation-building modernizers and attempt to build popular support as
well as strong economies, it can be expected that they will undertake
redistributive reforms and improvements in public health, education,
and housing. This would follow from the logic that the long-run
economic health of most Latin countries will require broader markets
and improvements in the quality of human resources if industrialization
and economic modernization are to occur. Given that it is in the self-
interest of the military regimes to be popular and to have strong
economies, then it will not be surprising if military regimes undertake ostensibly "radical" socioeconomic reforms. Of fundamental
importance of course is the concomitant impact on human rights.
As Brady Tyson emphasizes so convincingly (in Chapter 8), genuine
democratization is not likely to be included as one of the objectives
of military regimes.

It might be noted in passing that Latin "revolutionaries" have
ignored one potentially valuable strategy for achieving power. Because it is of the utmost importance to control the military and police
apparatus in order to force through rapid and radical reforms, one
possibility is that "revolutionaries" penetrate the police and military
officer corps from the inside rather than attempt to defeat them
through guerrilla war. This obviously is a difficult though not

impossible technique. If revolutionaries had infiltrated the officer
corps in large number some 20 years ago, the stage would now be
set for "revolutionary" coups d'etats, with monopolies of the instruments of coercion in the hands of "revolutionary" military elites.

The Middle Classes

An important phenomenon in Latin America is the expansion
of the middle classes. Statistical data for Mexico, for example,
confirm this growth of the middle class, which is also apparent to
the casual observer (see Table 1.3). From 1950 to 1963 there has
been a 50 percent reduction in the share of total pretax income of
the richest 2.4 percent of income receivers, while the share of the
poorest 40 percent of the income receivers fell by 24 percent. The
gainers have been that 37.5 percent of the population below the top
2.4 percent; their share of total income rose from 43.1 percent to
62.5 percent of total pretax income in these same years. The emergence of middle classes in other Latin American countries is similar,
though perhaps less pronounced. These middle classes (occupying
executive and technocratic positions in the domestic- and foreign-
owned economy, in the bureaucracy, in the professions, and in some
"labor aristocracies" in strategic sectors of the economy) aspire to
and are achieving a "modern" style of life of the North American-
West European variety. Relative to the rural peoples, to the unemployed or "spuriously absorbed" marginados, and to much of the
industrial labor force, the middle classes are in a privileged economic
position. Furthermore, these middle-income groups are usually
politically articulate.

The self-interest of various subgroups within the middle class
may motivate them to act in ostensibly contradictory ways. For
example, the middle-income groups may have no objection to nationalization (with or without compensation) of the landed and capital properties of the richest landlords and capitalists, as long as their own
positions are not threatened. Similarly, nationalization of particular
foreign-owned industries might be actively or passively supported by
those middle-class groups that would find increased opportunities
for promotion when the foreign personnel left their positions and
returned home. Executives in governmental bureaucracies may also
have little objection to nationalization, because expansion of the
governmental sector of the economy would improve their job opportunities. On the other hand, of course, the material self-interest
of the middle class or groups therein might be harmed if nationalization extended into areas of small business; if income redistribution
took place at their expense through expensive rural and regional

developmental schemes, taxation, incomes policies, etc.; or if foreign
exchange controls or import policies threatened their incomes and
life styles.

The middle-income groups, in short, acting upon their self-
interest, can be expected to behave in a variety of ways, depending
on their internal composition, on their historical traditions, and on
the way the political game is played. Thus it should not be surprising
to see substantial proportions of the middle-income groups supporting
the Brazilian generals, the PRI (Partido Revolucionario Institutional)
in Mexico, and the Peruvian military junta as well as President
Allende of Chile.

CONCLUSION

Despite the many similarities in the problems confronting most
of the nations of Latin America—income maldistribution, excessively
slow growth, high unemployment, and asymmetric interdependence—
the means by which these problems are tackled will probably be
highly pluralistic in the decade of the 1970s. Because of diversity
of historical traditions, economic bases, social structures, and power
configurations, it is most unlikely that the Latin American countries
will adopt a common route toward the good society. Moreover, conceptions of the good society and therefore the priorities assigned to
different developmental objectives vary between countries, and within
countries over time.

Theories such as those of A. G. Frank, which propose violent
political upheaval or guerrilla-style socialist revolution as a necessary (and perhaps a sufficient) precondition for the eradication of
external dependence and the achievement of genuine economic development are unduly simple and rigid, and do not capture the great diver-
sities among the Latin American countries. Indeed, violent political
upheaval may be neither a necessary nor a sufficient condition for
the achievement of prodevelopmental social, economic, and political
changes for a number of Latin American countries. Instead, reforms
that may cumulatively aggregate to "revolutionary" redistributions
of power and perhaps to "revolutionary" modifications in the nature
of political systems have been occurring, though excessively slowly
in too many cases. Due to the ambivalent and unpredictable behavior
of certain key political participants, it is likely that changes will
occur with surprisingly different coalitions of political groups supporting different reform measures in different countries during the
1970s.

2

**IDEOLOGIES
OF LATIN AMERICAN
MODERNIZATION**
David H. Pollock

Three introductory comments of an explanatory nature may help
to set the general parameters of the discussion that follows. First
of all, in trying to come to grips with the title, "Ideologies of Latin
American Modernization," it is necessary to define some terms. This
is particularly important because of the word "ideology," which, though
used often these days, is still a most bothersome word. Webster's
dictionary for instance has a number of definitions for it that include
"(i) the study of ideas, their nature and source, (ii) the theory that all
ideas arise from sensations, (iii) thinking or theorizing of an ideal-
istic, abstract, or impractical nature; fanciful speculation, (iv) the
doctrines, opinions, or way of thinking of an individual, class, etc."
This chapter ranges widely over that group of definitions. Indeed it
probably hovers a bit more than it should over the last: "etc." To be
as precise as one can when facing such a conceptual quandary I have
tried to adhere to a definition that Albert O. Hirschman put forward
in his excellent book published by the Twentieth Century Fund in 1961,
Latin American Issues, Essays and Comments. There he stated that
"The term 'ideology' [of economic development] is used here without
derogatory connotations to designate any moderately consistent body
of beliefs, ideas or propositions, tested or untested, that aims at
explaining Latin America's economic backwardness and at indicating
its cure." Perhaps one could be on safer ground by deleting the word
"Ideologies" in the title of this chapter and substituting the word
"Theses," or "Philosophies," or even "Policies." But Hirschman's
definition is all-encompassing, and has the desirable characteristic
of linking backward-looking explanations with forward-looking recommendations, and so I shall try to follow it.

Incidentally, no equivalent introductory definition can be put
forward for the word "Modernization" that also appears in the title

of this chapter. Probably, however, "Development" could be substituted for "Modernization" without doing too much damage to the idea behind my theme. And while on this matter of words, the thought has passed through my mind of trying to define "Development." But only fleetingly!

Secondly, the discussion touches upon various disciplines other than economics narrowly defined. In particular it alludes to certain sociopolitical issues, and does not dwell solely on the matter of economic growth.

Thirdly, a certain amount of intellectual tolerance is required on the part of the reader, since the chapter may appear to cover too many periods and too many areas of endeavor in too few pages. Yet I have tried to paint on a large canvas precisely because my objective is to look at different periods of Latin American history and describe—admittedly in very broad terms—some of the basic ideas that have shaped the pattern of Latin America's economic and social destiny from the nineteenth century up to the present. And even into the future. Remembering Webster's definitions, I have even gone a step further into "fanciful abstractions" and given a few ideas of my own as to what may lie ahead.

All this has been done with a view to providing—by way of a global tour d'horizon—some sort of a broad ideological framework into which more specific details can later be fitted. This chapter seeks to cover, albeit hurriedly, more than 100 years, so one must be patient if at that speed we see a panorama of Latin America's horizon, though in the process our view of the countryside becomes a bit blurred.

BEFORE THE DEPRESSION: THE ERA
OF THE CLASSICISTS

From the mid-nineteenth century through the first three decades of the present century the philosophic rationale underlying Latin America's pattern of economic growth stemmed largely from the classical theory of international trade.

In essence this thesis held that so long as foreign commerce took place without impediment and under conditions of international comparative advantage—which meant in reality that developing countries should concentrate upon exporting primary products in exchange for manufactured goods exported by developed countries—then it would inevitably follow that the gains from such trade would be optimized overall and simultaneously that each participating country would maximize its component benefits within the total.

Of basic importance to Latin America in this conceptual framework was the assumption that its internal economic growth would be
stimulated when foreign trade was dynamic. And conversely that
levels of Latin American domestic income and output would be correspondingly inhibited when external demand for its exports was stagnant
or falling. Under this approach therefore Latin America was destined
to occupy a more or less passive position in the international economic
scheme of things. The radiation of external stimuli into the region
depended on the functioning of the great economic heartlands of the
world. When those stimuli were positive and continuous, the Latin
American economy was given an impetus to a stable pattern of growth.
But when those external shocks faded in intensity, or evidenced themselves in cyclical or shorter-term waves of instability, then the
reverse happened and Latin America's internal economic situation
was adversely affected. Worse yet, the overall impact of international
shocks upon individual Latin American countries (or sectors within
those countries) was typically affected in some disproportionate
magnitude by the economic transmissions from abroad. When the
developed world sneezed, Latin America was indeed very prone to
catching pneumonia. Latin America not only became an appendage
to the economic system of the world's great industrial centers but it
was buffeted up or down by some multiple of the tremors reaching it
from those centers.

In retrospect then this phase of crecimiento hacia afuera* was
a period when an outside ideology (having intellectual roots in the
functioning of the post-industrial-revolution countries of the Western
world) was transplanted virtually holus bolus on the Latin American
scene. There it was accepted by governments, business, and academic
circles alike as being an inevitable as well as a desirable aspect of
an integrated and beneficial international economic order. This
acceptance, as stated above, took place largely without question in
Latin America, as indeed the classical theory had been accepted
throughout the rest of the parts of the Western trading world, developed and developing alike, until the early part of the twentieth century.

Thus it was that Latin America rationalized this basic ordering
of its economic structure: producing agricultural and mineral primary
products, offering them for sale in international commodity markets,
and then using the resultant foreign exchange proceeds to finance
imports from developed countries of those manufactured goods required for its consumption and investment needs. Exports comprised
Latin America's "engine for growth," at least insofar as growth in

---

*"Externally oriented" or "outward-looking" growth.

the Latin American monetary economy was concerned. The masses of the peasantry continued to slumber, far removed from modern economic activities, as indeed from virtually all of the region's social, political, and cultural activities as well.

But more on the latter at a subsequent stage. Up to here the point has been made that the concept of an all-pervasive, all-benefiting international division of labor was viewed essentially as a form of "invisible-hand" doctrine. Latin America did not dispute its ideological core; on the contrary, as I said above, the ruling segments of society accepted, promulgated, and benefited from the doctrine.

And so, until 1929 Latin America's growth was intimately conditioned by trends in international trading channels, and in particular by the way in which demand from developed countries affected those commodity markets of particular interest to Latin America. Latin America, like the rest of the developing periphery, functioned largely as an annex to the world industrial centers, providing the latter with basic foodstuffs and industrial raw materials and relying on them for most of its manufactured consumer and capital goods.

THE "GREAT CRISIS": A SYSTEM DISINTEGRATES

All this was to change abruptly with the advent of the "Great Crisis," as the decade of the 1930s is often called in Latin America. The impact of the depression was of course deeply felt throughout the world, but certainly it had especially severe economic repercussions south of the Rio Grande.

As internal economic activity declined in the United States, Western Europe, and other major industrial centers, and as their export earnings began to dwindle, those centers reacted in two separate but interconnected ways. On the one hand their demand for noncompetitive imports fell off commensurately with the contraction of their foreign exchange availabilities. And on the other their tariff and nontariff barriers rose on a great variety of goods, especially those of a direct or potentially competitive nature.

All this of course was very unfavorable to regions like Latin America that were so heavily dependent on external demand for their exports of only a few primary products. As world demand and prices for such goods tumbled to disastrously low levels in the 1930s, Latin America was led rapidly into a sequence of declining foreign exchange earnings, lower reserves, and a consequent fall-off in imports, consumption, investment, income, production, and employment. Latin America's era of crecimiento hacia afuera had disintegrated. The region's economic system was in total disarray and awaited a new and fundamental orientation to reshape its future pattern of economic growth.

The first principal indication of this reordering of Latin America's economic system began in the early 1930s. Since exports had now ceased to play the role that in more mature economies could be played by indigenous investment, policy makers sought to encourage such investment domestically and in particular to do so in the industrial sector. This was done to substitute (by production for home consumption) at least some of the imported manufactures that had previously been paid for out of export earnings. The phase of crecimiento hacia adentro* had begun.

As it did, the manufacturing sector took its inevitable step up the ladder of economic priorities. Thus policy makers saw in an emphasis on industrialization—as contrasted with the earlier emphasis upon agriculture and mining—a new strategy for reducing Latin America's vulnerability to external shocks of the intensity and duration that had been experienced during the initial years of the Great Crisis. Industry, it was felt, would become the "race horse" designed to lead toward development at a much more rapid pace than was possible from the larger but more sluggish "dray horses" of agriculture and mining. Both would continue to be utilized, but one would be given new preferential policy attention to reduce the dependency upon the other, that hitherto had been almost total.

Unfortunately however the need for a reorientation of Latin America's economic priorities was slow and disjointed in coming about. Specifically, the way in which the process of import substitution manifested itself in the 1930s was very ad hoc, with relatively few deliberate attempts being made to carry out medium- or long-term investment planning within any given country or between groups of them.

Let us consider one example, albeit a reductio ad absurdum. Let us assume that chewing gum had been imported into Latin America before 1929 but could no longer be paid for out of export earnings during the Great Depression. In consequence, someone with economic power and resources decided that it would be personally (even if not socially) profitable to undertake an import-substitution program for chewing gum. Typically, little or no thought would be given to alternative economic let alone social priorities. Should scarce domestic resources be allocated for investment in chewing gum rather than for some different direct consumption items with higher dietary value (powdered milk)? Or for the production of durable consumer goods having more utility from a household point of view (hand irons)? Or intermediate goods needed as inputs into the

---

*"Internally oriented" or "import-substituting" growth.

manufacturing sector (industrial chemicals)? Or simple capital goods
(inexpensive farm machinery)? Even less thought, unfortunately, was
given to criteria for allocating resources on an inter- or an intra-
country basis. As a result, at least three important problems emerged
to plague this initial wave of industrialization in Latin America. For
one there was an excessive amount of investment in the production of
manufactured consumer goods of doubtful economic or social value.
For another, where investment in the production of essential capital
goods did take place the scale of output was geared heavily to the size
and cost characteristics of protected individual country markets.
Under these circumstances it was very likely that the plants would
either be too large or too small for the dimensions of each sheltered
domestic market. The inevitable consequences were corresponding
degrees of under- or over-capacity, with price characteristics to
match. And finally, related to the latter was the problem that no
regional or subregional investment planning took place in Latin America. Hence, although industrialization advanced rapidly it did so in
an unplanned fashion within 20 separate "watertight compartments."
Economies of scale, through the utilization of larger economic spaces,
were conspicuous by their absence.

WORLD WAR II: A PERIOD OF HIATUS

Even though the shortcomings of an ad hoc policy of crecimiento
hacia adentro became increasingly evident in Latin America throughout the 1930s, efforts to evolve a new and more systematic approach
to growth and development were temporarily halted as a result of
World War II.

During the actual period of hostilities, the demand for Latin
American export products was substantial, limited mainly by shortages of international transport facilities. Additionally, the prices of
many key export items were maintained at fairly stable levels, through
forward purchasing and other forms of bulk sales agreements. However, although these factors combined to make Latin American foreign
exchange earnings rise to higher and steadier levels than had been the
case during most of the depression years, there was not a parallel
increase in Latin American imports. On the contrary, the retooling
of traditional U.S. and West European suppliers toward production of
military items, and the sharply diminished access to international
shipping, left Latin America with no alternative but to continue its
process of import substitution.

Moreover even during the initial years after the war relatively
little headway seemed to have been made as regards the evolution of
new growth models for the region. Many countries had accumulated

large foreign exchange reserves during hostilities, but these reserves began to disappear rapidly and in an unplanned way after 1945, mainly to make up for five years of pent-up demand for war-rationed consumer goods.

It is true that the ideas of Keynes had by then begun to make their imprint upon the Southern Hemisphere, even as they had begun to do in the north. But the uniquely Latin American way in which Keynesian ideas (especially as regards conscious intervention into the free play of market forces) were to be interpreted and implemented had not yet taken clear form. This process was to come soon, however.

THE 1950s: THE EMERGENCE OF AN
INDIGENOUS IDEOLOGY

One might say then that throughout virtually the entire first half of the twentieth century Latin American countries continued looking at the world from their own separate and distinctive orbits. Latin America was still a geographic grouping of individualistic and self-oriented nations, as yet unconnected by any indigenous ideology of development and modernization designed to unify and stimulate economic thought and action for the region as a whole. During the 1930s, it is true, a unifying thesis had evolved around the "internal-indus-trialization-via-import-substitution" route. But this essentially represented a defensive series of ad hoc reactions against external shock, and was not clearly thought out or efficiently implemented in either inter- or intra-regional terms. During World War II the export sector recovered some of its buoyancy, but Latin Americans seemed to be waiting for peacetime to satisfy their pent-up demand for foreign consumption goods whose importation had been blocked by hostilities.

However, the intellectual hiatus during World War II had not been total. Many Latins—noting the nexus between external and internal growth—were beginning to ask themselves what a return to peacetime conditions would mean to the region's future economic destiny. Modern técnicos had begun to move into the policy-influencing realm which until then had been dominated almost exclusively by traditional políticos. And the former were asking, "What should be at least some essential elements of a new and indigenous Latin American ideology of modernization?"

Thus events had moved to the point where Latin America resembled a team of disparate horses, waiting for a unifying driver. Into this disorderly but potentially very receptive field came the UN Economic Commission for Latin America which, under the direction of an Argentine economist named Raul Prebisch, was destined to have a significant impact in that regard.

The pros and cons of ECLA's influence on Latin American thought and action have been covered in many other writings, perhaps most bluntly and perceptively by Hirschman in the book I have mentioned. Below therefore follow only a few of ECLA's more interesting intellectual contributions, at least as I see them.

In essence ECLA's influence rested on two main elements, one ideological and the other tactical. International trade flows based on comparative cost and advantage, said ECLA, do not necessarily lead to the most efficient utilization of world resources, and certainly not to their most equitable distribution. On the contrary, the rules of the game as they were put forward by the classical theory of international trade were stacked against countries producing primary products in favor of those producing manufactured goods. Under such circumstances, ECLA maintained, many developing countries felt that trade had become a vehicle for global exploitation by a few countries rather than a means of maximizing welfare all around. This lack of economic symmetry—this bias favoring the "central" (rich) nations at the expense of the "peripheral" (poor) countries—had been overlooked, said ECLA, in traditional approaches to theories of trade and growth. Worse yet, this economic disadvantage was compounded by an additional element of political asymmetry. To redress the existing lack of balance in international commercial and financial policies, corrective negotiations were required between nations. Unfortunately however negotiations between sovereign nations did not necessarily imply negotiations between equals. Thus peripheral countries felt they had been maintained in a continuously secondary relationship vis-à-vis nations of the center, not only because of outmoded economic theories but also because singly they could not exert countervailing political pressures on the stronger and more unified industrial heartlands of the world.

As is well known, ECLA encompasses, within a single institutional framework, all the Latin American countries. Tactically therefore it came to provide a cohesive organizational framework for the (then 20) republics of the region. And simultaneously as stated above it synthesized into a single conceptual framework an indigenous developmental philosophy. ECLA provided, in short, for the first time in Latin America's history an economic ideology plus a political forum. Both were broad enough to encompass the region as a whole but flexible enough to encompass a wide variety of different national characteristics.

Putting aside the institutional aspect, it will be seen that by the end of World War II Latin America's grouping for a new and fundamental reorientation of its economic system had come to be satisfied by the so-called ECLA thesis. The latter in turn rested essentially on a sequence of separate though interrelated ideas, which will next be briefly traced out.

A basic goal of developmental policy should be to increase the rate of growth of product and progressively to diffuse the fruits of such growth. In so doing it was essential to reduce external dependency. One way was to seek external financial commitments via targets for international public loan capital rather than rely so heavily on the spontaneous flow of private direct investment capital. A more basic avenue involved a shift in the structure of production away from primary products—whose trends were too stagnant in the long run and too unstable in the short term—and toward manufactured goods. This would enable a diversification of exports and (highly important to Latin America at that particular time) would accelerate the possibility of industrial import substitution. During the postwar era however, unlike the decades of the 1930s and 1940s, such substitution should take place in some rational planning context within individual countries and between groupings of them.

In all of this ECLA had clearly parted ways with the hitherto prevailing notion that the free play of market forces would somehow facilitate a more economically efficient system and a more socially equitable one. In fact neither the economic nor the social goals had thus far been attained by Latin America through the unfettered workings of the market mechanism. Nor were there grounds for assuming that this situation would now change in some spontaneous manner. ECLA did not oppose private enterprise. On the contrary its writings stressed, from the very outset, the need to strengthen the role of the private sector. But, said ECLA, the private sector would respond better to economic and social imperatives if the latter were clearly laid out within the context of an indicative developmental plan. And in so doing, said ECLA, it was basic that Latin American private initiative—not foreign—be strengthened through deliberate acts of policy. It was in this context among others that ECLA stressed so often the need for intervention into the free and unfettered play of market forces.

One will, by the way, see some interesting parallels here with Canadian thought and action regarding foreign private investment during the postwar era, and in particular during the past few years.

THE ALLIANCE FOR PROGRESS:
ITS ORIGIN AND AFTERMATH

In a very schematic way therefore the basic components of ECLA's contribution to Latin American development might now be summarized under three main headings of goals, means, and mechanisms:

Goals: rapid economic growth and
          its equitable distribution.
Means: the need for simultaneous measures at home and abroad.
      Abroad: via trade—attain symmetry of trade benefits and
                  improve the terms of trade by diversifying exports
                  away from primary products toward manufactured goods;
                  via aid—increase certainty by setting volume targets
                  for public funds, and augment resource transfers by
                  easing terms and conditions; and
                  via technology—through selective inflows of foreign
                  private investments and a concomitant increase in
                  the role of the Latin American private entrepreneur.
      At home: via sectoral balance—effect structural transformations
                  of the agricultural sector, and in particular seek a
                  greatly accelerated pace of internal industrialization;
                  via larger economic spaces—by emphasizing import
                  substitution nationally and integration schemes
                  regionally; and
                  via social welfare priorities—e.g., better income
                  distribution and greater stress on employment,
                  education, health, housing, and the like.
Mechanisms: nationally—increased efforts by the state to promote
                  economic efficiency and social welfare, mainly via
                  developmental planning; and
                  internationally—exerting countervailing pressure
                  through multigovernmental forums, mainly in the UN
                  and the Inter-American system.

As an aside, it is no secret that this basic ECLA schema was, during the Eisenhower administration in the United States, received with many doubts and trepidations. Indeed what today would seem to have been a well-reasoned philosophy and a moderate set of action proposals was considered by many in the mid-1950s to be dangerously illusory, radical, and ill-conceived. To some, in fact, the stress on planning and the preference given to domestic entrepreneurs over foreign businessmen even served to invoke vexed cold war issues. Yet, despite all this the U.S.-Latin American atmosphere had changed so dramatically during the last few years of the 1950s that virtually all the points listed above were accepted by President Kennedy early in his administration. Indeed, as L. A. Rodriguez demonstrates in the spring 1970 issue of Growth and Change, the Charter of Punta del Este and the Alliance for Progress were predicated fundamentally on the points previously put forward by ECLA as prerequisites—internal and external—for Latin American development.

The United States and its tremendous resources had now become directly involved in a collaborative program of hemispheric development.

Thus whereas Latin Americans had entered the 1950s intent on evolving
a new and indigenous ideology, they looked optimistically to the 1960s
as a decade of operations; that is, a decade to translate ideology into
action. It is to be regretted however that illusion and reality differed
and, for reasons that have been covered in other writings, the actual
attainments of the Alliance fell short of the original goals. I do not
feel that this is the place to dwell in detail on why this was so. But
two thoughts may be worth noting on the matter, one dealing with
form and the other with substance. Regarding the first, the point
has already been stressed that the heart—the essential philosophy—of
the Alliance had originated within Latin America. Yet in the early
days of perhaps overly eager efforts of public relations men in
Washington, the Alliance was presented as a "made in the U.S.A."
contribution to Latin American development. As is well known in
Canada, an undue emphasis of that kind is often counterproductive,
since it tends to invoke a defensive reaction from smaller and less
powerful nations. This was a pity during the Alliance. By itself
however it probably would not have posed insurmountable difficulties
had it not merged into another and more fundamental problem. That
was the steady erosion of what initially had been intended by Latins
as a truly multilateral program (designed to promote the long-term
developmental goals of recipient countries) into a series of bilateral
programs (aimed increasingly at furthering the short-term economic
and political goals of the donor country).

Some very perceptive insights into the above can be found in a
book written by Juan de Onis and Jerome Levinson in 1970 for the
Twentieth Century Fund. Among other things that book made the
following points. First, the Alliance was initially intended to foment
the goals of economic growth, distributive justice, and participatory
democracy. Second, it was soon realized that a more equitable
distribution of the fruits of growth and an enhanced degree of mass
participation in the political system required deep structural transformations that would be inherently destabilizing. Third, in consequence, most attention was devoted to economic growth. As for the
two other goals, they were put aside as prime objects of policy and
in their places were put monetary stability and military security.
Fourth, the latter in turn were much more acceptable to the established groups holding resources and power during the years of the
Alliance. Fifth and last, the Alliance had therefore undergone a
fundamental metamorphosis, shifting its emphasis from a broad
socioeconomic transformation to a narrower stability-security
orientation. For such reasons, Levinson and de Onis have aptly
entitled their book The Alliance that Lost its Way.

For whatever the reasons, the Alliance did not measure up to
the hopes initially set for it. Indeed the slogan originally launching

the Alliance, "5 minutes to midnight," had counterproductive implications for the United States and Latins alike. True, that slogan
correctly posed a note of urgency. But it also conjured up a vision
of "instant development." Today in any case the Alliance lies dormant.
And so we find Latin America once again seeking a new ideological
framework. Once again the countries of the region represent a team
of horses looking for a driver. One Latin tersely but graphically
defined the situation to me at the beginning of 1970 as that of chaos
fecundo.

THE 1970s AND BEYOND: THE PAST AS
A GUIDE TO THE FUTURE

At this point it might be useful to briefly recapitulate by asking
two questions. What ideas have been among the most influential in
shaping Latin America's past development? What significance might
those ideas have for the region's future? To answer those questions,
let us begin by synthesizing the main points postulated for each of
the periods covered thus far:

1850-1930: Latin America considered itself as a more or less
passive annex to the developed heartland of the world's economic
system, and did not try to transform its subordinate position. Instead
it accepted its role as a supplier of primary products in exchange for
imports of manufactured goods. As went the external sector, so went
Latin America's internal growth.

1930-40: When this externally oriented system collapsed, Latin
America had to reduce its excessive dependency on trade and payments
decisions controlled primarily from the developed centers. It sought
to do this by attempting, through a process of accelerated internal
industrialization, to produce at home those goods it had previously
imported. But due to the suddenly vast dimensions of the task, many
shortcomings occurred, especially as regards criteria for investment
decision making. On grounds of neither economic efficiency nor social
equity was this—Latin America's first approach to developmental
autonomy—considered fully satisfactory.

1940-50: During World War II, Latin American export earnings
improved but imports continued to be limited by wartime shortages.
Hence import substitution continued apace. Meanwhile however, and
especially after hostilities ended, técnicos began to ask themselves
what elements of a new developmental policy could and should be
applied under peacetime conditions.

1950-60: During this decade, and influenced to a considerable
extent by the writings of the ECLA, Latin America finally began to
evolve its first truly indigenous approach to a developmental ideology.

Its elements were many but perhaps the main one involved an emphasis on achieving a greater degree of symmetry in central-peripheral economic relationships. Lack of symmetry had been particularly noticeable during the pre-1929 era when there was a heavy reliance on increasing primary product exports, and later when reliance was mainly on import substitution. In consequence a particularly high priority was assigned to accelerating the pace of internal industrialization. To do this with both efficiency and equity, national planning was encouraged in lieu of the past reliance on the free play of market forces.

1960-70: The decade of the 1960s began on a promising note as this new and distinctive Latin American ideology received initial support from the United States. When efforts to bring about deepseated and structural transformations confronted existing power structures however, problems began to emerge. Among other things involved was a struggle between Latin America and the United States concerning the basic long-run goals to be sought and the shorter-term means of attaining them. As events occurred, neither side was satisfied by the results obtained.

Admittedly the above is quite sketchy, but probably that is inevitable when more than a century of ideas is covered in a few pages. Even so, and after making all necessary caveats about generalizations, it is undoubtedly a useful exercise to look back and see whether history can help guide us into the future. From my point of view, in any event, this tour d'horizon has been useful in clarifying at least a few guidelines through the decade of the 1970s, and perhaps even to the end of this century. Let us look at each of them.

First and foremost, there now seems to be little doubt that Latin Americans will continue, and even accelerate, their past efforts at reducing dependency on the international system. These efforts, which began in the 1930s, did not attain the impetus in the 1960s that had been hoped for under the Alliance. During the 1970s and thereafter, I am certain that they will be emphasized once again by the Latins. In the international sphere, this will be attempted through the United Nations Economic Commission for Latin America and Conference on Trade and Development (ECLA and UNCTAD), through other inter-American entities (the Inter-American Development Bank, IDB, and Inter-American Committee for the Alliance for Progress, OAS CIAP), and through still other forums such as CECLA (Comite Especial de Coordinación Latinamericana). But basically these efforts will be nationally inspired. Incidentally, when I speak of "reducing dependency on the international system," this does not mean withdrawing from it but rather of modifying the existing terms of interchange. My point may be better made by comparing Central America with the Nordic countries, or Bolivia with Switzerland. In each case the

European countries are as fully, if not more fully, integrated into the international system than are the Latin countries—but largely on their own terms. And that is the crux of the matter.

As the quest for economic independence occurs, there could well be intellectual opposition from some developed countries. For example, one point that emerges quite clearly in looking back over past U.S. relationships with Latin America has been the resistance of the former to the ideas of the latter. Yet as I pointed out in the December 1970 issue of International Development Review, such resistance has often proved to be premature if not shortsighted. Indeed one should note the paradox that only 15 years ago the so-called ECLA thesis was considered unsound economically and dangerous politically. As events have shown however it was quite moderate economically, and by no means a cold war pawn in the political context. My second suggestion therefore would be for the United States to look carefully on new Latin writings as bellwethers for future goals of policy.

If further asked to put forward views on what should be some specific U.S.—or more broadly some Organization for Economic Cooperation and Development (OECD)—responses to Latin America's future economic growth requirements, my third point would be commonplace in prescription, though difficult in implementation, namely, to urge that the advanced countries keep their trade, financial, and technological channels as open as possible. As noted below, Latin America must radically augment its own process of domestic resource mobilization. But no matter how well this is done, it will be of no avail if the small but crucial external constraint continues to exist. To enable Latin America to help itself, international commercial policies, public financial flows, and private technological transfers must not become restrictive. This is a challenge to the rich nations of the world, a challenge that would be beneficial to them as well as to developing nations if it were met and overcome. One need not proceed further on this theme except to echo the emphasis given in the same regard by Lester B. Pearson, both in the now-famous 1969 "Pearson Report" but equally so in his fine 1970 book, The Crisis of Development.

And what of the Latins themselves? It is always a delicate matter for outsiders to give advice to developing nations, but for the sake of balance one might conclude with a few thoughts as to what lessons the past might show for the future.

One is that much of the existing ideology and institutional machinery is still valid for Latin America's future. Additions and renovations are unquestionably required, but the principal need is for better implementation of the existing domestic system. This is no light task—on the contrary, it is an extremely difficult one. But its difficulties lie in the area of commitments, not of conceptualization, a point of much significance for the 1970s and beyond. Another thought is that as planning proceeds, a basic decision is whether economic growth should be considered the main goal of policy, as has largely been the case until now, or a means to a different social goal, namely, to diffuse the fruits of growth to the disadvantaged masses of society. This is a point for instance on which employment policies become central to the whole issue of developmental planning. One important Latin American view on this fundamental issue can be seen in Change and Development: Latin America's Great Task, written by Raul Prebisch in 1970. Third, in all this preoccupation with developmental ideology the role of the economist should not be overemphasized at the expense of other disciplines. On the contrary as I see the matter, economists have played a most fruitful and positive role in the postwar years, but during the rest of this century the sociologists, political scientists, anthropologists, historians, and indeed a broad mix of all disciplines will be imperative. This interdisciplinary approach, especially at the sociopolitical level, is one that has been neglected in both North and South America until recent years and undoubtedly needs reexamination. Fourth and last, let us remember that man does not live by GNP alone, a point of much relevance to the Latin American developmental scene. Time and again in Latin writings one sees the emphasis being placed on issues other than those directly related to economic growth. For instance, what ethical and cultural values should imbue the Latin American citizenry by the end of this century? An audacious thought perhaps, especially at this particular moment when poverty is so much on everyone's mind, but not a premature one. Again, what to do about restructuring Latin America's political systems? How can they be tightened to enhance developmental discipline, but not at the expense of mass participatory democracy?

If, by the way, one were asked to give some "wishes" rather than "recommendations" for the future, two in particular merit consideration. First one would hope the United States could see that its long-run interests lie fundamentally in supporting Latin American long-term goals. Too often the causation has run in the other direction, that is to say with the United States seeking to influence Latin America's short-term actions in order to advance the more immediate interests of the United States. And second one hopes that Latin America will not let its struggles to reduce external dependency obscure the importance of its struggles to eliminate internal marginality. Indeed, looking ahead at the possible sweep of events during the crucial years still remaining in the twentieth century, a clear-cut interpretation of and a set of balanced priorities regarding these two concepts—dependency and marginality—are unquestionably of the highest domestic and international policy importance for Latin America's future growth and development.

KEY POLICY AREAS
FOR THE 1970s

3

**OBSTACLES
TO DEVELOPMENT
IN LATIN AMERICA:
AN EVALUATION
OF THE PLANNING PROCESS**
Harold A. Wood

It is generally assumed in the world today that problems can
be solved. Hence some consternation ensues when despite various
measures intended to be remedial an undesired conditions continues
to exist. Such is the case with the gap separating the underdeveloped
from the developed countries. Even though everyone professes a
wish to see the gap narrowed and even though developmental organizations and planning agencies exist by the score, at both national and
international levels, the poorer nations of the world continue to grow
poorer in relation to those that are better off and, in a few cases,
even in absolute terms.* It is not surprising therefore that in Latin
America attention is now being paid not only to an intensification of
planning and developmental efforts but also to an examination and
evaluation of the planning process itself as it relates to the problems
to be solved.

Of course every school of thought has its diehard devotees, and
a good many people still support the policies followed in recent years.
These policies have been directed primarily toward urban and industrial
growth, and it is true that their immediate objectives have been largely
achieved. Cities are growing at rates scarcely equalled anywhere in
all of world history, especially the national capitals, which in eight

---

*Figures released by the UN Economic Commission for Latin
America reveal that Latin America's annual rate of economic growth
has actually been steadily declining. Between 1945 and 1949, the rate
of growth was 5.7 percent per year. Between 1945 and 1949, the rate
of growth was 5.7 percent per year. It fell to 4.7 percent in the period
1950-59 and to 4.5 percent in 1960-69. Between 1967 and 1969 the per
capita rate of growth was only 1.1 percent per year.

countries (Argentina, Chile, Costa Rica, Cuba, Panama, Peru, Uruguay, and Venezuela) now contain over one fifth of the total national population. And industrial production is approaching or has indeed surpassed in value the agricultural output of most countries. Nevertheless the total direct and indirect costs involved in this development have been so high that many people now question whether the net benefits have been more than marginal. Specifically the following difficulties exist:

1. Latin American industry must perforce operate on smaller scales than do the industries of the more developed parts of the world. It also uses technologies that have filtered down from the more advanced countries and are therefore never quite as up to date as those in use in the centers of research and innovation. For these reasons Latin American industries cannot compete in world markets except in the sale of traditional products, based on local natural resources and made in plants using levels of technology that are relatively simple and labor-intensive. More modern, sophisticated industries exist, but even in domestic markets they must be protected from foreign competition. These industries must therefore be subsidized directly or indirectly by other sectors of the economy.

2. The necessity to purchase machinery and other capital equipment, plus various industrial supplies and raw materials, has created balance of payments problems so serious that many if not most Latin American countries have experienced continuing financial crises accompanied by inflation. As development proceeds, this problem is in part controllable, at least temporarily, as was demonstrated by President Carlos Restrepo in his adroit handling of the Colombian economy from 1966 to 1970. But even during the period 1967-69 the only Latin American republics with favorable trade balances were Chile, Peru, and Venezuela (with large mineral exports), Panama (where canal income is considered a service export), and Argentina and Uruguay (under strict controls).[1]

3. Most industries are of the import-substitution type, but the capacity of most countries to absorb the products of such industries has now been fairly well saturated. Hence further growth of manufacturing is impeded. Indeed, in the past 15 years, while world industry has grown at the rate of nearly 5 percent per year, the growth rate for Latin American industry was below that figure. Most manufacturing plants are now operating well under capacity and many at scales that are hardly economic. For example, Latin America uses 40 factories to make its 300,000 passenger cars per year, while in Europe or North America a single plant will turn out nearly twice as many.[2]

4. It has been impossible for the industrial sector, even during the years of its most vigorous growth, to provide employment for the hundreds of thousands of people who have left the rural areas and

migrated to the cities in search of work. In fact, between 1950-60
and 1960-65 the proportion of the total labor force employed in manufacturing fell, from 27.8 percent to 22.0 percent. Meanwhile the
proportion of the work force that is unemployed or underemployed
has been estimated at the staggering figure of 40.0 percent.[3] It is
in fact the presence of this vast "marginal class" that provides most
of the potentially explosive pressure in modern Latin American
society. Unless it attempts to deal specifically with this problem no
overall planning strategy can be considered to be adequate today.

Because of these difficulties it is realized that within Latin
America the policies that have guided the process of industrialization
in the past are not now sufficient to solve the more general problems
of development and therefore that other, additional approaches are
needed.

Yet unfortunately, in the opinion of the writer, the promoters
of industrialization are meeting these doubts by presenting the same
old developmental philosophy in different wrappings, with the suggestion that it is something quite new. Today's package is called
"economic integration" and it is currently being vigorously promoted
by a great many influential individuals and institutions.

A reasonably warm welcome was originally given to this proposal
because it appeals both to Latin American idealists and to foreign
investors. To the former the concept of Latin American integration
is emotionally attractive. It was, after all, a major objective of
Simon Bolivar over a century ago, and at the present time an integrated
Latin America might be able to exert considerable influence in a
world dominated by a few major powers. Perhaps integration would
even help to resolve some of the small but nasty disputes that now
set one Latin American country against another.

At the same time, the benefits of integration for the industrialist
are not only comparable in magnitude but also much more immediate.
Many major industries will find it more profitable to establish one
or two plants in strategic locations serving all of Latin America than
it would be to have to put a separate factory in each country. It is
not surprising then that the integration proposal was well received
and that the movement toward integration has been highly publicized
and well financed.

Nevertheless if, outside Latin America, the concept of integration as a necessary, desirable, and immediate path to be followed is
not often seriously challenged, for many Latin Americans the experiences gained in their first steps along this path have been deeply
disappointing. It is being realized more and more that economic
integration means, above all, industrial integration and that industrial
integration not only brings much profit to foreign owners of the industries concerned but also benefits especially those countries and

cities that have particular locational and other advantages. It follows, then, that integration will work to the disadvantage of the less-favored countries and cities. Thus economic integration, unless accompanied by demographic and political integration, can produce uncontrollable stresses and strains when it brings together component units that differ sharply in levels of income or development.

To some extent also, the emergence of severe economic problems in most of the Latin American countries has made each one more defensive and isolationist in its outlook. Those with fewer problems are unwilling to assume responsibility for those that are in greater trouble. And the countries with deeper difficulties do not trust their more affluent neighbors. More and more, intergovernmental meetings are being marked not by the warm glow of continental empathy but by tense, even bitter, interchanges.[4] At this moment in history no country feels that it can afford to sacrifice to its neighbors any of its potential for growth or to allow control over its destiny to pass into alien hands, even if they are Latin American hands. For this reason, the movement for integration, so widely heralded a few years ago, is now at best only a crawl. The Latin American Free Trade Association and the Central American Common Market are both in a state of crisis.[5] And if the Andean Group seems to show some vigor, one must remember that it has not yet properly begun to function. As a generator of general growth, there seems no reason to suppose that it will be much more successful than LAFTA as a whole. Some industries, of course, will benefit but the overall effect will be small. Distances are too vast and potential competition between member countries too great to permit any massive interchange of products and accompanying regional specialization.

On the whole, then, Latin Americans are somewhat disillusioned with the results of the past decade or so of developmental planning.* In their disillusionment they are not only losing faith in the strategies they have been using, on advice received from the developed world, but are beginning to question whether any so-called solutions to their problems, emanating from this source, will be relevant in the Latin

---

*A good example of this feeling among the masses was the wave of popular support for former dictator General Rojas Pinilla in the 1970 Colombian presidential election. Rojas Pinilla's image was that of a conservative with a traditional approach to the solution of domestic problems. His opponent, Pastrana, representing a modern technical approach to planning, was elected by only a handful of votes, even though he enjoyed the backing of the dominant liberal-conservative coalition.

American setting. The extremist would attempt to break all ties of
dependence on the advanced countries; the more moderate recognizes
a need for a constant flow of ideas, techniques, materials, and money.
But everywhere there is a growing insistence that the goals and procedures of the planning process be determined in Latin America by
Latin Americans, to fit conditions in Latin America, and that they no
longer be simply imported from abroad.* Even so it is clear that
bringing about the realization of these dreams is not easy. Apart
from obvious external difficulties there are serious internal ones.

In essence Latin America now realizes that it has to make up
its own mind not only on the question "What will we do?" but on the
more fundamental matter "What do we want to do?" And herein lies
perhaps a critical problem of Latin America today. Governments
are not sure. Not only is it difficult to establish firm planning procedures; it is difficult to reach any clear-cut decision about the
future path of development.

In the most general terms, one suspects, it would be fairly easy
to reach a consensus. The Second Seminar on the Regionalization of
Planning Policies in Latin America, meeting at Santiago in September
1969, placed in the opening paragraph of its conclusions the following
statement: "The objective of all development policies should be human
welfare. For this reason, any strategy should include, among other
objectives, the following: opportunities for employment at adequate
levels of remuneration, continually improving economic conditions,
opportunities for social mobility, and integration within the political
life of the nation through participation in the making of decisions."
Such a broad statement will find few opponents, but when one attempts
to come to specifics, disagreements arise.

At the level of spatial planning, one school of thought supports
the so-called horizontal developmental strategies, which promote the
geographical extension of development, to embrace new resources and
dynamize new territories, while others still wish to concentrate all

---

*Chile's Ambassador Pedro Daza Valanzuela spoke for much of
Latin America when he told the Tenth LAFTA Conference, "In order
to achieve their national objectives, affirm their own personality and
be able to take an active role in the construction of an international
society based on justice, the countries of Latin America must make
a great internal effort, as well as perfect a system of Latin American
cooperation. The guidelines and forms of this effort are a matter to
be determined by each of our countries; the choice of road is a
sovereign decision to be arrived at freely by each people."[6] Comercio
Exterior de México, February 1971, p.19.

attention on the major existing cities, where accessibility is best
and economies of scale are most evident.

In economic terms, those who believe in trying to reduce inter-
regional disparities in income confront others who consider it more
important to maximize national production, even at the cost of neglect-
ing many parts of a country.

In the area of politics, reformers who believe in the necessity
of violent social and cultural revolution are opposed by those who
feel that more meaningful progress can be made within the framework
of the status quo.

Granted, these are difficult alternatives. Nevertheless, they
are no more difficult than those which other countries are meeting
and having to resolve. Why, then, is Latin America so indecisive?

One basic structural difficulty is that all important decisions
in Latin America are made by national governments. Where a province
or state does have power to act, as for example in Brazil or Colombia,
the governor, we find, is appointed by the president of the republic
and cannot deviate widely from his wishes. Some local administrators,
as in the case of Chilean municipalities, are democratically elected
but the funds they administer are trifling and their responsibilities
do not go much beyond the provision of local services such as garbage
collection.

Yet despite their power the national governments are no longer
controlled by any single class or interest group. Rather they must
take into account simultaneously the interests of the rich and powerful in the maintenance of a system of privilege, the demands of the
middle class for stability and economic growth, the need of the poor
for some hope that changes in their favor will not be forever postponed, the aspirations of nationalists, and the requirements of foreign
investors. Without a clear vision of the best path to follow and
beset by this host of conflicting pressures, most governments can do
no more than react in a makeshift and ad hoc manner to meet emergen-
cies as they arise. New commissions are created and new programs
are set in motion—bodies and programs that tend to survive long
after the emergency that prompted their establishment has passed.
The result is the steady growth of a bureaucratic jungle that may
consume more national energy in the friction between its component
parts than is used in meaningful work.[7]

In Ecuador, for example, in 1970 there were 1,418 autonomous
governmental agencies which, between them, consumed two thirds of
the entire governmental revenue. When President Velasco seized
absolute power in June of that year he immediately abolished 700 of
them, dividing up their responsibilities among existing governmental
ministries.[8] At times it seems that Latin American countries actually
need an occasional escape from the inefficiencies of democratic

rule. Military juntas or other strong administrations often command wide support and, if they do not give up their power voluntarily, are usually brought down eventually not by popular uprisings but by palace revolts.

This political uncertainty is also related to various social causes, particularly the strong sense of pride, individualism, and desire for personal prestige which are typically Latin American. Whether he demonstrates his superiority by hiring an urchin to carry a parcel home from the store or by spending a year's salary on the wedding of a daughter, the Latin American is by tradition absorbed with the impression he makes on others and tends to use, for purposes of "showing off," resources that the North American materialist would put to more productive uses. Furthermore, perhaps because of the long history of class distinctions, a sense of real social concern is rare. To the rich, the poverty of others is not only tolerated but recognized as one of the elements that have permitted the accumulation of wealth in the hands of a few—and this attitude is copied by those lower in the scale. He who has become less poor tries to set himself apart from those who are now "beneath" him. Each person strives to attain his own independent advantage and tends to remain rather indifferent to the needs of society as a whole.

Obviously, many exceptions exist, but the exploitation of man by man is distressingly common in Latin America, and where exploitation is not conspicuous one may find an indifference that is not much better. Notably there seems to be little question that a majority of the large estate owners are more interested in the social advantages to be derived from their lands than in achieving maximum intensity of use, maximum production, or maximum income. Where such wealth is not used profitably, any economy is crippled.*

Perhaps the most frustrating situation of all occurs where these personal traits are carried over to the governmental level, and

---

*To illustrate, in the company of a group of planners, the writer once visited the Asuncion Mita area in Guatemala, where the valley floor, owned by seven absentee landlords, although it is provided with an irrigation system, is not intensively used since the owners do not wish to be bothered with the problems involved in organizing a real productive effort. Meanwhile, the thin soils of the surrounding hills provide a precarious living for a large peasant population. The planners concentrated all their attention on the hilly areas in the conviction that it would be impossible to persuade the large landowners to develop their holdings up to a level commensurate with their potential productivity.

spectacular projects are undertaken not because of the economic benefits they will bring but primarily to impress observers, both inside and outside the country. Probably Brazil is the greatest culprit in this regard and Brasilia the greatest monument to this philosophy. No matter how much one may admire the daring that established this magnificent city on the edge of the void, or the energy that is now carving the trans-Amazon highway out of the selva, one cannot but speculate on how much human development could have been achieved had the funds poured into projects such as these been invested instead in social and economic facilities in some of the poverty-stricken areas populated centuries ago but always neglected. Even in Costa Rica, thought to be a pretty level-headed little country, before a single road existed between San Jose and the Caribbean coast, a magnificent four-lane highway was built linking the capital city with the airport.

But the state of national indecision and the dominance of a philosophy of conspicuous consumption will not last forever. Everywhere the pressure of the populace is building up and their demands are clear: jobs, dignity, and security, both economic and social. Dramatically in Cuba and Chile but noticeably in other countries as well, the rich are being forced to withdraw from their position of political supremacy. At the same time the claims of foreign business to special privileges are being progressively denied. One way or another, Latin America is maturing politically and in its maturation many stumbling blocks to effective planning are being steadily eroded away. In time—possibly a rather short time—the goals of development may be provided with definitions that are unequivocal and corresponding adjustments will be made in the planning strategies. The final section of this chapter is an attempt to indicate what these new strategies are likely to be.

To do so requires first that the developmental objectives be spelled out to coincide with the predictable demands of the Latin American people. These objectives will probably include the following:

Reduced dependence on the developed nations of the world.

More complete integration at the national level.

More efficient use of both human and natural resources.

Of these three, the first cannot readily be pursued directly, since it is tied to world patterns of supply and demand, which are not quickly changed by the action or decree of a single country or group of countries. The failure of LAFTA in this regard has already been noted. It is therefore to the areas of resource use and national integration that efforts will first have to be directed. Only when these goals are close to realization will it be possible to reduce the degree of external dependence.

To elaborate, in this new perspective of national development principal attention will have to be paid not, as at present, to resources that will be exported for use by developed countries but to those that will be used within the Latin American nations themselves. The most important of these resources in terms of its contribution to employment is now, and for some time to come will continue to be, the agricultural land from which is derived the domestic supply of food and industrial crops. As all the densely populated rural areas of Latin America depend on agriculture, the modernization of this sector may contribute substantially to a more effective use of human resources.[9] The resulting increases in production and intranational trade would also constitute a major step toward national integration.

But, of course, agricultural development has always been considered desirable. That it has been so slow in coming is due to deficiencies in such related elements as social services to the rural population, transportation, marketing facilities, availability of fertilizers, machinery, credit, and the like. These must be planned in association with the development of natural resources and the planning effort must cover, at the very least, all populated areas. The specific term used to designate this kind of planning is "regional planning."

Space obviously does not permit a detailed discussion here of the theory of regional planning.[10] In summary, however, it may be stated that its full application involves the following five principal elements:

1. Each region requires a principal urban center, supported by centers of lower order. These towns serve as the essential points of contact between the region and the remainder of the country.

2. Adequate links must be established between the various regional centers so that they will be able to function as a system of interlocking units, each able to specialize in those activities for which it has the best comparative advantages.

3. Within each region, adequate links must be formed between the urban centers and the rural areas, so that the benefits of development may be transmitted to these rural areas.

4. To be an efficient planning unit, each region should also be an administrative unit, that is to say, a political unit.

5. If the people of the region are to be truly developed, as well as its natural resources, each region must enjoy a measure of genuine autonomy in the diagnosis of its problems, in the articulation of developmental objectives, in the selection of developmental strategies, and in the elaboration and execution of developmental projects.

Just when it will be possible to bring true regional planning to Latin America is difficult to say, for the concept is indeed revolutionary, in the best sense of the word. In almost every country there is some movement in this direction, but in most cases only the first two of the five steps are contemplated, and in others nothing more has been done than to apply the name of "regions" to a set of areas

used for statistical analysis.* The decentralization of authority is
not readily accepted by those who possess it, whether they stand to the
right or the left on the political spectrum. On the one hand, military
governments, such as those in Argentina and Brazil, believe in strong
central control; but so evidently does the Unidad Popular, Chile's
present ruling party, which has cut back sharply on the rather limited
freedom of action that had been assigned to various planning regions
in the comprehensive planning system that had been so carefully
worked out during the administration of President Frei.** Revolutions
seem unable to cope with more than a few problems at a time, and
the type of revolution implicit in the adoption of the five principles
of regional planning could proceed or follow a social revolution.
Alternatively, it might provide for the gradual achieving of fundamental
social change without the necessity of a cataclysmic upheaval.

It is submitted, however, that Latin America's future requires,
as an absolute essential, that the planning process be employed to
bring together all areas and all groups of people within every nation,
without the exploitation of one by another. Regional planning is an
integral part of this process.

Helio Jaguaribe, of the Instituto Universitario de Pesquisas de
Rio de Janeiro, writing in 1968, precisely summed up the choices
confronting Latin America when he defined three possibilities for the
future: dependency, autonomy, or revolution.[11] The present condition
of dependency is unacceptable because throughout recent history it
has not been able to create development on a sufficiently broad scale.
Jaguaribe predicts that revolution will come no earlier than 1978, but
no later than 1998, unless a condition of autonomy is reached first.
But in no way can the natural interplay of existing economic and social

----

*Honduras, Colombia, the Dominican Republic, Chile, and Uruguay
have regionalization schemes correctly linked to urban patterns.
Costa Rica is working on the establishment of such a scheme. Venezuela, Panama, Peru, and Argentina have "regional divisions" that have
no internal functional coherence and are therefore useful only for statistical analyses or as a part of the machinery for the decentralization
of planning activities on the basis of decisions made at the national level.
Brazil has developed to a superb degree the use of the regional concept
for spatial analysis but not for integrated regional planning.

**Communism is not, however, incompatible with regional
planning. Yugoslavia has probably gone further than any other country
in the world in giving to its various regions the responsibility for
planning their own development.

forces lead to such autonomy at either the national or the subnational level if planning does not go beyond its present preoccupation with cities, industries, and foreign trade and begin at last to give serious consideration to those aspects of development which cannot be defined in exclusively monetary terms. There is no guarantee that a revolution in planning will be able to forestall future violence. But unless the planning process is revolutionized, a collapse of existing social, economic, and political structures appears inevitable.

4

REGIONAL ALLOCATION OF INDUSTRIAL CAPACITY IN THE LATIN AMERICAN FREE TRADE ASSOCIATION

Jaleel Ahmad

The Montevideo Treaty which created the Latin American Free Trade Association in 1960 included as objectives "the expansion of present national markets, through the gradual elimination of barriers to intra-regional trade," and "efforts to achieve the progressive complementarity and integration of national economies on the basis of an effective reciprocity of benefits."[1]

It appears in retrospect that the initial commitment to the treaty by LAFTA members was not sufficient to ensure the full realization of these objectives,[2] even though a series of ad hoc measures since 1964 have attempted to broaden the scope of the treaty. The main difficulties seem to arise from the fact that the tariff-cutting commitments by member countries were interpreted to include only the commodities that already had a substantial volume in the intra-zonal trade, thus precluding the as yet nonexistent but potentially important categories of trade. Second, the process of product-by-product negotiations for tariff reductions in the "national" and "common" schedules turned out to be particularly slow. Despite the inclusion so far of 11,000 tariff cuts or reductions in the two lists, all efforts to introduce elements of automaticity in negotiating tariff cuts have proved futile.

The quantitative magnitudes of intrazonal trade in LAFTA between 1961 and 1969 are summarized in Table 4.1. The total value of intra-LAFTA trade increased from $1,078 millions in 1961 to $2,432 millions in 1969, representing an increase of 125.0 percent. The figures for 1969 represent an increase of 14.6 percent for exports and 19.6 percent for imports as compared with 1968.

Some would maintain that the intrazonal trade increases by 1966 had merely restored the magnitudes that had existed prior to the formation of LAFTA and thus neutralized the effects of a particularly severe trade cycle in the late 1950s.[3] Others would argue that

TABLE 4.1

Intra-LAFTA Trade, 1961-69

	1961	1962	1963	1964	1965	1966	1967	1968	1969
Exports									
(millions of dollars, FOB)	489.2	547.0	583.4	716.3	842.2	875.8	851.7	1000.4	1146.9
Index (1961=100)	100	112	119	146	172	179	174	204	234
Imports									
(millions of dollars, CIF)	588.3	643.4	706.7	841.9	985.9	987.3	995.6	1074.3	1284.6
Index (1961=100)	100	109	120	143	168	168	169	182	218

Source: LAFTA Newsletter, No. 3, September 1970.

trade liberalization alone, without corresponding measures to accelerate total development of the region, cannot be construed as the
sole objective of LAFTA.[4] A broader interpretation of the treaty
therefore recognizes that a regional investment policy must be built
into the tariff-negotiating structure to meet regional production and
investment targets and to ensure that all member countries benefit
fully from the integration processes.[5]

In fact, the Montevideo Treaty had recognized the paramount
necessity of a regional investment policy in the principle of "complementarity," whereby the member countries could coordinate their
plans for specialization and expansion through vertical and (or) horizontal integration of industrial sectors. Behind the principle of
industrial complementarity were two underlying objectives, (a) an
orderly development of productive activities throughout the region
with a view to correcting the fundamental structural disequilibrium
in internal and external sectors and (b) ensuring that such corrections
are compatible with an equitable distribution of costs and benefits
among the member countries that are at different stages of development.

The concept of "reciprocity" implied by an equitable distribution
of costs and benefits acquires central importance in the processes of
integration in the less-developed countries, due to an overt preference for industrial activity by all member countries regardless of the

stage of their development.[6]* The current difficulties of LAFTA, of which one symptom was the creation of the Andean Group, imply that continued momentum toward integration requires some reasonable equality in the distribution of gains within the region. The problem is difficult, since initial differences in structures and endowment between countries almost guarantee that reciprocity will be far from automatic, and hence will be achieved only by more direct and visible means of distribution. Indeed, it is certain that trade liberalization alone not only will prove ineffective in promoting reciprocity but may even aggravate the degree of inequality.

LAFTA has given only halting recognition to the problem by according preferential treatment to its less-developed members. But these preferential tariff measures are not even as generous as those given to Greece by the European Economic Community.[7] The smaller countries in LAFTA have generally been disappointed because of the difficulties in building viable industries within the framework of trade liberalization and complementarity. Some of the larger LAFTA countries understandably seem to be preoccupied with their non-LAFTA markets where close to 90 percent of their trade takes place.

There is general agreement that the industrial complementarity schemes in LAFTA have not been very effective. Perhaps the most ambitious and far-reaching of such agreements concerns the petro-chemical industry agreement entered into by Bolivia, Colombia, Chile, and Peru in July 1968. The four countries have agreed to distribute among themselves the production of 39 items of the petro-chemical sector, with a nonduplicating clause meaning that the industries alloted to one country will not be set up in others.

The agreements in operation to date are few in number and involve a narrow range of commodities** and only a small number of countries. Their prime concern has been the reduction of tariffs and nontariff barriers to trade, rather than the initiation of substantial new areas of production. In addition, some basic industries in the public sector, like steel, aluminum, and fertilizers, are left out of

---

*In trade theory, reciprocity is not necessary for the tariff-reducing country to obtain both efficiency and consumption gains from cheapening of imports.

**The other complementarity agreements in effect in LAFTA cover calculating and data processing machines; electron tubes; electrical, mechanical, and heating equipment for houses; and electronic communications equipment.

the integration process altogether.[8] It is clear, however, that the attainment of freer trade has very little to do with fundamental problems of structural development in Latin America. Far from promoting any coherent vision of regional development, the complementarity principle may have the effect of freezing the existing distribution of industrial capacity, which is far from optimal, and creating further rigidities in the continental production and trade flows.

The problem of the equitable distribution of potential industrial capacity within the framework of LAFTA and the Andean Group (Bolivia, Chile, Colombia, Ecuador and Peru) is now one of the most critical issues facing the integration movement in Latin America.* The problem then is the following: what general principles might be derived for allocating industrial capacity among the member countries on criteria that go beyond the mechanism of freer trade? In other words, is an equitable distribution of productive activities possible directly, without sole reliance on the mechanism of trade liberalization?

INDUSTRIAL POLICY IN LAFTA

First of all, the traditional customs unions theory[10] is inadequate to deal with this problem, insofar as it concerns itself with static gains and losses and excludes all dynamic considerations. But even the static gains from trade liberalization in LAFTA are not likely to be large, although it is too early to assess their quantitative magnitude. The experience of the European Economic Community in this regard is instructive, where nearly all estimates of the gains from trade(or alternatively, the costs of protection) are quite low. Tibor Seitovsky and Petrus Johannes Verdoorn estimate the potential gains from European economic integration to be of the order of less than 0.05 percent of the combined GNP of the member countries.[11] H.G. Johnson suggests that the potential gains to Britain from trade with the European Free Trade Association (EFTA) are no more than 1.0 percent of the British national income.[12] Edward Denison calculates that only 2.0 percent of the total increase in national income

---

*A detailed comparative evaluation of the procedures and performance of current schemes of integrated industrial development in the less-developed countries as well as a discussion of the ways and means of facilitating industrial cooperation is contained in a study sponsored by the United Nations Conference on Trade Development in Geneva.[9]

between 1950 and 1962 can be ascribed to the reduction of trade barriers in Northwestern Europe.[13] On slightly different assumptions, A. Harberger estimates the maximum free trade benefits to Chile of the order of 2.5 percent of her GNP.[14] Even if one allows for large errors in estimation, the gains in pure efficiency appear to be minimal.

But what about the "dynamic" considerations? The industrial policy in LAFTA is essentially a continuation of the earlier policies of import substitution within national borders. Only this time the national units have been replaced by a larger continental unit comprising the 11-member community. The basic weakness of the earlier national policies was that, due to market limitations, protection was given to the domestic industry only in the production of consumer goods. This protection to the consumer goods industry inevitably led to an increased requirement for imported intermediate products,* which were permitted at favored rates. There was thus a systematic discouragement to import substitution in the intermediate goods sectors, both by the lower level of protection as well as by higher effective rates of protection for finished goods. It was inevitable, therefore, that the national import-substitution process must stop when opportunities for investment in finished goods are exhausted. These opportunities were indeed exhausted fairly quickly, since the size of the domestic market in most countries was not large and export possibilities both within and outside the region were significantly limited.

The Montevideo Treaty had visualized that any further import substitution in the critical sectors of intermediate products and capital goods has to be based on the continental market rather than on the smaller national ones. Import substitution in the new context is seen as a change involving comparative advantage, factor endowments, increasing labor skills, and the economies of scale. Import substitution based on these long-run structural changes is quite different from the import substitution induced by policies of import licensing, quotas, and overvalued exchange rates in individual countries.

------

*One indication of the degree of responsiveness of imports to changes in domestic economic activity may be had by reference to a study by Clark and Wiesskoff. By means of a function relating imports to gross fixed capital formation they calculated an elasticity of 0.83 for Brazil for the period 1950-65.[15]

PROBLEMS OF SCALE AND EXTERNAL EFFECTS

One particular element of the trade liberalization policy—economies of scale—has received the most attention in LAFTA. The notion that the economies of scale, though not always amenable to precise quantitative measurement, are central to the integration process is widespread.[16] More recently, Bela Balassa has given a central place to the economies of scale in the context of LAFTA.[17] Allan Manne has estimated that in at least three manufacturing sectors the projected 1972 domestic market in Mexico appears insufficient to support even a single plant of representative size. Manne concludes that the three sectors—turbine generators, locomotives, and ships—"should either be delayed by Mexico or else initiated cooperatively with other members of LAFTA." Thomas Victorisz and Manne had estimated earlier that the projected fertilizer needs of Latin American countries in 1965 can be most efficiently supplied by a single integrated plant.[18] Similarly, it is estimated that the most efficient level of operation of a steel plant is over one million ingot tons—a level of output reached only by Brazil and Mexico.[19]

Actually, empirical evidence about either the size distribution of economies of scale or its implications for productivity is inconclusive, notwithstanding its theoretical plausibility. In Latin America there is a widespread belief, undoubtedly based on comparisons with the U.S. manufacturing conditions,[20] that production units are so small as to be inevitably inefficient. Goran Ohlin observes that "probably the operations of international companies are more than any other factor responsible for the impression that the existing national units are too small for effective economic operation."[21] There is, of course, no denying that in some industries and sectors there are significant economies of scale for the relevant range of output. But it is equally clear that in a large continent like Latin America small and big plants can survive in a symbiotic relationship.

The largely unwarranted claim for "efficiency" based simply on size, when combined with the search for "reciprocity," has created a schizophrenia in LAFTA's industrial policy. These two concerns have divergent consequences. The pull of efficiency impels industrial activities to concentrate in locations where rates of return are higher, while reciprocity tends to demand dispersal.

Failure to exploit economies of scale may raise the real cost of resources necessary to achieve a given degree of industrialization but with a relatively lesser concentration. But as Bhagwati[22] points out, it is not legitimate to describe the resulting situation as one of nonviability. The increase in real costs due to deliberately ignoring the economies of scale would then simply be the cost of reciprocity.* Pooling of markets via integration may reduce the joint costs of protection, and hence of industrialization, both in the case of constant returns and, a fortiori, in the presence of economies of scale. On the other hand, external economies, temporal growth of demand, and transport costs all suggest that diversification to serve the aim of reciprocity may be an equally desirable policy.[24]

It would thus seem that the preoccupation in LAFTA with the economies of scale and the allied notion of static comparative costs has acted as a straitjacket, precluding attention to other serious problems. One wishes that the ingenuity lavished on perfecting the arguments for "minimum efficient scale" had been devoted to more fundamental problems of regional balance and stability. The problem was never so serious in the EEC or in EFTA, simply because the level of disparity in economic structure is relatively small. In an economic union of unequal partners like LAFTA it is almost axiomatic that (a) countries that can theoretically "go it alone" because of their competitive strength will tend to accumulate most of the benefits of freer trade, and cannot realistically be expected to forego them unless required to do so by subsequent arrangements; and (b) the relatively less-developed countries need extra-trade-liberalization measures to "equalize" the benefits and cannot be expected to continue to commit themselves to the union in the absence of such measures.

A greater readiness to recognize the tradeoffs between economies of scale and other distributive gains between member countries would have the effect of mutually reinforcing each others' economic viability and ensuring the continued existence of the union. Any success in devising such measures may have the effect of rendering trade liberalization superfluous apart from its cohesive, catalytic role.

STRUCTURAL DISABILITIES

The traditional trade theory with its reliance on smooth processes of continuous adjustment fails to recognize the structural problem. There is no need to recapitulate the arguments here. Essentially it is asserted that a trading country can always convert

---

*In steel industry, for instance, assuming a minimum efficient size of one million ingot tons annually, costs are approximately 18 percent higher for capacity levels of half a million tons and 33 percent higher for a level of a quarter of a million tons.[23]

exportables into importables at international price ratios, assuming a favorable spectrum of elasticities. Given this continuously differentiable transformation locus, the production and demand policies of the country can be separated.[25]

These conclusions rarely amount to more than a preference for free market forces which would be easy to share if the markets—domestic and international—were indeed free or even in operation. In any event, marginal reallocation of resources resulting from changes in international price ratios are clearly no solution to the problem of structural disequilibrium and consequent long-run instability.

Latin American economies have suffered from structural imbalance for too long to let simple trade liberalization correct the situation. Structural disequilibriums arise because of the failure of the economy to adapt its production structure and trade patterns to the factors that condition its future development.[26] This form of disequilibrium results from flaws in the adjustment mechanism by which excess demands and excess supplies are eliminated. The present imbalances in Latin America are clearly the result of past failures to adjust the structure of production and trade consistent with changes in external and internal data. While the internal causes of disequilibrium may have had an external origin (e.g., an unanticipated fall in exports or unexpected difficulties in obtaining capital inflows), a continuing failure to reallocate resources can only cause further rigidities.

Regional integration policies can mitigate the rigor of some of the most binding constraints to development in Latin America. A common denominator in the new domestic policies in Latin American countries is the concern with structural changes in production, trade, employment, and growth.[27] Deprived of the instruments of commercial policy in the wake of trade liberalization, the Latin American governments are being gradually led to a prolonged and detailed attention to their domestic structures. This policy relies on direct measures to correct distortions in labor and capital markets.[28]

In principle it is thus better that the locus of attention is shifting from the external to the domestic sectors. This policy carries the possibility of promoting industrial development and reciprocity rather better than trade liberalization. One is forced to recognize, however, that the required degree of control over economic forces will in some cases entail a sacrifice of conventional economic efficiency, at least in the short run. But there is also the indication that as long as the emphasis is on the long-run adjustment, social and economic objectives will coincide.

EQUITABLE DISTRIBUTION OF
REGIONAL ACTIVITIES

The rather poor record of post-LAFTA progress in industrial complementarity suggests that the search for developmental policies that do not conflict with market forces released by trade liberalization has been an elusive goal. At the supranational level there is the obvious problem that potential measures of cooperation defy any attempt at precise definition, despite the fact that economic interests of any one country are profoundly affected by the policies of another.

Arbitration at the supranational level would certainly be necessary, since in a world of imperfect competition what is good for LAFTA is not necessarily the summation of what is good for each individual country. This nonconvergence may arise from several causes. First, in the face of composite objectives the preference function of any one country would be different from that of another, since they are likely to attach different weights to different objectives. No spontaneous interregional "ordering" thus emerges and gives rise to the "Condercet paradox." Second, even if one were to admit that a common criterion exists, it might be that a key activity in one country need not coincide with the one necessary for supranational growth and stability. Third, the differential rates of productivity between countries may guide foreign capital to areas of higher productivity and thus accentuate regional imbalance.

It is clear that some form of bargaining process will have to be incorporated into the trade liberalization policy as a means of distributing industrial capacity. But what should be the bases of such an arbitration? One radical alternative, of course, would be the creation of a supranational planning agency that could modify the international price ratios to serve the purposes of regional balance. The European Coal and Steel Community is an example of such a regional planning agency. But at least in the near future in Latin America this must remain only a distant possibility. "Neither the Latin American governments nor any international agencies envisage an over-all Latin American planning which would coordinate twenty different national plans."[29]

The method of lump-sum transfers to the disadvantaged groups in an integration area has also been suggested.[30] First of all, such schemes cannot be relevant if no institutional means exist for their implementation, as is typically the case in LAFTA. Second, even if such transfers were possible, they will not solve the problem of structural viability in the receiving countries.* Here the most

---

*The continuing difficulties and disappointments with foreign

important if not the only means of redistribution may consist of increasing the rate of industrial development.

In one fundamental sense there is no essential contradiction
with comparative costs if one takes comparative costs as a principle
of bargaining, rather than simply a result of market forces. Then
one could not only include all foreseeable elements of "dynamic
comparative advantage" but also incorporate direct economic tradeoffs
between the countries. One possible means of effecting this kind of
arbitrage based on economies of scale and reciprocity is to provide
for staggering of investment projects over time and space. David
Kendrick suggests an illustration where "Chile might construct a
new steel mill and Peru a new petroleum refinery at the same time
and begin trading in these products with the understanding that so
many years later Peru would build a new steel mill and Chile a petroleum refinery and the flow of products would be reversed." Another
possibility cited by Kendrick is, "When a country installs a new automobile plant it might build a very large plant in order to take advantage of the economies of scale. It could then export for a time
with the expectation that exports will decrease as domestic demand
grows. Neighboring countries might agree to stagger the installation
of large production facilities over time in a complementary fashion." [31]

Latin America provides several examples of the sequence and
ease with which new industrial units can be established in formerly
unindustrialized areas. The development of the Chilean automobile
assembly industry in Arica in Tarapaca Province—a virtually underdeveloped area—is a representative example. If economies of scale
are important, the comparative advantage will have to be determined
at a specified level of output, depending on partial or complete access
to the continental market. Alternatively if the external effects are
believed to be sizable, comparative costs should be determined for
alternative combinations of investments rather than for individual
projects. Further, one must have some notion of the long-run opportunity costs, since neither market prices nor current shadow
prices are likely to reflect real costs.

In theory at least it is also possible to lay down a Lange-Lerner-
type "rule" for international prices within the region. The producers
would then base demands and supplies on "profit" maximization
at prices given by the region, and the prices are revised in proportion
to excess demands. It is not necessary that these "prices" are set
by a supranational planner; they can be arrived at and agreed to by a

---

aid among both the donor and the receiving countries is a warning
against such facile notions.

process of iterative bargaining which involves communication between the parties. In most such situations it would only be necessary that a regional point of view prevails. In other words, member countries when making individual decisions should attach some weight to the preferences of the region, i.e., the collective entity of all members.* In problems involving multiple criteria with no possibility of a collective ordering, a "third" party (in our case, the region) with equal weight but with a different point of view can always obtain a consistent ranking without any intervention.[32]

The distribution of production activities by levels of technological complexity of the production processes is a case in point. The more-advanced countries are naturally in a better position to establish technologically more-complex industries manufacturing intermediate and capital goods. But light manufacturing industries, e.g., electric bulbs and radios, can be initiated virtually anywhere in the LAFTA region. There are also numerous possibilities for interproduct specialization in the case of multiproduct industries like the iron and steel industry. If regional weights are appropriately taken into consideration it would be desirable for each individual country—regardless of its level of development—not to manufacture the whole range of products but to specialize in a few selected lines and trade with the others. It is necessary to emphasize that this kind of specialization does not require a supranational mechanism; it requires only that all parties involved agree to allow some weight to broader LAFTA considerations, and base their individual decisions on information supplied by each other. Reciprocity would be achieved when a set of countries mutually provide markets for each others' goods.

One may expose oneself to the familiar criticism that such trade may lead to the exchange of high-cost products for other high-cost products. There is no presumption that this will necessarily be so. On the contrary, interproduct specialization is equally likely to lead to production below international costs (i.e., costs outside LAFTA) by a more intensive utilization of capacity in specific lines of operation. Even if the costs are "high" in the transition stage there is no reason to suppose that they will always remain high.** In any event, the

---

*This should be distinguished from the "rule of the majority" which would be prejudicial to national sovereignty.

**The purists may contend that the absence of discipline provided by international commerce may eliminate the incentive to reduce costs. But carrots are often as effective as sticks and domestic discipline within LAFTA may be equally effective.

comparison with international costs is somewhat spurious, since it assumes that on the margin domestic resources can be converted into necessary foreign exchange. This assumption of continuous transformation, however, is not very realistic, particularly in view of the extreme weakness of the export sectors in Latin America.

It is obvious that the variety of circumstances and relative valuations of reciprocity make it nearly impossible to lay down universal criteria. It is equally clear, however, that plausible bases do exist to deal with the problem of efficiency and equity in distributing the gains from regional integration. The choice among them necessarily depends on the particular issues and parties involved.

5

THE PEARSON AND PREBISCH REPORTS: THE CRUCIAL ISSUE OF UNEMPLOYMENT

David H. Pollock

INTRODUCTION

For reasons of space limitation this chapter does not attempt to delve deeply into two documents of such detail and complexity as the Pearson Report* and the Prebisch Report**. Instead it limits itself to sketching in broad strokes what appear to be some of the main points of similarity and difference between the two reports. It then draws a few overall conclusions therefrom, emphasizing in particular the growing and urgent issue of unemployment.

This has been done with the goal of trying to present in comparative form what might have been the substance of a dialogue if these two distinguished citizens of the Western Hemisphere—one from the developed north and the other from the developing south—had in fact met to put forth some personal variations around the basic theme of development. At this historical juncture, only one generation away from the end of a wartime era and with only one other generation separating us from the beginning of the twenty-first century, many people throughout the hemisphere are trying to clarify old thoughts and evolve new ones about relations between rich nations and poor. Therefore it seems timely to reflect upon what these two internationally

---

*Partners in Progress: President's Report. (President of the Commission on International Development.) (New York: Praeger Publishers, 1969.)

**Change and Development: Latin America's Great Task, Report submitted to the president of the Inter-American Development Bank, 1970 (New York: Praeger Publishers, 1971).

renowned thinkers have recently written about problems of development, globally and in a regional context, and how each of them would
design strategies to overcome such problems. It is in short a
pertinent time to ask how Pearson and Prebisch—viewing the world
from their different vantage points—might find elements of divergence
and convergence as they try to evolve a common set of developmental
goals and then come up with policies and programs to implement
those goals.

THREE POINTS OF FUNDAMENTAL IDENTITIES

In at least three basic respects the Pearson and Prebisch reports complement and reinforce one another.

The "Partnership" and "Convergence"
Principles

In the title of his report as well as elsewhere, Lester Pearson
stresses the need for a " . . . new partnership based on an informal
understanding expressing the reciprocal rights and obligations of
donors and recipients." On his part, Raul Prebisch emphasizes that
" . . . in reality, development calls for a number of covergent measures
which must be adopted by both groups of countries if it is universally
acknowledged that the problem is common to all." Thus both reports
highlight the fact that development depends on the simultaneous application of a series of joint actions—both internal and external—that must
be taken by rich and poor countries alike. They have common responsibilities and hence all must adopt and apply a series of converging
measures if any global strategy of development is to be truly effective
and not merely a list of rhetorical platitudes.

Why do the Pearson and Prebisch reports repeatedly emphasize
such seemingly obvious facts as the existence of "reciprocal responsibilities" and the need for "convergent measures?" The reason is
not difficult to see. Far too often during the postwar years both
national and international measures aimed at development have emerged
in a piecemeal fashion. They were disjointed and ad hoc and had no
organic structure. This was wasteful in terms of time, talent, and
capital resources. Measures emerged that were without cohesion or
order and did not reinforce each other, but rather surfaced, then
subsided, depending on the moods and characteristics of the moment.
For want of a better phrase, and for those who are over 30 years of
age, one might refer to this as the "seesaw syndrome." That is to
say, one particular approach or emphasis gained tremendous weight

to the detriment of others which, in consequence, were pushed far into
the air and even out of sight.

Let us consider a few examples. One past practice, fortunately
less prevalent today, has been that of telling a recipient country in
effect that it must first check inflation and then—only then—would a
donor give it a much-needed loan. Yet it might have been precisely
such an external loan, taken in conjunction with related internal
measures, that would provide the extra margin of resources needed
to stop the inflation. As other examples, one might think back over
the years about the way in which donors have put forward individual
measures, each as "the" approach to development; for instance, price
and exchange rate stability, fiscal reform, the Green Revolution,
family planning, attracting private foreign direct investment, and the
like. On the other hand, one can also remember how often governments and exporters in developing countries have in past times
focussed their attention so closely upon external (commercial policy)
constraints that must be eliminated before they would take the internal
self-help (production) measures needed to improve their commercial
competitiveness.

The point at issue is that none of these emphases—whether put
forward by developed or developing countries or by intergovernmental
agencies—should be viewed as correct or incorrect taken by themselves. Clearly the impact of such measures is reduced, if not lost
completely, when they take place one by one and without order. All
individual strands of policy have their places but they must be woven
into an integrated framework of converging measures, to be applied
simultaneously within some finite period. In a word, Prebisch and
Pearson insist that development must be viewed in a global planning
framework as others (Tinbergen and Myrdal for instance) have also
stressed. Here then—in their stress upon "convergent measures
simultaneously applied"—is the first basic way in which the Prebisch
and Pearson reports strengthen one another.

Mutual Reinforcement Politically

One of the more unusual aspects of a comparison between the
Pearson and Prebisch reports relates to the political configuration
of the two authors and the way in which that configuration reinforces
the impact of their respective recommendations. At first glance,
this idea may not seem evident, since their political symbolism is so
different. On the one hand appears Lester B. Pearson, former prime
minister of Canada, Nobel Prize winner, heading a panel of prestigious
commissioners mostly from the Development Assistance Committee
(DAC), the "rich man's club" of the Organization for European

Cooperation and Development (OECD). And on the other hand there is Raul Prebisch, long a controversial spokesman for the developing world and, as the Washington Post recently said," . . . independent enough to include Che Guevara among his sources."

Yet note how in fact these disparate backgrounds interconnect in a most effective fashion when each man directs his recommendations largely (though not wholly) at his "own camp" and not at the others. Thus we see Pearson admonishing and exhorting the developed OECD countries about their international responsibilities while Prebisch does the same vis-à-vis the Latin countries in terms of their internal responsibilities. In my view this was a very wise tactical approach. Had Pearson unduly lectured to the developing countries his report would have been received very cooly by them, if received is the word. In the case of Prebisch, he could lecture Latin Americans about their need—and competence—to evolve their own destiny by their own hands. Thus Prebisch did not cavil at the rich, nor did Pearson at the poor. Both aimed their principal fire where it would have maximum receptivity rather than the reverse. It is in this sense that I use the phrase "mutual reinforcement politically."

Intellectual Agreement on Specific Measures of International Economic Collaboration

It has been highly interesting to note the progress achieved during the past half decade or so regarding intellectual agreement on key areas of a global policy for development. This is a matter of much fascination to developmentalists—theoretical and applied alike— as has been briefly noted in a paper recently published by the Society for International Development. In that paper the point was made that as recently as 1964 many if not most of the new approaches to international commercial and financial policies put forward by the UN Conference on Trade and Development (UNCTAD) had been greeted with much skepticism and even outright hostility by the developed world generally. Consequently when these ideas—which were considered heretical and even counterproductive in 1964—were implicitly endorsed and recommended by the Pearson report in 1969, this was really an intellectual watershed, a true act of international statesmanship on the part of Pearson and his commissioners. As stated in my article:

> Not only the underlying philosophy of UNCTAD (in particular the basic thesis of minimizing the external constraint to growth of developing countries within a policy of convergent measures) but also most of its specific measures

have now been given the salutary respectability that follows
from receiving the implicit endorsement of this recent
and prestigious international commission.[1]

This is an issue of very great significance and undoubtedly explains
why Pearson largely concentrates his report around the three subheads
that follow below—all of which deal largely with international policy
issues—whereas Prebisch largely accepts them as given and hence
concentrates his attention on what should be done internally within
the developing countries of Latin America.

It is of course well known that these intellectual advances have
not been followed proportionately in political terms, that is to say,
in the sense of firm commitments to transfer a specific volume of
resources within a specified period. On the contrary, while the
thinkers' comprehension has grown, the legislators' decisions have
deteriorated. In real terms, for instance, the value of global aid was
reduced by more than 50 percent between 1962 and 1968. Nonetheless,
the desirability of larger and more continuous real resource transfers
is no longer in question, only the feasibility of selected approaches.
And even there, the heresy of yesterday is becoming the accepted
wisdom of today. Bear in mind for instance that current international
discussion about negotiating a system of nondiscriminatory, non-
reciprocal global preferences represents a significant reversal of
the situation existing as recently as the 1964 UNCTAD session when
discussions on preferences were rejected by several major developed
countries solely on grounds of principle. Remember too that the idea
of a Special Drawing Right (SDR) "link" was rejected out of hand only
two years ago but is now under study within the International Monetary
Fund (IMF) and the International Bank for Reconstruction and Development (IBRD) as well as in OECD and UNCTAD regarding alternative
approaches for possible implementation. Indeed, there is now a rather
surprisingly broad-based agreement to an array of international
financial and commercial measures that both the Pearson and Prebisch
reports have supported. Some of them are listed below.

Financial Policy: Public Funds

Volume. With progressively fewer reservations, the international
community is now accepting "targetry" as a basis for determining
the volume of global capital flows from rich to poor countries. This
includes the 1.0 percent of GNP target, of which 0.70 to 0.75 percent
is to be in public form and of which 0.20 to 0.30 percent should be
transferred via multilateral channels. Even where targetry is not
acceptable to congresses or parliaments it is now largely accepted that
there should be at least a "reversal of the recent downtrend" in international public flows.

Terms and Conditions. Here many advances have been made regarding the need to increase the concessional element in capital flows (through, for example, more grants, lower interest rates, and longer grace and maturity periods). Similarly, there is a greater awareness of the need to untie aid: at the minimum, to enable aid extended by developed countries to be used for purchases in developing countries. Increasingly, moreover, efforts are being made to ensure a greater continuity in aid flows, for example by two- to five-year instead of annual appropriations. And finally, the evaluation of performance criteria is being considered more and more in terms of the developmental needs of recipient countries rather than the political criteria of the donor countries: more and more too, this is being done through multinational rather than bilateral forums.

Debt Rescheduling. There has been an explosive increase in the external debt of developing countries and its concomitant servicing burden. This is particularly evident in Latin America. The need therefore to effect organic debt rescheduling programs—on the average as well as at the margin—is now widely accepted as an urgent political and economic datum.

Other Financial Policies. Often, recommendations that are considered unrealistic and illusory at a given time are found to be both desirable and feasible not long afterward. In this category reference should be made to the schemes for "complementary" and "supplementary" financing by the IMF and IBRD, respectively; the "Horowitz Plan" for establishing an interest equalization fund; assistance by multigovernmental agencies on the prefinancing of international buffer stocks; and the SDR "link" proposal designed to transform some of the newly created SDRS directly into international development assistance through, for instance, bonds purchased from the International Development Association (IDA) or regional development banks.

Foreign Private Direct Investment Policy

New Studies. These should be undertaken to assess both the costs (e.g., what are the direct balance-of-payments costs and what are the political costs, such as those concerning the impact of multinational corporations on regional integration groupings within the developing world?) and the benefits (e.g., how to transfer "internal" technology in the form of scientific or managerial know-how and how to transfer "international" technology regarding production, marketing, and distribution techniques?).

New Operational Formulas. Additionally there are the needs for evolving new and better formulas that would permit some form of peaceful coexistence between foreign and domestic entrepreneurs. This might entail the use of traditional formulas (such as joint ventures and management and patent agreements) or newer formulas (such as those specifying the need for phased disinvestment through prior negotiations, in order to transfer some specified degree of equity control from foreign to local hands).

Trade Policy

Short-run. Both the Pearson and Prebisch reports stress the importance of short-term stabilization of export earnings of primary products (through, for example, formal commodity agreements, informal commodity arrangements, buffer stocks, and other national and international market control techniques). Uncertainty poses a direct economic cost, and therefore short-term stabilization would redound to the benefit of planners in the developing world.

Long-term. In addition to minimizing fluctuations around the trend, however, it is of fundamental importance to increase the trend itself. This might be done through a number of avenues, such as imposing a "stand-still" on those impediments that still inhibit access to the markets of developed countries; by directly expanding market access through global preferences and through other schemes designed to reduce tariff and nontariff barriers to the markets of developed countries; export promotion measures; and of course the need to inaugurate structural (production and export) diversification programs in developing countries.

My point in reviewing the international policy subheads above is this: given the different structure and orientation of the Pearson and Prebisch reports, if both of them are in basic agreement with those headings then there is an a priori basis for concluding that the issue for the 1970s is quite different from the issue for the 1960s. Earlier it was to obtain intellectual agreement on new approaches to policy; during the 1970s it is to ensure political commitment. In this context, the joint abrazo given by Pearson and Prebisch to the first and third subhead topics and—though to a lesser degree—to the second strikes me as very significant indeed.

FOUR POINTS OF DIVERGENCE

In four different though interconnected ways the Pearson and Prebisch reports differ in structure, substance, or emphasis.

An Inventory of Recommendations versus an Organic Ideological Framework

The Pearson report basically entails a listing of 68 specific policy recommendations, each one supported by separate statistical and

analytical coverage. With relatively few exceptions (such as those
pertaining to the matter of private foreign investment), I think they
are excellent recommendations considered one by one. On the other
hand, however, I feel that they lack a central philosophical or ideological core. Indeed, there is almost an element of clinical detachment
to this particular "inventorying of measures" approach. The Prebish
report is quite different: almost the reverse in fact. On the one hand,
for instance, the Prebisch report possesses an organic ideological
framework encompassing economic, social, political, and cultural
considerations, but all contained within the contours of a specifically
structured developmental strategy. And on the other hand, there is
the matter of style and presentation. The Prebisch report is far
from being clinical and detached. On the contrary, it is very Latin
in the intense, vigorous, and one might even say passionate way in
which its case is presented. As Albert Hirschmann once said of an
earlier Prebisch report, this is another in his series of "veritable
manifestos," although here, for reasons of both form and substance,
I would rephrase this as a political as well as an economic manifesto.
I think Paul Rosenstein-Rodan put the matter very well when he said
"The Prebisch report is like a seismographic apparatus sensitively
registering social tremors." It is no disservice or criticism of the
Pearson report to say it has a very different "tone."

There is an incidental institutional collorary to the above. One
aspect of the Pearson report that troubled many readers sympathetic
to its case was that it did not provide any built-in institutional mechanisms designed to perpetuate itself and hence its recommended
objectives. This is an important matter in the bureaucratic channels
within which such reports must float or sink. Again, to quote the
Washington Post, international reports on development too often
"resemble the proverbial bee which, stinging once, dies." The Prebisch
report did not come fully to grips with this problem either. However
it has undoubtedly contributed directly to certain new and important
types of institutional machinery, for instance, by suggesting the
creation of a new subsidiary of the Inter-American Development Bank
(IDB) and by recommending a broadening of the country review
mechanism beyond current Inter-American Committee for the Alliance
for Progress (CIAP) dimensions. In addition it has been placed on
the agenda of a forthcoming ECLA meeting, thereby requiring formal
consideration by the 20 governmental members of that commission.
Both the Pearson and Prebisch reports of course lead to various
follow-up actions within the IBRD and IDB, respectively. But the
other measures just mentioned should help in particular to sustain
the momentum of the Prebisch report's broad policy recommendations.

Six Percent Versus Eight Percent Growth Rates and
Their Underlying Rationale

The Pearson report puts forth a 6 percent rate of growth for
the developing world during the decade of the 1970s. Somewhat
surprisingly, however, the report does not present a theoretical
model—neither quantitative nor qualitative—to support that particular
number. I must confess that I am a bit puzzled as to the rationale
underlying the 6 percent target. Not that I am necessarily in disagreement with it as a target for the developing world as a whole (after all,
it exceeds the 5 percent target put forward by the United Nations
General Assembly for the so-called First Development Decade), but
rather I do not know why 6 percent. Why not 5.5 percent, or 6.5 percent, or 10 percent, or whatever? Thus, in the "Conference on
Development in the 1970s" held at Columbia University and Williams-
burg, February 15 to 21, 1970, L. Dominguez made the following point
about the Pearson report:

> One would want to know more about such things as why the
> 6% target was selected. Not that quantitatively precise
> answers are necessarily possible but an explicit presen-
> tation of the growth scheme underlying the Commission's
> analysis would have helped to understand the internal
> logic of what otherwise appears as a loosely connected
> number of proposals of obviously varying importance.

The Prebisch report, for its part, presents a target fully one-
third higher than the Pearson report, namely, an 8 percent GDP (gross
domestic product) growth rate. This is a target of very major
proportions, since among other things it presupposes an increase in
Latin America's investment from its present rate of 18 percent
(close to that of Canada) to a future rate of almost 27 percent
(approaching that of Japan). However, my point here is neither to
support nor to criticize the magnitude of the projected investment
and income growth targets put forward in the Prebisch report.
Difficult as it will be to attain them—and it will be very difficult
indeed—the background data and underlying assumptions for those
targets are presented in the Prebisch report. This is done in general
analytical terms as well as in the form of an econometric model
specifying levels of domestic and foreign savings; export and import
requirements; the volume, terms, and conditions of foreign loans;
changes in per capita productivity and aggregate output in different
economic activity sectors; and the like. One can argue with the
assumptions postulated in the Prebisch report but there they are, for
all to see and query.

Another and even more basic issue emerging from the two different growth rates has nothing to do with the scale of the numbers as such but rather with their socioeconomic policy significance. This is a rather delicate political issue and one that can easily be misunderstood. However, I feel that an absolutely fundamental point is involved, and one which must be treated in this chapter, albeit in brief and general terms. Note that the Pearson report presents its economic growth target (6 percent) as a prime goal of policy. The Prebisch report conversely puts forward its growth rate (8 percent) as an economic means to a social end. Thus in the latter report a computer was asked what rate of economic growth would be required to bring about a new and different pattern of employment and income distribution in Latin America. The very core of the Prebisch report, in short, is to maximize social welfare and distributive justice. To do this, the absorption of marginal and redundant manpower becomes the central focus of policy.

As an aside, it is interesting to compare Prebisch's policy focus in this report with his two main reports as secretary-general of UNCTAD. In UNCTAD, his policy net was thrown widely over a number of external (trade and aid) issues, but central to it all was his emphasis on filling the foreign exchange gap of developing countries. In this report his net is also thrown widely, but this time over a number of internal policy issues (at the heart of which is the issue of unemployment). Growth is basic, but it is viewed by Prebisch as an economic means to the fundamental social end of a more equitable diffusion of the fruits of progress.

Elements of a New Development Policy That Extend Beyond the Economic System

With relatively few exceptions, I believe the 68 recommendations in the Pearson report to be both desirable and feasible. Excellent as they are, however, they seemingly accept as given that the social, political, and cultural mores of our times will be extrapolated through the next few decades. Prebisch questions this thesis and asks instead what type of society, indeed what type of man, does the developing world wish to evolve by the turn of this century. For me, as a North American, it is most suggestive, audacious, and I must add admirable that—in a long technical report aimed at stimulating the economic and social development of Latin America—the entire final chapter (before the conclusions) is devoted to the matter of "transcendent values" which extend as the report says "beyond the economic system."

These values—cultural, philosophic, artistic, ethical—will have a great appeal to the youth in Latin America who, like our own youth

here, do not believe that man lives by GNP alone. Another basic
difference between the Pearson and Prebisch reports, then, is that
the latter seeks to illuminate society's countenance in the developing
world of the future and asks what human values should lie behind that
countenance, an aspect which was not, I felt, treated with the same
perceptiveness in the Pearson report. Of course, the Pearson report
was not intended to devote itself to Latin America per se, and it did
make reference to various elements analogous to the so-called
transcendental values of the Prebisch report. But even so, the ways
in which the Pearson and Prebisch reports view this important issue
differ noticeably—in my opinion at least—in intensity, emphasis, and
compassion.

Another difference in coverage concerns the extent to which the
Prebisch report probes deeply into certain operational aspects of
existing political systems. Thus the report is bluntly and unequivocally
critical of "immediatism" (the unduly short-term time horizons of
many politicians who respond to day-by-day problems through improvisation rather than by rational long-term planning); of "developmentism"
(the almost fatalistic assumption that if an economic system is
growing at a satisfactory pace social welfare will be maximized
through the spontaneous play of market forces); and hence the need
for much tighter "political discipline" (whereby all income strata—
upper, middle, and lower—combine their political participation to
bring about the structural transformations needed to optimize investment through domestic resources). One must be careful in interpreting
this latter point. The Prebisch report at no stage suggests one or
another type of economic system needed for greater political "discipline." That is the sovereign prerogative of each nation. However,
he does ask a question as pertinent to Canada as to Latin America in
these troubled times, namely, whether ideologies will influence the
course of events or vice versa. Whether by design or accident one
does not get the impression that such matters were of equal importance
in the Pearson Commission's scheme of things.

Areas of Special Policy Priority

To pursue the matter of growth rates a little further, and again
at the risk of unduly simplifying these two very complex reports, it
is reasonable to say that among its many areas of policy emphasis
the Pearson report places agriculture and population control very
high on its rank order of priorities. Thus, as stated by M. Lipton in
the December 1969 University of Sussex Bulletin, "Donors and
recipients must work together to concentrate the national development
programme on sectors with satisfactory returns, properly used. But

what are these sectors? The sectors to which the Pearson report
devotes relevant attention are agriculture and population policy."
(Emphasis added.) The Prebisch report conversely postulates industrialization and employment policies as primus inter pares. Not that
these differing emphases are necessarily in conflict: one might even
say that they are the mirror image of each other. Yet it is precisely
the differences in emphasis and in priority that are basic. For
Prebisch, like Pearson, is unequivocal about the need for a structural
transformation of Latin America's agricultural sector to make it
more dynamic in the future than in the past. But—and this is perhaps
the most important single "but" one can use in comparing the two
reports—Prebisch expresses much more concern about what will
happen to the rural labor force when agricultural productivity rises
under the stimulus of a Green Revolution.

　　Here is the crux of the matter. Prebisch is disconcerted to
find the tendency recorded during the past 20 years, when a steadily
rising share of the labor force left the farms and became marginal
and redundant in the cities. There they were overtly unemployed, or
else were underemployed in very low-productivity service activities.
Conversely, the share absorbed in secondary sector activities (industry, construction, and mining) has fallen steadily since 1950. Such
contradictions should not be allowed to continue, according to Prebisch,
for three different but interrelated reasons: economic (the redundant
work force makes a minimal contribution to the growth of GNP, if
indeed it makes a contribution at all), social (large and ever-growing
numbers of under-or unemployed laborers distort still further an
already highly-skewed pattern of income distribution), and political
(the "marginal ones" cluster together in urban slums where they
constitute a seemingly inert mass, but one that can be only too easily
ignited by sparks of political tension).

　　Perhaps two of the figures appearing in the Prebisch report
will illustrate this letter point more clearly (see Figures 5.1 and 5.2).
These two figures portray dramatically the manpower-absorption
problem so central to the report. Thus, a seemingly inexorable
characteristic of the developmental process involves a decline in the
share of the total labor force engaged in agriculture. Although the
intensity of the phenomenon differs as between countries it has
characterized virtually every region of the world, regardless of the
economic and social systems involved. Whether because of the
attraction of city lights or because of higher levels of agricultural
productivity—especially when coupled with increased mechanization—
the end result has been a faster and faster exodus of workers from
farm to city. As is well known, this phenomenon has been widespread
in Canada as well as in Latin America; my own province, Saskatchewan,
has provided a vivid illustration of this during the past 20 years. In

FIGURE 5.1

Distribution of the Total Latin American
Labor Force

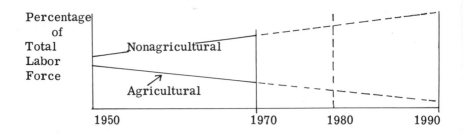

FIGURE 5.2

Distribution of the Nonagricultural Latin American
Labor Force

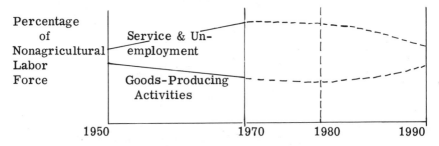

any case, as Figure 5.1 shows, a continuation of that trend is projected
for Latin America throughout the next 20 years. However, although the
the trend will undoubtedly continue its intensity will vary greatly,
depending on numerous factors. If, for example, agricultural productivity rises sharply, as will be the case if the Green Revolution is
successful, then the exodus of workers from farm to city will be
correspondingly accentuated.

    And what happens to these people who are marginal on the farm
and then become even more redundant in the cities? As shown in
Figure 5.2, some find employment in goods-producing activities
(industry, construction, and mining). Unfortunately however, a larger
and larger share of them move into tertiary sector activities, typically
at very low levels of output and remuneration (such as household
domestics or underutilized labor in public administration) or are

unemployed. Note in Figure 5.2 how the share of the nonagricultural labor force engaged in the production of goods fell from 35 percent to only 30 percent between 1950 and 1970, and therefore the share represented by services or unemployed rose from 65 percent to 70 percent during that same interval. It is precisely to check the disparate trends of the two lines in Figure 5.2 that the Prebisch report postulates the need for Latin America's GDP to rise from its postwar rate of 5.2 percent to a future rate of 8.0 percent by 1980 and beyond. But as Figure 5.2 also shows, even if this massive acceleration in economic growth can be achieved it will still require two more decades (from 1970 to 1990) before Latin America will have been able to recover from the effects of the past two decades (1950 to 1970) where there was no de facto employment policy, broadly conceived. One full generation of time, in other words, will be required to make up for a generation of time lost, at least as regards employment policy.

Thus the Prebisch report postulates a line of reasoning that begins with a Green Revolution but ends with a plea for industrialization to absorb the labor force displaced by the Green Revolution. Reflect for a moment on the following. The Pearson report states quite explicitly that "the main burden of absorbing the increase in the labour force falls inevitably on agriculture," a statement that contrasts noticeably with that in the Prebisch report, reading "The idea of placing the emphasis on agriculture and paying little attention to industry is dying hard, but it is indefensible." Here, as presented in the title of my chapter, is one of the most crucial issues distinguishing the policy emphasis of the two reports.

TWO CONCLUDING POINTS

Internationally: Economic Ingenuity Versus the Need for Political Commitments

On reflecting back upon the various points of similarity and difference characterizing the Pearson and Prebisch reports, two issues seem to merit special attention. One has to do with future priorities on the part of the international community and the other concerns national policy priorities within the Latin American context.

Looking first at the international side, there no longer seems to be the need that existed as recently as a decade ago to invent ever-longer and more novel lists of new commercial and financial policy recommendations designed to foment the economic growth of developing countries. A comprehensive list of such recommendations now exists on which intellectual agreement is widespread. The problem

here, on which both Pearson and Prebisch are in accord, is therefore
one of political will rather than of ideological content or economic
ingenuity. This problem is assuredly one of global dimension, and
its resolution lies in the hands of legislators in rich nations, as was
noted so often in the Pearson report.[2]

Nationally: The Importance of Restoring Sectoral
Balance Between Agriculture and Industry

The second point concerns the responsibilities of Latin American
legislators to resolve their own manifold internal development problems. The Prebisch report presents a broad ideological framework
of means and ends in this regard, all the while urging Latin governments to look beyond their day-by-day problems to establish basic
priorities for the longer pull. And it is here that the Prebisch report
postulates employment as the crux of the matter. It is not that this
report is in conflict with the more current and popular stress on
family planning and the Green Revolution, as was emphasized in the
Pearson report. Rather it is that Prebisch notes two important
caveats often missed or glossed over by supporters of those different
approaches.
This: (1) Even if a truly effective family planning program
could be implemented immediately—as should be the case—its effects
on the labor force would evidence themselves only after a time lag of
15 or 20 years. True, there would be certain immediate beneficial
effects, such as those on private household budgets (especially important for poorer families) and on social overhead expenditures by the
state (especially for investment in housing, health, and education).
But one must also bear in mind that a birth control program will not,
in its initial stages, correct existing distortions in the structure of
employment, nor will it alleviate unemployment in the short run. The
mothers have already been born who will have children within the
next two decades, and so a certain amount of time is inevitably
required before any demographic policy can show definitive results
in terms of working-age population. Family planning, in other words,
is a long-run complement of, and not a short-term substitute for,
an organic developmental policy. (2) Essential as the Green Revolution
is—and the Prebisch report gives it unquestioned support—the point
nonetheless remains that as fewer and fewer people produce more
and more agricultural output the exodus of marginal manpower from
farms to cities will speed up even further beyond its already-excessive
pace.
There is an old parable, "Be careful of what you ask: it might
be given to you." Prebisch like Pearson asks for a Green Revolution,

but he goes much further than Pearson when he asks "What should be done if that particular revolution is successful?" In a nutshell, his answer is to plan for a vastly increased industrial investment program to absorb Latin America's ever-burgeoning numbers of marginal manpower.

It is here, in my view, where the two reports disclose an area of crucial divergence in priority. And yet it is also here where the Pearson list of international measures and Prebisch's domestic policy framework can and ultimately must converge.

6

PLANNING
FOR FULL EMPLOYMENT
IN LATIN AMERICA
Paul N. Rosenstein-Rodan

The existing and growing unemployment in much of Latin America prevents a stable solution of the problems of those countries. Even an otherwise "respectable" rate of growth may not provide the path toward full employment. There is general agreement, both in economic theory and in developmental policies, that not only the so-called economic but also social objectives should be clearly formulated. The objectives are not only maximum output but also better income distribution and, notably, full employment. The two objectives (income and employment levels) are only in part complementary, and may in part be in conflict. Thus, to obtain a 5.5 percent rate of growth over the next five-year period may (because of market imperfections and adverse factor endowment) be only compatible with 10.0 percent unemployment, while the reduction of unemployment to a level of 5.0 percent may only be compatible with a rate of growth of 4.5 percent. The analysis has, moreover, to be intertemporal. More employment in the next five-year period may (because of lower capital accumulation) mean less employment than would otherwise have been possible in the second five-year period.

NON-EUCLIDEAN PERFECTIONIST
ECONOMICS OF THE LONG RUN

Modern technology is characterized by fixed coefficients of production. The costs of efficiency are capital-intensive methods of production. Technological progress in the form of new types of less capital-intensive methods of production might reverse the trend in the future. But we cannot wait for this to happen: we have to plan on the basis of existing technology. On that basis, there can be a conflict between maximizing output and maximizing employment. The social

welfare function may well impose <u>some</u> sacrifice of growth for the
sake of a better income distribution and notably fuller employment.
It is easier, however, to achieve a better distribution of <u>increases</u> in
income than to redistribute existing income. In this sense we are
<u>desarollistas</u>, not merely <u>distribucionistas</u>.

The divergence between maximum output and maximum employment can be reduced substantially by a better economic policy. Wages,
interest, and foreign exchange rates more closely corresponding to
shadow rates might lead to a choice of a more labor-intensive technology
and of a more labor-intensive product mix. With a few exceptions
however, the differences in productivity between different methods of
production are so great that the proportion of labor directly employed
at the machine would change only if wages were reduced enormously
(e.g., 40 percent). The only variability of coefficients of production
applies to labor indirectly employed in bringing raw materials to the
machine and to handling and packaging the product from the machine.
While it is difficult to quantify, it seems that the scope for market-
induced employment creation in industry is rather limited. The same
applies to shadow rates of interest in the private sector. Industry in
this sector already operates at shadow rates of interest; a project
which will not "repay" in five years is not undertaken. More important
would be realistic foreign exchange rates and fiscal measures authorizing LIFO (Last In, First Out) instead of FIFO (First In, First Out)
to prevent undercapitalization and suboptimal dimensions of firms in
inflation-ridden countries. On the other hand, it is important to apply
shadow pricing of interest in the public sector.

Wages and interest rates would have to change substantially to
have an appreciable effect on employment. Even if it were possible
to introduce such changes, the effect would be limited and slow.

Similar limitations apply to changes in product mix. Cross-
elasticities of demand between different sectors are very low, although
they may be quite high between different goods of the same sector.
Income redistribution would have to be very considerable to produce
a net widening of the market sufficient to raise employment on a
substantial scale. Even in communist countries with their certainly
considerable income redistribution, the product mix is astonishingly
similar to that of other countries. The employment and welfare
impact depends very much on the manner in which income is redistributed. It will be greater if real incomes are increased by lower
prices due to more efficient production, realizing economies of
scale.[1]

Regional integration and an increase in exports are important for
that reason. They reduce the limits put on by local demand conditions.
Moreover, the lowering of industrial prices is the most important
condition for stimulating agricultural expansion with its considerable

employment potential. Today the national terms of trade between industry and agriculture are even more unfavorable to the latter than the international terms of trade. Only their improvement can lead to a more balanced development and better employment conditions in agriculture.

While the employment effect of shadow pricing and of changes in product mix due to income redistribution is limited and slow—and that of economic integration and export policy somewhat greater—we cannot afford to neglect them. Combined operations of various measures are needed to solve the employment problem. The sum total of various second orders of magnitude may add up to a first order of magnitude.

The main instruments of growth and employment are, however, (a) a critical rate of growth, including measures to spread work in two shifts in industry, supplemented by (b) special measures of labor-intensive public works in construction, transport, and agriculture; and (c) regional developmental measures in favor of small enterprises (trading estates and industrial zones).

The existing technology severely limits the scope of substituting labor for capital. In most cases, labor-intensive methods are possible only at high expense of productivity. A woman working 10 hours a day at a hand loom in India produces 3 yards of woven cloth, while a worker on an automatic loom produces over 300 yards in the same amount of time. While there are several sectors in which labor-intensive methods are not as "expensive" in terms of output (secondary roads and hydro-electric dams built without bulldozers; other construction methods with spades and hammers instead of machines; and rural as well as some urban public works like well-digging, terracing, bunding, and slum clearance), the employment scope of those methods at the present state of organization is rather limited. It is vitally important that these methods be used. A different and efficient organization is needed for that purpose, but it seems that such methods may well absorb one fifth or one quarter of unemployment (it would be no mean achievement), but not more than that. It was calculated, for instance, that rural public works in India could provide employment for 5 (out of 20) million unemployed for 100 to 150 days a year.[2]

The unemployment problem gave rise to a public discussion in Italy in 1950. Italy had at that time an open and disguised unemployment of between 15 and 18 percent of her labor force. One possibility was to reduce this unemployment drastically within the next 3 years by using the unemployed in subsidized and technologically inefficient handicrafts and public works. The required subsidies would, however, absorb the bulk of investible funds, so that little would remain for investment in modern, technologically efficient but capital-intensive industries. The price for reducing unemployment quickly would be a low rate of growth (2.5 to 3.0 percent) with no hope of raising income and the standard of living in the longer run. The alternative (adopted by Italy) was to give up the rapid reduction of unemployment during the first 5-year period and to raise investment in highly productive, modern, capital-intensive industries that would raise the rate of growth to a "critical" level which, by the sheer bulk of investments, would in 10 years absorb unemployment while at the same time bringing about a growing standard of living at a 5.5 percent rate of growth. A sectorial income and employment multiplier study[3] estimated that the income multiplier was between 1.80 and 2.00, while the employment multiplier was in the short run only 1.23 (because of underemployment in industries) and in the long run was 1.44. Yet a 5.5 percent rate of growth would lead in 10 years to full employment. These ex ante projections were compared with the ex post results in Italy in 1961, showing a margin of error of only ± 4 percent.

Italy in 1950 had an even higher unemployment rate than most Latin American countries (except the Carribean). On the other hand, her rate of population increase was only half that of Latin America. Italy had also a better outlet for emigration. If a 5.5 percent rate of growth solved the Italian employment problem, a 6.5 to 8.0 percent rate could suffice in Latin America.

We suggest that a similar study of what is a critical rate of growth that would bring about both a rising income and employment should be undertaken for several Latin American countries.

The underdeveloped countries are at a crossroads. There are only three possibilities for them:

1. A system of distribution of poverty, obtaining full employment without appreciable growth of income per capita, which would be obtained through subsidized, widespread, labor-intensive projects. (Compared with the present situation, it would be better if no other solution were in sight.)

2. A communist system. Whatever its drawbacks, this system can provide both a high rate of growth and full employment.

3. Attaining a "critical" rate of growth that would provide both growth and full employment.

It is believed that rates of growth of between 6 and 8 percent could realize these objectives.

IMPLICATIONS OF A HIGH RATE OF GROWTH

A "critical" (threshold) rate of growth is the necessary though not sufficient condition for reaching full employment. In some countries a 6.0 to 6.5 percent rate may be sufficient. In many of them, however, a 7.5 to 8.0 percent rate will be needed; is there any chance

to mobilize sufficient resources for it, quite apart from the problem
of organization and absorptive capacity?

Today* the rate of growth in Latin America is around 5.0 to
5.5 percent and requires gross investment at the rate of 19.6 percent
of GNP. Almost 90 percent of the gross investment is financed by
national resources, so that national savings equal 17.6 percent of GNP:
10 percent of investment is financed by external resources which equal
2.1 percent of Latin America's GNP and is composed as follows:

> 1.0 percent, aid (Agency for International Development,
> Inter-American Development Bank (IBD), International
> Bank for Reconstruction and Development (IBRD), Europe,
> etc.);
> 0.6 percent, private international investment; and
> 0.5 percent, short- and medium-term credit.

To reach a 7.5 to 8.0 percent rate of growth, gross investment
of around 25.0 to 26.0 percent of GNP is needed, i.e., it has to increase
by 30 percent! That takes into account already-better planning, shadow
pricing, and a better international division of labor that might lower
the ratio of gross capital to output from 3.6 to 1 to 3.2 to 1 or perhaps
even 3.1 to 1.

If 85 percent of this "heroic" development target were to be
financed by national effort, there would be a moral claim for a supplement of 15 percent from external resources.

85 percent of gross investment has thus to be financed by national
savings, which have to rise by over 25 percent to form 22 percent of
GNP.

If external resources are to finance 15 percent of the investment,
they must amount to 3.2 percent of Latin America's (increased) GNP,
i.e., they have to rise by 50 percent.** They might be composed of:

----

*"Today" refers to 1966-69 and may well represent an over-
estimate up to 10.0 percent.

**In absolute money amount, external resources have to rise
by 100 percent in 1975 but more later on. Latin American income
will be 100 percent higher in 1980. And in nominal dollars such resources would have then to increase by 32.5 percent. The developed
countries' income should however be 60 percent higher by 1980, so that
the proportion that aid forms of their GNP would have to increase
by 135 percent. It would then approach the 1 percent of GNP target
of the UN Conference on Trade and Development (UNCTAD) and of
the Pearson Report.

aid, 1.7 percent of GNP (an increase of 70 percent);

international investment, 0.9 percent of GNP (an increase of 50 percent); and

medium- and short-term credit, 0.6 percent of GNP (an increase of 20 percent).

CAN THESE TARGETS BE MET?

National savings would have to be raised by 25 percent. However ambitious, such a target can be met by new measures such as the following:

1. Severe fiscal measures to increase revenue and public savings (higher taxation and better price policy of public enterprise).

2. Incentives to voluntary savings.

3. Forced savings of the working class, by forming a national investment trust. Twenty-five percent of each increase in high wages and 15 percent of each increase in low wages would be paid in investment trust certificates. A better distribution of income would thus avoid its main drawback, due to the lower propensity to save of persons with low incomes. Taxing the rich is needed, but it cannot yield enough.

4. Development of national capital markets (including bonds having constant purchasing power and new forms of equities).

External resources as a percentage of Latin American GNP would have to be increased by 50 percent. The moral claim for this would be overwhelming if the ambitious target of a 25 percent increase in national savings were met. It is to be remembered, moreover, that the flow of foreign capital into Latin America was very low in the 1960s and that the increase is needed for only one or two decades; it is not a bottomless pit remaining forever. It is fully compatible with targets proposed by the Pearson Report.

Work in two shifts in industry requires a great deal of organization and industrial extension. It is very important, however, as a method of additional efficient production without corresponding additional investment. It is the best way of lowering capital requirements and of lowering the capital-output ratio. The main bottlenecks here are not the generals or the colonels (the managers and skilled workers); training (also abroad in firms delivering machinery to Latin American countries as a condition to win the tender) and organized immigration are essential.

The managerial problems of passing from one to two shifts (and the much more difficult ones of passing from two to three shifts) were well studied in Italy during 1955, distinguishing between sectors, sizes of firms, and regional location (Lombardy, Piedmont, and Ligure).

Employment in agriculture has to be increased and made more attractive. Even an 8 percent rate of growth and a 12 percent increase in industrial production cannot provide enough for full employment. A rate of urbanization of 7 percent per year cannot be sustained. The flow into towns can be reduced only if more and better employment is created in agriculture. Rural industrialization remains a utopian dream under present technological conditions. Output and employment in agriculture are at present below equilibrium; they have to be increased, although in the longer run the percentage of labor force in agriculture will fall. The main reason why agricultural development is "lagging" in most under-developed countries is the fact that the domestic terms of trade between industrial and agricultural products are even more unfavorable to agriculture than the international ones. Protection of infant industry raises the prices of industrial products, while agricultural prices are at the world market level. If it takes twice as many bushels of wheat to buy a ton of fertilizer, a farmer acts as a homo economicus and does not buy it. The tariff policy must be changed to create lower industrial prices if full employment is to be reached. Various forms of regional and subregional integration are as essential for that purpose as are other measures to improve the international division of labor by facilitating and promoting exports.

Balanced 7.5 to 8.0 percent growth for Latin America as a whole (although not for each single country) implies about 5.0 percent growth of agriculture.

Short-term measures must supplement those of the long term. They are sketched in the "Notes on a Short-Term Employment Program" that follow. For the next decade or two, special measures and organizational forms are needed for labor-intensive methods in construction of feeder roads and rural public works without bulldozers, in slum clearance and construction at discriminatory lower wages (shadow pricing of labor). Those are the only sectors in which a substitution of labor for capital is possible without an overwhelming loss of efficiency. The better should not be an enemy of the good. Any reduction of unemployment without undue lowering of the standard of living is good. Better, more equitable, and more equal wages can then be reached in the last decade of this century.

NOTES ON A SHORT-TERM
EMPLOYMENT PROGRAM

How to reach full employment is recognized as the main problem of the second developmental decade. In theory one may assume that there is a "critical rate of growth" (7 to 8 percent or more) which, if reached and maintained, would lead in the long run to full employment.

There are two snags however: (1) The rate may be too high to be reached, and changes in economic structure and strategy (such as organizing work in two shifts and changing product mix) which might reduce the critical rate of growth to a feasible level—say 7 but not 8 or 9 percent—may not be worked out or applied. (2) Social stability cannot be maintained for so long a period: before people are dead in the long run, they will revolt in the short run. Special measures with immediate effect must be taken where unemployment is severe. The main concern is that they should not unduly lower the rate of growth and should not impede a long-run policy aiming at both full employment and a rising standard of living. An emergency program of useful employment should be an addition to, not a substitute for, a long-run plan.

The choice between different but efficient methods of production is very limited and practically confined to few sectors. "Intermediate" and labor-intensive technology at not too high a cost of efficiency may emerge as a product of research, but it is not available for an immediate operation in most industrial sectors. A change in the product mix (producing more goods with a higher labor content) will be helped by free trade and tariff preferences for developing countries, but for a larger impact it requires an income redistribution not feasible in the short run and not suitable for a "crash program."

A program should be established for an immediate and short-term action as well as for long-term policy. It is important that works undertaken immediately should create useful employment. While a study of the short- and long-run problems should be started simultaneously, they encompass different tasks. The following remarks refer only to the immediate and short-run action.

Apart from a high rate of growth, more labor-intensive investments are at once possible in these sectors: (1) Construction and transport—building of secondary roads and hydro-electric dams, as well as river navigation and flood control projects, without earth-moving machinery and bulldozers; slum clearance; and building of barracks. (2) Rural public works and community development—especially in slack periods for, say, 100 to 150 days a year. (3) For a longer-run program, a planned dualism in agriculture, organizing a coexistence of a twenty-first- and a nineteenth-century agriculture. (4) Creation of trading and industrial estates for small enterprises—using experiences of "special" areas in England (after 1934) and in southern Italy—joined with incentives that create investment opportunities for small enterprises, for example, a ship-repairing yard.

The substitution of labor for capital without undue loss of efficiency is possible in the construction of secondary and feeder roads, hydro-electric barrages and in river navigation and flood control measures. Labor provided with spades and building materials but without bulldozers or other earth-moving machinery can build secondary

roads in the way the Burma road was built. It is true that such roads
have to be maintained almost continuously, especially in countries
where torrential rains wash away a good part of them. But the very
much higher maintenance costs are compensated for by saving on
fixed capital. It has been calculated in some tropical countries (e.g.,
India) that if wages were 40 percent lower than the going rate and
interest rates were not higher than 6 percent, the costs of a secondary
road built that way would not be higher than the costs of a normally
built road. Higher maintenance is, of course, no objection in countries
with considerable unemployment. The main trouble is the fact that
it takes six or seven times as long to complete a 300-mile road or a
hydro-electric barrage (per cubic foot).

There are three reasons, however, why the opportunity of using
such labor-intensive methods is not seized in this field. First, long-
run developmental programs indicating where roads will be useful by
1976 or 1977 hardly exist. Long-run planning is either too aggregative
or still very deficient. Second, every minister, member of parliament,
governor, or mayor wants to see results in his electoral period. A
completion of a project in six years has no political appeal. Third,
contractors do not like to have to tackle problems of labor supervision;
they will always prefer bulldozers. When contracts are awarded by a
ministry of public works on a "cost plus profit" basis, bulldozers will
always be preferred. It is important, therefore, that contracts in the
case of feeder roads should specify a labor-intensive method, not only
for roads financed by an external loan but also for all those financed
by internal resources.

There is practically no experience of such road building in the
United States. But U.S. army engineers who were in China during
World War II might remember how Chinese authorities built such
roads to transport guns and ammunition to Chungking. Canadian
authorities also have experience of such road building in the western
part of Canada. Technical assistance from those quarters can be
mobilized.

Rural public works at a distance of not more than 20 to 25 miles
from a village and community development have been studied and
planned in India. While nowhere near enough has been done, some
experience is available.[4] Since such works can be undertaken in
slack periods of seasonal unemployment and since workers are disguised and seasonally unemployed living with their families, a low
wage rate (30 to 40 percent of an urban wage rate) can be paid. Many
land improvement operations (terracing, bunding, etc.) which do not
"pay" at the going wage rate might become feasible at such an "incentive shadow rate." Indian experience also shows that hydro-electric
dams can be built without bulldozers. The quality is satisfactory,
but it takes seven to eight times as long to construct 1,000 cubic feet.

The main difficulty here is organization. A Communist party or an army can solve it. Let us hope that another form of organization could deal with the task as well.

Even a "critical rate of growth" may not be sufficient to reach full employment—it is a necessary but not sufficient condition—unless supplemented by specific measures, such as those outlined earlier in this chapter. Relying on changes in technology (via better shadow prices of capital and labor) and on changes in product mix (due to integration, export push, and some income redistribution) may also have only a limited scope in the short run, although each should play its part in a longer-run employment plan. Industrialization alone will not provide sufficient employment, and a 6 to 7 percent rate of urbanization cannot be sustained. Better living and employment conditions have to be created in agriculture. That is possible only if we arrange for a "planned dualism" in agriculture, with wages in the nineteenth-century agricultural sector very much lower than those in agrabusiness. Such price discrimination in the labor market makes sense. After all, we are accustomed to discriminatory tariffs where one kilowatt-hour of electricity is sold at different prices according to its use. The idea, of course, is not new; it just applies shadow pricing to the labor market. But two problem areas arise: first, how to "optimize" this price discrimination; second, how to "sell" it, i.e., overcome the resistance of trade unions, public opinion, etc. All kinds of institutional gimmicks like calling it national service or youth service, with a daily or weekly pay which should not be considered as wages, must be considered; they may require different formulas in different countries.

Another field of labor-intensive activity could be a growth of small enterprises, including some handicrafts. Such investments do not emerge spontaneously on a sufficient scale. They require both prenatal and postnatal control. The organization of trading and industrial estates, such as was undertaken in England after the Special Areas Act (1934) and in southern Italy, provide useful experience. One of the successful measures, for instance, was the construction of 40 or 50 factory buildings, with movable walls so as to fit different dimensions, which were offered to small enterprises for rent. Since the factory building usually immobilizes 40 to 50 percent of a small firm's capital, the possibility of renting a factory building that can be vacated at a three-month notice represented a substantial reduction in risk and was eagerly taken up.

Incentives for small enterprise in industrial estates should be geared not to capital invested but to investment and employment opportunities created by subcontracts. The pattern of industrialization differs today from what it has been in the past. An up-to-date, large, industrial unit often comes first and induces investment in small firms which find a market in subcontracts of the large firm. Subsidies for small enterprise only may thus be insufficient.[5]

In a long-run program considerable attention should be paid
to work in two shifts in industry. Scarcities of skilled workers and
foremen are bottlenecks here (more than managers) which can be broken
only in the longer run.

It might be said this is nothing but a Works Progress Administration (WPA) program. That program under the New Deal was in
essence a good policy under the circumstances. Our task is not to
be original but to be effective. With better planning, and in some
cases like rural public works consciously applying wage discrimination
(wages lower than the going rate but, in towns, higher than the unemployment benefit), and with projects that have economic value, it can
achieve good results.

Organization is more of a bottleneck in this action than capital.
Technical assistance has to be provided from many quarters: the
Canadian government; the IBRD, which might mobilize those who had
experience of road building by the Chinese during World War II; English
and Italian experience on trading and industrial estates; Japanese and
Italian assistance on construction of ship-repairing yards, etc. The
UN International Labor Office of course would participate in the
overall and larger new planning of a full-employment policy.

While no complete shadow pricing of wages will be applied,
careful explanation to public opinion and labor organizations is needed
about wages which must in many cases be even lower than the going
wage rate.

A large part of financing should be provided by aid. The World
Food Program (and (or) P. L. 480) can provide a proportion—25 to
40 percent—of wage payments (for example, as in Tunisia). Soft loans
from IDB, IDA, and bilateral loans should provide for a high proportion
of the costs. We envisage as an example: 25 percent of aid in kind
(food); 25 percent as soft loans; 10 percent of loans from aid agencies;
and 40 percent from national resources.

CULTURAL IMPERIALISM
AND DISESTABLISHING
EDUCATION IN LATIN AMERICA
Ivan Illich

When Cortez arrived in the Americas in 1519 with his 16 horses
and 553 soldiers, some 18 million people lived on the territory now
under the Mexican flag. Forty years later this population had been
reduced to only 3 million. This, of course, happened before the age
of penicillin, when healthy populations still adapted flexibly to a new
balance with the environment produced by a new economy. For three
and a half centuries the population stayed around 8 million. Only in
the present century did Mexico regain a population of 20 million—
which has since been more than doubled.

The original population had lived on a highly labor-intensive
agriculture. The yield per acre, cultivated by hoe, was high and
ritual laws kept the loss of produce on the way to the consumer very
low. Marginal land must have been cultivated in order to have supported so large a population before iron, cattle, or the plow were
known. With all that agricultural labor there was still time available
for tens of thousands of people to build hundreds of pyramid temples
to placate their gods and to engage periodically in ritual wars to provide them with human sacrifices.

The two fundamental life processes, production and reproduction,
were balanced to provide all members with sustenance through small
but equal and stable shares in the limited stock of wealth available in
Mexican valleys. Though the warrior and the priest were not engaged
in production they were everywhere regarded as essential to the task
of keeping the sun on its course. Their individual shares to consumption were not much greater than those of everybody else.

This neolithic life style depended on a short individual life
expectancy of relatively able-bodied men. It depended on an ecological
balance—or "health"—far superior to that possible under any higher
technology of later ages.

Pre-Hispanic social goals found their expression in ceremonial
laws which each "god" imposed on his own territory; laws which set

97

the rules for the calendar, the market, the protection of the harvest
and seed grain—even for the survival of children. The gods were
local guardians of a mature ecology in each valley, but all directed to
conservation, recycling, and balance. These local rules were destroyed
by the arrival of the Spaniards.

Four centuries later, the same territory had of course once
again become capable of sustaining 20 million inhabitants, each with
a longer life expectancy. But this had been accomplished at the expense
of a triple degradation, physical, social, and psychological. The physical environment suffered depletion and pollution. Social polarization
developed through unequal distribution of wealth and status. The
absolute and the relative shares of each individual in the economy had
moved apart. People had learned to content themselves by seeing the
size of their absolute shares increase ever so little, while their relative shares continually shrank.

The Spanish plow permitted bringing more land under cultivation
but it reduced the yield per acre, and the Spanish cattle had to be fed
some of that yield. Sickness, too, no doubt caused many deaths. But
the central cause for the destruction of the original high ecological
balance may well have been the disruption of the old rituals by the new
religion imported from Spain.

The Spaniards came not only as conquerors but also as mission-
aries for a worldwide religion. Paradoxically the expansion of agriculture and mining reduced the yield of sustenance for the Mexicans,
and with their land they themselves went out of production. Mexico
was fitted into Spain's world market, the Aztecs were degraded into
a part of "mankind," a mankind which inhabits not a valley but the
earth.

Simultaneously the local elites were destroyed. Only 25 years
after the conquest of Mexico the first university opened its doors to
the sons of native princes. They were taught a world language, promised a heaven equal for all men, and trained for minor positions in
the bureaucratic hierarchy of the Hapsburgs whose empire now
spanned the earth. Local divinities, who had been guardians of a local
balance of maintenance values were replaced by a universal ideology:
Gold and God.

The Tlalamantines, the four wisest men the Mexicans could
muster to talk with the Spanish friars, reflected the sentiment of a
dying people. They said, "You come from afar and you are very wise.
You say that our gods are dying. Well, if that be so, let us die with
them." They had no choice. The gods of Mexico represented social
goals that did not mesh with the imperialist goals of the new ones.
The Mexican gods stood for the values of high maintenance, stability,
and quality of life. These are, of course, the very same goals of
which Boulding speaks when he refers to a "spaceman economy,"

necessary for the generation that has learned to look back from the
moon with the nostalgia of men suddenly experiencing just how small,
how limited our green planet is. The goals of the pre-Colombian gods
are thus fundamentally the same as those which the rich nations will
now have to choose, unless they want to choke in their own wastes.

Unfortunately, these goals—common to the Tlalamantines and
the wise men of today—are not the goals that rich nations export in
the name of development into the poor world today. They are not the
goals that the educational ministries of Dakar or La Paz redistribute
through their schoolhouses to the last outposts in the jungle and the
high desert.

The school system today performs the threefold function common
to powerful churches throughout history. It is the repository of
society's myth, the institutionalization of the contradictions of the
myth, and the locus of the ritual that reproduces and veils the disso-
nances between myth and reality. Today the school system, and
especially the university, provides ample opportunity for the criticism
of the myth and for rebellion against its institutional perversions. But
the fact that, above all, school is the ritual that induces tolerance of
the fundamental contradictions between myth and institution still goes
largely unchallenged. Yet, neither ideological criticism nor social
action can bring about a society which both is "modern" and remains
"rural." Only disenchantment and detachment from the central social
ritual and ritual reform can bring about radical change.

THE MYTH OF INSTITUTIONALIZED VALUES

School initiates to the Myth of Unending Consumption. This
modern myth is grounded in the typically urban belief that progress
inevitably produces something of value and that, therefore, production
necessarily produces demand. School teaches us that instruction
produces learning. The existence of schools produces the demand
for schooling. Once we have learned to need school, all our activities
tend to take the shape of client relationships to other specialized
institutions which in their totality constitute the city. Once the self-
taught man has been discredited, all nonprofessional activity is ren-
dered suspect. Rural, self-reliant, polyvalent problem solving is then
viewed as autodidactic incompetence. In school we are taught that
valuable learning is the result of attendance, and that this value increases with the amount of input. School is of one piece with growth
economy and industrial production. Inevitably the initiation to social
reality through the ritual of schooling teaches the transfer of responsibility from tradition and self to planning and institution. Inexorably,
schooling destroys a rural subsistence-oriented ethos and substitutes
for it an ethos that fits industrial agriculture.

As a matter of fact, learning is the human activity which least needs manipulation by others. Most learning is not the result of instruction. It is rather the result of unhampered participation in a meaningful context. Most people learn best by being "with it," yet school makes man identify his personal, cognitive growth with elaborate planning and manipulation.

Arnold Toynbee believes that the decadence of a great culture is usually accompanied by the rise of a new World Church which extends hope to the domestic proletariat while serving the needs of a new warrior class. School seems eminently suited to be the World Church of our decaying culture. No ritual could better veil from its participants the deep discrepancy between social principles and social reality in today's world. Secular, scientific, and death-denying, it is of a piece with the modern mood. Its classical, critical veneer makes it appear pluralistic if not antireligious. Its curriculum both defines science and is itself defined by so-called scientific research. No one completes school—yet. It never closes its doors on anyone without first offering him one more chance: at remedial, adult, and continuing education.

The rural schoolteacher in today's poor countries is no less well motivated and no less destructive than was the missioner of old. He stands at the outpost of the consumer-city, as the latter stood at the outpost of the Spanish empire. He is no less destructive of regional ecological stability, and he cannot even offer the redeeming aesthetics of colonial culture. His main task is the modernization of hunger. A traditionally hungry man has an empty stomach; a modernized hungry man is trained to knock the bottom out of his belly.

School serves as an effective creator and sustainer of an urban, industrial myth because of its structure as a ritual game of graded promotions. Introduction into this gambling ritual is much more important than what or how something is taught. It is the game itself that "schools," that gets into the blood and becomes a habit. A whole society is initiated into the Myth of Unending Consumption of services. This happens in the measure that token participation in the open-ended ritual is made compulsory and compulsive everywhere. School directs ritual rivalry into an international game which obliges competitors to blame the world's ills on those who cannot or will not play. School is a ritual of <u>initiation</u> which introduces the neophyte to the sacred race of progressive consumption, a ritual of <u>propitiation</u> whose academic priests mediate between the faithful and the gods of privilege and power, a ritual of <u>expiation</u> which sacrifices its dropouts, branding them as scapegoats of underdevelopment. Economic backwardness of an area is blamed on the low level of schooling of the poor; and the poor themselves quickly learn to attribute their inferiority to their lack of schooling.

Even those who spend at best a couple of years in school—and this is the overwhelming majority in Latin America, Asia, and Africa—learn to play at culpable underconsumption. In Mexico six grades of school are legally obligatory. A child born into the lower economic third has only 2 chances in 3 to make it into the first grade. If he makes it, he has 4 chances out of 100 to finish obligatory schooling by the sixth grade. If he is born into the middle third, his chances increase to 12 out of 100. With these proportions, Mexico is more successful than the great majority of the other Latin American republics in raising this modern pyramid of 16 grades in all of its provinces. The children know that they were given a chance, albeit an unequal one, in an obligatory lottery, and the presumed equality of the international standard now compounds their original poverty with the self-inflicted discrimination accepted by the dropout. They have been schooled to the belief in rising expectations and can now rationalize their growing frustration outside of school in terms of their rejection of scholastic grace. They are excluded from Heaven because, once baptized, they did not go to church. Born in original sin, they are baptized into first grade, but go to Gehenna (which in Hebrew means "slum") because of their personal faults. As Max Weber traced the social effects of the belief that salvation belonged to those who accumulated wealth, we can now observe that predestination is reserved for those who accumulate years in school. This same dynamic holds true, a fortiori, for the distinction between urban and rural schooling, with added caste-bias thrown in: advanced education is reserved to those who move into the city. Inevitably, conversion to the tenets of school inculcates a sense of inferiority to those who live far from the city.

THE COMING KINGDOM: THE UNIVERSALIZATION OF EXPECTATIONS

School combines the expectations of the consumer expressed in its claims with the beliefs of the producer expressed in its ritual. It is a liturgical expression of a worldwide "cargo cult," reminiscent of the cults that swept Melanesia in the 1940s, injecting cultists with the belief that, if they but put on a black tie over their naked torsos, Jesus would arrive in a steamer bearing an icebox, a pair of trousers, and a sewing machine for each believer. School fuses the growth in humiliating dependence on a master with the growth in a futile sense of omnipotence so typical of the pupil who wants to go out and teach all nations to save themselves. The ritual proclaims the coming of an earthly paradise of never-ending consumption, and at the same time inculcates to the wretched and dispossessed a sense of guilt for their exclusion from it.

Epidemics of insatiable this-worldly expectations have occurred throughout history, especially among colonized and marginal groups in all cultures. Jews in the Roman Empire had their Essenes and Jewish messiahs, serfs in the Reformation their Thomas Munzer, dispossessed Indians from Paraguay to Dakota their infectious dancers. These sects were always led by a prophet, and limited their promises to a chosen few. The school-induced expectation of the kingdom, on the other hand, is impersonal rather than prophetic, and universal rather than local. Man has become the engineer of his own messiah and promises the unlimited rewards of science to those who submit to progressive engineering for his reign.

But there is a further important distinction between messianic cults and rituals of other times and the growth of rural schools today. Traditionally, messianic movements were endogenous to rural areas. They are now imposed by the city-bred schoolman. Peasant leaders arose in Germany and the northeast of Brazil and rural clerics assumed the charismatic leadership of messianic crowds. In the latter case city bureaucrats introduce disruption into the stable-state ethos of agricultural areas.

Each nation is responsible for its own deschooling, and this power resides only in the local community. No one can be excused if he fails to liberate himself from schooling. Men could not free themselves from the Crown until they had freed themselves from the established Church. They cannot free themselves from progressive consumption until they free themselves from obligatory school.

The fundamental set of options is clear enough. Either rural nations continue to be indoctrinated to the belief that learning is a product that justifies unlimited investments, or they rediscover that legislation and planning and investment, if they have any place in formal education, should be used mostly to tear down the barriers that now impede opportunities for learning.

In Latin America, most countries spend one quarter of their national budgets on schools, make five years of school attendance obligatory, and provide a school system that must deny two thirds of their young with the opportunity to complete a minimum elementary "quantum" of schooling. It really doesn't matter at which level you drop out to accept your inferiority if you have accepted the belief that more investment of school hours makes another man more productive and therefore entitles him to more consumption. The same amount of money, if spent on various devices to render the total environment more educational and to provide intensive skill-drills for persons once they are self-motivated, would provide more education, less alienation, and less degradation.

The following rules might serve educational policy making for rural areas:

First, burden the city with the full cost of introducing the immigrant to its myth instead of requiring rural contributions to the urban economy by shifting to rural areas part of the cost of schooling for city life.

Second, increase expenditure to enrich the "field academy" of rural areas, which corresponds to the informal "street academy" of the city, where most things valuable for survival are even now learned among peers. This enrichment is primarily a matter of the following investments:

1. Distribution of a bill of goods with high repair-intensity.

2. Increase of educational games, illustrations, books, and (in more advanced areas) tapes and other communication equipment which can provide everybody with equal chance to communicate and receive communication.

3. Provide payoffs for those who share their know-how, rather than follow the present custom of paying students to acquire a certificate which permits them to monopolize teaching.

4. Increase the guarantees for free speech. The discussion of controversial key words, as Paulo Freire has shown, is the fastest way toward creative organization—with literacy as a by-product.

5. Provide rural elites with the opportunity to develop ethos and skills which are not transferable to the city. This, of course, would be opposed to the present attempt to provide the national elite with a recruitment base extended to every nook of the territory, providing every peasant a chance to rise in this pyramid. While his personal chance now inevitably decreases with the square of the distance of his village from the urban center of power, his degree becomes that more valuable among his family members, and thus contributes to nation building.

The use of modern technology to assist in the rise of a counter-culture has been feebly attempted by urban splinter groups in the 1960s, and already constitutes one of the major challenges to the culture of growth, efficiency, escalation, and total passivity of the scientist and hard-hats. The great opportunity of the 1970s is the conscious consolidation of a rural counter-culture that opposes growth-economy and incorporates technology to increase the quality of rural subsistence.

If the agricultural technologist and his schools prevail, 3 billion people will have to say, with the Aztec Tlalamantines, "Since our gods of stability and personal encounter are dying, let us die with them."

8

THE EMERGING ROLE
OF THE MILITARY
AS NATIONAL MODERNIZERS
AND MANAGERS IN LATIN AMERICA:
THE CASES OF BRAZIL AND PERU
Brady Tyson

It is difficult to categorize—much less to adequately describe—contemporary events, if for no other reason than that our categories are derived from past events and may even obscure the essential nature of contemporary events more than fit them. Doubly difficult, then, to try to predict even the short-range events on the basis of categorizations. Even so, the effort is probably as valid as intuitive predictions. Furthermore, observations of contemporary events and attempts to categorize them are necessary for the formulation of working hypotheses of more rigidly scientific inquiry. The emergence of an apparently different type of military regime in Latin America is the case in point.

THE "NEW MILITARY" IN BRAZIL AND PERU:
SIMILARITIES AND DIFFERENCES

The first attempts to analyze the seemingly increasing number of military-dominated governments, which began about 1964 with the Brazilian coup, tended to use the concepts inherited from the pre-World War II study of military dictatorships in the same area.[1] It was usually assumed that any military government was a stand-in for the traditional oligarchic forces and seized power largely to prevent the spread of liberal democracy. The generally unexpected posture of the Peruvian military government since it seized power in 1968 has provoked some efforts to distinguish this type of military government from "rightist" ones, and hence such phrases as "military populism," "military modernizers," and "military nationalists" have been used to describe the Peruvian (and for a while the Bolivian) military regimes.[2]

Furthermore, seven years of observation have begun to produce some
new evaluations of the Brazilian army in power and some attempts
to describe the new role of that army in its nation's political system.[3]
There has been one serious article comparing the sociological backgrounds, the professional attitudes, and the educational and training
programs of the Peruvian and Brazilian army officer corps, written
by undoubtedly the best-qualified and most articulate student of
military-civilian relations who has an interest in both Brazil and
Peru.[4]

It is the intention of this chapter to expand on some new categories suggested in the literature and to develop a set of concepts that
this author believes fit both the Peruvian and Brazilian governments.
Even though the military governments of Brazil and Peru are wary of
each other—if not somewhat antagonistic—my thesis is that the two
officer corps are tending—and will tend even more—to be similar in
style and program. And moreover, that the differences between the
approaches and programs of the two governments are largely the result of the different historical contexts in which they seized power
and the consequently different political allies they have sought in their
own countries. It is also the thesis of this chapter that both officer
corps will increasingly tend to institutionalize a permanent, authoritarian, managerial approach to national modernization; will tend to
adopt more explicitly a corporatist concept of society; and will tend
to use nationalist and technocratic plans of modernization. Thus the
characterizations of the Brazilian government as "rightist" and the
Peruvian regime as "leftist," "nationalist," or "populist" will be
related in this chapter to specific national and international political
dynamics rather than used as indicators of supposedly basic differences.

SOME HISTORICAL PERSPECTIVE TO THE
PRESENT REGIMES

The Brazilian government is commonly thought of as a rightist
military regime because (1) it took power by overthrowing a populist,
leftist-reformist regime; (2) it openly sought an alliance with the
United States in an anticommunist bloc to protect the free world.*;
(3) domestically, the Brazilian government since 1964 has adopted
strong repressive measures against any residual populist or leftist
tendencies, including a law and order rhetoric; (4) the Brazilian

---

*Though this was more true in the administration of Castelo
Branco than at present.

military government has openly adopted a "neo-capitalist" road to
"national development"* and has often seemed to ally itself with
national, international, and foreign big business and banking interests;
and (5) the aloof, apolitical and technocratic style and policies of the
ESG and ADESG** have given an aura of elitism to the Brazilian
government (especially in the Castelo Branco period). Furthermore,
fears of potential Brazilian expansionism (political and economic,
and even military—based partly on history) among her neighbors
(including Peru) have helped to define Brazil as at least potentially
"imperialistic" and therefore rightist. It should also be mentioned
that the corporatist model a la Salazar and Franco[5] and the model
of the Estado Novo of Getulio Vargas (1937-45)[6] lend Brazil a natural
aura of potential fascism and (or) corporatism.

---

*Unfortunately, the words "development" and "modernization"
are often used (especially in the United States) almost interchange-
ably. In Latin America many writers make a distinction, reserving
the word "development" for a process that might be called "modernization plus humanization through the transformation of the existing
structures of society and the creation of structures of self-determina-
tion to replace the structures of dependency." "Modernization," on
the other hand, means the adaptation of modern technology by the
existing socioeconomic political structures to achieve greater efficiency and productivity. The words will be used in this sense in
this paper. The words are increasingly used in this sense also among
certain North American academics. See for example Norman Jacobs,
Modernization without Development: Thailand as an Asian Case Study
(New York: Praeger, 1971). The publicity for this book says that
the author believes that modernization "is the maximization of the
potential of a society within the existing social and cultural framework; development on the other hand disregards limits set by the
fundamental structure of the society to offer an open-ended commitment to productive change." Jacobs compares Thailand's experience
with that of the western countries and Japan, where modernization
accompanied development.

**ESG: Escola Superior de Guerra (Advanced War College).
ADESG: Associacão dos Diplomados da Escola Superior de Guerra
(Association of Graduates of the Advanced War College). An article
by Frank McCann and books by Alfred Stepan and Ronald Schneider
(see note 3) refer to this school repeatedly. Probably its influence
has somewhat declined since 1968, though a serious study of this is
still to be done.

On the other hand the Peruvian regime has been characterized
as in some basic ways different from a rightist military regime because (1) it has been more anti-United States—at least in its rhetoric;
(2) it has been reasonably free of political repression of the type that
has come to be identified with the present Brazilian regime; (3) it has
much more consistently followed a policy of economic nationalism;
and (4) domestically it has adopted a rhetoric and programs that have
appropriated many of the populist programs of the Acción Popular
Revolucionaria American (APRA). Furthermore, in the field of
foreign policy Peru has reestablished relations with Cuba and other
nations of the socialist camp, and in general might be said to be
following an "independent foreign policy" similar to that once practiced
in Brazil.[7] Further, the antipersonalist, antiaristocratic, and mystique-
of-a-national-plan characteristics of the social scientist military
officers of the Peruvian CAEM,* has been seen as leftist by some who
identify rightism as the posture of "antiintellectual gorillas" and
leftism or a "progressive government" as somehow inherently tied
to social sciences and intellectualism. Perhaps the most significant
claim to being leftist is the nationalism of the Peruvian army, at least
as compared with the less-nationalist attitudes of the Brazilian army,
or the populist rhetoric of the Peruvians as compared with the "doc-
trinaire antipopulism" of the Brazilian military.[8]

But if there are differences, there are also some similarities.
Both the Peruvian and Brazilian armies took the decisive step of
seizing power only when the military corporation itself seemed to be
threatened by contagion with the current atmosphere of divisiveness,
corruption, and spreading populism. Both army officer corps had
become thoroughly disillusioned with civilian politicians in general,
and not just those in power at the time. Both had become convinced
of the dangers of old-style caudilhismo or political personalism, and
patronage politics, and had succeeded in building up in the officer corps
a strong sense of esprit de corps that continues to work strongly in
favor of "new professionalism"** and against the Peronist or Nasserist

---

*CAEM: Centro Alto de Estudios Militares (Center of Advanced
Military Studies).

**Alfred Stepan defines the "new professionalism" as a belief
that there is a fundamental interrelationship between social, economic,
and political life and the concepts of "internal security" and "national
development" in the minds of the "new professionals," and that they
further perceive an important role for the armed services in certain
situations. Thus, the "new professional" has become highly politicized

deviation from the decision-making pattern in both the officer corps, which is collective but still hierarchical.

Both army officer corps have come to be dominated by the assumption that a rational, disciplined systematic approach to national problems, on the part of a specially selected and trained elite, could provide the guidelines for a sound policy of national development. As Alfred Stepan has noted, Brazil and Peru are the only countries in Latin America "to have developed fully an ideology relating internal security to national development, and to have institutionalized that ideology within the military."[10] Both armies show a decided reliance upon technocratic and social science approaches to devise the plans for national development, and both have relied to a high degree on high-level war colleges (ESG in Brazil and CAEM in Peru) to develop unifying theories, approaches, and plans to orient their national programs. "The two countries are strikingly similar when analyzed from the perspective of the central part played by their respective war colleges in the process of military role-expansion."[11]

Both armies have accepted the "third mission" of the army* as an inevitable result of the decline and (or) decadence of the political systems of their respective nations, and are aware of a need for efficient and rapid national modernization if the nations are not to fall even further behind in the competition between the developed and the less-developed countries.

Though the political styles have been different (Brazil: aloof, apolitical and authoritarian-technocratic; Peru: populist rhetoric, "new nationalist" policies, open advocacy of such normative goals as social justice), the two military regimes are both paternalistic at their best and hierarchical-arbitrary at the worst. It can be well argued that both seized power "to make the revolution before the people make it."[12] It is one of the basic assumptions of this chapter that military paternalism as practiced by the new professionals can

---

through the application of technological concepts of "national development," even if these new concepts were developed in the name of a political professionalism.[9]

*The "third mission" of the army (explained to this author by a Brazilian army colonel as an idea derived from the Peruvian military) is the one that "naturally" follows from the first two. First mission: to defend the national frontiers against external threats. Second mission: to defend the national order against internal subversion. Third mission: to assume the role of the vanguard of the nation in the national modernizing ("developmental") process.

easily become populist.* Most previous models of modernizing authoritarian-populist regimes have centered on a charismatic leader (Peron, Nasser), but one of the characteristics of the "new professional" may be the utilization of populist rhetoric and programs at a certain stage of the institutionalization of a stable authoritarian regime without the potentially unstable element of a charismatic leader. At the present moment both the Brazilian and Peruvian military governments show some signs of utilizing populist rhetoric, but this is much more true in the Peruvian case and only slightly and recently in the case of Brazil.

There have been significant differences in the factors that have contributed to the responses of these two military governments to the responsibilities of nearly unchallenged political dominance in their respective nations. Stepan has summarized the principal factors contributing to the different policies of the Brazilian and Peruvian military regimes as being: (1) the impact on the Brazilian army of World War II and close involvement with the U.S. army in Italy, the Peruvian army having no similar experience, (2) the reliance of ESG almost entirely upon U.S.-trained leadership, under the dominance of veterans of FEB (the Brazilian Expeditionary Force to Italy in World War II), while CAEM "often sent its military officers to United Nations civilian-directed schools in Chile," and the fact that the private industrial sector was more heavily represented at ESG than at CAEM, (3) the greater size and dynamism of the Brazilian private industrial sector, and (4) the concern, on their taking power in 1964, of the Brazilians, who were "largely concerned with repression, which by 1968 had become institutionalized torture," while the Peruvian army was more nationalist and developmentalist.[13]

---

*The word "populist" is used somewhat differently in common practice in Latin America than it is in the United States. In the United States, "populism" usually means something like "a movement of relatively powerless and poor groups considered socially inferior in the existing dominant system, with some allies from other groups and classes, that places its confidence in the common sense of the common man as opposed to the claims of any elite."
In Latin America, "populism" is often used to designate a movement created or manipulated by opportunistic politicians who offer simplistic perceptions of problems and solutions to relatively powerless and poor groups. Also, a primitive form of class consciousness, immediatist, nonideological, and superficial.
In this study, "populism" is more often used in the second sense, and since it is not the favorite definition of this author it is placed in quotation marks.

One acute observer of the Peruvian scene has observed,

> It seems as if Peruvian history predestines its actors to
> move out of historical phase. The nationalist bourgeois—
> the civilians—entered on the scene after their turn had
> passed. The populist movement that APRA sought, on the
> other hand, appeared before its time—which would be
> today—and now its role has been seized by new actors.[14]

Accepting this interpretation of historical timeliness, certainly Peru
has been out of phase with Brazil. The Brazilian army fought the
battle of oil in the 1950s and did so in the name of nationalism, earning
the popular reputation as an incorruptible, disinterested protector of
the national interests. The Peruvian military fought the same battle
in the 1968 crisis over IPC (International Petroleum Company) and
were able to claim for themselves the mantle of "nationalists and
revolutionaries."[15]

The Peruvian army had dealt with a populist movement so long
(since 1918) that they had seen the movement grow almost "reformist,"
had dealt effectively with a guerrilla, subversive movement splintered
from APRA (1963), and had had time to reflect upon and study the
causes of the discontent upon which they felt APRA fed. They had
watched while the middle sector and enlightened oligarchy had vainly
tried (through Belaunde Terry) to initiate and sustain a dynamic
developmental process. When this reformist government faltered,
they were able to seize power in the name of popular aspirations. "We
had only a formal democracy, dominated by a favored minority, that
always ignored the true necessities of the people. The people were
absent from the great decisions, the old privileged groups and the
great injustices were maintained," said General Velasco.[16] It was
the failure of the liberal, democratic reformers that gave the Peruvian
army its opportunity to seize power.

In Brazil, on the other hand, populism had been so thoroughly
domesticated by the sistema established by Getulio Vargas that the
Brazilian army recognized it as a threat only when it appeared in a
more virulent (and perhaps opportunistic) guise in the Quadros-Goulart
years. The populists suddenly seemed to be on the verge of toppling
the whole system—and even were talking about democratizing the
army. There was no time for the "security and development" ideology
(that was being developed in the ESG) to adopt a populist rhetoric for
the purposes of gaining (for the army) potential support from the
peasants, urban workers, and intellectuals against the landowners,
the foreign and domestic industrialists and bankers, and the "political
class." The trauma of 1963-64 was, indeed, so deep that often the
rhetoric of O Estado de Sao Paulo (which favors a return to the "liberal"

system of the "old republic,") was adopted, even though the army
was instinctively drawn to reestablish (and modernize) the system of
the Estado Novo.

Part of the populist movement that had so frightened the Brazilian
army was the "independent foreign policy" that sought closer alliances
with socialist countries. This policy became identified with Cuban-
exported professional subversion efforts in the minds of the army
officers, whereas the Peruvian APRA had steadfastly been anticommunist for generations. Therefore, the Peruvian army did not have
the deep reservations about "an opening to the east" that their Brazilian
counterparts had.

It probably will be more fruitful in a few more years to try to
compare the programs and institutions of the two military regimes—
thus giving them (especially those of the Peruvians) more historical
exposure. Certainly, how the first succession crisis is resolved—
who is chosen, and how he is chosen—will indicate the internal cohesion
of the Peruvian army and will give a deeper indication than any one
policy of the directions in which the army is tending.

BASIC ATTITUDES TOWARD SOCIAL CHANGE:
THE MODERNIZING MENTALITY

This brief comparison of recent national historical experience
is offered as a hypothesis to be more thoroughly tested by historians.
For the purposes of this paper the hypothesis is offered that the basic
attitudes toward social change—toward the historical process and toward political authority—and the perceived sociopolitical identity of
the two army officer corps will in the long run outweigh the historically
imposed differences between the Peruvian and Brazilian military
regimes. It is not so much the military nature of the two officer corps
as it is the managerial cum bureaucratic-technocratic cum new nationalism (security and development) cum corporatist vision of society that
is basic to the attitudes mentioned. It happens that in both Brazil
and Peru the most effective (best-armed, for one thing) and best-
trained (peacetime officer corps have little else to do but go to school)
bureaucracies in their respective nations are the army officer corps.
The two armies are, and probably will remain, competitors (unless
there appears an agreed-upon common enemy—like the U.S. economic
presence in both their countries), since they represent different and
sometimes conflicting national interests. Furthermore, it is inherent
that an army corporation must have as part of its basic ideology some
concept of nationalism (just like a corporation executive can correctly
assume that the corporation has as its basic assumption the pursuit
of profit). If it is true that the new professionalism "contributes more

to the military's general attitude toward political action than to specific policies,"[17] it may also be assumed that the different policies are therefore derived more from the socioeconomic and political context than from the "mentality" or attitudes will probably also tend, over a substantial period of time, to develop its own characteristic institutions and programs. And it is the mentality and attitudes of the new professionalism that the two officer corps have in common.

New professionalism is not a mentality or a set of attitudes limited to professional military officers who have become concerned with national security and development, or who operate naturally in a bureaucratic-technocratic milieu, or who view society as something to be managed from above. Both the Peruvian and Brazilian officers have found eager and willing supporters who share this mentality. Therefore in an attempt to better understand the distinctive mentality of the new professionals or "militechnocrats",* they will be considered as a part of a "modernizing" mentality that has many other manifestations. Many "international development" technicians and planners for instance can well be included in this category (though many more probably share some of the characteristics of the "liberators," as outlined in Table 8.1). Many corporation executives, bankers, educational administrators, and government officials are probably more modernizers than liberators or traditionalists.[18] The comparison of these three approaches may shed some light on the consistencies and antagonisms of each. Table 8.1 attempts to deal more with mentalities and group attitudes than with ideological systems or institutions, and is intended to show some aspects of the mentality of the new professionals as a typical response to typical challenges of our historical period.

It can be asked in this scheme: where are the liberals and where are the Marxists? Both groups are certainly present in both Brazil and Peru, and both groups have their influence. It is the hypothesis of this writer that neither liberalism nor Marxism any longer represents conceptual schemes significantly correlated to contemporary social, economic, and political dynamics, at least in the two countries under consideration. This is not to say that the concepts of either are irrelevant, or that as attitudes or ideologies they will not be influential. In fact, both have had (and will continue to have) an influence on the articulations, ideologies, and attitudes of even the traditional mentality, and much more so on both the modernizing and the liberating mentalities. But the historical phase in which liberalism and Marxism were the most useful sets of categories, either to plan and organize

---

*The term is used by Stanislav Andreski.

TABLE 8.1

The Three Competing Cultures or Mentalities

	Traditional	Modernizing	Liberating
Source of authority	Tradition, social standing, "old" church	Rational scientism, technocratic norms	Populist consensus and (or) humanist value system
Type of army	Old professionalism	New professionalism vanguard, third mission concept	People's army
Philosophy of Education	Transmission of cultural patrimony	Training of necessary technocrats and specialists for national development	Realization of individual and group values and potential
Approach to political change	To strengthen the rule by the traditional elite	Through national planning, directed by professional managers	Through participatory democracy, with intellectuals and technocrats as consultants
Approach to social change	Only through the incremental "civilizing" process	Directed according to a master plan by social engineering	Follows cultural and communitarian dynamics and (or) humanist vision
Ideal state	Administrative state at the service of the ruling aristocracy	Administrative state at the service of the planners and technocrats	Representative, pluralist, political, and populist
Ideal Social system	Pyramidal, with an aristocracy of leisure time for culture at the top. An organic, harmony model of the society	A bureaucratized society, run as a meritocracy, like a corporation. Nation and state as part of an integrated efficient system	A communitarian and participatory model
Prime virtues	"Culture", wisdom, and tradition, (roughly synonymous)	Efficiency, planning, and integration	Cultural creativity and spontaneity, communitarian solidarity
Basic strategies	Rule through traditional symbols of authority and legitimacy	Establishment of functional, bureaucratic agencies in a political ambience	Share social skills with the masses for self-determination
Heroes	The patrician, the bacharel, the "notable," the man of letters	The organization man, the technocrat, the manager. Tendency to anti-personalism	The charismatic leader—Dom Helder Camara, Emiliano Zapata, Father Hidalgo, Salvador Allende, Camillo Torres

social change or to research and understand it, appears to be closing,* even though their main emphases will naturally be absorbed (as well as many of their concepts adapted and utilized) by the three mentalities suggested. If, indeed, it can be agreed upon (if not very well demonstrated) that in this postideological phase of the world's intellectual history comprehensive conceptual systems have lost their hold on masses and intellectuals alike, it may also be imagined that there are still some different attitudes or mentalities that sometimes even cut across ideological lines.

Some Marxists for instance are more modernizers than liberators, as are some liberals—and vice versa. The basic distinction between the two is probably whether a person inclines more toward confidence in populist democracy (as distinct from middle-class, liberal, and reformist democracy), or toward some form of technocratic guidance from above. It is the difference between Lenin and Rosa Luxembourg. It is an assumption of this paper that the democratic hope has escaped its middle-class retaining institutions of "old liberalism" and (more-or-less) regulated capitalism, and that today democracy tends to mean social, economic, and political egalitarianism and participation—at least more so than at any time in the past.

Two other characteristics might offer clues to distinguishing between the modernizers and the liberationists. The modernizers incline toward social scientific, rational, and bureaucratic solutions. The liberationists conversely tend either toward humanist (Marxist or Christian) values as goals or toward a popular will as generated from popular culture as the determinant. If it is argued that there is no inherent contradiction in the two mentalities, it can still be maintained that they represent typical approaches to the search for

---

*This interpretation is the same as that of some of the Brazilian and Peruvian (and more specifically, Greek) military intellectuals, who hold that both liberalism and Marxism are not only "foreign" (and therefore unsuitable to their nations), but "out of date." A new, national, self-generated ideology must be developed to fill the "ideological vacuum," and aid the nation to realize its hitherto frustrated national greatness. The national mission is seen as unity and development. Needless to say, this author does not accept the corporatist solution advocated by these military intellectuals, even though he agrees with the broad outline of their criticism of the contemporary political scene. It is perhaps the basic political dilemma of our time to reconcile the "modernizing" and the "liberating" approaches into a truly developmental process.

solutions. The second clue is in the style of human relations. The
modernizers seek bureaucratic or civil service type relations as
more rational, scientific, and amenable to technocratic planning and
efficiency. The liberators tend to try to place "the movement" (to use
U.S. terminology) or "Consciousness III"* ahead of the bureaucratic
relations, i.e., to emphasize the dynamic, creative, communitarian
style of human relations. Mao's populist "Cultural Revolution" was
used to try to overcome the tendency toward remandarinization of
the state apparatus. When asked what was the chief enemy of the
"revolution," Che Guevara replied simply, "Bureaucracy."

Every student of Latin America is familiar with the traditional
culture and social, economic, and political systems, based on domination by a group of land-holding families (latifundistas). It has been
common to contrast this traditional system and mentality with "revolutionary" forces, though especially since the rise of Fidel Castro there
has been a great deal of difficulty in deciding what the nature of the
revolution is. In the old dichotomy between democrats and dictators,
back in the days when "Her banners made tyranny tremble, when
bourne by the Red, White, and Blue," and the United States was (at least
publicly) applauding the downfall of old-style dictators, the word
"revolutionary" meant liberal and constitutional. But the old concept
of liberal democracy (a constitutional order dominated by a large
middle class, built on a capitalist and imperialist economic structure
somewhat attenuated by liberal and reformist tendencies) no longer
excites revolutionary fervor except at the annual conventions of the
Daughters of the American Revolution. The search by the awakening
"masses" for a meaningful political and social identity, and the
widespread longing for social justice, has made the concept of a state
whose only function is to provide and protect political liberty for
those who already have it seem somewhat quaint, vis-a-vis the
overwhelming and mounting necessities for social planning.

The traditional culture was certainly not a liberal, democratic
one. But the conservative desire for order, stability, and tradition
still represents (unlike old-style liberalism) a living culture or
mentality, in Peru and Brazil. Many of the modernizers for instance
seem to long for only the modernization of the traditional order, to
ensure its continued power and to protect it from its enemies. In the
old order or mentality, authority was founded on an alliance between

----

*The reader is invited to do his own correlation—if he is in-
terested—with Charles Reich's "three consciousnesses."

property, family, the "old" church,* and the "old" army.** Some
authoritarian modernizers, especially in Brazil, seem to have in
mind some modern version of the traditional society.

---

*The "old" church was (and is) that church dominated by the
mentality and interests of the land-holding classes—triumphal, paternalistic, unashamedly authoritarian—that preaches the submission of
the poor to the existing socioeconomic and political system as a
religious virtue. It was (and is, where it continues to flourish) the
guardian of morals and doctrine, and still thought of itself as occupying the "Queenly" position in society of the traditional Iberian church,
though in fact it was (and is) more of a useful tool to "King Oligarchy"
or "King Latifundista" than a partner. The old church is, of course,
the dominant strain before Vatican II, Pope John XXIII, and the Medellín
Council. It still persists, and probably still is dominant in both Rome
and Latin America, in spite of the great attention given to the new
church. The new church is the group that seeks to carry forward the
spirit and work of Vatican II and Pope John—an ecumenical spirit, a
concern for social justice, and a general openness to change and new
ideas. The distinctions are, of course, not always clear. As in the
case of Peru today, some churchmen might be both nationalist and
authoritarian—thus making them more modernizers than liberators.[19]

**The "old" army is that mentality and structure which preceded
even the old professionalism, much less the new professionalism, or
the rise of the "militechnocrats." The old army was personalist, and
its chief officers usually gained their rank through political or family
connections. It was closely identified with the existing social hierarchy
and political system and, in general, did not develop a sense of a
separate identity or profession. This came only with the rise of the
old professionalism. The most complete study of the transformation
from the old army to the old professionalism has been that of the
transformation of the Mexican army from the old army of Porfirio
Diaz to the "old professional" army that emerged under Calles and
became an established institution under Cardenas. The work of
Edwin Lieuwen has detailed this transformation. Perhaps it is a
sign of the decadence of the traditional latifundista class that they
allowed the officer corps to slip away from their control and to
develop its own identity, even though the old professionalism might
ostensibly have been seen as a way of removing the military as a
potential source of interference in the status quo.

THE NEW PROFESSIONALS: A HYPOTHETICAL
ILLUSTRATION AND FIVE EXPLANATORY
MODELS

The impact of modernizing attitudes on a traditional mentality
might be illustrated by a hypothetical Brazilian army officer, who is
probably not atypical. The ambitious son of a conservative and
parochial small-town or small-city, lower-middle-class, family, he
grew up in a period (the 1930s and the 1940s) in which the local parish
priest was a somewhat distant but universally known authority figure,
the channel of rulings and attitudes on most important questions of
the day. Along with the established political order, guaranteed by a
police power that was benevolent toward middle-class transgressions
but arbitrarily and unpredictably harsh when dealing with the poor,
the priest was a common reference point in the community, and stood
for decency and order. Since Vatican II, however, this has seemed
to change. The church that once stood against communism and im-
morality has itself become the home of some groups whose attitudes
and daring innovations affront the sense of decency and the respect
for (or fear of) authority and an established order in society that the
army officer learned while still a child. The church, that should be
an ally of the army in its mission to combat communism, chaos, and
corruption, actually seems, in some cases, to be abetting the subver-
sives. Without daring to articulate the possibility, it might be suggested
that the army officers see themselves as the "new priesthood" of a
national religion, with development rather than salvation as the goal.
The new liturgy is social science, national planning, and "moral and
civic education."[20] Instead of the priests (the church has fallen into
decadence and internal divisions), the army officers are the paragons
of virtue, and the new virtue is selfless patriotism and loyalty to the
officer corps. There is even something in the positivist traditions
of the Brazilian army that might contribute to such attitudes, if not
to an open ideology.

Perhaps by nature the modernizers incline to be authoritar-
ians.[21] The vision of society as a system potentially efficient, rational,
and modern seems to endow the holder of that vision with a belief
in his capacity to contribute significantly to the planning of the process of modernization. But there are still varieties of modernizers.
They can perhaps be divided roughly into two groups; the statists and
the capitalists. (Many Marxists, in the opinion of this writer, would
have to be considered primarily statist-modernizers, while others
are more "liberationists" or populists.) In Brazil, because of the
historically determined antipopulist nature of the military seizure of

power, the army at first (especially during the Castelo Branco period)
made common cause with big and even international (usually U.S.)
business and banks. And though the Brazilian government still
officially endorses capitalism as the best road to development, it has
been acting in a slightly more nationalistic style in more recent years.
It has been prudent, though, not to let its rhetoric outstrip its need
of U.S. and other foreign capital, and its present posture reminds
one somewhat of the Mexican approach in this regard: a balanced
attempt to attract foreign capital and allow reasonable profits while
attempting to strengthen the national bourgeoisie, and a symbolic
rhetoric of independence of "Uncle Sam" balanced with a careful
estimate of the dangers of provoking a negative reaction in the United
States.

That there is a tension between the developmentalist aspirations
of the officer corps of Brazil and Peru and their new nationalist* goals
seems evident. The Brazilian government attempted for some years
to use an anticommunist rhetoric of solidarity with the free world
and Western civilization to paper over the gap between dependence
on international and foreign capitalist governments and corporations
and its aspirations for national modernization. The Peruvian military, gaining its initial popular support from its nationalist posture
in the International Petroleum Company crisis, continued to use a
much more nationalist rhetoric, even though they have shown a
willingness (and a need) for foreign capital. Their strategy "seems
to be the diversification of sources of capital in the capitalist world.
The nationalist component of the ideology of the Junta is subordinate
to the development perspectives." [22]

It is perhaps not surprising that the two military regimes can
work in alliance with capitalist systems, though inherently they would
seem both to tend to statist direction of the economy rather than a

---

*The new nationalism tends to be as much economic as purely
political, and seeks to augment national efficiency, productivity, and
autonomy. It usually begins by attempting to direct national resources
to the development of the economic infrastructure, and by attempting
to regulate or expropriate foreign investments that are critical to the
nation's economy. The term is used to distinguish it from the older,
cultural and literary sense of nationalism that was largely limited
to the upper classes. It is clear that the new nationalism is also a
response of and to the politicization of hitherto marginal groups in
the less-developed countries, whereby these people are seeking a
relevant political-historical identity to enable them to cope with their
new knowledge of the world.

laissez-faire capitalism.[23] It certainly is not without historical
precedent that capitalism is aligned with authoritarian statism in
one country and with liberal democracy in another. Capitalism, by
its very hierarchical nature, is flexible enough to seek temporary
alliances for tactical reasons. Indeed, it may well be a conscious,
tactical decision to make common cause with a future opponent on
the part of the army officers as well, because of present need. That
is, the first steps of modernization may seem to demand an alliance
between corporations and the military regimes, simply because the
military have assessed the situation and calculated their immediate
resources—without allies—as inadequate to the task. Thus, the
greater strength of the Brazilian industrial and banking sector and
of foreign investment in Brazil, plus the size and complexity of the
nation, may have seemed to the army intellectuals to demand an
alliance at this time, whereas in Peru the relative weakness of the
same sectors made it possible for the army to choose the nationalist
path immediately.[24]

In 1965 a Brazilian army major, talking with this writer,
explained the general plan of the army as the following: "First,
we make an alliance with the latifundistas, the American corporations, and Brazilian business, to get rid of the corrupt politicians
and the communists. Then, we make an alliance with the American
and Brazilian business interests to get rid of the latifundistas.
Then, we make an alliance with Brazilian business to get rid of
the American business interests. Then we get rid of the Brazilian
business." This indicates the same mentality as that described by
a recent commentator who wrote that the Peruvian officer "is steeped
in a new type of military paternalism by which he believes that the
armed forces are not only the most organized and efficient organ-
isms within the body politic, but the most socially enlightened, as
well."[25] If such an elite was open and pretentious in its claims it
might be easier to analyze. Even admitting that it may be incipient paranoia, nonetheless, the possibility of a new elite (built in
a close-knit, meritocratous bureaucracy with a belief in "collective
leadership" as opposed to personalism; taught to think strategically
and tactically; and taught to calculate resources before undertaking projects, holding to a tradition that its plans are rightfully kept
secret in the national interest) is enough to give one pause.

The common mentality or approach of the new professionals
of the Brazilian and Peruvian army officer corps is the result of
many different influences and factors. An important one is the sociological backgrounds of the officers, the schooling and military socialization they experience, and the internal dynamics and structure of the
officer corps.[26] Given the increasing difficulty in researching these
matters, the amount of data available is surprising, and the results

are readily available. Less attention has been paid, however, to the
sources of the concepts and attitudes, as intellectual history, of the
new professionalism.[27] Some suggestions as to the sources of the
modernizing culture may be offered as possibly aiding understanding its nature and the behavior of those who belong to this group.
Let it be emphasized, however, that in both Peru and Brazil the
military modernizers are quite deliberately setting out to create a
new, national, modernizing culture.* Though the attempt here is to
isolate the intellectual and historical sources, it is present cultural
attitudes or mentality derived from these sources that are the real
goal. One of the characteristics of the modernizing mentality of the
new professional is a certain praxiological approach that tends to use
ideology instrumentally. Theory is held to be necessary, but the dynamics of history and experience will dictate new theory, and thereby new practice. The "permanent" in this experience is the "party"—
in this case the ongoing officer corps, the guardian and bearer of national values and safekeeper of the national mission to find salvation
through development. Thus, doctrines become of less importance—
perhaps—than attitudes or mentality. But each of the sources listed
here is a set of attitudes as well as an apology or ideology. If it can
be assumed that the particular ideological manifestation of an attitude
(corporatism, for instance) is historically conditioned by the national
situation, the contemporary intellectual struggles, etc., then it can perhaps be imagined that there are characteristic and enduring attitudes
of a, say, corporatist mentality.

The first source is the Iberian concept of an organic yet hierarchical society. It has had many names historically—Catholic conservatism, corporatism, the medieval "harmony model" or "guild
(syndicalist) model" of society. Italian, Austrian, and Portuguese
fascism have all shown strong traces of this. The Spanish state under
Franco is a clear example of a marriage between a modernizing,
authoritarian state, and a vision of society as an organic, interdepen-
dent, almost mystical, whole.[29] In Brazil today the concept of "national
integration," espoused by President Medici, seems to be a counterpart, in systemic terms, of the belief in the importance of harmony

_____

*This attempt in Brazil is an interesting parallel to the attempt
of ISEB, Institute Superior de Estudos Brasileiros (Advanced Institute
of Brazilian Studies), to do the same thing from a liberal-populist
(and sometimes technocratic) stance at an earlier time. Though the
new doctrines of security and development of the ESG are ostensibly
an answer to the ISEBian doctrines, still there are many similarities
that could be studied with profit.[28]

of the whole as a prerequisite to security and development. In Peru, there is also the evocation of an almost mystical sense of "Peruvianism," in which a sense of national strength and purpose will be found. Though very few of the Peruvian officers are <u>cholos</u>, still there is a mystical (if probably romantic and condescending) desire to integrate the Indian into national life—for the same.reasons of national development.

Second, there is a belief in reason and science as the means through which problems can be solved. In Brazil, especially in the army, there was a strong positivist influence, though it is difficult to measure how significant this was in the formation of the mentalities of the present senior officers. The pragmatic know-how approach of the American manager (be he corporation executive or army colonel) is not unlike the positivist approach, in some ways, and the transition has been fairly smooth. In Peru, a newer but equally pervasive (if also impossible to evaluate) influence of social science as a guide to social engineering is the equivalent. The vision of a nation as a total system that can be regulated and developed by rational planning from the top has helped answer the frustration of the Peruvian and Brazilian officers with the slowness of national development in their respective countries.

Much akin to the belief in social science and planning is the set of attitudes that are characteristic of a professional managerial class. A brand of military professionalism that exalts competence, that promotes on a merit basis, that educates (or trains), not limiting itself to traditional military questions, but that takes for granted the necessity of applying managerial skills to the whole society, brings with it a certain set of attitudes. Both the U.S. corporation and the U.S. military have been sources of the managerial mentality—especially in Brazil. Both U.S. corporations and the U.S. government and military have provided examples and training in public and business administration.*

The mentality and attitudes of the new professionals are both the result of and an influence on the changing roles of the officer

---

*Alfred Stepan has thus described very well what is, to him, the real significance of U.S. aid to Brazil:
"While many other factors have also played a part in the expanding role of the military in Latin American politics in the last five years, on balance it appears that U.S. military policies which have encouraged counterinsurgency and nation-building tasks for the military have not been conducive to a political military 'professionalism,' but rather have been implicitly supportive of increased military managerialism in the political system."[30]

corps in politics. The "new autonomy" of the army,* achieved as
a result of the rise of the middle sector in Peru and in Brazil that in
turn followed upon a three-way political impasse, accelerated the
articulation of new role possibilities on the part of the officer corps.
Up to this time both officer corps seem to be significantly motivated
by a desire to achieve national integration, though there have been
some different emphases on the content of modernization, and more
significant and dramatic differences in the style used to pursue that
end. Five models (sometimes overlapping) may be suggested to help
explain or understand the approach of the Brazilian and Peruvian
army officers to their own role in the process of national modernization. Again, it is not the rhetoric or the ideology of the mission of
the army, or of national development, but the attitudes toward self,
the mentality, which is sought.

First, the officer corps can be seen as a club or a clan, with
a strong sense of corporate identity and a high esprit de corps. It
hardly need be mentioned that political loyalties will flow to the group
that can afford the most social security, political protection, and
status. Thus, the extended family operated (and still does for some)
as a "social security system" for members of the traditional class.
The officer corps provides many of the same services, including the
sense of identification, for many army officers, and given the very
early age at which military socialization begins[33] it is hardly surprising that the officers feel and act so much a part of the corporation
of military officers.

Second, the army officer corps can be seen as the body of
executives of a corporation (in the business sense), organized bureau-
cratically and hierarchically, run by senior executives who have
been promoted up through the grades. It is a corps that has shifted its
measure of excellence and criteria for promotion from the old
professional concepts of personal leadership of men to the new
professional concepts of managerial excellence. If, as has been
argued, "the army is the only cohesive force in many Latin American
republics," then it means that the force of tradition has dissolved,
that the force of a strong national consensus never existed, and that
inadequate institutionalization of conflict-management and political
compromise is the rule, then the group that is best organized and
that has the monopoly of the tools of violence will dominate. The
officer corps of Brazil and Peru can be seen as groups of closely

---

*Cotler[31] and Petras and Rimensnyder[32] develop the argument
that the Peruvian military is a more middle-class, modernizing movement than a radical, nationalist phenomenon.

organized managers, commanding the means of coercion, who have
found themselves existing in a relative power vacuum. The monopoly of fire power is not the only advantage that the army officers
have over all the other corporations that are potential competitors.
They tend to have the best (most systematic, rational, and purpose-
ful) personnel selection, training, and promotion processes. They
are able to spend more time in training and education than any other
managerial corps; they have taken it as their mandate to study the
whole society and have available to them critical and sometimes
classified information.

Third, the army tends to see itself as a national cadre, helping
the whole nation get organized for its struggle against subversion
and then to achieve national development. Naturally, the officers
tend to project their style of organization and concepts of development on the nation, and their final goal as some sort of national,
permanent, boy scout encampment, with the generals as the big scout-
masters and the whole nation singing as it pursues production goals.
Like the Grand Inquisitor, it may be for the love of their people that
the officer corps would deny their people the burdens of liberty, and
have in exchange given them Brazilian and Peruvian versions of Fatima,
fados e futebol. The Grand Inquisitor gave to his "little people"
mystery (in religious rites they did not understand), bread, and
little carnal pleasures. A Brazilian version of the "corn and circus"
might be futebol, carnaval, and cachaca. In Peru, there is more of
an attempt to offer a national religion that is more emotional, that
appeals more to the vanity of the "little man." If the Brazilians are
stern Calvinists, the Peruvians are nearly Pentecostals. In both
cases, the "bishop-generals" are still basically authoritarian—
paternalistic.

Fourth, the army officer corps can be seen as a democratic-
centralist political party, paralleling the state administrative structure and reserving to itself all basic political decisions, which
will be implemented, however, by the apolitical administrative apparatus. The role of the social-science-oriented "think-tanks" (ESG
and CAEM) plus the usually informal club of high-ranking and influential generals, is an interesting division of most of the tasks
usually assigned to the general committee of the party in a "demo-
cratic-centralist" Marxist state. To date, in Brazil and in Peru, the
president has been always the "first among equals" of a small group
of senior generals. He is, in other words, the head of state (a symbol
of the military presence, of continuity, of order and authority) as well
as "chairman" of the central committee (though in Brazil the alto
comando of eleven generals acts independently of the "retired"
general-president in crises). The political power of the president,
and his executive mandate, comes from his membership in the "club."

He also fills the largely symbolic role of incarnating national unity
and purpose and of legitimizing the programs decided on or approved
by the "party." He also acts as regulator of the state apparatus, as
its chief administrator, to ensure its fidelity to the indicated programs. Other key military personnel are also designated to penetrate the state apparatus and the business establishment at key places.
These are often graduates of ESG or CAEM, and part of the alumni
associations of such. In Brazil, many civilians have been "militarized,"
and obviously find much satisfaction in belonging to the ADESG cadre
in every ministry and in bearing the overall guidelines and philosophy
to their offices. They are, in effect, commissars. Another pene-
trating agency, also with cadres in each ministry (as well as in major
corporations) is the SNI, the National Informational Service, in Brazil,
It is more concerned with subversion (rather broadly defined) than
with tutoring the administrative structure, but like ADESG it is
basically responsive to the military corporation—the "party"—and
not to the state.

Fifth, the army can be seen as a self-designated candidate for
the role of an authoritarian and authoritative national church, establishing the doctrines and practice necessary for the mobilization of
the people for the national mission—in Brazil, the struggle against
subversion and then on to development; in Peru, an emphasis on
development. Especially in Brazil, the army has sought the role of
seeking out and protecting society from deviants and heretics and
those who reject the authority of the army to set the national norms
and philosophy.

CONCLUSIONS

An apologist for the new role of the Peruvian army has explained
in this way the new role of the army in that nation, and expressed very
well an attitude toward it:

> The army—the armed forces—have always had the role
> of protagonist in Latin America. It was the armed part
> of the nation that led the struggle to create the national-
> ities. Its task now is to bring about profound changes,
> of structure, in the economic and social sphere, generat-
> ing political conditions for democracy. The reactionary
> forces, on the other hand, expect the army to support
> the status quo, which is linked to external dependence.
> The first "option" affirms sovereignty, creates the
> conditions of qualitative growth, and diminishes the

specter of gratuitous violence. This last because the
power of change is exercised in the name of the total
society, channelling it into a project of sovereignty.
The second "option" leads to the reenforcement of
social tensions, to a greater amount of subversive
activity, and to the fate of being a colony, whether prosperous or not.[34]

Both the Brazilian and Peruvian army officer corps claim to be leading
the nation back to democracy (in the case of Brazil, the army apparently has adopted the view that pre-1930 Brazil was a democracy-
in-development, interrupted by the Vargas era) or forward to democracy (in the case of Peru). The essential preconditions are the curing
of corruption, the containment of subversion, "fiscal responsibility,"
and "social tranquility." The period of "tutorship" in which the army
monopolizes political power is still thought of as "exceptional" in
both nations. It is the contention of this author that the basic managerial
and authoritarian mentality of the two officer corps will lead in both
countries to a permanent Salazar-like authoritarian regime. It would
be a mistake to take too seriously the present rhetoric of the Peruvian
(and some Brazilian) officers. Sincere they may be, but the implications of some of the populist-liberationist approach they use may not
be fully seen.
　　　A probably apocryphal story recently appeared in The Guardian.

One of the clearest illustrations of the military-civilian
contradictions concerns a zealously revolutionary
colonel who visited the aristocratic and exclusive Club
Trujillo to speak to the landowners of the region about
the reforms of the government.
He said he was very happy to visit the famous club, but
felt he had to point out that its members were no longer
in step with the times. Peru had changed and the landowners should admit peasants and small farmers to the
club, which should cease to be the preserve of the rich
and well-bred. The president of the club assured the
colonel that the membership entirely agreed with
this revolutionary principle and said they were waiting
only for the Circulo Militar in Lima to admit private
soldiers.[35]

It can be doubted that either the Brazilian or Peruvian army
officers are really capable of establishing an open, democratic
society. It also remains to be seen if they can carry through

even the modernizing program they have announced as their intention. But certainly neither nation will ever be the same as before.
It is no profound social revolution that either is experiencing, but
instead the substitution of a series of inept, weak and (or) decadent
elites by a single, homogenous, organized elite, possessed of a
managerial mentality and imbued with a nationalist and developmentalist spirit. It can thus be said that both Brazil and Peru have passed
irrevocably beyond the old, oligarchic rule and beyond the experiments with middle-class liberal democracy that characterized the
post-World War II period in both countries. The power of the old
oligarchy is broken (or just decayed) and the bankers, industrialists,
and businessmen never dedicated enough energy, brains, and resources to the task of building their desired form of government to
compete with the army officers. For a while in both countries a
political class, of reformist tendencies, tried to act as more or less
"honest" brokers between the competing interests and sometimes
exploited emerging populist tendencies. In both countries the populist
leadership was too unskilled or weak to organize a political base
strong enough to lead the country. It was into this vacuum that the
two armies stepped.

An acute observor of the Brazilian scene predicted soon after
Medici assumed the presidency that the new president "will find
himself increasingly pushed toward a hard line nationalism of the
Peruvian type, which is not leftist but much like rightist nationalism
in the United States."[36] The Peruvian model is more Nasserist
than the Brazilian model at present, because it has and uses a popular rhetoric. The two regimes will no doubt significantly modify
the structure of the two nations, where they find themselves in
nearly absolute power. A new, mixed military-civilian oligarchy of
technocrats and bureaucrats will appear. A stable authoritarian state,
more efficient and modernizing than Salazar's or Franco's but
resembling them in many ways will emerge. Perhaps the two
governments will achieve some more economic development and
administrative efficiency. But it will be only a case of creating a
new overclass. There is very little in the mentality and attitudes
of the new professionals to indicate any possibility of really building a society of freedom, participation, and equality. As Victor
Alba has concluded: "The only antidote to pseudo-leftist, technocratic
and military paternalism is to educate and organize the people so
that they acquire the capacity to make their own decisions."[37] Even
though in October 1970 the Peruvian government announced its intention to begin a massive program of "social mobilization," the manipulation of the mass through the use of symbolic acts and populist
rhetoric is not the same thing as helping the people "to acquire
the capacity to make their own decisions." It remains to be seen if

either the Peruvian or Brazilian armies know how to allow democracy
to flourish in their nations. The typical attitudes of the new professional are hardly reassuring.

9

THE CATHOLIC CHURCH
IN LATIN AMERICAN POLITICS:
A CASE STUDY OF PERU
Carlos A. Astiz

It is the author's assumption that, at least among political
scientists and other interested scholars, the position is no longer
accepted that the Catholic church does not involve itself in politics
(however one defines the political realm). The political involvement
of the Catholic church in Latin American countries is very pronounced.
When the Vatican confirms the excommunication of Paraguayan officials
who attacked faculty and students of the Catholic University of Asuncion, as well as clergy who had participated in processions and other
acts said to be politically motivated; when Cuban bishops demand that
the trade boycott of Cuba be lifted; when the National Confederation of
Peasants, one of the three sectors of Mexico's ruling party (PRI),
engages in a heated exchange with the First Congress of Theology
over the political participation of the peasantry in Mexican politics—
it becomes apparent that the Catholic church of the Latin American
countries is deeply involved in national, as well as regional and local,
politics.1 The recent growth of the literature dealing with this topic
confirms the widespread recognition that the Catholic church is
involved in that which is Caesar's and that in turn Caesar is involved
in that which is the church's.

Within its space limitations, this chapter will explore various
avenues and mechanisms employed by the Peruvian Catholic church
to participate in politics, the course and extent of its power, the
processes employed to articulate its interests, and the possibility of
altering its political role. This analysis will focus on one country
only, and hence its findings may not have validity beyond the case
considered here. It is the author's opinion that much data needs to
be uncovered before broader comparisons can be made, although he
looks with sympathy on those willing to make the attempt.

It is not necessary to discuss here the historical factors that
gave Catholicism a religious monopoly in Latin American countries

and converted the Catholic church into an essential element of the
national struggles for political power. It should be noted, however,
that the close church-state relationship transferred to this region by
the Spanish political system at the time of conquest was adjusted,
but not essentially altered, by the processes of independence.[2] The
political elites of the republics that finally emerged saw fit to retain
the close relationship inherited from the colonial powers, and the
Catholic church found the maintenance of the status quo equally attractive.

Some writers maintain that the Catholic church is simply one
more pressure group operating within the traditional political systems
of Latin America. It is maintained here that such a view is simplistic
and fails to explain the essential role played by the church in the
domestic politics of Latin American countries. The political power
of the Catholic church is derived from the fact that, throughout these
countries' history, it has been the provider of a conservative political
ideology. Thus the traditional upper class and other groups favoring
the maintenance of the status quo have not had to develop an ideological
base that would intellectually justify their privileges.[3] A principal
character of a recent Spanish novel, for instance, provided a blunt
description of the relationship between the holders of political and
economic power and the national Catholic church which this author's
thesis implies, "I go to Mass to serve as an example, I give alms to
the priests, I protect an orphanage. Religion is useful. We help
priests to live, and they defend us from the poor with the threat of
hell."[4] A keen observer of the Peruvian political scene provides
evidence that Peruvian landowners seemed, at least until recently, to
be thinking along the same lines. He writes that in the Peruvian
Sierra,

> The chapel is the required complement of the landlord's
> residence; mass is celebrated there when there is a
> priest available, and always on the festivity of the Patron
> Saint who protects the fields, harvests and cattle, pre-
> vents droughts, and offers heaven in exchange for obe-
> dience and resignation in this world; these are the Chris-
> tian virtues which the priest emphasizes in his sermons.[5]

Three decades ago, the Archbishop of Peru actually spelled out
the ideological role being played by the Catholic church in relation
to the poorer sectors of Peruvian society and polity. He told them
that poverty was the road to eternal happiness, and based the solution
of socioeconomic problems on the ability of the state (and apparently
the church) to make the poor recognize the virtue of their economic
plight.[6]

In discussing the political role of the Catholic church, we can refer to three distinct levels from which ideological pronouncements in fact originate: the supranational level, essentially the Holy See and the international church gatherings; the national level, mainly the archbishop, the bishops acting jointly, and the hierarchy usually located in the capital city; and the local level, especially the parish priest but also all religious personnel in direct contact with the faithful.

It would be unfair and erroneous to say that Catholicism's main objective, as a world religion, is either the maintenance or the alteration of the political, social, and economic status quo. Catholicism, as are practically all religions, is made up of a collection of texts, often obscure and contradictory, which lend themselves to varying interpretations. At least their basic documents can be and are interpreted in so many different ways that they appear to support different and occasionally contradictory interests.

It must be remembered, however, that access to these pronouncements (often made at the supranational level and occasionally by the national hierarchy) requires both a high level of education and the availability of sophisticated sources which provide texts and background commentaries. These sources are available only to a small minority of Latin Americans, principally those with enough training, time, and means to keep up with Catholic reinterpretations of the dogma. Most believers (members of the lower class and of the lower-middle class) do not belong in this category. In the particular case of illiterates, but also for the majority of those who have received elementary schooling, Catholic dogma is what the local priest says it is. In other words, the local level is in a position to actually remake the political ideology to which all good Catholics are expected to subscribe. Obviously the national level can operate as an ideological filter regarding supranational pronouncements. It also has the power to police the interpretations transmitted by the local level.

Available evidence indicates that the local level of the Catholic church in Latin America has long employed these powers to give specific political meaning to general supranational and national pronouncements, as well as to downplay those which would interfere with their political role. In the case of Peru local priests have tended to come out on the side of the status quo and against those who favor effective reform. When APRA developed as a reformist party in the 1920s and 1930s, with a political ideology running counter to that of the Catholic church, each sermon became a forum to denounce APRA whose leaders and followers were accused of planning to murder priests and laymen, to burn churches, and to rape nuns. When elections were on the horizon, the clergy, often speaking from the pulpit, threatened with damnation those who would disobey their political

directives by supporting APRA. One witness reports, "I heard a
priest's sermon in one of the churches of Huancayo in 1932; he was
addressing the faithful on political subjects. He showed that APRA
was the work of the devil, and that it should be feared and hated since
its own leader, because of his nose profile, looked exactly like Satan."[7]

Timely pastoral letters reminded Peruvians of the errors in
APRA's ideology and platform, as well as of the consequences (both
in this life and after death) of going along with those errors. Since
World War II, as APRA shifted its stand and became a defender of the
status quo, the Catholic church of Peru directed its attention to more
immediate ideological threats, i.e., other political organizations such
as APRA Rebelde, the Movement of the Revolutionary Left (MIR), the
Frente Revolucionario Izquierista (FIR), and some peasant groups
became the new rivals. It has been reported that, in the early 1960s,

> The Catholic Church, at least at the parish level . . . joined
> in this campaign against the peasant movement. The priests
> of the region refused to baptize the sons of those peasants
> who belonged to the unions directed by Hugo Blanco. . . .
> If the cultural level of the Cuzco peasantry is taken into
> account and if the religious beliefs of the Peruvian peo-
> ple in general are remembered, the fear felt by these
> peasants because of the priest's refusal to baptize their
> children will be easily understood.[8]

PRESSURES FOR CHANGE

The traditional position of the Catholic church in Peru as the
ideological supplier of the traditional upper class has been subject to
increasing pressures since the late 1950s. Domestically, the "revolution of rising expectations" has reached some of the lower levels of
Peruvian society. In so doing it has contradicted that interpretation
of the dogma which counselled patience and resignation on the grounds
that little can be done to upgrade the status of those who were not
getting their share of socioeconomic rewards. When educated outsiders
told the peasants that they were in fact entitled to own the land they
were working and to receive a larger share of the profits for their
work, the peasantry found nothing wrong with the idea. When ideological
struggles developed between these "outside agitators" and the local
clergy, the peasants had to choose between what they thought was just,
fair, and in their own interest, on the one hand, and the mandate of the
Catholic church, on the other. One should not be surprised that a
significant number chose that ideology which offered them (at least
on paper) an immediate solution to their economic plight, even if it
meant foregoing salvation after death.

The limited data available indicate that a similar choice has been made by their urban counterparts. The traditional position of the church in Peru and elsewhere in Latin America has caused it to lose followers. According to a representative of the conservative sector of the Peruvian church,

> It cannot be denied that the percentage of adults who attended mass weekly is low, and the percentage of those who follow the precepts of yearly confession and communion is even lower. . . .
>
> The Protestant propaganda, particularly that of the Adventists, Baptists, Jehova's Witnesses, Mormons, but above all Marxist and atheist propaganda have grown greatly. This propaganda has had contributing parties, unbelieving intellectuals, and press organs. It increased . . . after the triumph of Castroism in Cuba. . . . Although in the 1940 census, those who stated that they did not have any religion were very few, I fear that their number has grown a great deal in the last twenty-two years.[9] (Emphasis added.)

More important, a study conducted by social scientists of the Catholic University of Peru in the department of Puno found that only 27 percent of a representative sample were aware of the religious organizations available in their communities, 8 percent showed appreciation for them, and 6 percent actually belonged to at least one religious organization (one third of those who belonged indicated that they were somehow coerced into membership). The researchers concluded that, "The religious organizations seem to have significantly less importance than we thought before beginning to conduct this research. Only one-third of the sample is aware of their existence, and less than one-third of these appreciate and belong to them."[10]

Inasmuch as the political efforts of the Catholic church after the late 1950s were directed against its ideological competitors, the parties of the left, it should be noticed that the above testimony and data are confirmed by electoral returns in various elections held just before the military takeover of October 1968. Although the left-wing parties (because of their own inability and political incompetence, compounded by police hostility) had been unable to show any electoral strength until the mid-1960s, in the 1966 municipal elections their candidates obtained 20.7 percent of the vote in Arequipa, 12.8 percent of the vote in Cuzco, and an impressive 33.9 percent in Puno, where, as we showed, religious organizations were found to be extremely weak. These electoral returns acquire even more significance when it is remembered that illiterates are not allowed to vote and that more than 80.0 percent of the population of Puno was classified as illiterate. Only 7.8 percent of the total population and 15.2 percent of the voting-age population exercised the franchise in Puno; since 15.8 percent of the voting age population was legally permitted to register, the percentage of those entitled to vote but who failed to do so was minimal.[11] Those deprived of the franchise belong to the lower layers of society, which is where the ideological conflict between Catholic dogma (as interpreted by the local level) and anti-status-quo political philosophies collide. Therefore, it is fair to assume that in the last few years left-wing candidates would have done better had more people been enfranchised and had other elections been held.

IDEOLOGICAL CHANGES WITHIN THE
PERUVIAN CATHOLIC CHURCH

The deterioration of the church's position, particularly among the Peruvian lower and lower-middle classes, did not go unnoticed by the clergy. The parish priests and other religious personnel, such as nuns working in free schools and hospitals, perceived that Catholicism was losing out to anti-status-quo ideologies. Relatively little was done within the church until the late 1960s, although mention should be made of two clergymen who were pioneers in this matter.

Salomon Bolo Hidalgo, organizer and leading figure of the country's National Liberation Front, apparently started his opposition to the traditional role of the Catholic church in politics during the 1950s. Although Bolo Hidalgo has not been taken seriously by most of his fellow countrymen, he developed a blunt line of reasoning which, in recent years, has been adopted by the reformist group within the Peruvian clergy (a group, needless to say, that is far from being politically homogeneous). At one time he wrote,

> I consider that it is absolutely necessary for the clergy to place themselves decisively on the side of the peasants, on the side of the unprotected and the forgotten, instead of prostituting themselves before grants spotted with blood. It is very sad for me to see that, when there appears a priest who, conscious of his duty, follows Christ in his condemnation of imperialism and the oligarchy, those at the top of the Church hierarchy are the ones who condemn an attitude which they should back. . . . I feel that, if Christ were to come to this earth today, he would take the side of the Peasant Leagues, he would take the side of those who earn their food with their sweat, of those who earn salaries of hunger and misery.[12]

Bolo Hidalgo has repeatedly disclaimed that he is a communist or even a fellow-traveler, an accusation hurled at him by some conservative Peruvian newspapers. In doing so, he uses an argument which constitutes one of the potentially most powerful weapons of the Catholic Left: that they cannot possibly have anything to do with communism because they are devout Catholics.* He has consistently emphasized that communism has nothing to do with the political insecurity that exists in Peru. Instead, he blames it on the extremely uneven distribution of wealth and other socioeconomic rewards and he has not hesitated to attack the cardinal, the nuncio, and the clergy as a whole for their position on these matters.

> Those bishops who issue pastoral letters to take votes away but do not issue them to require the wealthy to give something to the poor, to pay just salaries, to stop the exploitation of miners, peasants and workers; those bishops who photograph themselves with the "jet set" but who forget the undernourished children and do not issue pastoral letters against those responsible for the massive illiteracy and tuberculosis; those bishops who gain plenty of weight but only remember in their pastoral letters to favor the powerful in this country; those bishops, I repeat, are only merchants of religion.[15]

The second priest to be mentioned here is the Jesuit Romeo Luna Victoria. He is more of an intellectual reformer and less of a "doer" than Bolo Hidalgo. Luna Victoria at one time taught political science at a normal school and he has published an interesting manual dealing with the theory and practice of revolution, addressed to political leaders. He provides both a theoretical justification and specific techniques to carry out a revolution. Although he does not single out any one country, outlining instead only a series of conditions for violent revolution, other writings make clear that Peru was foremost in his mind.[16] Luna Victoria rejects the idea that Catholic doctrine forbids participation in strikes or in a bloody revolution. Indeed, his opinion is that the contrary is true and that the advice to "offer the other cheek" does not apply to sociopolitical matters. He concluded, "There may arise the unfortunate and sad situation in which,

---

*Although Bolo Hidalgo has long employed this argument,[13] since the 1968 military takeover he stresses the point that, although a radical reformist, he is as far from communism as he is from the traditional upper class.[14]

to carry out that which is experimentally correct, unquestionably just, and extremely urgent, which we are sponsoring throughout this study, there may not be, in some areas of the world, any other alternative but to resort to armed revolution."[17] Luna Victoria has recommended the redistribution of certain types of property: those items given by nature and not produced by an individual's work (which he calls "elastic property") are subject to confiscation or at least the rent they produce is so subject.[18] Finally, he has shown the same frustration expressed by Bolo Hidalgo toward the Peruvian Catholic church; he has pointed out that, when this institution receives money or other economic advantages from the state, the result often is "a 'satisfied' and 'silent' Church." "I do not wish to cite contemporary names because I prefer to avoid damaging discords and arguments. The spectacle of a religious hierarchy that does not speak up when it should, that remains silent when it must denounce the obvious violation of sacred human rights, is extremely depressive."[19] The political position of these two forerunners, and their disagreement with the Peruvian Catholic church, was further emphasized in 1965 when guerrilla groups began to operate in the Peruvian Andes. Both Bolo Hidalgo and Luna Victoria supported, or at least defended, the guerrillas' position which contradicted that of the hierarchy. An organization led by Luna Victoria even rejected the government's branding of guerrillas and supporters of communism as traitors.[20]

During the 1960s, most of the (few) laymen and clergymen who favored drastic reforms in Peru tried to channel their political activities through the Christian Democratic party. This alternative, incidentally, gained popularity after the 1964 presidential victory of its Chilean counterpart. However, it soon became clear that the Christian Democratic party of Peru would be unable to develop the popular following or the political influence for which these Catholic reformers had been hoping. Furthermore, the party was partially co-opted by Belaunde Terry's Accion Popular, and consequently was blamed for the errors of his administration. More recent divisions of the Christian Democratic party have further diminished its political potentialities and, in any case, the present military regime placed a cloud over the future of all existing political parties.

Meanwhile, the ranks of the Catholic reformers within the clergy seem to have grown substantially in the late 1960s. They have organized themselves and entered their country's political arena as a group. Their activities became particularly noticeable when the post-October 1968, military regime showed that it was prepared to carry out certain reforms. In a sense, the influence of the forerunners has been reduced (or, better said, superseded) by a more highly organized group which, although still a minority of the clergy, no longer relies on a few individuals. The organization articulating what

these reformers believe the political ideology of the Peruvian Catholic
church should be is the National Office of Social Information, or ONIS,
after its Spanish initials. It is difficult to obtain a complete list of
its members, but 100 would not be an unrealistic figure, apparently
all of whom are members of the clergy. Their message on agrarian
reform (issued on June 20, 1969, shortly before the Peruvian military
regime announced its Agrarian Reform Act) has 82 signatures. It was
possible to obtain some information on 72 members of ONIS, which is
summarized in Table 9.1.

Some characteristics of this group are readily apparent. Its
members are clearly young priests, a majority of whom are located
in the Lima metropolitan area. The proportion of those with very advanced training in the social sciences and the humanities is high. Of
those located in Lima, the overwhelming majority were in either the
Arequipa or the Trujillo diocese. In fact, some of the signers participated in an incident in the city of Trujillo during March-April 1969,
when they supported striking blue-collar workers and ran into a conflict with an upper-class club. The priests involved were attacked
by the papal nuncio, who denounced them to the hierarchy and to the
military government. The episode ended when the government and
the hierarchy refused to intervene, thus forcing the Vatican representative to leave his post.[21]

These reformist elements widely publicized their perception
of what the position of the church was and should have been. One leading spokesman of this group has outlined in no uncertain terms the
traditional role of the Peruvian church as follows:

> The Church has been an easy, and often complacent, prey
> of those who, in the name of a "western and Christian"
> world, have used it to protect their interests and to defend
> an order created for their own benefit. It could be admitted,
> at the most, that the Church presents certain ethical require-
> ments in the building of the eternal city; and this only when
> these requirements do not openly contradict the interests of
> those who have the reins of the economic and political domi-
> nation of the people.[22]

On the other hand, he sees the new role of the Peruvian Catholic
church as that of a provider of "a theology of man's liberation."

> To preach the evangelical message is not to preach an eva-
> sion of this world. On the contrary, the Word of the Lord
> tends to make deeper, to radicalize, our commitment in
> history. And this, concretely, means for us to solidarize
> with the oppressed of this continent, to participate in their

TABLE 9.1

Comparison of ONIS Membership and
General Peruvian Clergy

	ONIS Members	All Priests
Percentage native Peruvian	57.5	56.8
Percentage located in Lima	62.5	32.5
Age breakdown—percentage distribution		
to 40 years of age	56.9	43.7
41 to 50	33.3	22.7
51 to 60	6.9	17.1
61 or more	2.8	16.5
Average age	40.3 years	45.9 years

Source: Data made available by the Peruvian Catholic church.

efforts to become free, with the understanding that the
history of salvation is a liberation in process.[23]

THE CATHOLIC CHURCH AND CURRENT
PERUVIAN POLITICS: A POSSIBLE
COURSE OF ACTION

A careful exploration of events within the Catholic clergy of
Peru shows that the "liberationist" position constitutes the vanguard
of the reformist group. It cannot be ignored, however, that the Peruvian reformists and their more conservative colleagues are currently
facing a very special situation. It is not too difficult for the Catholic
church to place itself to the left of those in control of the government
in countries such as Brazil and Paraguay. They can do this without
radically shifting their political ideology and without necessarily
alienating the bulk of their upper- and upper-middle-class supporters.
The abuses of power committed by those in control provide attractive
short-term issues, without forcing the church into a consideration of
the more crucial redistribution of socioeconomic rewards.[24] But in
Peru, since October 1968, the Catholic reformers and the rest of the
clergy in Peru have been operating under an authoritarian military
regime which has presented itself as the country's developmental
elite. Furthermore, the Peruvian military officers now in control
of the government have taken actions in certain fields (such as

agrarian reform, tighter control of foreign investment, and greater
supervision of foreign exchange operations) which lend some credence
to their avowed intentions.[25]

The only situation analogous to that being faced by the Peruvian
Catholic church is the Castro takeover in Cuba and his later embrace
of communism. But this situation is not directly comparable. Both
the supranational authorities of the Catholic church and their national
counterparts have indicated their opposition to communism, although
the church has continued its activities in countries controlled by those
who subscribe to that ideology. The Peruvian military leaders, however, have stated that, while they are not too responsive to the wishes
of one superpower, they have not moved very much closer to the other.
It must also be remembered that some of the officers now occupying
responsible government positions were active in the elimination of
the left-wing guerrilla bands in 1965. Therefore, the Catholic church
of Peru and particularly its reformist wing are faced with a regime
that is taking the limelight away from them. The alternative of siding
with the traditional upper class is hardly an alternative at all, either
for the reformist wing or for other members of the clergy. If the
church was competing unsuccessfully with left-wing ideologies when
it could count on the resources of the state for help, and when it could
accuse its ideological rivals of being communists, how could it expect
to compete successfully against a noncommunist military government
that was able to convey a reformist image? To oppose reform would
be to alienate an even greater percentage of the lower and lower-
middle classes, and probably of the few technocrats who still subscribed
to the Catholic faith.

The choice was not difficult for the reformist wing. Since its
members noticed that there were policy cleavages within the armed
forces, the reformists placed themselves clearly to the left of the
military regime. They supported those measures they considered
sufficiently reformist and selectively criticized those which did not
go far nor fast enough. Consequently, ONIS's declaration on agrarian
reform appeared a few days before the military government issued
its Agrarian Reform Act, but when it was vox populi in Lima and the
rest of the country that a decision on this matter was forthcoming.
The declaration states: "It is our duty, as servants of the Lord's
Word, to announce to all those who in one way or another return
dignity, bread and justice to the peasant, that in doing so they are
doing it to Christ himself."[26] The implication that ONIS is more
reformist than the military is emphasized by Gutierrez, who indicated
in October 1969 that the steps so far taken by the government were
"interesting, important, but insufficient." An authentic transformation
suggests, for instance, greater popular participation; such a transformation cannot be made only from the top down. A public declaration of
ONIS dated October 4, 1969, read as follows:

Social transformation is not merely a revolution for the
people; the people themselves—particularly the peasants
and the blue collar sectors, exploited and unjustly mar-
ginated—should be agents of their own liberation. . . .
The steps recently taken in Peru [nationalization of the
International Petroleum Company and agrarian reform]
suffer obstacles and limitations in their application,
owing to the pressures and the involvement of those
sectors affected by these measures and to the negligence
of some public officials. . . . We call the public's attention to the distrust and even the repression shown against
just demands of unionized labor.[27]

More recently, when the government was involved in negotiations
with American corporations regarding the extraction of copper from
the Cuajone area, ONIS warned the military that further concessions
should not be granted. Members of ONIS have assisted workers who
were striking for higher salaries or who had been laid off, while the
organization questioned the military government's policy of ignoring
the high unemployment rate and maintaining the freeze originally
decreed on wages.[28] Thus ONIS seems to have been successful in
maintaining the initiative in terms of reformism and in remaining
disassociated from the present regime. A similar attitude has been
followed by Luna Victoria, recently living in London but writing often
in the magazine Oiga. This political position has had its consequences;
Father Harold Griffiths Escardo, sympathetic to the reformists, indicated,

The powerful economic groups, for instance, have rejected
this new attitude of the Church and have refused, in retalia-
tion, their economic assistance to the works of the Church.
This attitude, however, has only served to assess the depth
of the belief of many of those Christians and to painfully
ascertain the limitations of the serious training provided
in Catholic schools and pulpits. . . . Unfortunately, the
January calls of Medellin and of the national hierarchy
have not been sufficiently heard or sufficiently implemented.[29]

What may be more surprising is that the main bulk of the Peruvian Catholic church, represented by the hierarchy, has maneuvered
into a position that parallels that of its reformist wing, albeit a few
degrees to the right. This equivocal attitude of the Peruvian hierarchy
has been in existence since the 1960s and was reflected in the public
positions taken in the Second Vatican Council (see Table 9.2).

TABLE 9.2

Public Positions of Peruvian Representatives
in the Second Vatican Council

| | Conservative | | Liberal | |
	Number	Percentage	Number	Percentage
Cardinals	4	66.6	2	33.3
Bishops	3	50.0	3	50.0
Total	7	58.3	5	41.7

Source: Information published in Xavier Rynne, Letters from Vatican City (New York: Farrar, Straus, Giroux, 1963-66), four vols.

Thus, while the hierarchy did not punish early reformist priests, such as Luna Victoria, and did not support the papal nuncio's attack in the Trujillo episode, it did nothing to prevent the use of the faithful in combatting left-wing organizations, particularly in the Sierra region.

The relationship of the hierarchy and the military government has been, at best, an uneasy one. Cardinal Juan Landazuri Ricketts, the head of the Peruvian Catholic church, supported those measures which had obvious popular appeal, such as the takeover of the assets of the International Petroleum Company and the conflict with the United States over the purchase of military equipment. His support of governmental actions on the IPC question, however, was coupled with a call for prompt elections and a return to civilian government.[30] The bishops of Chimbote and Cajamarca took the side of workers and peasants and severely criticized the authorities. They also stated that the Agrarian Reform Law passed by the military regime had serious deficiencies and called for its improvement. Indeed, the bishop of Chimbote's position in favor of blue-collar workers was so forceful that he was reported to have been detained by Peru's secret police.[31] Auxiliary Bishop Bambaren, who was appointed bishop of the shanty towns not too long ago, heads an organization that advises shantytown dwellers on possible improvements. When General Artola, then minister of the interior (and thus in charge of internal security), tried to develop popular support by distributing presents among these people, he was rebuffed by Bambaren, who pointed out that "instead of calming the poor with cake and used clothing, it is necessary to reform society."[32] General Artola ceased in his attempts.

The conflict between Auxiliary Bishop Bambaren and Interior Minister Artola came into the open once more in May 1971. Shanty-town dwellers occupied urban land in a newly developed area of Lima.

While Bambaren does not seem to have encouraged the move, he went to the area being occupied, made some apparently inflammatory remarks and celebrated mass. Artola took an ambivalent attitude toward the episode, but finally decided to authorize the use of force to expel the invaders. When the confrontation took place, Artola accused Bambaren of being an agitator and ordered him jailed. Although President Velasco freed the auxiliary bishop that same evening, the event caused the urgent return of Cardinal Landazuri Ricketts from abroad; urgent meetings between the principals; apologies; and, after a few days, Artola's resignation. In the process, the participants made certain remarks which indicated that the settlement had been, at best, a tactical one. President Velasco reiterated that the land invasions had been the work of agitators, planned by enemies of the government; however, Bambaren was not involved and everything had been a misunderstanding. In fact, according to the president, the clergy was supporting the administration and there was no problem between the two. Bambaren issued a press release in which he discriminated between the government and the minister of the interior. The auxiliary bishop was apparently willing to absolve the former but not the latter, and reminded the public that he had not been treated in accordance with his position. Cardinal Landazuri Ricketts, after meeting with President Velasco, tried to play down the episode (he had complained bitterly and publicly at the airport upon his hurried return to the country). In general terms he agreed with the president and indicated that there was no confrontation between church and state. He then stated,

> What we should make very clear is that to solve the problem posed by the land invasions, lack of respect for private property cannot possibly be admitted; if private property is not respected, then the juridical order, the legal procedures established in our nation, are attacked. If there is no respect for private property, guaranteed by the Constitution, by our laws, then, naturally, there will be chaos, lawlessness. [33]

Perhaps the most serious conflict between the hierarchy and the military regime came about due to university reforms enacted by the government. Students of the Catholic University demonstrated in opposition to the new law, and the police entered the buildings and beat up faculty, students, and even the university president. Cardinal Landazuri Ricketts chastised the government, even after apologies were made. The conservative newspaper La Prensa, which articulates the views of the coastal sector of the traditional upper class, praised the cardinal's position.

These exhortations should be taken very much into account, because they show the preoccupation of the primate of the Peruvian Church with the commission of acts which injure the rights that constitute the spiritual and human patrimony of Peru's Catholics, as citizens.

But the newspaper felt that it should distinguish between the cardinal and the reformist wing. In a different article, printed in the same editorial page, La Prensa attacked change in the church.

In wanting to renew the Church in order to bring it up to date, those who wish an "incarnation" of the Church as close to the present world as possible, as modern as possible, should remember what happened in the Middle Ages: a tie between the Christians and what then was "the present" world. And it cannot escape our attention that, in those procedures, there was a large share of legitimate drowning of the Christian in the profane; and this is what is dangerous in a too definitive "incarnation," in too steep a renewal toward that which is temporal.[34]

When it came to deeds that affected their immediate interest, the hierarchy was extremely cautious, and the reformist wing lost its precision and sense of urgency. ONIS agreed in October 1969 "to make a very real effort to eliminate in our communities the system of payments for the administration of sacraments."[35] A meeting of Peruvian bishops held in July 1969 agreed to review relations with the state and indicated that a committee was studying the matter of church property in relation to urban reform. At the same time the bishops demanded social security and other social benefits for the clergy. Cardinal Landazuri Ricketts decided to move from his official residence into a less pretentious house. He also donated suburban land near Lima to build 600 houses for people of limited means (although it was not made clear to whom the donation had been made or who was going to build the houses).[36] More recently, ONIS has continued in this general line by criticizing as insufficient the reformist measures taken by the military regime and by calling for effective popular participation in national politics and collective ownership of the means of production.[37] Even so, there was no indication of the measures that ONIS was prepared to take toward solving concrete problems such as the system of payment for the administration of sacraments. Finally, in May 1971, a meeting of Catholic organizations (including ONIS) concluded,

It will be necessary to change the privileged situation occupied by the Church, expressed in its properties, in its union

with the State, in the congregations which maintain schools
for the wealthy, and in certain pastoral ways which are
repressive, since they prevent the materialization of a
committed Faith. . . . Currently, there still prevail the
unjust structures of the capitalist system and there exists
an incompatibility between "our Christian being and the
maintenance of an unjust situation."[38]

   In spite of this aggressive rhetoric (or perhaps because of it),
the shortage of specific deeds, as well as episodes such as that of the
"600 houses," have prompted accusations of deception by anti-Catholic
writers.

TABLE 9.3

Percentage Changes in Religious Personnel in
Latin America, 1960-68

Country	Priests		Nuns	
	Period 1960-68	Yearly Average	Period 1960-68	Yearly Average
Argentina	7.64	0.95	- 7.65	- 0.96
Bolivia	- 2.86	-0.35	41.37	5.17
Brazil	10.42	1.30	14.89	1.86
Chile	8.21	1.03	11.24	1.40
Colombia	18.31	2.28	22.00	2.75
Costa Rica	59.92	7.49	57.04	7.13
Cuba	-69.57	-8.70	-90.83	-11.35
Dom. Republic	56.53	7.06	36.67	4.58
Ecuador	19.66	2.45	7.67	0.96
El Salvador	37.10	4.63	62.82	7.85
Guatemala	44.02	5.50	94.24	11.78
Haiti	-12.96	-1.62	5.00	0.62
Honduras	30.52	3.81	-40.45	- 5.05
Mexico	23.25	2.90	15.38	1.92
Nicaragua	18.31	2.29	- 9.98	- 1.25
Panama	26.38	3.30	-37.80	- 4.72
Paraguay	5.16	0.64	33.52	4.19
Peru	28.91	3.61	3.08	0.38
Uruguay	0.72	0.10	.00	.00
Venezuela	41.44	5.18	55.70	6.96
Latin America	14.07	1.75	12.08	1.86

Source: Data made public by the Catholic church.

The Church pretends, through spectacular postures such as the already-mentioned encyclical [Populorum Progressio], to place itself in a more or less "advanced" strategic position. In such a way, it plans to imitate what happens in road bicycle races, when a team captain sends one of his assistants to lead the group, in order to slow it down with the appearance of giving it more impetus.[39]

This line of thinking, however, would appear to be erroneous. If the core of the Catholic church's political power in countries such as Peru has been derived from its being the provider of a political ideology, ratified by the word of God, which justified the status quo; and if the "revolution of rising expectations" has reduced the effectiveness of that ideology and turned people away from the Catholic faith, as this author maintains; then it would seem that the only realistic alternative, if those souls are to be regained, is to shift the ideological content of Catholicism in order to turn it into a political ideology of change. This shift in content can be achieved at the national and local

TABLE 9.4

Vacant Parishes in Selected Areas of
Peru and in the Entire Country, 1969

Location	Total Number of Parishes	Total Number Vacant	Percentage Vacant
Lima[a]	114	0	0.0
Arequipa[a]	41	9	22.0
Trujillo[a]	35	4	11.4
Callao[a]	9	0	0.0
Piura[a]	34	2	5.9
Abancay[b]	37	23	65.2
Puno[b]	37	21	56.8
Ayaviri[b]	29	15	51.7
Sicuani[b]	22	12	54.5
Chuquibamba[b]	20	10	50.0
Entire Country	991	234	23.6

[a]Urban and (or) relatively developed areas.
[b]Rural and relatively backward areas.

Source: Data made available by the Peruvian Catholic church.

level by adequate interpretation of such existing documents as Rerum
Novarum, Quadragesimo Anno, and Populorum Progressio. This
interpretation is (in most cases and particularly in reference to the
lower class) the responsibility of the parish priests and of all other
religious personnel working directly with the poor. It is they who have
to be convinced of the necessity to shift, before the Catholic church as
an institution can provide ideological support to social and political
reform in Peru.

The general tone of this contribution may give the impression
that the only problem of survival faced by the Catholic church as a
political institution, both in Peru and in the rest of Latin America, is
the type of ideological guidance it provides to the faithful. However,
at least a brief reference should be made here to the problem of
personnel recruitment, which also threatens the existence of the church
as an institution and as an important actor in Latin American politics.
Table 9.3 shows recent evidence of a trend that has existed for a long
time in most of the Latin American countries. Table 9.4 shows that
parish priests in Peru tend to concentrate in the large cities and in
the more highly developed regions of the country (data for Chile and
Colombia indicate the same preference). Without religious personnel,
the Catholic church will be unable to provide any political ideology,
thus surrendering its political power by default.

While many reasons account for the inability of the Catholic
church to attract personnel, it could be suggested that its traditional
political philosophy plays a role here too. After all, religious personnel tends to be recruited from among the strongest believers. Hence
the more cleavages the political role of the church produces among
Catholics, the smaller the pool from which to recruit. Similarly, the
greater the doubts about the validity and relevance of the institution,
the fewer who would be willing to become its active representatives.

Existing data indicate that the majority of the clergy in Peru and
in the other Latin American countries do not yet favor the ideological
change proposed by its reformist elements. In the case of Peru, it is
realistic to assume that the presence in power of a group of military
officers prepared to carry out some reforms, the neutrality of the
hierarchy, and the pressures that develop at the supranational level,
will give ONIS and similar groups an opportunity to develop the widespread support among their colleagues that is required to effect the
desired ideological shift. Regarding the rest of Latin America, diagnosis has to be reserved until more research is done on a country-by-
country basis.

10

LITERATURE AND SOCIETY
IN SPANISH AMERICA:
TRADITION AND CHANGE
Robert J. Glickman

Whatever some ingenuous revolutionaries may believe, the future, despite its multifarious novelties, is essentially an extension of the past. Therefore, the accuracy of any prediction concerning the future depends, of necessity, on the degree to which the prognosticator is conversant with the past. Although it may seem paradoxical, even the nature of revolutionary events and the ostensibly novel institutions to which they give rise are determined by cultural forces that have long operated, and will continue to operate, beneath the surface of daily reality as "protean constants"—that is, as social energizers which, though capable of assuming many guises, remain fundamentally unchanged for extensive periods. After giving due recognition to the power of individual creativity and after paying obeisance to the role of chance in human affairs, we find that the protean constants that function within a given culture are just as active and just as crucial in literature as in any other area of the culture. Hence, if we are to predict what Spanish American literature will be like in the 1970s we must first understand what that literature and its cultural context have been like in the past.

CULTURAL INFIRMITIES

At times overtly and at times by implication, Spanish American writers have portrayed their culture as something weak, sickly, or deformed. Thanks to a confluence of factors—among them, the rapid development of various biologically oriented sciences—this image became quite common in the late nineteenth century. It was used so widely, in fact, that, after doing extensive research, one renowned scholar of our own generation found it appropriate to begin his monograph on patterns in the Spanish American essay of ideas (1890-

1960) with a chapter entitled "The Sick Continent and its Diagnosticians." As the following paragraphs attest, this image of Spanish America did not disappear at the end of the nineteenth century, but continued well into the twentieth.

Excessive Spirituality

In El problema de la cultura americana,[2] Alberto Zum Felde of Uruguay examines what many people believe to be the essential difference between North Americans and Spanish Americans. The former are said to be characterized by utilitarianism, an ethical position which is rooted in Anglo-Saxon Protestantism and which translates itself into "practical" norms of conduct. Spanish Americans, on the other hand, are reputedly distinguished by their spirituality, a fundamentally aesthetic trait which is nurtured by a refined sensibility and a keen imagination, but which does not generally result in "practical" activity. Although Zum Felde is proud of the spirituality of Hispanic culture, through his imagery he tacitly confesses that the culture as a whole is by no means in perfect health. As he sees it, the problem stems from an excessive imbalance on the side of spirituality; therefore, to improve the situation, he prescribes the injection of a few drops of pragmatic optimism and Yankee will-to-do.

Tropicalism

Like his Uruguayan colleague, although with far less sympathy, the Venezuelan essayist Mariano Picón Salas also speaks of the imbalances and infirmities that are present in Hispanic culture. In "America y el disparate,"[3] he criticizes the nations of Spanish America for reasons that are well known to North Americans: industrial output and the rate of commercial development are low, while agricultural and extractive production are high—and the most intensively cultivated product of all is Rhetoric! Picón Salas considers the superproduction of Rhetoric to be symptomatic of "tropicalism," a contagious disease that is endemic in Hispanic culture. Inwardly, tropicalism is characterized by the incapacity to call a spade a spade, by verbal delirium, and by deformation of facts and ideas. Outwardly, it manifests itself in a sustained emotionalism as well as in the constant use of long, vacuous substantives, poorly chosen adjectives, tiresome repetitions, and extravagant exaggerations.

"Huaynacapaquismo"

Taking the statements of Zum Felde and Picón Salas a step further, one might add that hyperspirituality and tropicalism are

often accompanied by "huaynacapaquismo."[4] This culturally transmitted
malady is related to machismo and is commonplace in the population.
Its principal characteristic is the deep-seated need to prove one's
verbal and intellectual superiority. The individual usually tries to
satisfy this need by taking up a lofty position on a podium, balcony,
or cloud; by representing himself as an incarnation of the cosmic
forces of illumination; and by dazzling his audience with glowing words,
brilliant images, and resplendent concepts. Although Spanish America
has always produced individuals of this type in abundance, one who
carved a particularly impressive reputation for himself was Guillermo
Valencia, Colombian poet and politician. When Valencia rose to
speak, his listeners realized at once that they were in the presence
of a man of verbal potency. His voice had an electric quality that
could galvanize any audience, his hands sensuously caressed every
sentence that he uttered, his whole being became transfigured as he
spoke.[5] Of course, his impact on the public was tremendous: men
were awed by his learning and his oratorical vigor, and, we are told,
"ladies swooned over him like young girls over a matinee idol; a
word, a gesture was enough to enrapture them."[6] This was a real man!

HYPERVERBALISM: SOME
CAUSES AND EFFECTS

In good measure, huaynacapaquismo is widespread in Spanish
America because each person belongs to a network of associations
which prompt this kind of conduct. Among these associations are
the family; the extended family (compadrazgo); special interest
groups, such as labor unions; and clubs that have social, cultural,
political, and (or) religious aims. With much greater frequency
than their counterparts in North America, these associations not
only encourage histrionics and exaggerated oral behavior, but they
also back the establishment of formal organs of expression, such
as newspapers and journals. When decisions are taken concerning
who will be granted an outlet for expression, the first requisite is
membership in the group; the second consideration is the individual's
standing with the powers that govern the group; and the third consideration is the degree of talent he possesses. This order of priority,
which lies at the root of literary nepotism, is by no means exclusive
to Spanish America. Nevertheless, because it tends to be more
widely supported there than in the countries of Anglo America, it
poses a more serious threat to the well-being of each nation. Simply
stated, it promotes subjectivism and extreme partisanship, it fosters
the production and circulation of material that is intellectually and

aesthetically inferior, and it causes many writers of outstanding talent to become alienated from the society in which they live—a society that gives preference to those with connections rather than ability.

"Caudillismo"

Because success depends so greatly on having good connections, it is not uncommon for writers to support a strongman in the expectation that he will grant them a certain measure of security or at least flatter them with his attentions. Indeed, nowhere does nepotism flourish more vigorously than in the garden of the caudillo. This is a problem of long standing in the Hispanic world and many examples of it may be given. One of the most graphic statements, however, is Esteban Echeverría's description of conditions in Buenos Aires during the dictatorship of Juan Manuel de Rosas:

> "así como Rosas ha hecho una federación y una
> dictadura a su modo, se ha formado también en ese
> Buenos Aires una literatura de Rosas, y las
> inteligencias deben seguir el impulso que Rosas quiera
> darles y moverse en la orbita que les trace. . . .
> Para comprender mejor el fenómeno, figuraos
> que Buenos Aires es un órgano de viento, que
> alli no hay más que un organista y ese organista
> es Rosas."*

Today, of course, we might choose names such as Perón, Trujillo, and Fidel Castro to illustrate the phenomenon that Echeverría so aptly described more than a century ago.

It must be emphasized, however, that there exists another type of caudillismo. In this case, instead of seeing a literary claque

---

*"just as Rosas has formed a federation and a
dictatorship in his own style, a literature of Rosas
has also come into existence in Buenos Aires, and
all thinking beings must go in the direction that
Rosas might wish to prescribe for them and must
move in the orbit that he might wish to trace for
them. . . . In order to understand the phenomenon
more clearly, imagine that Buenos Aires is a pipe
organ, that there is but one organist and that organist
is Rosas."[7]

applauding the exploits of some local strongman, we find the voters
raising a man of letters to a position of political eminence because
of his forceful manipulation of words and ideas. The election of
Rómulo Gallegos to the presidency of Venezuela in 1947 is an outstanding example of this tendency. In part, this occurs because
mastery of the word is equated with virility, and virility stands high
on the scale of Hispanic values. Nevertheless, this is not the only
factor at work. For instance, it must also be recognized that the
artful manipulation of words is greatly esteemed by Spanish Americans
because their culture, by tradition, is humanistically oriented.

Perhaps no one has enunciated the common ideal with greater
clarity than José Enrique Rodó. In his essay _Ariel_, Rodó expressed
the hope that Spanish Americans would some day become truly well-
rounded individuals—whole men, like the citizens of ancient Athens:

> "Cada ateniense libre describe en derredor de sí, para
> contener su acción, un círculo perfecto, en el que
> ningún desordenado impulso quebrantará la graciosa
> proporción de la linea. Es atleta y escultura
> viviente en el gimnasio, ciudadano en el Pnix,
> polemista y pensador en los pórticos. Ejercita su
> voluntad en toda suerte de accion viril y su
> pensamiento en toda preocupación fecunda."*

Of course, if this ideal is not realized as perfectly as it should be—
and, as we all know, the probability of attaining perfection in anything
is indeed remote—society can expose itself to very serious hazards.
Not the least of these is _dilettantism_. As Manuel González Prada so
trenchantly explained, amateurish dabbling in areas that demand the
precise skills of specialists can lead to national disaster and humil-
iation:

---

*In order to give form to his life, each free
Athenian describes a perfect circle around himself—
a circle in which no unruly impulse will shatter the
graceful proportion of the line. He is an athlete and
a piece of living sculpture in the gymnasium, a citizen
in the Pnyx, a polemicist and thinker in the meeting
places of the city. He exercises his will in every
kind of manly action and his intellect in every area
of fruitful concern."[8]

Sin especialistas, o más bien dicho, con aficionados que
presumían de omniscientes, vivimos de ensayo en ensayo:
ensayos de aficionados en Diplomacia, ensayos de
aficionados en Economía politica, ensayos de aficionados
en Lejislación, i hasta ensayos de aficionados en Táctica
i Estratejia. . . . Vimos al abogado dirijir l'hacienda
pública, al médico emprender obras de injeniatura, al
teólogo fantasear sobre politica interior, al marino
decretar en administración de justicia, al comerciante
mandar cuerpos d'ejercito. . . ¡Cuánto no vimos en esa
fermentacion tumultuosa de todas las mediocridades, en
esas vertijinosas apariciones i desapariciones de figuras
sin consistencia de hombre, en ese continuo cambio de
papeles, en esa Babel, en fin, donde la ignorancia
vanidosa i vocinglera se sobrepuso siempre al saber
humilde i silencioso! *

In spite of González Prada's forceful argument, however, there still
has been no definitive answer to the question of whether more can
be done for the general welfare of Spanish Americans by the utility-
minded specialist who operates within a very limited sphere of
activity, or by the multifaceted humanist who, like Bartolomé Mitre,
might serve in the army, establish an independent newspaper,
translate a foreign literary masterpiece, and play an active role in

---

*"Without specialists, or rather, with amateurs
who imagined themselves omniscient, we lived from
experiment to experiment: experiments by amateurs
in Diplomacy, experiments by amateurs in Political
Economy, experiments by amateurs in Legislation,
and even experiments by amateurs in Tactics and
Strategy. . . . We saw the lawyer conduct public
finance, the physician undertake works of engineering,
the theologian give free reign to his imagination in
the area of domestic politics, the seaman pass decrees
regarding the administration of justice, the merchant
lead the army. . . . What didn't we see in that tumultuous
fermentation of all kinds of mediocrity, in that vertiginous
appearing and disappearing of figures completely devoid
of human substance, in that continuous changing of roles—
in short, in that tower of Babel, where conceited and
vociferous ignorance always overpowered modest and
quiet knowledge!"9

the government of his country. Undoubtedly, a strong case can be
made for each side—which suggests that a certain mixture of materialistic specialization and humanistic generalism is desirable. But
whether there is a mixture or not, one thing seems inevitable: in order
to win the support of his compatriots, the leader of the future, like
the leader of the past, will have to be a strongman in the verbal arts
as well as in other areas of endeavor.

The need to have caudillos manifests itself within every social
group: even men of letters issue manifestos, name themselves
preceptors, and seek disciples who are willing to follow their lead.
In view of this, one cannot fail to be impressed by Rubén Darío's
1896 refusal to publish an aesthetic manifesto and to welcome a band
of slavish imitators into his artistic camp. Said the poet,

> "Yo no tengo literatura 'mía'—como lo ha manifestado una
> magistral autoridad—, para marcar el rumbo de los
> demás: mi literatura es mía en mí; quien siga servilmente
> mis huellas perderá su tesoro personal y, paje o esclavo,
> no podrá ocultar sello o librea. Wagner, a Augusta
> Holmes, su discípula, dijo un día: 'Lo primero, no
> imitar a nadie, y sobre todo, a mí.' Gran decir.*

Ironically—yet inevitably—Darío's unwillingness to become a literary
caudillo was ignored by his contemporaries, who, depending on their
aesthetic inclinations, either extolled or maligned him as the "leader"
of the Modernist Movement.

Words as Weapons

History shows us that modernists like Darío, Najera, Casal,
and Valencia saw themselves as gladiators struggling against ferocious
predators in the arena of life. Although this image is no longer as

----

*"I do not have a literature 'of my own'—as has
been alleged by one supreme authority—designed to
show the way to others: my literature is uniquely
mine; whoever servilely follows in my footsteps will
lose his personal treasure and, since he is a servant
or a slave, will be unable to hide the brand or colors
of his master. Wagner once said to Augusta Holmes,
his disciple: 'First of all, imitate no one—especially
me.' Great words."[10]

fashionable among men of letters as it once was, it reminds us of a basic cultural fact: Spanish Americans are an extremely pugnacious and litigious people. This is reflected in many features of their culture, among them, the quantity of attorneys produced by Hispanic universities; the frequency of verbal attacks, debates, and polemics; the recurrence of palace revolutions and military coups; and the extraordinary number of political parties that are formed when free expression and association are permitted. The most commonly used weapon in the arsenal of aggression is the word, spoken or written. Like the gaucho's facón or the soldier's rifle, the word is to be caressed if it is ours, honored if it is our friend's, and feared if it is our enemy's. And rightly so, for, when astutely employed, it can arouse the masses, sway judges in our favor, or destroy our enemies more effectively than any other instrument available. How meaningful, therefore, is the exclamation, "Mi pluma lo mató!," which Juan Montalvo uttered on hearing of the assassination of Gabriel García Moreno, or Picón Salas's damning assertion that, at the drop of a hat, Spanish Americans are prone to mobilize "una verdadera artillería de palabras."*

Genres and Subgenres

Since the beginning of the nineteenth century, when almost all of the present-day republics attained political independence, the literate population of Spanish America has been small, but the relative amount of literature produced has been large. All of the major genres have been cultivated, and some of them, like poetry and the essay, have been cultivated both intensively and extensively. One point, however, generally escapes the attention of literary critics and social scientists alike: cultural factors such as caudillismo, nepotism, and the communal failure to impose verbal restraints have made Spanish American literature particularly rich in subgenres. Among the forms that are produced with notable regularity are the biography of Lilliputian luminaries, the memoirs of boastful nonentities, the sycophantic dedication, the partisan prologue, the commemorative allocution, the abusive review, the open letter, the manifesto, the insurrectional proclamation, and, after considering the frequency with which they are written in some countries, one is tempted to add, the constitution.

---

*Montalvo: "My pen killed him!" Picón Salas: "a veritable verbal artillery."[11]

Conclusive proof that literary subgenres must be taken seriously by critics is given by Manuel Puig, who has fashioned an entire novel out of them. That novel is Boquitas pintadas.

In order to understand Spanish America better, we must study both the genres and the subgenres with great care, for no matter what form it comes in, literature is revelation. The lyric poet unveils the mysteries of his deepest thoughts and feelings; the memorialist makes public the words, deeds, and motives of himself and others; the epic poet reveals the heritage of greatness from which his compatriots may draw inspiration; the novelist brings to light important features of social reality and human nature; the critic exposes the virtues, defects, and significance of another's work; the composer of manifestos and constitutions discloses his cherished vision of how things should ideally be; and so forth. Let there be no mistake, however: despite protestations to the contrary, there is no single truth. Our grandfathers overthrew Absolutism and placed the scepter of authority in the hands of Relativism. Therefore, any attempt—by partisans of the right, or the left, or any position in between—to reinstate the deposed ruler of a bygone age is anachronistic and should be judged as retrogression. Each man is the product of a unique mixture of personality-shaping influences; for this reason, his views must also be unique. Each author may be sincere in his convictions, but when we read a piece of literature we should remember that the views expressed therein cannot coincide completely with those of anyone else. It is important to keep this point in mind, because Spanish American writers, with their marked inclination toward huaynacapaquismo and caudillismo, are extremely prone to literary ventriloquism.

The Writer as Ventriloquist

Since the middle of the nineteenth century, when it became fashionable to make a public display of one's social consciousness, Spanish American writers have devoted considerable energy to the creation of ventriloquists' dummies. In general, this type of literary figure has Indian, mestizo, or negroid features; is dressed in tribal, regional, or lower-class garb; and is used to express the author's impression of what is in the mind and heart of the social group whose external characteristics have been reproduced in the dummy. Usually, the author's motives are to provide information about the nature of life among the victims of social injustice and, by shocking the power elite or winning its sympathy, encourage changes that will redound to the benefit of the voiceless masses. At times, a writer manages to document himself so thoroughly and to capture the spirit of the underdog so completely that even the underdog believes the writer to be one of his number. This was the case with José Hernández who, after publishing Part I of his gaucho epic, was addressed as Martín Fierro on more than one occasion, because people thought he was the very character that he himself had created. Martin Fierro, however, belongs to a very special category, for, until now, most literary works have never become known to the unfortunates whose lot they have been designed to improve. This is quite understandable because, with the exception of an extremely small minority, the inhabitants of Spanish America have been nonreaders. Even if we agree that the novel, for example, has tended to be a "documento denunciador, cartel de propaganda doctrinal, llamamiento de atención hacia los mas graves y urgentes problemas sociales," as José Antonio Portuondo says, how can we possibly imagine that it can incite "the reading masses" to action?* There are no reading masses in Spanish America. As Angel Rama points out,

> "los distintos países del continente se mueven con
> públicos lectores muy reducidos, de pocos miles, que
> en los hechos corresponden a la estructura de los mismos
> transmisores de la cultura: profesores, maestros,
> algunos funcionarios y algunos profesionales. En un
> país de 35 millones de habitantes (México) un público
> de 5 o de 15 mil compradores es insignificante, y,
> como indicamos, corresponde al ambiente educativo
> que rodea el fenómeno literario. . . . [E]1 novelista
> podrá engañarse . . . pero ello no altera la verdad:
> escribe para su grado social algo ampliado. De
> ningún modo escribe para la sociedad entera de su
> pais, y, menos aún, para la de la comarca
> hispanoparlante.**

---

*A "document of denunciation, a poster for doctrinal propaganda, a means to call attention to the most serious and urgent social problems . . . the reading masses."[12]

**"The various countries of the continent operate with a very limited number of readers, a few thousand, who really belong to the same social groups as the transmitters of culture themselves: professors, teachers, some civil servants, and some professional people. In a country of 35 million inhabitants (Mexico), a reading public that consists of 5 or 15 thousand buyers is insignificant, and, as we indicated, corresponds to the cultural environment that surrounds the literary phenomenon. . . .

If these points are kept in mind, no one will falsely assume that the
Indians of Spanish America speak through novels such as Huasipungo,
El indio, El mundo es ancho y ajeno, and El callado dolar de los
tzotziles. In works of this type, non-Indians (the authors) are speaking
to other non-Indians (a small portion of the literate minority) in
behalf of—but not with the voice of—multitudes who at present do not
express their thoughts, feelings, and aspirations in a written literature
of their own. With few qualifications, the same can be said of all
other groups found at the lowest end of the socioeconomic scale: the
literature that speaks of them and, presumably, for them is not
created by them. Therefore, the reality presented in that literature
is particularly susceptible to falsification. In short, what literature
cannot now do in Spanish America is accurately represent the views
and wishes of all segments of society. If it is directed to those at
the top, so that they might be prompted to initiate reforms, those
reforms will still be an imposition from above for the imagined
benefit of the nonliterate masses; and if, in some way, it is used to
incite the nonliterate masses, it will be little more than an instrument
of manipulation wielded by persons who do not belong to the groups
whose cause they are championing.

PROSPECTS FOR THE 1970s

The foregoing considerations bring us to the main point at
issue: what are the prospects for the 1970s with regard to Spanish
American literature? As may be inferred from the opening paragraph
of this chapter, I am convinced that the same cultural forces that
have been operative in the past will remain operative in every country
during the coming decade, no matter what changes occur in the
political, economic, or social order of things, or how drastic those
changes appear to be on the surface.

Because of the fact that verbal skills have constantly occupied
a preeminent position in its scale of values, Spanish America has
produced a greater quantity of literature than might be expected
from the size of its reading public. In the 1970s, Spanish American
society will continue to foster cultivation of those skills and will
continue to provide its members with numerous outlets for verbal
expression.

The novelist may delude himself . . . but that does not
alter the truth: he is writing for his own social group,
somewhat enlarged. In no sense is he writing for all
the people of his country, and, even less, for the
Spanish-speaking world as a whole." 13

Although the word does have great importance in Hispanic culture, there is little evidence to support the impression of writers that, as writers, they play a key role in effecting or guiding revolutionary change within their society. As a matter of fact, the repeated failures of the most outstanding literati in this respect strongly suggest that men of letters in Spanish America have consistently deluded themselves about the ability of literature to generate or direct radical change. In politics, the literary activities of Echeverría, Sarmiento, and Mármol did not bring about the fall of Juan Manuel de Rosas; the investment of a quarter century of literary effort by José Martí did not lead to Cuba's liberation from Spanish colonial rule; belles lettres did not cause the overthrow of Porfirio Díaz or give direction to the Mexican masses during the revolutionary holocaust that followed his deposition; and no single writer or group of writers can take credit for toppling the regime of Fulgencio Batista in Cuba or for bringing Salvador Allende to power in Chile.

And with regard to socioeconomic change, it is clear that the books, pamphlets, and articles that flowed from the pen of Sarmiento cannot be represented as the direct cause of Argentina's educational and mercantile reforms. These came about only when the man himself succeeded in occupying positions of power within the structure of government. The novels of Rómulo Gallegos did not bring "civilization" to the Venezuelan countryside nor did they induce the rural population to resist the call of Venezuela's urban centers and remain proudly attached to the land. And the works of Jorge Icaza and Ciro Alegría—not to mention those of Clorinda Matto de Turner and Manuel González Prada, who demonstrated the nature and seriousness of Andean socioeconomic problems some 50 years before—have not, to this day, improved the lot of the indigenous masses in Ecuador and Peru. Unfortunately, these lessons, which history so eloquently teaches, will have little influence on the writers' self-image. Guided by a system of values that has remained essentially constant for generations, they will continue to believe that the word has some magical power to change reality. Given the system, it is logical for them to hold this belief, for, by so doing, they can avail themselves of a fundamental vehicle for publicly demonstrating their manliness. The result seems obvious: since there will be no rupture in link between verbal skill and machismo, and since there will be no diminution in the power of machismo to condition behavior in Spanish America, the rate of literary production will continue to be high during the 1970s.

The Spanish Americans' deep-rooted uncertainty about their inherent worth—a feeling derived from the circumstances surrounding their origins in the sixteenth century and accentuated by the embarrassing duration of their colonial status—has caused them to look more sympathetically on what comes from abroad than on what is produced at home. Nevertheless, their tendency toward syncretism— another characteristic that can be traced back to the age of conquest and colonization—has consistently led them to Americanize everything that they have imported. Since belles lettres are no different from any other facet of Spanish American culture, it seems reasonable to expect that the literature of the 1970s, like the literature of previous epochs, will be affected by both of the abovementioned tendencies. In many ways, it will be profoundly influenced by the writers' need to feel themselves a part of the literary mainstream, which, as they see it, is not to be found within Spanish America, but abroad. Yet in the end—its cosmopolitan qualities notwithstanding—the literature they produce will have an unmistakably American cast.

For its part, the reading public will continue to encourage men of letters by responding to their efforts in a vigorous and enthusiastic manner. Furthermore, anticipated increases in literacy during this decade, together with expected advances on the economic and technological fronts, will most probably raise the level of literary consumption throughout the area to heights never reached in the past. In spite of this, extraliterary factors will exert much more influence than literary ones upon the conduct of the individual when he passes from the role of reader to that of citizen.

History reveals that organizations which form part of the power structure of Spanish American society normally react to the man of letters in three ways. When the writer's words and deeds are not interpreted as a real threat to the organizations in question or to the individuals that head them, little effort is made to interfere with his freedoms. When there is some concern about the writer's capacity for disrupting the established order, attempts are made to render him harmless by incorporating him into the system or by encouraging his departure from the country.* And when the targets of the writer's attacks become convinced that he is really a menace to their survival, they deprive him of as many freedoms as necessary to reduce him to impotence. Depending on circumstance, the same three reactions will continue to manifest themselves during the remainder of this decade. In the interest of accuracy, however, a special note must be added to this appraisal of the situation:

---

*Occasionally, incorporation into the system and expulsion from it are united in an interesting way: writers of stature whose presence within the country is considered dangerous are offered posts as diplomatic representatives of that very country abroad.

revolutionary regimes are not especially tolerant of gadflies. Indeed, they exhibit a marked inclination to equate criticism with subversion, no matter what the motivation of the criticism may be. In Spanish American societies that have just had a revolution, this tendency will pose special problems for writers who belong to the generation that made the revolution. Having been conditioned by prerevolutionary society to see themselves as members of an elite corps that has special access to the Truth, they will expect to be granted unlimited freedom to act as critics of the revolution in order to help achieve the ideals for which they so ardently fought. This expectation will soon be frustrated by the regime, whose major purpose—despite the lofty claims which it constantly broadcasts—is to perpetuate itself in power. Frustration will soon lead to disillusionment and, ultimately, to disaffection. On the other hand, in societies that have already institutionalized their revolution, writers who have been produced by the revolution will be looked upon with increasing suspicion by the establishment, for, as they gain dominion over their art, they will make more and more suggestions for change. This is inevitable because, as Mario Vargas Llosa reminds us, literature is by nature a product of discontent and, therefore, the writer cannot help rebelling against the status quo:

> El escritor ha sido, es y seguirá siendo un descontento.
> . . . La vocación literaria nace del desacuerdo de un
> hombre con el mundo, de la intuición de deficiencias,
> vacíos y escorias a su alrededor. La literatura es
> una forma de insurrección permanente y ella no admite
> las camisas de fuerza. Todas las tentativas destinadas
> a doblegar su naturaleza airada, díscola, fracasarán.
> La literatura puede morir pero no será nunca
> conformista.*

What is meant is that literature cannot be converted into an instrument of propaganda especially designed to serve a given ideology. All that

---

> *"The writer has been, is, and will go on being a
> malcontent. . . . The literary vocation comes into being
> as a result of one man's lack of harmony with the world,
> as a result of his ability to perceive deficiencies, gaps,
> and wretchedness in the world around him. Literature
> is a form of permanent insurrection and does not
> accept straitjackets. All attempts to force its
> irascible, recalcitrant nature into submission will fail.
> It is possible for literature to die, but it will never
> conform." [14]

this can produce is an inferior grade of art and a biased image of reality, such as is found in works of "socialist realism." Spanish America cannot possibly benefit from the kind of limitations that such a practice would entail, for a literature that is placed in bondage cannot inspire men to anything but servitude.

11

**SOME OBSERVATIONS
ON LATIN AMERICAN
GUERRILLA MOVEMENTS**
J. C. M. Ogelsby

The activities of guerrillas in Latin America have been receiving a great deal of attention in recent years. The six-month chase of Ernesto ("Che") Guevara in Bolivia; the wave of terrorism in Guatemala; the activities of the Tupamaros in Uruguay; and the techniques as exemplified in the actions of the Brazilian guerrillas have been the chief centers of attention. They have been added to the crisis atmosphere in which we are living. However, I wonder if there is not too much being made of these guerrilla activities, and I believe the following six points concerning Latin American guerrilla movements ought to be considered before we succumb to the purveyors of crises:

1. That Guevara has been given more publicity than he deserves or warrants.

2. That guerrilla movements lack the ingredients of success as long as the governments offer a reasonable, even if very slow, hope for social change.

3. That any guerrilla movement that hopes to succeed in Latin America must have both a historical tradition and a charismatic leader.

4. That alien ideological positions will not succeed.

5. That guerrilla movements are the best guarantee for evolution rather than revolution.

6. That to make revolution and counterrevolution is good business for those engaged in it. In other words, it is a way of life.

Che Guevara was a romantic figure. He also was a professional revolutionary whose emotions rather than his mind dominated in the end. He was consumed by his own visions and probably by the image projected by the international press. He thrived on publicity to the extent that he was willing to sacrifice his most recent movement in order to have that publicity.[1] He also violated his own principles of guerrilla welfare:

First, by launching a movement in Bolivia: "Where a government has come into power through some form of popular vote, fraudulent or not, and maintains at least an appearance of constitutional legality the guerrilla outbreak cannot be promoted since the possibilities of peaceful struggle have not yet been exhausted."[2]

Second, by not having the peasants firmly on his side: "The guerrilla leader needs full help from the people of the area. This is an indispensible condition."[3] In the latter case I think it is important to remember than in all cases of his activities (whether in Guatemala, Cuba, or Bolivia) Guevara was a foreigner, an Argentine, and therefore virtually incapable of gaining the complete trust of the nationals within the area in which he worked. He would have no success among the Indian populations of America (those who make up the majority of the Andean populations and Guatemala), and while he could work with Castro it would be wrong to imagine that Che could have ever substituted for Fidel.[4] Che was a victim of his own guerrilla-oriented personality and he believed in his own dictum that "What is decisive is the determination to struggle." It was decisive for him! And for the reasons stated above it was erroneous of Debray, and Castro, to assume that Guevara, who perhaps would be the unquestioned political and military leader of a guerrilla band, could be the leader of a revolution.[5]

It is impossible to deny that he is still a symbol for some (whether for or against the revolutions), but I would stress that I believe it is unwarranted within the framework of Latin America and this focus is based upon a misinterpretation of what is important to the success of guerrilla movements there.[6]

My third point has really two components and is based on Castro's overthrow of the Batista regime. Whatever the faults of Batista, Castro had two things in his favor that no other guerrilla leader in Latin America has had. The first is the fact that guerrilla movements in Cuba have a historical tradition. Cuba remained in the Spanish Empire longer than the rest of the Spanish American republics, and between 1823 and 1898 there were a number of attempts at removing Spain's hold on the island. It is ironic, I think, to see how much history seems to repeat itself in Cuba, where a rebel force invading with the help of U.S. citizens in 1852 landed 50 miles west of Havana and was captured. The rebels' intelligence reports stated that once the landing was made Cuban supporters of their cause would flock to the beachhead and the government's overthrow would be assured. Of greater import, however, was the movement that issued its cry, the Grito de Yara, in the foothills of the Sierra Maestra in October 1868. This rebel movement helped keep the island in a state of war

for the next 10 years. That rebellion failed to achieve its goal of independence, but it helped inspire the activities of a young Cuban of
Spanish parentage, who provided the charisma needed for a second
attempt to gain independence. That man, of course, was Jose Marti,
and it is interesting to note, I think, that his revolution began in
Oriente province and used the Sierra Maestra as well. Marti died
in the first few months of that struggle, but the U.S. intervention
tipped the scales in favor of the rebels and Cuba gained its independence from Spain, only to lose its freedom of action to the United
States.[7]

What is important is that Cuba had its romantic legacy. Castro
had that to aid him, and he certainly used Marti's name, and his own
Oriente background, to the full. Yet Castro had that other essential
ingredient for success—a personality that inspired men and women
to follow him.[8] As Andre Suarez's recent book, Cuba: Castroism
and Communism, 1959-1966 goes to considerable length to point out,
Castro had no communist inspiration in his revolt against Batista,
and those who supported him were not doing so because of an ideological direction in the rebellion. His immediate followers in the
Sierra Maestra were doing it because he was Fidel.[9]

Of those guerrillas operating at this moment only the Nicaraguans
have a successful historical tradition to which they can turn for inspiration. The others have only Castro's example (and his was a
Cuban example). Castro may not really mean much to Guatemalans,
or Bolivians, or Venezuelans, or Peruvians, if an indigenous historical
tradition and (or) personality is being sought. Hence the rather futile
attempt by the Peruvian MIR (Movement of the Revolutionary Left)
guerrillas to invoke the rebellion of Tupac Amaru II as a symbol to
attract the Andean Indian to its revolutionary goals. Tupac Amaru II
was a mestizo, but Indian-oriented, cacique (or chief) who in 1780-81
rebelled not against the crown but against the abuses of its local
representatives. The Spanish executed Tupac Amaru (as they had
his ancestor, Tupac Amaru I, 200 years before); the Peruvian government forces crushed the guerrilla movement.[10] This point might
be noted by the obviously romantic, and widely publicized, Uruguayan
Tupamaros.

At this moment no guerrilla movement has an indigenous leader
who has that charisma required for its possible success. In fact,
it appears that the system advocated by Carlos Manighella in his
"Minimanual of the Urban Guerrilla" is designed to avoid producing
such a leader. The creation of individual and anonymous cells, such
as employed by Quebec's Parti Quebec Libre (PQL), precludes the
emergence of a dynamic and exciting leader, and therefore, I would
argue, any chance of success.[11] Only Colombia appears to have
raised a figure comparable to Fidel, and he was Camillo Torres

Restrepo, who was killed before he had an opportunity to demonstrate his abilities.[12]

Camillo Torres Restrepo is perhaps as good an example as any for beginning my fourth point, that alien ideological positions will not inspire success, for it is a historical truth that men and not ideas matter in Latin America. Torres was a priest who reacted against the lethargy and conservatism of his leaders in Colombia and saw social revolution as the only means to relieve the majority of people. Marx, Mao, Lenin, or Castro can always be cited for his efforts, but what is meaningful to a Colombian or a Peruvian is not an alien example but one drawn from his own environment and from his own experience. And thus one of the difficulties faced by the guerillas is how to reach the people.

It is all well and good for Radio Havana or the Voice of America to talk to the Quechua of Bolivia and Peru or the Mayan of Guatemala in his own tongue, but unless the radio announcer is from a specific village and aware of the situation within the immediate environment of the people to whom he is addressing himself, his sponsors are wasting their money. To speak to all is to speak to none. What is meaningful to the peasants is what they are familiar with. In countries with a large Indian population the problem is greater because of the Indian's distrust of anyone who is not an Indian.[13] Therefore, it is more remarkable that Guevara could have chosen Bolivia for his attempt and that the Tricontinental Solidarity Conference in January 1966 focused attention on Guatemala as a country ripe for increased guerrilla activity. In the latter case there was a spate of guerrilla action which led the Los Angeles Times of November 21, 1966, to headline "Guatemala Red Threat Worst in Latin America."[14] But it should be pointed out that Guevara and the leaders of the Guatemalan movements chose to operate in areas where mestizo peasants, rather than Indians, resided. However, the Guatemalan MR-13 (November 13 Movement) acted contrary to Guevara's suggestion to avoid heavily populated areas by choosing such a place for their activities. More hunted than hunting, MR-13 probably collapsed completely with the death of its leader, May 16, 1970.[15] Guatemala still has its leftist Rebel Armed Forces (FAR), which withdrew from rural areas in 1966 or early 1967 to concentrate on terrorist tactics in the cities. FAR has no monopoly of terror there, however, for it has to compete with right-wing guerrillas. Both sides contribute to instability in Guatemalan life, but instability in Guatemala is virtually institutionalized and one has learned to live with it.

I think it also worth reemphasizing that too much fear is generated in North American minds, among others, by the guerrilla movements. The guerrilla aim, of course, is to produce instability and fear, but a more positive position can be taken and I think ought to be taken. That is that guerrilla activity is the best means of keeping an army engaged, and when the military in Latin America are engaged they have little time for plotting. Venezuela is perhaps the best example of this. President Betancourt was the first Venezuelan chief executive to pass the presidential sash to his successor, Raul Leoni, not solely because of the Venezuelan peoples' love for the democratic process. Betancourt survived because he recognized that the army leaders had to be appeased and did so. But he was also fortunate because the army was kept very busy during his term of office (1959-63) keeping down terrorists and chasing guerrillas in rural areas.[16]

One of the most striking aspects of guerrilla activity with regard to Latin America is the composition of its membership. Young men, usually students or former students, take to the hills or to the sewers to have an adventure. That they have a goal of revolution justifies their activities and appeals to their ideals, and thus they avoid the odium of being regarded as bandits. They try, therefore, to deal honestly with the people whom they say they are fighting for, but one wonders if there is not a certain irresponsibility about guerrilla activity, an element of adventure in it all. I am reminded of U.S. Ambassador John Bartlow Martin's amazement and disappointment at finding a young doctor in the Dominican Republic who had left the town of Higney because he preferred the life of a guerrilla to the running of the community's only clinic.[17] Che Guevara also was a trained doctor. I do not want to be too hard on dedicated social reformers, for many honestly believe that violence is necessary to overturn the status quo, but it is all too easy to make revolution and far harder to use one's training and talents in a more prosaic but important way.

Also in that direction I might take a long hard look at those exiles who sit around making the counterrevolution. It seems to be institutionalized (in the case of Haiti and Cuba) and a not uncomfortable way to make a living. I wonder how many Cuban exiles in the business of counterrevolution really want to go back, if it means giving up their business? I must admit I do not know and can only speculate.

The counterrevolution also benefits senior military officers in the republics. The purchase of arms and the support they receive from those with vested interest in the status quo merely add to the officers' power and prestige and make them more willing to preserve their own position.

Our North American values color our point of view with regard to Latin America, and I am sure values alien to Latin America color the views of European specialists. I am not sure that we have the correct point of view but, assuming we do, then what is the alternative

to guerrilla activities and the violent revolution that so many theo-
reticians and writers see as the only alternative to the present situation
in so many of the republics? If historical examples have any lesson,
then the one institutional force that has continually played a vital
political role in Latin America is the military. Everyone expects the
military to move "to protect the constitution" or "preserve the republic"; this is traditional. What is not traditional is having the
military act as a force for social change. (One need only look at the
apolitical constabularies created by the U.S. occupations of Nicaragua,
Haiti, and the Dominican Republic, and what happened when their
leaders used their position to take over control of the country for
individual ends.) But even Castro has declared that the military
leaders ought to be the ones to take charge of the revolutionary
process, for he has stated "To those who show military ability, also
give political responsibility."[18] I am sure he did not have the Right
kind of military leader in mind—he undoubtedly meant the Left kind!

It has not been my intention to dismiss guerrilla movements
as unimportant, for they are here to stay. But I do believe that they
ought to be considered in relation to the societies in which they exist,
and it may well be the present movements are laying the foundations
for future successes as they build a tradition and search for a leader.

12

**THE DIPLOMAT AS HOSTAGE:
REFLECTIONS ON POWER
AND VIOLENCE
IN LATIN AMERICA**
G. S. Smith

THE GENERAL VULNERABILITY
OF MASSIVE POWER

The recent wave of kidnappings and other assorted acts of violence directed by Latin American guerrillas against internal and
external enemies may first be appreciated within the context of a
general vulnerability of power during the 1960s. In this topsy-turvy
decade, strong nations discovered suddenly that their strength tended
to work against them; meanwhile, several weaker nations emerged
that possess new strength.

This paradox resulted from some fundamental changes in global
politics, changes that have invalidated what observers not too long
ago termed immutable realities of the cold war. In short, by the end
of the decade national power was no longer being defined as a matter
of pure might. Nowhere was this point clearer than in the respective
positions of the United States and the Soviet Union. Having made each
other mutually vulnerable to nuclear destruction, Washington and
Moscow stood at an impasse. Neither nation could augment its power
vis-à-vis the other simply by increasing such power variables as
weapon supplies, gross national products, armies, or populations.
This being the case, the two superpowers had lost a degree of superiority over the weak. And, as New York Times columnist Max Frankel
and several historians pointed out, it suddenly seemed that the greater
a nation's power, the greater was that nation's weakness.[1]

Examples of the impotence of Soviet and American power are
at once apparent. Arab terrorists have stymied Soviet policy in the
Middle East by keeping Moscow's potential allies at one another's
throats. The Russian invasion of Czechoslovakia in 1968 occurred in
large part because East German party boss Walter Ulbricht realized

that his position would become untenable if another Soviet-bloc country succeeded in breaking out of the satellite orbit. So also did Soviet power prove incapable of embarrassing independent-minded Rumania during the mid-1960s. Nor was Moscow able to rescue Egypt from ignominy during the Seven Days' War of 1967.

Things have been no better from the vantage point of American policy makers. The most powerful nation in the world failed to overthrow Fidel Castro or to defeat North Vietnam. The practice of gunboat diplomacy, long a simple American answer to problems in the Western Hemisphere, backfired loudly in 1965 after President Lyndon Johnson ordered a full, military intervention in the Dominican Republic. And two years later American leaders appeared helpless when North Korea captured the crew of the U.S.S. Pueblo.

Reflecting these changes in international politics, the practice of diplomacy—at best a difficult art—has become increasingly problematic, and in some cases nearly impossible. Leaders and representatives of strong states have encountered new problems in dealing with underdeveloped nations and once-compliant smaller countries. At the same time representatives of both larger and smaller nations have themselves proved unable to control proliferating interest groups within their own borders. This latter problem is especially true of Latin America, a geographical area seemingly marked by equal measures of anarchy and agony.* In a milieu where governments have been ineffective in exercising constructive power, there is good reason why foreign diplomats and prominent officials have become targets of terrorist organizations. Contemporary Latin guerrillas, like Palestinian terrorists, radical bombers, and airline hijackers in the United States, and cells of the FLQ in Canada, have discovered that by applying force at a vital pressure point they can render helpless the most powerful nations of the world, embarrass leaders in their own countries, and frustrate the sophisticated methods of institutional diplomacy.

Considering America's dominant role in the Western Hemisphere, it might seem appropriate to blame the United States for the recent outbreak of Latin terrorism. It is true, for example, that the Alliance for Progress has not achieved its goals and that inter-American diplomacy directed from Washington has often prevented social reform by buttressing groups favoring the status quo. But to ascribe the current crisis to roads taken and forsaken by policy makers in Washington is to credit them with inordinate control over complex

---

*Of course this generalization does not apply to all Latin American countries.

historical events. In other words, the Latin American's cry of Yanqui imperialismo! may contain some substance, but the epithet might also be a politician's ploy to win votes at election time, or a Latin American ruler's cover for his own failure to solve very real national problems.

In any event, a total explanation of Latin American terrorism as a response to American imperialism, so fashionable with contemporary "New Left" revisionists, ignores what historian Ramon Eduardo Ruiz terms an uncontrollable historical factor—"the internal dynamics in the history and societies of the Latin American countries themselves."[2] In these days of the futility of American omnipotence, therefore, one should not search for the devil at 1600 Pennsylvania Avenue or within the inner chambers of the Pentagon or State Department. On the contrary, it is more useful to test the heat of the Latin American inferno itself.

To assess the full meaning of violence in its Latin American milieu, an impossible assignment in these few pages, one must first assess several fundamental political and social differences between North and South America. Although Hannah Arendt has suggested that within the last few years North Americans have lost their revulsion for violence, most Canadian and U.S. citizens historically have felt themselves to be members of political groups who are in basic agreement with ends to be pursued for the common good and upon the framework in which social change is to occur. For these individuals, public policy is something that evolves through regularly held elections and political activity is guided by shared assumptions stressing personal liberties and the sanctity of private property.[3] In this context violence is by definition an abberation. Violence has not defined collective group interests; nor has it provided an acceptable mode of political behavior.[4] Thus when North Americans have discussed violence generally, they have usually ascribed to the term a "revolutionary" connotation. For them the appearance of widespread violence, especially in a political context, heralds the emergence of a force for abrupt change, usually resulting in a sharp cleavage with the past.[5]

This pattern contrasts significantly with the situation in many Latin American countries. There, violence and "revolution" have provided legitimate means for the pursuit and exercise of power. For statistical evidence one need only consult the historical record, which reveals the successful prosecution of 115 revolutions between the independence movements and World War I, and 58 more overthrows of incumbencies between 1931 and 1950.[6]

In conjunction with myriad other manifestations of political violence that have fallen short of revolutionary consequences, ranging from street riots to barracks revolts, these figures indicate that Latin American violence is noteworthy for its diffuseness.[7] In fact,

collective violence has been put to numerous uses in the political life
of the republics to the south. The employment of immoderate force
has changed political personnel, eliminated the influence of social
classes, shaped the nature of public policy or prevented its execution,
determined the ability of certain interest groups to obtain power,
and transformed entirely systems of government. Because of the
wide application of violence, moreover, it is difficult to distinguish
between its perpetrators, whether they be public officials, professional
soldiers, committed ideologues, or the ubiquitous caudillo. The point
is that all of these social types are accommodated by what political
scientist Merle Kling has termed a Latin American "culture of violence."[8] In the words of another analyst, Harry Eckstein, expressions
of Latin violence emanate not so much from "specific objective conditions and not even from the loss of legitimacy by a particular regime,
but from a general lack of receptivity to legitimacy of any kind."[9]
In this sense, violence in Latin America has become, over the years,
a political and social style that is self-perpetuating.[10]
    The compatibility of violent means with such highly diverse ends
is perhaps the crucial historical quality of violence in Latin America.
Yet if collective strife seems to have produced changes in the lives
of many citizens, it has also served as the area's greatest force for
continuismo. Paradoxically, in perpetuating patterns of institutional
instability, violence has produced a peculiar situation of stasis in
which social, economic, and political inequities remain substantially
unmitigated. It is not surprising, therefore, that large segments of
Latin populations deny cynically the possibility of change through
established channels.[11] For them, 400 years of history, including
150 years of political independence, have not amounted to much.
Political reform remains a phantasma. All too often "revolutions"
have resulted in the substitution of one rascal for another.
    Unfortunately, men who are capable of adapting and willing to
adapt traditional institutions to modern functions—social scientists
call them "modernizing leaders"—have not assumed significant
leadership roles in Latin American life.[12] Political power generally
has remained in the hands of neo-colonial oligarchies that for reasons
of self-interest have perpetuated traditional structures and ways of
life. Rather than employing the spirit of nationalism to produce
structural changes that would improve their societies, for example,
conservative and liberal leaders alike have played on nationalistic
aspirations to prevent reform. Describing the stillbirth of Latin
American nationalism, Victor Alba notes that Latin Americans have
evolved into "nationalists without nations." Politics, he writes, has
been "conducted in a vacuum, with the people taking no part."

Hence, coups, counter-coups, mutinies, plots, and in-
trigues could take place without jeopardizing the
survival of the oligarchy; politicians and military men
could play for power and seize it. It was all in the
family. New proclamations were issued and new
constitutions were framed, but the people were not
even aware of them; they seldom knew anything about
such matters. This accounts for the picturesque style
of Latin American politics. Newspaper readers in
other countries, seeing reports of coups, shrug their
shoulders and say, "Those Latin Americans, always
so tempestuous."[13]

It follows that if nationalists without nations have nothing to lose
by attacking their governments, they are able to act with astonishing
impunity. Like other groups that have produced tremors in the global
nervous system during the past decade, some of these people have
abandoned law for what they regard to be the higher authority of
their own revolutionary goals, as ill-defined as these may be. Not
surprisingly, the foreign diplomat and public official, as representative
symbols of hated institutions, become ideal targets through whose
abduction guerrillas seek an immediate position of bargaining equality
with their alleged oppressors. Just as recent airline hijackings have
been defended by their perpetrators as "political" acts, the kidnappings
of foreign diplomats and prominent Latin American citizens often have
been interpreted not in criminal terms but as a means to a specific,
"political" end, such as the release of prisoners or the outright
destruction of the government that holds them.

FOREIGNERS AS HOSTAGES: FROM
POLYBIUS TO TUPAC AMARU

The use of foreigners as hostages has historical precedent.
Leaders of the Greek city-state of Carthage, for example, first
developed the concept of employing captured leaders of other states
along Carthaginian borders to prevent surprise attacks. Later, the
Romans took and held prisoners for ransom so as to ensure respect
for peace treaties. In their destruction of Macedonia, Roman leaders
rounded up 1,000 senior Greek politicians, including the celebrated
historian Polybius, and condemned them to spend the remainder of
their lives in Italy, rather than endanger the ensuing peace settlement.
More recently through the documentary study of the Mafia The Valachi
Papers, edited by Peter Maas, and Mario Puzo's lurid novel The
Godfather, we have seen that before important "family" meetings,

hostages are exchanged to prevent one group from double-crossing
the others.

In these examples it is important to note that the use of hostages
is an integral part of a preventive strategy. The current use of hostages by Latin terrorists, on the other hand, is more complex in
meaning. Of course an easy approach to the problem would be to
define such activity as criminal and be done with it. But to capture
and execute the kidnappers is too simple an answer. It might be a
just reward, but such a solution ignores the important symbolic and
collective meaning of this latest version of Latin American violence.

In the first place, a primary justification for kidnapping as a
legitimate guerrilla activity seems to be taken directly from the text
of Frantz Fanon, the late Algerian revolutionary who interpreted
violence as a cleansing force that freed the native from his inferiority
complex and from his despair and inaction. Born in Martinique in
1926 and trained as a psychiatrist, Fanon saw first-hand the human
wreckage recovered from the battlefields of French Algeria. From
his clinical experience with both the colonizers and the colonized he
came to realize that only through revolutionary violence could the
self-hate of oppressed colonials be transformed into self-respect.
The exquisite hatred of one's own people, which is the lot of all
colonial populations, became for Fanon the source of a millenarian
vision in which colonizers would be liquidated and dignity obtained
by native populations. According to this romantic prophecy, violence
became therapeutic. Its unleashing would mark Day One of the New
Calendar; its appearance would herald the beginning of the end of
racism, imperialism, and all types of inequity and brutality; and its
success would allow the colonized man to discover his freedom, his
identity, and his future.14

Unlike Fanon, who was vitally concerned with the difficult period
of reconstruction that would follow the demolition of colonial empires
(and who thus recognized that violence could be counterproductive),
contemporary guerrilla warriors have often demonstrated lack of
similar compunctions. For them violence has become an end in
itself—a symbolic and spiritual way to obtain self-respect and community. This meaning of violence has itself been clarified by the
coincidental emergence, on a global scale, of alienated groups pro-
fessing to be self-contained tribes. Reacting against traditional modes
of institutional and economic control and attempting to discover some
meaning in life, members of these organizations—be they Hippies,
Yippies, Palestinian patriots, Uruguayan Tupamaros, or even Charles
Manson's bizarre "family"—have rejected the possibility of reforming
their societies from within. Rather, they have moved onto higher
ground, envisioning an entire cultural reorganization of the social
order. Yet in their necessary rejection of uses to which governmental

violence has been put in the Latin American past, contemporary Latin
terrorists have created a milieu in which the proliferation of violence
is inevitable. These "new men," therefore, are not so new. In waving
their banners, individuals who claim to be oppressed inexorably
assume the characteristics of their oppressors, and life proceeds
as usual. In other words, Hannah Arendt's dictum that, unlike Achilles'
lance, violence cannot heal the wounds it has inflicted, well describes
a serious flaw in the guerrilla's line of argument.[15]

Nowhere have the negative aspects of indiscriminate violent
action been as notable as in Guatemala, a country that has been under
virtual martial law since November 1970, four months after the
accession of President Carlos Arana Osorio.[16] Here, as in other
countries, the situation is exceedingly complex; but the tolerance and
use of violent methods—both by the government and by the government's
friends and opponents—since the assassination of President Carlos
Castillo Armas in 1959, has resulted in tragedy. As Victor Perrera
has written, la violencia lies at the core of Guatemalan society: "The
situation is rotten. Ya no se compone."[17]

Strong feelings generated by cold war tension remain strong—
bitterness exhibited by reformers after the ouster of leftist President
Jacobo Arbenz Guzman in 1954, leftist disgust at the continuing American military and intelligence presence, and divisive ideological feelings
for and against communism. When the glow of Castroism spread over
Central America in the early 1960s, Guatemala became a testing ground
for two guerrilla movements, the pro-Chinese November 13 Movement
(MR-13), and the pro-Cuban Rebel Armed Forces (FAR). By 1965 the
latter organization had emerged the stronger and began receiving
support from Indian field workers in San Marcos Province. A year
later the commander of the Zacapa Military District, future-President
Arana, initiated counterinsurgent warfare and within two years, aided
by American Green Beret units and local, vigilante "death squads,"
the counterattack had left 4,000 persons dead, most of them campesinos
and professionals sympathetic to the FAR Among other things, this
campaign forced remnants of the two guerrilla factions into the cities.
Here they encountered more organized, right-wing opponents who also
believed in the use of terror. These organizations, the Armed Nationalist Organization Movement (MANO.), and the subsequent Ojo por Ojo
group, had a singular advantage over their radical adversaries: they
carried on their operations with tacit government approval.

And these latter groups were ruthlessly effective in their work.
Inexorably, with the FAR and MR-13 groups striking back to vindicate
fallen comrades and protect themselves, the conflict intensified to the
point where the country seemed to be approaching national suicide.
With the stakes of this internecine war being survival, the visiting
diplomat suddenly discovered himself to be an unwitting pawn. In 1970

the kidnap-murders of Ambassadors Gordon Mein of the United States and Karl von Spreti of West Germany shocked the world. But what most outside observers missed in their indignation was the fact that both Mein and von Spreti had fallen victim to a force that a majority of Guatemalans now took for granted. In death the two men had become casualties of a politics of violence that had escalated into "a systematic, mutual slaughter of front-rank Guatemalans of all political persuasions."[18]

With the passing by the congress of the Law of Public Order in November 1970, and the numerical attrition of radical forces, conditions seem to have improved. Yet only time will reveal if such deep-rooted cleavages are really healed. The likelihood is that if the FAR is capable of strengthening itself insensate violence will again break out and things will return to normal.

While a climate of unrestrained violence was responsible for the deaths of Mein and von Spreti, that point has not been reached in Brazil, where the idea of diplomats being held to force the release of political prisoners has been a popular one. Since 1964, successive military governments have grown increasingly sensitive to charges that the country's notable economic growth has not benefited the Brazilian populace, especially in rural areas. In the eyes of the government, critics of depressed wages and the high cost of living defame the government and the nation; their dissent is tantamount to subversion. In other words a cold war mentality narrowly circumscribes the views of Brazil's leaders. Opponents more often than not have been identified with the menace of international communism and, where necessary, have been silenced.[19] In the past three years the military government (now led by President Emilio G. Medici) has imprisoned and tortured hundreds of citizens. These dissenters—usually university students, young workers, and members of Catholic populist elements and the Dominican Order—have encountered the grossest brutality. Indeed, the situation has been compared with that existing in Greece under the ruling junta of colonels.[20] According to documents gathered by the American Committee for Information in Brazil, in the use of electric shock "therapy," water torture, and beatings the government has engaged in "a flagrant denial of human rights and dignity."[21]

This ideological rigidity and repression of dissent has provoked a response from groups of urban guerrillas—critics of the regime forced to go underground to continue their opposition. Their use of kidnapped diplomats as hostages has two purposes: to call world attention to the plight of the Brazilian people and to obtain the release of comrades held in government prisons. In the former intention the guerrillas have had moderate success. Reliable information concerning the situation is now more easily available through the offices of groups like the Committee for Information. In their latter pursuit the National Liberation Alliance has been even more effective. While justifying its kidnappings as acts of "legitimate defense" against prison torture, the group has caused the government to bend to a greater degree than any other Latin government currently facing the general problem of ter- roristic kidnapping. In June 1970, for example, in return for the abducted German Ambassador Ehrenfried von Hollenben, Medici's government released 40 political opponents and flew them to Algiers. Six months later, as payment for the release of Swiss Ambassador Giovanni Bucher, the government flew another 70 prisoners to Chile.[22]

More illustrative of the use of violence within the tribal context mentioned above are the Tupamaros of Uruguay, until recently one of the most technically advanced and prosperous of the Latin American republics. Unlike most other Latin terrorist groups, the Tupamaros have attempted to endow themselves with legitimacy by constructing a usable past. They style themselves as spiritual descendents of Jose Gabriel Tupac Amaru, himself a descendent of the last Inca. In 1779 Tupac Amaru led a rebellion of overworked and terror-driven Peruvian Indians against a hated Spanish corregidor, Arriaga, ending in the latter's death. Two years later, however, the rebel leader and his followers were completely routed and, as a warning against further opposition to Spanish rule, his tongue was cut out, his body dismem- bered, and his bleeding remains left in public view. The execution initiated open warfare that lasted for many months and caused the death of more than 80,000 persons.

Most historians would agree that in view of Tupac Amaru's previous experience in negotiating with Spanish officials he could not have hoped to obtain improvements in the intolerable economic con- ditions of the area, even from a position of strength after Arriaga's death. Having concluded that change within the existing system of Spanish colonial administration was impossible, therefore, Tupac Amaru and his followers probably wished to create their own realm within but separate from Spanish control. In other words, Tupac Amaru gave up on political reform and, making common cause with the poorest of his Indian kin, moved toward a complete reorganization of society, from the bottom up.[23]

The contemporary Tupamaros claim to be working for a simi- larly directed change. Until the last three years, in fact, this group could best be described as a moderate organization composed of youthful members of the labor force and university students who felt and articulated their anxiety amid Uruguay's deteriorating economic position. Once a premier exporter of woolen and meat products, the country had fallen on hard times in the early 1960s, and it was this factor, more than any other, that posed a threat to one of the more democratic traditions in Latin America. Led by Raul Sendic Anto- naccio, who became well known as a left-wing union leader in the

northern part of the country, the Tupamaros entertained hopes of
political reform until 1968. When President Oscar Gestido and his
successor Jorge Pacheco Areco refused to accede to their demands,
however, the group suddenly embarked upon a campaign of terror.
The government, now under Pacheco, would not be cowed. Declaring
a state of siege early in 1968, the president also partially suspended
the constitution, closed for unspecified periods numerous secondary
schools and banks deemed incapable of defending themselves against
Tupamaro looting expeditions, froze prices and wages, and instituted
strict press censorship.

The battle thus joined, the Tupamaros initiated guerrilla warfare
in an attempt to destroy the Uruguayan state. Attempting to create
a "revolutionary mentality" among the populace in and around Montevideo, the group adopted symbolic actions to lay bare the alleged
corruption of national life under President Pacheco. To arson and
bombings, methods that were already established, the Tupamaros
added robbing banks in order to reveal financial misdeeds, and kidnapped U. Pereira Reverbal, president of the State Electricity and
Telephone Monopoly, to point out irregular dealings by the government.
In August 1970, after Pacheco announced his government's resolve
not to negotiate with the rebels until they constituted a legitimate
political force, the Tupamaros gave their answer in the form of a
kidnapping spree. Within a period of three weeks Brazilian diplomat
Aloysio Dias Gomide, American agronomist Claude L. Fly, and Daniel
Mitrione, an American adviser to the Uruguayan National Police,
disappeared from sight. Fly and Dias Gomide were subsequently
freed by their captors, but Mitrione was found murdered or executed.

This program of terror, part of a deadly testing of wills between
Tupamaro terrorists and the government, continued well into 1971.
Prominent persons who "enjoyed" the hospitality of the urban guerrillas included British Ambassador Geoffrey H.S. Jackson, Attorney
General Berzo, and for the second time, the ill-fated Pereira Reverbal.
Yet at no time did Pacheco's resolve flag. His police garrison and
national armed forces searched tirelessly for the kidnapped men; at
the same time, however, state officials seemed almost to ignore their
captors. In September 1971, 106 imprisoned Tupamaros, including
Sendic, made a spectacular escape through a tunnel that had been dug
beneath them by friends on the outside. Since that time, with national
elections fast approaching, the Tupamaros have chosen to lay low,
awaiting the outcome.[24]

One suspects that like the warriors of Tupac Amaru, the
Tupamaros are involved in a battle they cannot win. And yet, despite
this fact there is something more than destructive cynicism behind
their motto; "If there is no fatherland for all, there will be none for
anyone." Within this statement, in fact, courses the anarchist's

glorification of violence for its own sake and the realization of both personal and group identity in acts of violence directed at his tormentor.

VIOLENCE VIEWED IN CRIMINAL
AND (OR) POLITICAL TERMS

In this context, stealing and even murder do not violate moral precepts and do not carry criminal connotations. Such activities are, rather, justified as political in nature. To the extent that they are collectively executed, furthermore, they take on increased meaning in the minds of their perpetrators. As the slave of yore stole from the master and earned approval and admiration from his fellows, so the Tupamaros and other terrorists resort to bank robberies and political assassinations to survive in both a corporeal and a spiritual sense. Of course we all know that individuals rob banks to support themselves. But we might also consider that as the looters pool and distribute the money, the entire process takes on added importance. It is, finally, the act of looting and distributing, even more than the money itself, that belongs to the group. In a similar vein, but with a great deal more at stake, a diplomat is kidnapped, held, and assassinated. There results from this process a sense of vicarious participation in violent activity which itself contributes to the creation of a collective identity about which the terrorist can boast (often it is the only thing about which he can boast). Significantly, inasmuch as he and his fellows have wreaked momentary vengeance upon their oppressors, the terrorists have become more closely knit and—ironically—they have discovered community in murder.

Be they Tupamaros in Uruguay, leftists and rightists in Guatemala, opponents of military regimes in Brazil and Argentina, or followers of Marcus Garvey, Jr., in Jamaica, Latin guerrilla terrorists are attracted to violence because in their world there is no concept of cause-and-effect relationships in politics. In short, there is no pervasive belief that governments exist to satisfy the basic needs of people. The lives of these people, as North Americans understand them, are abnormal. They are unable to obtain relief or redress of grievances through government. Therefore their lack of knowledge of or confidence in legal systems having consequences other than evil must necessarily lead some of them to demand recognition of their identity, a demand that often explodes in violence.

The outside observer's appreciation of the meaning of violence as an end in itself—as a political statement par excellence—is also facilitated by the realization that unlike North Americans who tend to internalize their aggressive impulses Latin Americans wear their emotions openly and unabashedly. These feelings may be manifest anywhere—at bullfights, in a raucous confrontation on a Tijuana street-corner at midnight, in never-ending verbal repartee that always amazes the visitor from the north. It is less than astonishing that from this cultural tendency there has emerged a politics that is noteworthy for its maleness. It is, in fact, the cult of machismo and not a sense of noblesse oblige that generally spurs the Latin American along the trail of politics. · On the way it is his right, indeed his duty, to prove his virility—in Norman Humphrey's words, "in an immediate, direct, and normally violent way."[25]

In addition, Latin Americans approach death in a way that helps to clarify their acceptance of violence. Unlike the norteamericano who fears death and attempts to escape it at every turn, Latin Americans have been forced to accept death as a part of their way of life. Death is given real and symbolic meaning in the daily lives of the people, whether in the form of infant mortality statistics in Northeast Brazil or in widespread religious festivals and processions, death masks, and skeletal figures employed in funeral rites. Death, in the form of chapin (Guatemalan) fatalism, walks with the civil secretary or intellectual, who goes through his daily routine knowing full well that he has been marked for death. Death is always close at hand, as is evident in Oscar Lewis's recent anthropological study, A Death in the Sanchez Family. As the Mexican writer Octavio Paz explained in his Labyrinthe of Solitude, "To die and kill are ideas that rarely leave us. We are seduced by death."[26]

Perhaps, in summary, it is the combination of these three broad factors—the Latin acceptance of open aggression, the prevailing cult of machismo, and the omnipresence of death—that has created a society in which violence is the norm and not the exception. In any event, the foreign diplomat residing in many Latin American countries now appears to face what Merle Kling aptly called "an active minority engaged in political violence . . . inhibited neither by a political system that brands such acts as illegitimate, nor by internalized values that censure resorting to violent methods."[27] Given the diverse ends to which violence has been put in the Latin American past, it is not at all astonishing that the visiting diplomat has now been chosen for special attention. The only surprising thing is that it took so long for the terrorists to single him out. The big question of the 1970s is whether sophisticated, institutional diplomacy will be able to cope with the stealthy attacks that are bound to come, without having to resort to the primitive methods of the terrorists themselves.

13

RECENT DEVELOPMENTS
IN BRAZIL:
A PERSPECTIVE
Maris Pone

The military government of Brazil has been the subject of much
critical and some derisive reporting.[1] Charges levied against the
regime have ranged from its abolition of viable democratic processes
to the use of repression as an instrument of national policy to administrative ineptitude. There is no doubt a great deal of truth to these
charges and (except for the last one) even defenders of the regime
are willing to concede that there is substance to them. Yet in addition
to some contrived exultation, official and sycophantic, the government
does, somewhat perplexingly, enjoy considerable popularity in the
country, and its leader, President Medici, receives the strongest
support any president has received since the heyday of Getulio Vargas.*
The object of this chapter therefore is to shed some light on the above
paradox and to speculate on the likely course of future politicoeconomic
developments in Brazil. Part of the explanation of the regime's
unexpected popularity is no doubt the fact that many Brazilians have
been cajoled into inertia by rising affluence** and seem quite willing

---

*In the absence of meaningful polls and (self-) censorship of the
press and other media, these conclusions are admittedly rather risky
and largely impressionistic but are elaborated in the body of this
paper.

**One need hardly point out the fact that Brazil is still an
underdeveloped country with a low per capita income and a large
segment of the population outside the market economy. There are
striking regional and other inequalities in income distribution:
whereas Sao Paulo does indeed resemble Chicago, as the saying goes,
many villages in the Poligono das Secas resemble nothing on earth in

to entrust their fate—even in a nonparticipatory political vacuum for
a time—to a technocracy whose main claim to competence has been
its ability to provide a rising standard of living. It is impossible,
however, to understand what is now happening in Brazil without
reference to past events, particularly the crisis of 1963-64 and the
role of the military in its solution.

A BACKGROUND TO THE CURRENT MILITARY GOVERNMENT IN BRAZIL

The crisis that led to the revolution (i.e., the military take-over)
had an economic dimension and intertwined and mutually aggravating
political dimensions. These were as severe as they were unexpected,
and only with the benefit of hindsight can we speculate that the crisis
was to some degree inevitable. For a long period preceding it,
Brazil had experienced a remarkable mix of economic growth and
political calm, disturbed, it is true, by the tragic suicide of Getulio
Vargas in 1954 and the suspense surrounding the assumption of power
by Juscelino Kubitschek but without the loss of administrative continuity.* Growth of the economy was sustained at high rates for
most of the postwar years. Between 1947 and 1962 real domestic
product grew at a rate of 6.0 percent per year and output of secondary
industries at a rate of 9.5 percent per year. Incidentally, it was
during this period that Brazil ceased to be primarily an agricultural
country as industry surpassed agriculture in terms of sectoral contribution to aggregate product.

The rapid inflation that accompanied this growth was accepted
with equanimity as the price to be paid for rapid economic growth,
although little of substance was offered to rationalize this view. In
retrospect a transfer of relative income does seem to have occurred
from wage-earners to profit-takers, thereby encouraging capital
accumulation.[2] Whether this outweighed the growth-retarding effects
of bottlenecks, dislocations, and economic inefficiencies occasioned
by the inflation is, however, doubtful.[3] The rate of inflation, which

---

wretchedness and destitution. Much of the criticism directed at the
military regime is, in consequence, really a criticism of the symptoms
of underdevelopment.

*The next political disturbance, the resignation of Janio
Quadros, is properly an integral part of the crisis itself, despite
preceding it chronologically.

had averaged 10 percent per year during the 1940s and 20 percent per year in the 1950s, accelerated to 50 percent per year in the late 1950s. By 1963, prices were rising at the rate of 90 percent per year and during the first quarter of 1969 at an annual rate of 165 percent.

There seems to be little doubt that much of the blame for initiating the runaway phase of the inflation rests with the energetic Kubitschek. "Fifty years of Progress in Five" was his motto but it unfortunately applied to prices as well as growth. In his haste to build the new capital city and access routes to Belem and Fortaleza, to cure the chronic problems of the Northeast, and in general to catch up with countries already developed, his administration incurred colossal deficits.* These grew tenfold between 1955 and 1960 (from 7.6 billion to 76.7 billion cruzeiros). Between 1958 and 1960, currency in circulation increased by 67 percent and sight deposits by more than 100 percent. Prices followed suit: the consumer's price index rose by 85 percent over these two crucial years of accelerating inflation. The slowdown of growth in real terms which became acute in 1962-63 was however more immediately felt than the dislocations caused by the inflation.

No single factor was to blame for the downturn. On the one hand, there was an exhaustion of possibilities for import substitution** which helped to mark an end to the boom of the industrial sector. Reflecting this, there was on the other hand a decline in foreign private investment,*** which reduced opportunities for complementary domestic investments as well. The decline in foreign investment could not have come about at a worse time. Brazil's trade balance (in U.S.

---

*Not all the governmental deficits were due to enlarged developmental spending. There was, for example, an ever-increasing need to absorb the operating deficits of government-supported railroads and other means of passenger and freight transportation.[4]

**Brazil considered itself self-sufficient by the early 1960s, and for a good reason: domestic output accounted for about 90 percent of the total supply of industrial goods, 95 percent of consumer goods, 90 percent of intermediate industrial and 80 percent of the capital goods available on the Brazilian market. This was viewed with a sense of triumph, but many in the end have contributed to trouble, as discussed below.

***Direct foreign private investment fell from $108 million in 1961 to $69 million in 1962. In 1963 it had been reduced to $30 million no doubt reacting to the Profit Remittance Law passed in October 1962.[5]

dollars) had shrunk from $320 million and $437 million in 1955 and 1956, respectively, to -$89 and $112 in 1962 and 1963, respectively; the current account balance changed from -$27 to $7 and from -$491 to -$219 during the same pairs of years. Foreign capital inflows, which had made the current deficit tenable, remained at slightly less than accustomed rates in 1962, only to collapse the next year as agitation against foreign capital grew more vociferous, itself a reflection of growing despair over the incipient payments crisis.

The difficulties on the trade account were attributable to the failure of Brazilian exports to rise. And this was to a degree brought about by the government's policy of discriminating against exports through manipulation of the exchange rate and, in the case of manu- factured goods, by quotas as well. Central to the decline of export earnings was the protracted and continuous fall, since 1956, in the price for coffee, by far the chief source of external revenue. By 1963 the New York price for a 100-lb. bag had fallen to $28.98 (in 1958 it was $40.35). Prices of cotton and cacao also declined, the latter falling by 1963 to 50 percent of its 1958 value.* For all such reasons, foreign exchange was exceedingly scarce. It may, indeed, have been the case that the inability of some sectors and industries to obtain essential foreign inputs, because of exchange rationing, was an important factor retarding the economy as a whole.7 It became apparent in early 1963, however, that no amount of rationing of the foreign exchange was going to enable Brazil to meet the substantial liabilities that would shortly become due to foreign creditors unless there was a massive refinancing operation. And Brazil's ability to renegotiate the debt hinged on its adoption of a creditable stabilization policy, long unpalatable to the vacillating men in charge and later— as derangements in industrial relations became widespread and the political situation convulsive—impossible to implement.

The beginning to the political crisis8 must be sought as early as the (last popular) presidential election of October 1960. There were no new faces among the candidates: Henrique Lott (supported by the PSD),** with "Jango" Goulart as his running mate (supported

---

*In fact, even though the performance of coffee was unsatisfactory, exports other than coffee, taken as a whole, performed worse than coffee during the postwar period. Between 1947-49 and 1960-62, real aggregate output had grown by 140 percent. But while the value of coffee exports had risen only 34 percent, other primary product exports (cocoa, cotton, tobacco, sugar, hides, rubber, timber, beef, etc.) had actually fallen slightly.6

**The abbreviations PSD, PTD, UDN, and PSP stand for Partido

by PSD as well as PTB); the popular Janio Quadros (supported by UDN plus some minor parties and the Janista movement, the Movimento Popular Jañio Quadros); and another oldtimer, Adhemar de Barros (supported by the PSP). Quadros received a very strong mandate: 48 percent of the popular vote, or nearly the combined total cast for the other two candidates. In the largely independent vice-presidential race Goulart won a marginal victory with 36 percent of the total vote.

Quadros began with seemingly boundless energy. The change at the top was felt at the lowest level of federal administration. He seemed intent on sweeping inefficiency and corruption out of the government, just as he had promised he would. The country was willing to submit to the hard work and self-discipline required at this time. Even less-popular reforms, such as banning of gambling and beauty contests, were accepted with unaccustomed equanimity. Once the euphoria generated by the election subsided, however, murmurs of discontent began to be heard concerning the effects of the earnest antiinflation program that had finally been undertaken by a Brazilian government and which—as stabilization programs always do—involved a number of measures sure to make the administration unpopular (such as a wage freeze, a credit freeze, and the reduction of import subsidies). In addition there was little agreement with respect to a profound reorientation of foreign policy. This was particularly so with regard to the resumption of diplomatic relations with Russia and the Soviet bloc countries, support of the admission of China to the United Nations, and pursuit of a policy of nonalignment with respect to Cuba. Most of these developments were heatedly discussed in the press and there was considerable criticism of this change of orientation, particularly after Quadros had awarded the highest Order of the Cruzeiro do Sul to Che Guevara.

Criticism took a new form on August 24, 1961, when Carlos Lacerda (king-maker, journalist-turned politician, now governor of the state of Guanabara) hurled serious accusations on TV and radio regarding the conduct of Quadros's justice minister, alleging that he had solicited support for a "Gaullist" solution to his problems with the congress, namely, an expansion of presidential power. The minister, Oscar Pedroso D'Horta, was commanded by the congress to appear and answer these charges. On August 25, to the astonishment of the nation, Quadros resigned from the presidency.* Next in line

---

Social Democrático, Partido Trabalhista (i.e., Labor) Brasileiro, Uniao Democrática Nacional, and Partido Social Progressista, respectively.

*No satisfactory explanation for this unexpected act was ever

to power was Vice-President Goulart who happened at that time to be out of the country on an official visit to the Peoples' Republic of China. Because of this, Ranieri Mazzilli, president of the chamber of deputies, was sworn in as provisional president. There was ample time, therefore, for a thorough discussion of the pros and cons about allowing the legitimate successor to power to return. The main opposition to Goulart's succession came from the military ministers (retained from Kubitschek's administration). Although their intransigence was not shared by a great many of their subordinates, it raised the spectre of civil war.

Opinion was certainly divided in these crucial days. Many prominent people (the legalistas) steadfastly held that, for better or for worse, the constitution should be upheld. However there was such widespread and profound mistrust for Goulart in influential circles that impasse was resolved only by a compromise: Goulart would be allowed to return but a constitutional amendment (the Additional Act) would vastly abridge his powers. A new post was accordingly created— that of a prime minister—to be chosen by and answerable to the congress. Under this new arrangement, effective control of the cabinet would rest not with the president but with the congress.

Needless to say, Goulart was less than satisfied with the dilution of his powers* but agreed to accept the parliamentary solution when he was presented with it in Paris, before his unhurried return. The parliamentary experiment began with Tancredo Neves who became Goulart's first prime minister. Judging from his nine-month tenure, the parliamentary system was not in the least an effective form of government for Brazil at such a crucial time. Perhaps this was so, however—as critics were quick to point out—because Goulart himself was intent to prove the new system unworkable.

Neves resigned, and in June 1962 San Tiago Dantas, the vigorous foreign minister of Quadros's independent policy, was nominated to the post. His candidacy was rejected by the congress after a bitter debate despite the threat of a general strike in support of Dantas's

---

offered by Quadros or his perplexed supporters. It is a sad commentary on Brazilian politics that Quadros, the man who had bitterly disappointed the vast electorate whose allegiance he had commanded, now discredited and without party support, did nevertheless attempt a political comeback (and, incredibly, almost got elected governor of Sao Paulo).[9]

*Cartoonists quickly seized on this aspect of the "solution" and depicted him in Queen of England's garb.

appointment. This turned out to have been more than a bluff. The strike was called and resulted in paralysis of transportation, food shortages in metropolitan areas, riots, looting, and deaths; the Army forces went on alert, Goulart requested special powers, and politicians blamed each other for the widespread unrest.

Goulart turned next to Senate President Mauro de Andrade, but he lasted only two days in the prime minister's post before resigning. In July 1962 another compromise candidate, Brochado da Rocha, was nominated and became the prime minister. His hands, too, were quickly tied as a number of his legislative proposals—somewhat irrelevant, given the civil disorders, rampant inflation, and threat of international bankruptcy—were turned down by the congress. He resigned in early September to be replaced by Hermes Lima, the last in the parade of short-lived prime ministers.

The parliamentary system was by now totally discredited. Naturally, advocates of an early plebiscite to settle the important question—of whether Brazilians wanted to retain the parliamentary system or to return to presidentialism—steadily grew in strength, but the timing of the plebiscite itself generated much dissension and ill-will. After much wrangling, it was finally held on January 6, 1963, and as universally expected the parliamentary regime was rejected by a majority of five to one.

With the resumption of full powers by the president there was reason for some optimism, as Goulart enlisted the aid of a number of able deputies, notably San Tiago Dantas and Celso Furtado, the latter being the main author of a Three-Year Plan that was to form the backbone of economic policy and on the workability of which the government placed much faith and perhaps staked its future. The plan aimed at reducing inflation, fostering reasonable economic growth, and improving the country's financial and international credit positions. It was an ambitious plan but it failed. The reasons for failure were the same as those which had led to the abandonment of earlier stabilization attempts in 1958 (Lopes and Campos) and 1961 (Quadros), namely, the government's inability to withstand criticism over the unpopular features of antiinflation programs, particularly the reduction of governmental deficits and its resistance to wage demands. By the end of May not a single group could be counted on to support the government's antiinflation campaign. The 40 percent guideline adopted for wage increases came under scathing attack as civil servants and the military demanded at least 60 percent and then—in conjunction with an ultimatum to the congress—demanded 70 percent, which was granted in July.

By then the planning ministry had been dissolved, San Tiago Dantas replaced by Carvalho Pinto in the finance ministry, and Celso Furtado relegated to the sidelines. Despite heroic efforts, no major

policy initiatives undertaken by Pinto met with any success, and he
resigned in December. The president, in endorsing the Three-Year
Plan, had committed himself to a program of reducing inflation and
promoting development. Now, bewildered by the financial briefings
and correctly assessing the political liability of continuing the former,
he turned to "basic reforms" in his quest for a political following.
One such agrarian reform had been an important component of the
Three-Year Plan and had elicited considerable sympathy from many,
as befitted a bill that had the twin objectives of creating greater social
justice and increasing productivity in agriculture. In the form in which
the bill was submitted to the congress, however, it would have required
a constitutional amendment (because of the bond, not cash, financing
of land redistribution) which would have required a two-thirds majority
for approval. Unfortunately, since this came at a time when more
immediate issues demanded action and when memories of violence
associated with Francisco Juliao and his Peasant Leagues were still
fresh in legislators' minds, passage of the bill was impossible. In any
case, it was equally disliked by both extremes—scorned by the left
as inadequate and denounced by the right as theft.

Consensus politics was becoming increasingly difficult and the
president more isolated. Goulart was widely deemed to be incapable
of governing, and defense against criticisms of his administration
from both the right and left was increasingly undertaken by his deputy,
San Tiago Dantas. Goulart himself stayed strangely aloof, or in
search of a political base. Party association had ceased to be an
index of political stance. Majority opinion in and out of the congress
all along seemed to be centrist but it had no nucleus around which to
gather and therefore to develop a cogent position. Perhaps it was too
late for Goulart himself to enlist the allegiance of representatives of
the centrist position but he seems hardly to have tried, choosing
instead to attempt to silence some of the outspoken critics* and
reaching outside organized politics to grassroots for support.

There was little to attract Goulart to either of the more extreme
positions if for no other reason than that these groups were faction-
ridden. This was particularly true on the left where many groups,

---

*The October orders had been issued from the Presidential
Palace for the arrest of Miguel Arraes and Carlos Lacerda, left- and
right-wing governors of Pernambuco and Guanabara States, respectively. Because of poor planning, an information leak, and questionable
allegiance of the dispatched troops, the attempts at arrest ended in
no more than well publicized fiascos, hardly adding to the government's respectability.

both in and out of the congress, maneuvered for position and vied for popular support, some having little to lose and much to gain from the current crisis. The attractions offered by the "positive left" were dubious. The orthodox policy measures it had recommended had not been implemented and now the sensible positions that this faction espoused politically—represented by the viewpoints of Celso Furtado and San Tiago Dantas—held little promise. Whether this was going to continue was unclear, since San Tiago Dantas, even while critically ill, did his utmost to find sufficient common ground among the leftist groups still dedicated to the constitutional process and attempted to organize a broad coalition, the Frente Unica. The "negative left" could not agree on a spokesman, but its views were more or less represented by those of Leonel Brizola.* While Goulart vacillated, disillusionment with politics and politicians steadily grew, as did the feeling that the solution to essential problems had been indefinitely postponed and that somebody should be held accountable for allowing the visible spread of anarchy and violence, not unlike the French experience in the spring of 1968.**

---

*If a single man could be held responsible for the military coup it would likely not be Goulart, nor any generals, but Brizola. He was Goulart's brother-in-law, but that did not endear him to the president. Brizola, earlier governor of the state of Rio Grande do Sul, was elected to the federal congress to represent his arch antagonist Carlos Lacerda's state: Guanabara. With him demagoguery reached new depths and ordinary political discourse became impossible. He was too arrogant, self-righteous, and uncompromising to assume the leadership of the radical left but he did use to the maximum the special powers intransigence bestows. He liked nothing better than an abusive, public and frequently pugilistic confrontation with his "respectable" colleagues whom he despised, to threaten the use of force when in its charge, or to urge the mob to it when not, and it would never have occurred to him that for him as an elected representative to incite crowds to violence was irresponsible. He largely preempted the left, extinguishing any hope more statesmanlike leftists, including Dantas and Goulart, had to establish a consensus platform and to organize a following.

**Indicative of the erosion of authority, sensed everywhere, has been the September rebellion in Brasilia, involving noncommissioned officers and enlisted men. During this rebellion, no more than a few hundred men almost seized control of the government, a fact that could not pass any potential plotters unnoticed.

By March 13, 1964, Goulart had made up his mind to ally his political fortunes with the far left. The occasion chosen for the announcement was a huge public gathering, the first of many such planned, to be held in front of Rio's Dom Pedro Segundo railway station and largely organized by the illegal Comando Geral dos Trabalhadores (CGT). Governmental assistance was not lacking, as army units were called in to protect the proceedings from disruption and as trucks of the state oil monopoly (Petrobras) were used to cart listeners to the meeting from as far away as Sao Paulo. Some 150,000 listened to many speeches while Goulart tried to arrive late—so as to avoid the embarassment of hearing Brizola's harangue. He only partly succeeded. His own speech was as impassioned and inflammatory, and although the two decrees there promulgated were modest in their effects the tone with which they were announced left no doubt that a significant change in the political posture of the president had occurred. Essentially, he had vowed to bypass the congress and to proceed unilaterally by decree.

In response to, and to express disagreement with, the views expressed at the Rio meeting, a huge rally was organized in Sao Paulo at which the president of the senate, Auro de Moura Andrade, condemned Goulart's attempt to short-circuit congress and his failure to cope with the chaotic situation prevailing in the country. A similar meeting was planned for Rio on April 2. By then the breakdown of discipline was fairly general and 3,000 sailors mutinied on March 25, 1964, to demand greater political rights. Two days later, 1,400 were still striking and were encouraged to continue by the offer of a general sympathy strike by the CGT. Astonishingly, Goulart professed to back not the men engaged in restoring order and discipline but the mutinying sailors, and announced that they would not be subject to punishment.

Military intervention, long rumored (on behalf of "continuists" as well as "coupists") and in the end seemingly courted by the defiant Goulart, began on March 30. It started out with much suspense, since only one of the four military regional commanders had been part of the conspiracy. With the joining on the side of the rebellion by Amaury Kruel, long a friend of Goulart and commander of the Second Army from Sao Paulo, the amicable meeting of rebellious troops and those despatched to intercept them, and the sudden realization all around that the far left (to which Goulart had committed his political future) had vastly overestimated its real strength and sources of support, the outcome was clear.

The CGT called a general strike but everybody worked as usual. The justice minister pleaded over the radio for people to go out on the streets and resist, but those who did were more curious than bellicose. Brizola urged armed resistance from the balcony of the Porto Alegre Town Hall, but nobody listened.

Goulart fled to Brasilia, then to Rio Grande do Sul, and by April 4 he was in exile in Uruguay. Third Army units, ambiguous to the last, occupied Porto Alegre, capital of Goulart's home state, without firing a shot. The meeting planned for April 2 in Rio for the purpose of protesting against the government developed into a day of celebration while a number of people believed to be responsible for the anarchy and agitation were rounded up by the military. Others fled the country (among them Brizola) and (or) sought sanctuaries in foreign embassies. On April 15, 1964, with the acquiescence of the congress, General Humberto Castello Branco was selected by the recently formed military supreme command of the revolution to finish the term of Quadros and Goulart.

THE 1964 INTERVENTION: NEW ECONOMIC AND POLITICAL PRIORITIES

While the ouster of President Goulart was widely regarded as a solution to the political chaos, the country still faced vexing economic problems. We would have to agree with Furtado's statement.

It would by no means be easy to demonstrate that social and political factors were of only secondary importance in the decline of the growth rate discernible in Brazil since 1962, and . . . it would be even more difficult to demonstrate that these factors were the prime or principal cause of this decline.[10]

As indicated earlier, economic and political problems were closely linked and mutually aggravating. The return to comparative serenity and the installation of a strong government did not, of course, mean that economic recovery and a stifling of the rampant inflation would follow by itself. On the contrary, the situation facing policy makers had the elements of what has been described as an economist's nightmare: recession cum inflation. For 1963 as a whole, prices had risen by 90 percent (and at almost twice that rate at the time of the coup) while the industrial index held stationary, the manufacturing index showed a slight decline, and real per capita income fell 1.6 percent. Further, the inflationary process had been institutionalized with price rises universally anticipated, making it fairly obvious that any swift and vigorous action to eradicate it would aggravate the recession and lead, almost inevitably, to a disenchantment with the new regime.[11] It was easily decided, however, that the inflation, which had reached the hyper stage, was too disruptive not to be attacked first.

The initial measures were directed at what was believed to be the chief source of the galloping price rise: the inordinate monetary expansion concomitant with the government's method of financing

its deficits by borrowing from the monetary authorities. Other measures were directed at reducing the rate of commercial credit
expansion and the rate of increase in wages and salaries. As the
effects of the antiinflation program were diffused throughout the economy,
pinch became pain. The tightening of credit soon produced a sharp
reduction in the purchase of durables, notably automobiles and household appliances, and in the level of consumer and business inventories.
The major industrial centers felt the decline in production and employment rather severely, particularly in the early months of 1965. The
recession was sharp but short-lived and by 1966 things had very much
returned to normal.

After the contrived but purging interlude of economic retardation,
growth has resumed at good rates: approximately 5 percent, 8 percent
9 percent, and 9 percent at constant prices for 1967, 1968, 1969, and
1970, respectively. The high rate is expected to be maintained. It
was known in advance that inflation would be stubborn and difficult to
erase due to its institutionalization over the years. It has been. The
austere budgeting and incomes policies have been successful in
reducing inflation considerably (albeit at a price). In 1964 the rate
of rise in consumer prices of 87 percent fell to 45 percent in 1965
and the wholesale price increase fell from 84 percent to 30 percent.
The initial results were impressive, the more so when one considers
that at the same time some prices, the rise of which had been previously suppressed (such as agricultural products, rents, utility rates,
and favored imports) were allowed to rise to reflect real scarcities
and help eliminate previous bottlenecks, thus laying the foundations
for balanced growth. The rate of price increase for both 1968 and
1969 was 24 percent per year, failing to decrease in the latter year
partly due to the effects of a severe drought on food prices. For 1970
the rate was 20 percent and, government planners forecast, should
be no more than 10 percent in 1973.

As for the foreign trade sector, the improvement in Brazil's
balance of payments has been remarkable, with reserves exceeding
$1.5 billion in mid-1971. What was believed to have been a major
source of trouble—the lag in adjusting the exchange rate to reflect
new price structures—has been eliminated. There were 8 small
exchange rate adjustments in 1969 and 10 in 1970. With the changing
business climate, long-term lending to Brazil reached unprecedented
heights ($557 million in 1969), the large influx allowing the govern-
ment to exercise considerable latitude in sifting foreign investment
proposals. Exports, due to a good performance of cotton, iron ore,
cacao, and manufactures, also have risen well in recent years. The
country has become less vulnerable to the vicissitudes in the coffee
market, as that crop's share of export values declined (to 34 percent
in 1969) and as other nontraditional items (meat, machinery,

manufactures) have come to constitute a large and growing share. Given the long list of severe economic maladies besetting the Brazilian economy at the time of the national crisis—stagnation, hyperinflation, industrial relations, and balance of payments problems—and the fact that available policy tools were not simultaneously compatible with the many policy goals, economic recovery has been at least as good as was hoped for. Unfortunately, recovery of the economy, and the likelihood that its growth will continue, has not been accompanied by political liberalization.

In the early days of the military takeover, while there was a political vacuum and the country clamored for leadership, it was not surprising that the heirs to power should be given exceptional powers to deal with an exceptional situation. To begin with, a vaguely worded Institutional Act was issued by the supreme command empowering the new president to remove congressmen and to suspend the political rights of individuals for 10 years if it was deemed to be "in the interests of peace and national honor". In the first round, 44 federal congressmen lost their seats and over 250 individuals were deprived of their political rights. There were well-known men among them: Joao Goulart, Janio Quadros, Juis Carlos Prestes, Leonel Brizola, Miguel Arraes, Celso Furtado, Francisco Juliao, and Osvino Ferreira Alves. Later, on June 8, Kubitschek also lost his political rights, despite a petition drawn on his behalf and signed by hundreds of thousands of Brazilians.

Castello Branco, on the whole, was not popular but highly regarded all around and if one is prepared to accept his treatment of dissenters as a necessary evil one can say that his rule had been effective. Predictably Branco's harsh economic and social controls made him less popular toward the end of his (once prolonged) tenure and when on March 1967 power was transferred to the jovial General Arthur da Costa e Silva the change was widely regarded as timely, for Brazil seemed to be ready for a less autocratic rule.

At this point the military still held 11 of the 22 cabinet posts and the change could not be construed as a movement toward civilian rule. Costa wanted to "humanize the administration," to use his own words, and to strike a better balance between control of inflation on one side and national economic development on the other. He was successful to some degree in all three endeavors. Costa e Silva's term of office ended abruptly on August 30, 1969, when he suffered a stroke. The civilian vice-president, Pedro Aleixo, who under the 1967 constitution should have assumed power, was however imperiously brushed aside and a military triumvirate was set up consisting of the ministers of the three armed forces. Transfer of power was legalized by the Institutional Act No. 12, on August 31.

After a brief scuffle, the supreme command nominated General Emilio Garrastazu Medici to succeed Costa e Silva. Not to forget the trappings of legitimacy, the congress, suspended as a result of the passage of Institutional Act No. 5 on December 13 the previous year, was ordered to reassemble and on October 25 it formally elected the new president and Admiral Grunewald as vice-president for terms running to March 1974. A week earlier a new constitution, the second in five years, had been promulgated. It differed from the previous one in that it incorporated and codified most of the amendments to the constitution and executive powers assumed by the government since December 1968.

Congressional immunity was not to apply to congressmen charged with breaches of security or "crimes of honor". The death penalty and the right to exile and to confiscate property in the case of subversion or revolutionary warfare were retained and incorporated in the new constitution, in addition to the permanent provisions of all the Institutional Acts. It stipulated further that the president and vice-president would be elected indirectly and the state governors directly (except in 1970). Congressmen's terms were limited to two years, with no provision for reelection. And, of course, the president retained powers to issue decrees in all matters involving national security, public offices, and public finances.

THE VIEW FROM WITHIN: "ORDER AND PROGRESS TODAY" BUT WHAT OF TOMORROW?

What has been the outcome? President Medici, by virtue of his constitutionally granted decree-issuing powers, buttressed by censure laws, and having at his disposal an impressive internal security police (now merged with the security divisions of the armed forces), is an absolute ruler, more so than Castello Branco or Costa e Silva ever was. There is now only one civilian in the cabinet with any power, Delfim Netto, and so long as he is able to keep up the current growth rates his position as minister of finance is secure. Not that the military itself is immune: Institutional Act 17 of October 14, 1970, empowers the president to transfer active officers to the reserve. The forebearance with which the citizenry has accepted these developments has many causes.

The most obvious one is, of course, that the government simply cannot be voted out. But would it be if it could? The answer would depend on what alternatives were offered. If the same test were applied that is frequently used in connection with Cuba (i.e., in the Brazilian context, whether Brazilians would vote for the return of

Goulart), then the answer would be "no." It is easy to pontificate
about the governments we would like others to have: participatory,
just, nice, espousing this or that ideology. The Brazilian government
doesn't fit into the above nor any other easy categories. The government sees as its chief task the supervision of the economic and social
development of the very large country where its 95 million people
live, a country beset by enormous but hopefully surmountable problems.

Brazilians are fond of saying their country will always have a
bright future. This is being reworded now to cease being a joke.
Economic development, its students have painfully learned, is not
likely to bring with it, as early fruits, social contentment. Perhaps
the opposite is more nearly the case. It is hard to find "national"
goals, and interests are sure to conflict. For one thing, policy makers
have extremely difficult decisions to make. Many of these are of
a strategic nature. Indeed in the Brazilian case they are the same as
those issues faced by Quadros and Goulart* as well as the current
regime: should policy favor industry, or agriculture? Which sectors
and groups should be the main contributors of the savings necessary
for capital accumulation? Should foreign savings be used and what
should be their composition and extent? What should be done about
regional imbalances, particularly the poor and plagued Northeast?
What distribution policies should be adopted? How, in fact, could the
resources needed for nation building be effectively mobilized and
sustained while assuring a modicum of social justice? More prosai-
cally, how could all that, plus rapid and steady growth, be maintained
with a minimum of inflation?

Critics have been all too cavalier with these prosaic matters.
It is easy to be smug about the evils of inflation, as many seem to be,
having never suffered through one which exceeded 6 percent. It is
easy to dismiss high growth rates as trivial matters. But there is a
world of difference whether this is done by someone living in a

---

*After his fall, Goulart was depicted as the man who in team-
like fashion has picked up Quadros's banner upon his (willful) fall,
and continued the fight against their common antagonist, the entrenched
interests. This is a gross oversimplification. Despite some common
elements, neither the issues nor the opposition were the same. As
for being members of the same team, this was an accident of Brazilian
electoral law which had permitted Goulart's election over Quadros's
own running mate (Milton Campos). The two men had campaigned
against each other and (to Quadros), Goulart represented nothing less
than the corrupt establishment he was fighting against. A few months
after taking office Quadros did not shirk from implicating his "own"
vice-president in a financial scandal involving pension funds.

developed country. The military regime has given the country the milieu in which economic growth can resume, and it has done so. This is no mean accomplishment and Brazilians know it. There are other changes: administration has been improved; tax collection has been simplified and its coverage extended (e.g., to 6 million people for income tax in 1970, up tenfold from 1965). The country is on the move. There is a massive housing program, obviously inadequate but significant given the high birth rate (2.7 percent over the 1960s) and the absence of birth control. Education, an integral part of which is the nationwide literacy program, now takes the largest single share of the budget: 12.7 percent. For one reason or another the government has expanded the scope of its economic activities, nationalizing some firms (such as those constructing the 8 1/2-mile bridge across Guanabara Bay), adding to its large holdings in steel and oil, and moving into new areas such as aircraft manufacturing and tourism.

It partakes, frequently using military personnel, in a host of developmental projects* such as the incredible 2,500-mile Trans-Amazonian highway which could, planners hope, help to relieve the population pressures in the Northeast. A plan for land reform in the Northeast, long the red herring of Brazilian politics, also has been announced. It provides for (compensated) expropriation of large land holdings for redistribution to landless farmers, and financial and technical assistance to get them started. Another redistributive innovation is the Social Integration Program whereby part of firms' profits are deposited in workers' accounts. But this is hardly the place for an evaluation of the various programs. Suffice it to say that the military government is proud of what has been accomplished and has developed a sense of mission to continue the work. It vows to protect it from disruption from whatever sources, including from the few who have had the temerity of offering armed resistance.

There is no reason to doubt that the government's efforts to eradicate terrorism meet the approval of most Brazilians, although overreaction on a number of occasions is costing it dearly in terms of popularity. The appearance of the first terrorist incidents date back to 1966 when a bomb was thrown at Costa e Silva while he was visiting Recife. For over a year and a half following that incident, various terrorist groups dedicated to the forceful eviction of the government assaulted armories and robbed banks. On September 4, 1969, a new tactic made its appearance: Charles Elbrick, the U.S.

----

*Brazil has now become the largest borrower from the World Bank with over $1.6 billion outstanding.

Ambassador to Brazil, was kidnapped. Other kidnappings followed.*
For obvious reasons, it is difficult to assess the size and importance
of these underground groups. It may be that the government has
succeeded in annihilating or dismantling them.** Much adverse sentiment has developed due to the extreme eagerness on the part of the
authorities to apprehend the members of such groups, going so far
as to be willing to condone infliction of torture on suspects.*** This
has been particularly repugnant because at the same time the government, rather ambivalently, has been less than zealous to apprehend
right-wing mobsters, the members of the Death Squad.**** It is

---

*On March 11, 1970, that of the Japanese consul general in
Sao Paulo; on June 11, 1970, of the West German ambassador to
Brazil; and on December, 7, 1970, of the Swiss Ambassador. All have
been released in exchange for political prisoners flown either to
Mexico, Algeria, or Chile. There have been two unsuccessful attempts
against United States Consuls in Porto Alegre and Recife, on April 5,
1970, and July 24, 1970, respectively. One American officer, Capt.
Charles R. Chandler, was murdered on a Sao Paulo street.

**Two were reportedly destroyed last year: National Liberation
Alliance (ALN) and Popular Revolutionary Vanguard (VPR, also known
as the Palmares Group). Remnants of this group later joined with
another (Colina) to form Var-Palmares. The group claiming responsibility for the Elbrick kidnapping was called Revolutionary Movement
8th of October (anniversary of the death of Che Guevara). There are
a fair number of dead or arrested leaders whose names are well
known: Carlos Marghella, Guimaraes de Brito, Jose Mariani Ferreira
Alves, Joaquim Camara Ferreira, Yoshitama Fujimori, Jose Raimundo
da Costa, Aldo da Brito de Souza Neto. On September 17, 1971 the
best known and most elusive of all, Carlos Lamarca, met his death
in a shootout in Bahia.

***The subject of torture was first brought to the public's
attention in November 1969 with the publication in Brussels of a report
on the subject by the International Association of Democratic Jurists.
Some 500 people are estimated to have been subjected to mistreat-
ment or torture so far. The government's position has been that,
whereas it admits that there may have been isolated instances of
torture, it asserts that steps have been taken to combat their incidence.

****Members of this and other vigilante groups such as Operation
Bandeirante and Communist-Hunting Command have been credited

unlikely that terrorism will completely die more easily in Brazil than elsewhere. If it does not, it will be yet another reason to prevent quick liberalization from taking place.

All said, the outlook seems to be for another decade of some kind of military rule. It is well to remember that Brazilians have had a long and sad experience with corrupt, irresponsible, and inept leaders, however popularly certified. It was in Sao Paulo that Brazilians, in disgust, nearly elected a rhinocerous to the city council. The sustained economic expansion dates back no further than to the advent of military rule and nobody, it seems, wants to spoil the run. Brazilians remember well the tenure of Goulart, who chose to agitate rather than to administer, and the indecisiveness of the parliamentary system. The military government, if anything, is overly decisive. But at the same time that it has shown itself paternalistic and self-righteous it has also been reform-minded and austere. "Order and Progress" reads the inscription on the Brazilian flag. While they are given both, Brazilians themselves seem to be willing to tolerate the Draconian features of the first.

---

with some 1,000 assassinations during the 1960s. There is indication that things have changed for these individuals. On October 4, 1970, 16 of them were charged with murder. A year later a well-known police chief, Sergio Paranhos Fleury had been indicted and the first conviction (a 19-year sentence) registered; two others followed in January, and in March, 15 Sao Paulo policemen were indicted on charges of murder.

14

THE MILITARY
ESTABLISHMENT
AS A POLITICAL ELITE:
THE PERUVIAN CASE
Carlos A. Astiz

The military establishment has played a crucial role in the politics of most countries of Latin America. Peru is no exception. From independence in 1821 until 1971, 51 of the 77 occupants of the presidency of the country have been military men. Furthermore, more than half of the civilian presidents achieved office through the use of force and depended on the military to remain in power.

In most countries of Latin America the armed forces are not merely "another pressure group," unless the meaning of that expression is to be altered. In situations where constitutional "rules of the game" are not fully supported by the overwhelming majority of the political participants, those who have a near-monopoly on the means of violence and are willing to use them within the polity are in an obviously privileged position. In the case under study, history shows that the type of "pressure" that the Peruvian military is capable of applying surpasses the ability of the constitutional authorities to resist. Furthermore, the success which the armed forces usually have in associating their interests with those of the nation often makes their pressure even more nearly irresistible.[1]

In such circumstances pluralism becomes an impossibility. True pressure groups are unable to counterbalance the actions of a power factor such as the armed forces when there is agreement among the members of such a power factor regarding the demands to be made upon the political system and the intensity with which these demands should be formulated.

PERUVIAN MILITARISM IN HISTORICAL
PERSPECTIVE

The domestic struggle for power which ensued after Peru's independence made the line between the national armed forces and the

personal troops of various <u>caudillos</u> very difficult to draw. There
were very few "career officers." Indeed, this expression only meant
that they were willing to remain in the armed forces for a long time.
As elsewhere, politicians and men with ambition and power became
generals, often overnight; officers who had achieved their personal
objectives withdrew, sometimes to administer their newly acquired
land or business. The national army happened to be that army whose
<u>caudillo</u> was in control of the capital city and therefore had access to
the national treasury. Soldiers and noncommissioned officers joined
because there was nothing better to do or because they were forcibly
drafted. In brief, throughout the nineteenth century the country had
armed groups but not a national army as the expression is now understood.

It has been emphasized that the military <u>caudillos</u> were not
members of the traditional upper class. This was particularly true
immediately after independence, as Victor Villanueva points out.

> The civilians subordinated themselves peacefully and with
> pleasure to the generals-made-<u>caudillos</u>. The landlord,
> somewhat impoverished as a consequence of the war, pre-
> fers to withdraw to the hacienda to rebuild it and to im-
> prove his damaged economy; he does not see the military
> <u>caudillo</u>, who relieves him of acting in politics and gives
> him guarantees defending his property, in a bad light.[2]

Evidence of this alliance (or at least agreement of interests)
can be found in the various measures which, in fact, reinstated slavery
until the <u>mestizo</u> dictator, Castilla, abolished it in 1854. During this
time the officer corps was open to all those with courage and a strong
desire to move upward in the socioeconomic scale. While the nineteenth-century Peruvian military were willing to risk their lives to
improve their individual status, nobody, not even Castilla, took steps
to alter the status quo or to take power away from the traditional upper
class. It would seem that a tacit accord developed early in Peruvian
history between Creoles who replaced the Spaniards and the military
officers, its main objective being to preserve the structure left by the
Spaniards. In exchange, the upper class provided ample reward and
relatively easy admission into the "good families" for those military
officers who distinguished themselves in preserving the status quo.
The upper class also provided military regimes with a certain degree
of legitimacy. Needless to say, disagreements occasionally developed
between some <u>caudillos</u> and certain upper-class cliques. However,
military officers who occupied high political positions surrounded
themselves with upper-class civilians, as they were the only ones
adequately trained to administer the country.[3]

The relationship between the upper class and the caudillos was upset in the 1850s and 1860s. In 1872, the Partido Civilista wrested the presidency from the caudillos. Once in direct control of the government, this coastal upper class tried to subordinate and counterbalance the influence of the military by creating a national guard and various military schools designed to unify and professionalize the armed forces and convert them into an effective and reliable fighting force. These actions were only partially successful. The defeat in the War of the Pacific and the inability of the upper class to provide effective national leadership brought the military back to power, although this time they were less willing to be guided and advised by the traditional upper class. Yet there was no attempt to modify the traditional sources of power, particularly the land grants and the laws that permitted this stratum to maintain and enlarge its power base.

An explanation of this behavior is that the military officers wanted to join the upper class and share its privileges. They had no intention of introducing changes in the sociopolitical structure. In any case, the abuses and lawlessness which ensued in the process of building up personal fortunes at the expense of the public treasure caused a reaction against the military caudillos. This reaction materialized in the coalition between the upper-class Partido Civilista and the Partido Democrata, a conglomeration of lower-and middle-class elements. In 1895 the army was defeated in a popular uprising and a civilian— Pierola—was installed as president. As it had done with the military before, the coastal upper class influenced this civilian caudillo who continued the attempts of the Partido Civilista to control and professionalize the armed forces. He hired a French military mission in 1896, created a national military school and training centers for non-commissioned officers, enacted a Law of Obligatory Military Service, and rationalized the promotions system. The net result was less popularity though more professionalism in the armed forces, a development that led to limited civilian control.

These events altered the political thinking of the military officers, who realized that they lacked the political power to oppose a popular leader backed by the coastal plutocracy. But the presidential election of 1912 showed the beginning of a split between the upper class and the Partido Democrata. The latter's winning candidate took steps (support for the eight-hour working day and a reduction of the military share of the national budget) that widened the split and developed an obvious community of interests between the upper class and the armed forces. The Lima garrison revolted in February 1914. Colonel Oscar R. Benavides captured the presidency and was escorted by the Prado brothers, his "civilian advisers." This event marked the beginning of a new period of mutual assistance between the military establishment and the coastal plutocracy, with the apparent support of the Sierra landowners.

It has been claimed that the 1914 coup, which overthrew President Billinghurst, marks the moment when the military became the defenders and protectors of the upper class. This may have been the case, as later revolts against dictator Leguia and President Bustamante y Rivero tend to show. This argument, however, cannot be considered the whole case. The military had come to realize that the traditional upper class (when allied with a popular movement) could subject them to civilian control or at least could deprive them of the legitimacy provided by the approval of the "good families" and the "distinguished citizens." The military also knew that a government that challenged the interests of the upper class would be no more responsive to the budgetary needs of the armed forces than would a government that attained office by a coup, particularly if the coup was led by a military man or if the military establishment participated in it. It cannot be ignored that while former dictator Leguia had encouraged the development of a competing industrial base at the expense of the traditional upper class he also granted military commissions and rapid promotions to his followers, created a civil guard, and purchased expensive military equipment for the navy and air force to counterbalance the army's effectiveness in internal affairs. This redistribution of military funds becomes particularly important if it is remembered that, although he increased the military share of the national budget to 22.1 percent in his first year in office, it had dropped to 17.6 percent when he was overthrown. The part played by the military budget in civilian-military relations is emphasized when it is pointed out that President Jose Prado (the candidate of the Partido Civilista elected in 1915 with military backing) was overthrown in 1919 after having reduced the military share of the budget, from 25.2 percent to 17.9 percent.

The different reasons that directed the upper class and the armed forces toward each other were made clear by their respective spokesmen in 1914. The proclamation issued by the coup's military leadership emphasized the poverty of the military establishment, i.e., the ragged appearance of the troops and even their lack of shoes.[4] On the other hand, in a banquet honoring the Prado brothers (considered to be the "political commissars" of the revolt[5]) organized by their peers of the coastal upper class, the keynote speaker concluded that the military revolt had been fundamentally directed "against the irreverent, insolent, and demolishing audacity of the lower classes, which had almost eclipsed the ruling class."[6]

Other coups d'etat carried out in this century further demonstrate the existence of this community of interests. Dictator Leguia was overthrown by Colonel Sanchez Cerro, a mestizo from a well-to-do family. It did not take long for the colonel to be co-opted by Lima's upper class, which "makes Sanchez Cerro dizzy with the glamour of its gatherings, swells him with pride with its flattery, seduces him with the 'love' of some of its ladies and places the commander totally at its service."[7] The flattery included admission to the exclusive Club Nacional five weeks after Sanchez Cerro overthrew Dictator Leguia, as well as a huge banquet attended by nearly every important person in Lima.[8]

Sanchez Cerro raised the military share of the budget to 24.1 percent (at the expense of other sectors), had himself elected president in 1931, and was killed in 1933. His place was taken by General Oscar Benavides, who had shown his responsiveness to the wishes of the traditional upper class. A number of revolts were attempted in the 1930s and early 1940s, many of them sponsored by the political party APRA, but they failed. In the process, APRA made the mistake of appealing to the noncommissioned officers and the soldiers against the officer corps. In the Trujillo revolt of 1932, organized by Aprista elements, most of the officers taken prisoners were executed. Two years later a "conspiracy of the sergeants," again under APRA sponsorship, was discovered in Lima. APRA became (particularly after the Trujillo revolt) unacceptable to the armed forces and, because of its reformist ideology, it was also unacceptable to the traditional upper class. Thus at least until the 1950s the desire to keep APRA out of power reinforced the community of interests between the military establishment and the upper class.

The successful coup d'etat of 1948 shows a similar pattern. President Bustamante y Rivero, a middle-class provincial intellectual with strong Catholic leanings, was elected in 1945 with APRA votes in exchange for APRA's participation in the legislature and in patronage appointments. But the alliance was extremely shaky. Bustamante y Rivero got along neither with APRA nor with the traditional upper class. His own popular appeal suffered significantly as a consequence of the postwar economic dislocations. It was widely reported that APRA attempted numerous conspiracies and made contacts with young officers and noncommissioned officers. It did not appear to have been successful with the officers, but elements of the Peruvian navy revolted on October 3, 1948. The revolt ended in failure, triggering a reaction on the part of the traditional upper class which, fearful of APRA's victory, had already joined forces with some senior officers. The result of these efforts was the overthrow of Bustamante y Rivero on October 27, 1948.[9] Once more, the community of interest was functioning. The military establishment had feared the inability and (or) unwillingness of Bustamante y Rivero to handle APRA, which had broken relations with the existing regime and was plotting against it. But in the last month of his administration the president outlawed APRA, jailed many of its leaders, and moved tanks into San Marcos University to control Aprista students. These moves may have been prompted by pressure from the army and the traditional upper class.

The military proclamation that overthrew Bustamante y Rivero also justified its actions by mentioning, somewhat vaguely, attempts to "weaken the power, diminish the prestige, and destroy the unity of the armed forces." It also accused the Bustamante y Rivero administration of "not having built even one military base," of refusing to purchase "weapons, materials, equipment, and even elements which are needed for military training," and of having adopted "the inconceivable project of reducing the military forces by one-third, for economic reasons."[10] In reality, the military forces' share of the national budget declined from 25.6 percent to 19.9 percent during the three years of the Bustamante y Rivero administration.

The grievances of the traditional upper class, and particularly of its coastal sector, were equally important. APRA was still projecting the image of a revisionist party with large popular support; it wanted to alter the nation's structure radically. It had previously indicated some willingness to resort to violence and it was plotting again, particularly among noncommissioned officers. But there were other reasons for being unhappy with Bustamante y Rivero. He had enforced exchange controls which, in fact, were a tax on exports, i.e., a tax that could not be passed on to the buyers because of competition from other countries. The money (particularly the hard currencies) thus obtained by the government was partially allocated to subsidize industrial development.

The connection between these grievances and the coup d'etat is evidenced by the key measures taken by General Odria shortly after assuming leadership of the new military regime. He ruthlessly persecuted the Apristas, increased the military share of the budget to 23 percent, enabled the officers to engage in business operations, and awarded them sizeable bonuses upon retirement. Last, but not least, he eliminated the exchange control system, thus more than doubling the net profits of Peru's exporters.[11]

WEAKENING OF THE COMMUNITY OF INTERESTS

The joint actions by the armed forces and the upper class to eliminate governments that were insensitive to their respective interests came to a temporary end in the 1950s. This may have been due to the abuses and the growing unpopularity of the Odria regime, especially in his attempts to develop a more permanent political base and his repressive legislation (originally directed toward the Apristas) against individual members of the coastal upper class.

Furthermore, the alliance became less and less necessary when APRA lost its reformist zeal and turned its energies to fighting communism. Perhaps the partial reconciliation between APRA and the coastal plutocracy caused an unfavorable reaction within the military establishment. By 1955, the break between the Odria government and those within the traditional upper class, which "guided" him to power, was total. The newspaper La Prensa attacked the regime constantly, and many of those associated with it were leading the opposition. Their candidate, Manuel Prado, received the APRA vote and defeated Hernando de Lavalle (who was preferred by Odria) in an election supervised by the armed forces. It may be more accurate to speak of a break in relations between Odria's military clique and members of the traditional upper class, led by La Prensa's director Pedro Beltran, with the armed forces left in the middle. Some have thought that events prior to the 1956 election implied the repetition of the coalition of the late 1890s between the traditional upper class and Pierola's Partido Democrata, with a "domesticated" APRA providing popular backing. By the same token, some military officers could have felt that one objective of this coalition was going to be the settlement of scores with the military establishment. The coastal plutocracy might not have been prepared to forget the closing of La Prensa, the police action against the Club Nacional and other affronts. The Apristas certainly would not forget the killing, torture, imprisonment, and exile of many of their leaders and followers. Although both APRA and the upper class lost no time in reassuring the armed forces, the military establishment started a profound reexamination of its role in Peruvian society and politics.[12]

THE CENTER OF HIGH MILITARY STUDIES

A key element of this reexamination within the military establishment was the Centro de Altos Estudios Militares (CAEM). Created in 1950 to prepare the high military command for national defense, the center became a military school of public affairs.* The faculty, comprising many civilians, subscribed to a wide diversity of political philosophies.[13] The center concentrated on the study of social, political, and economic problems of special relevance to Peru. At the same time the number of younger officers attending the universities increased and presumably contacts developed between them and

---

*In a conversation with the author, a civilian member of the CAEM faculty pointed out that it was "the only school of political science in Peru." The curriculum was quite advanced for Peru and indeed for many other Latin American countries, where political science is only beginning to exist as an independent discipline.

civilian students. The military attending CAEM concentrated on studies of current problems facing the country and prospects for the future. Their findings were apparently disappointing, at least as these intellectual pursuits appear reflected in the articles published by the Revista Militar del Peru, the journal of the Peruvian army. A comparison of articles published in 1949-51 with those included in the early 1960s shows that approximately one sixth of those published in the later issues deal with national development and related sociopolitical problems. No reference to these topics conversely are found in the earlier issues. The general thesis of these later articles indicated that,

> The new military ideology proposes the improvement of social and economic conditions so that the grievances on the basis of which revolutionary groups can obtain support will be eliminated. If the new perspective toward development is a nationalistic one which includes purely military aims, it also includes a modern economy and social structure as the necessary supports of a modern military organization.[14]

The CAEM interests in socioeconomic problems were not received favorably by the traditional upper class. In the 1950s the curriculum of the center called for a 10-month course: 7 dedicated to social, political, and economic matters and 3 to military subjects. In 1960, when Pedro Beltran became premier in the Prado administration, it was changed to 9 months of military and 1 month of nonmilitary topics.[15] This sensitivity of the traditional upper class to the activities of the center may have been prompted by the antiaristocratic sentiment developing among the officers, who began to feel that they had been "used" by the traditional upper class, without being given an adequate share of the benefits.[16]

This feeling was undoubtedly encouraged by the social origin of the majority of the officer corps. While the Peruvian armed forces have been reluctant to authorize systematic data-collection within the military establishment, officers come from the middle class, with an overrepresentation of the interior over the capital city. The available data show that 82 percent of those reaching the rank of general between 1955 and 1965 were born in the provinces and 56 percent of the total in small towns of the Sierra and Selva regions. Furthermore, 75 percent of all army officers come from public schools and only 4 percent of the total have attended the exclusive private schools. This last figure is somewhat higher among navy and air force officers: 12 percent and 7 percent, respectively, although the difference does not seem to be too significant.[17]

There is a logical explanation for the social background of the
Peruvian military officers. Military life is too regimented and disciplined for the youngsters of the upper class, who already have at their
fingertips almost all of the rewards a successful military career could
bring them. The same reasoning may be applied to a large portion of
the upper-middle class found for the most part in the large urban areas.
On the other hand, practically all those who belong to the lower class
are excluded, i.e., they cannot meet the formal educational requirements for admission to the Peruvian military academies. These
factors in effect reserve the military academies for the middle class.
Moreover, Lima and the other large cities offer other comfortable
educational and business alternatives which are scarce in the small
towns. The abundance of scholarships at the service academies (in
contrast with the universities) further attracts those who have financial
difficulties.[18]

Nevertheless, the significance of the social background of the
military has probably been exaggerated. There appears to be something mysteriously powerful about the forbidden data. Most writers
in the field accept the idea that, given a certain social origin, only one
kind of political behavior will take place among the officer corps of
the Latin American armed forces.[19] This deterministic cause-effect
relationship does not seem to be present in Peruvian politics. The
social origin of the military does not explain the changes in political
behavior and the cleavages existing in the Peruvian armed forces.
The issue is not in what class the officers were born, but rather whom
do they represent? Whose values do they share? What view of the
ideal Peruvian society do they hold? If the problem is seen in these
terms, then it can be said that the country's armed forces reflect
some of the contradictions of its middle class, heavily mediated by the
institutional interest of the military establishment itself.[20]

The armed forces constitute the most solid and cohesive of all
organizations of middle-class origin, much more so than the few
white-collar workers' unions and the small businessmen's organizations. The officers are not brought together by a common economic
interest, although it has been demonstrated that the protection of the
institution's economic well-being is an important factor in their political actions. The future officers enter the military schools between
the ages of 16 and 18, and thereafter their contacts with the civilian
world are kept to a minimum. While this is probably very good from
the professional point of view (since it intensifies the specific socialization process), it greatly reduces the officers' ability to deal with
civilian matters (particularly in the field of politics). The ultimate
goal of the process of military socialization is the development of a
strictly military outlook that sets the military establishment apart
and above the rest of the national society, equating it with the "sacred

interests of the fatherland." Available evidence for Peru corroborates
Jacques Lamber's dictum that in the last 40 years the military officer
corps has been "as distant from the aristocracy as from the masses."[21]
    A further element of potential discord between the military
establishment and Peru's traditional upper class is the image the
military officers have of the Peruvian armed forces as a fighting
force. Placed between the extremes of Argentina or Brazil on the one
hand, whose armed forces consider themselves (rightly or wrongly)
capable of carrying out the traditional mission of protecting their
country's security from almost any type of aggression, and El Salvador
or Honduras on the other, whose armies cannot possibly believe that
they can withstand any serious attack, the Peruvian military would
seem to have been torn between their needs for domestically manufactured supplies and the traditional reluctance of the upper class to
encourage industrialization. Thus, if the Peruvian military officers
consider themselves closer to their Argentine or Brazilian counterparts (and personal observation indicates that they do), they are forced
to become industrial promoters, regardless of the social, economic,
and political consequences that rapid industrialization usually brings
about. On the other hand, there are signs that the traditional upper
class is aware of the consequences of rapid industrialization (e.g.,
in Argentina) and has shown little desire to allow the military or any-
body else to promote it. This discord has been reflected in the studies
conducted at CAEM and in the program changes introduced in it by
Prime Minister Beltran. It acquired overt political manifestations in
the 1962 and 1968 coups d'etat.

THE 1962 MILITARY REVOLT AND ITS AFTERMATH

    In exchange for the electoral support given to Manuel Prado in
1956, APRA was permitted to participate fully in the 1962 elections.
Haya de la Torre once again became its presidential candidate. Former
dictator Odria was Union Nacional Odriista's hopeful, Bernando
Belaunde Terry led the Accion Popular ticket, and there were four
other candidates from minor parties. The military was unhappy about
the organization of the election, and divided over the candidates. There
was almost total rejection of Haya de la Torre, and remarks were
made before the election to the effect that he would not be allowed to
consummate his expected victory. Beyond this virtual veto, the military appeared to have been divided in their preelection preferences.
The officers active in CAEM favoured Belaunde Terry. Those who
had benefited under the previous Odria administration were naturally
inclined toward him. A large number seem to have doubted the whole
process and remained undecided.

It would take too long to detail the armed forces' involvement in
the electoral process. It began with their investigation of irregularities
in voter registration, included electoral surveys, and ended with a
rejection of the results and the overthrow of the Prado government.
The military takeover took place on July 18, 1962, 10 days before
Prado was to have turned the presidency over to the victorious candidate. The coup was directed not against Prado but against his successor who (according to an agreement reached the day before between
APRA and the Odriista party) was going to be Odria. Because none
of the candidates had been able to obtain the required minimum of one
third of all valid votes cast, the election was to have been decided by
the congress, which has the constitutional authority to choose the president from among the three candidates with the largest number of votes.
No single party enjoyed a majority in the newly elected congress, a
fact which was compounded by the armed forces' veto of Haya de la
Torre (who had obtained the largest number of votes and controlled
the largest number of seats in both chambers). The veto was announced
by Haya himself on July 4. After conversations between the three
leading candidates, the leader of APRA instructed the party senators
and representatives to vote for Odria, a decision which would have
ensured the latter's election.[22]

General Odria was the candidate most acceptable to many members of the traditional upper class, in spite of his difficulties with
some of them in the mid-1950s. After an unsuccessful attempt to
organize an upper-class electoral machine (the National Independent
Movement), the large landlords had distributed their support between
Odria and Haya de la Torre. However, they were evidently aware of
the military's position regarding a possible victory by Haya, and when
the veto materialized they were essential in persuading APRA to support Odria, who had persecuted the party ruthlessly until the mid-1950s.
As one writer put it,

> The coup d'etat finally took place. It took place regard-
> less of the understanding between Haya and Odria. There
> are those who believe that it would have taken place in
> any case, even if the understanding had been reached
> sooner. It took place, above all, against Odria, who at
> noon of July 17 virtually was president-elect.[23]

The only candidate acceptable to those officers who carried out
the coup was Belaunde Terry, whose electoral tactics paralleled those
of the military. Before the election he had openly recognized the
military's role as election arbitrator, by stating that he would accept
defeat at the polls only if the armed forces accepted the result.[24]
Since it was apparent that his main competitor was Haya de la Torre

and that APRA's victory was not going to be accepted by the military
establishment, Belaunde Terry was apparently counting on his military
supporters to extricate him from an electoral defeat or to guarantee
his victory. The day after the election Belaunde Terry, on the basis
of early returns, went on radio and television to thank the Peruvian
population for their votes and the national electoral jury and other
authorities for having conducted a clean election. As later returns
changed the picture, he denounced the electoral process and openly
encouraged the military to intervene. His invitations grew louder
after the understanding between APRA and Odria became likely.*
Whether Belaunde Terry led the military or simply announced publicly
bits of political gossip is extremely difficult to establish. But the
coup d'etat took place, Odria did not become president, and Belaunde
Terry was given a new opportunity in 1963, which he did not waste.

THE NEW MILITARY IN POWER

From the moment the 200 Peruvian Rangers (counterguerrilla
troops) took over the presidential palace, it was evident that there
were important breaks with traditional military revolts. While the
army was still the more important of the three services, true collective leadership existed in the junta. Four co-presidents, the chairman of the joint chiefs of staff, and the commanders of the three
branches acted jointly on all policy decisions with the chairman
(General Perez Godoy) acting as chief of state. No individual caudillo
appeared and when Perez Godoy showed an inclination to become one
he was dismissed from the junta and his responsibilities were transferred to General Lindley, the army representative.

Other breaks with tradition were the unusual effort made by the
three services to consult the officer corps, and their desire to show
at least a facade of unity in the military establishment. In the three
or four months prior to the coup, numerous steps were taken by the
military leadership to familiarize itself with the views of officers at
all levels in regard to the developing political situation. A written
questionnaire of the objective type was even circulated and all officers

---

*Belaunde's erratic behavior was widely reported in the daily
press. He went so far as to barricade himself with a few youngsters
in the center of his hometown, Arequipa, while announcing that he
was beginning the movement to overthrow the Prado government and
annul the elections. The government ignored him and, without any
armed forces reaction, he gave up and went home.

were encouraged to answer it anonymously. The military leadership
probably used this information in selecting a course of action satisfactory to a majority of the officers in active service. In this sense,
it can be affirmed that the 1962 coup d'etat was institutional in its
inception and in the policies it produced. The military had no popular
backing, nor did they pretend to have it. But popular support against
the coup could not be mustered either. An attempt by APRA to call
a general strike elicited almost no response although the party controlled a large number of unions, or at least their leadership.[25]

It seems apparent that the members of the military junta and
their backers, particularly at the middle level, had either been involved in CAEM or influenced by its activities. During the first few
months of their administration there was no repression of individuals
or ideologies. Perhaps owing to outside pressure, fair elections were
promised within a year. Although their declared objective was to
invalidate the 1962 election, the military decided to try to solve some
of the problems identified as most pressing, according to the files
developed at CAEM. The announced goals were agrarian reform,
better distribution of wealth, improvement of the educational system,
and reductions in the price of foodstuffs and basic items.[26]

The opposition attempted by APRA and a few minor parties during
the first few days was handled effectively and with minimal threats to
individual rights. Delegations representing most unions were invited
to visit the presidential palace and meet with key officers, and on
August 21 a decree-law ordered pay increases and other benefits for
white- and blue-collar workers in industry, commerce, and the service
sector. This action pacified discontented union members. Other
workers were promised a minimum salary statute as soon as studies
were completed. A new plan to reduce illiteracy was devised and
1963 was decreed "Literacy Year." Taxes on corporation income
and the fishing industry were enacted and the minister of government,
General Bossio, even brought up in public the possibility of annulling
the International Petroleum Company oil concessions at La Brea and
Parinas.

However, as time went on the measures announced or enacted
by the junta were either forgotten or altered. In the last weeks of
1962 and the beginning of 1963 the compromising attitude was abandoned and a large number of left-of-center elements, some of them
involved in the articulation of miners' and peasants' interests, were
summarily imprisoned. These groups had not yet received the salary
raises and other improvements promised earlier by the military
rulers. The educational reforms to be carried out during the "Literacy
Year" were somehow shelved, after the nomenclature was printed in
all official correspondence. Only the equivalent of $400,000 was
appropriated to get the program under way.

The new taxes were unanimously opposed by commercial industrial, and landowners' organizations and by the newspapers that articulated their views. These revenue measures were either reversed or
substantially altered for the benefit of the prospective contributors.
Finally, General Bossio, who had publicly announced his intention to
annul the foreign oil concessions, resigned in mid-October "for reasons
of health."

The imprisonment of left-of-center politicians and labor leaders
was indicative of both the changing mood of the military government
and the success of the traditional upper class. The latter, after dis-
agreeing with the coup d'etat, challenged the legitimacy of the government and demanded that it prove itself by taking measures that would
diminish or eliminate the effectiveness of the reforms which CAEM
considered necessary. In the area of labor policy, the newspaper La
Prensa emphasized the danger of a communist takeover of the labor
movement and stressed that since the labor organizations were going
to be involved in partisan politics anyway, they may as well be led by
men of "democratic tendencies." Inasmuch as control of the labor
movement was being disputed by Apristas and communists, it was
clear La Prensa was asking the military to assist APRA in ousting
the communists. General Bossio, who represented CAEM thinking
within the military government, left his cabinet post after having been
opposed by La Prensa. Following his departure, the newspaper continued its denunciations of communist involvement in labor and peasants' organizations, and of the junta's deficit-spending program.[27]
The exhortations were finally heeded by the military leaders, who
moved forcefully, first against the peasants and later against the
miners and other workers who had gone on strike. After suspending
constitutional guarantees the junta conducted a widespread dragnet in
the first week of 1963, netting close to 2,000 political prisoners who
were accused of planning sabotage, subversive activities, and the
violent overthrow of the government. The prisoners were slowly
released. As far as can be ascertained, not even one of them was
ever found guilty of these charges by either a civilian or a military
court. Indeed, only 62 were brought to trial before a military court,
in highly irregular proceedings, with the junta unable to provide the
evidence it said it had.[28]

However, the military leaders achieved (with this action) a number of objectives. First, they satisifed the highest priority demand
of the traditional upper class: the repressive measures greatly diminished the effectiveness of organizations that articulated lower-class
interest, particularly in the rural areas, where the peaceful occupation
of haciendas was threatening the landowners' economic base. Second,
powers derived from the suspension of guarantees were directed
against the National Liberation Front and other left-of-center, minor

parties and nonpartisan organizations. Though their voting strength
was small and diffused, in the absence of participation by these parties
and organizations, most of those votes would have to go to Belaunde
Terry, the candidate least repugnant to the left-of-center voters. In
view of the results of the 1962 election, these votes were important.
Finally, the junta quieted the annoyance of powerful foreign investors
(particularly oil companies and mining enterprises) with the nationalistic tone prevalent in some CAEM studies.

While managing these changes and counterchanges the military
did not forget their economic interest. The Prado administration
had, approximately one month before it was overthrown, decreed
salary increases for the military, with the provision that they go into
effect in 1963. The military junta, however, ordered that the increases
go into effect immediately, but they were not made applicable to retired
officers as had been legally mandated heretofore. Furthermore, the
junta took away from retired officers a number of privileges (including
free medical treatment at the military hospitals and the opportunity
to purchase low-price, duty-free goods at military stores). This
change of policy regarding retired officers further illustrates the
differences between those who carried out the 1962 coup d'etat and the
previous military leadership.

One promise that the military did fulfill was the holding of free
elections within a year of its takeover. The voting registration pro-
cedure was improved and the number of registered voters dropped,
thus indicating that at least some of the irregularities denounced before, during, and after the 1962 election, may in fact have existed. A
new electoral law was passed, and the total number of senate and
house seats was reduced, with some redistribution among departments,
though the most backward departments, mainly in the Sierra continued
to be overrepresented.[29] The most important electoral event was the
agreement reached between the Popular Action and the Christian
Democratic parties whereby the latter agreed to vote for the former's
presidential candidate, Fernando Belaunde Terry. This coalition
together with the decision by minority, left-of-center parties to back
Belaunde gave him the margin of victory.

The military turned power over to Belaunde Terry, who had
been able to put together a majority coalition and to attract most of
the left-of-center votes. But it should be emphasized that the individuals who participated in the transfer of power of July 28, 1963, had
moved away from the mandate that produced the 1962 coup d'etat,
even if some of the top political offices were occupied by the same
individuals. In spite of their reformist zeal the CAEM alumni and
particularly the so-called Nasserites were unwilling or unable to
establish linkages with those civilian political groups which could have
assisted them in gaining lower-class support. This inability of the

reformist military officers to carry out any of the proposed reform programs was not an accident. Credit should be given to the outstanding campaign of division and psychological warfare that brought enough key officers around to the traditional upper class's point of view to drive a wedge between the military establishment and the civilian reformists.

THE ARMED FORCES UNDER THE BELAUNDE ADMINISTRATION

Since Belaunde Terry was the most popular (or the least dis-tasteful) of all presidential hopefuls, his 1963 victory in an election which none of the leading participants challenged appeared to have satisfied the political desires of the military. Ostensibly they returned to their bases and surrendered the governing to what many Peruvians considered the country's new modernizing elite. In reality, however, they were involved in the decision-making process, not only in those matters related to national defence but in every major political move made by the Belaunde Terry administration. Although the president expected that the military were going to assist in having his proposed reforms approved by the legislative branch (dominated by a conserva-tive APRA-Unión Nacional Odriista (UNO) alliance), in fact the opposite happened. The traditional upper class, which had effectively divided the military establishment and backed the group that shared its view of Peruvian society, continued its rapprochement with the military leadership by signaling a new basis to renew their community of inter-ests: the danger of a Castro-communist takeover which was said to be developing in the Sierra region as an outgrowth of the occupation of land by the peasants' organizations. There was enough truth in the claim to make it believable, particularly to a Peruvian military establishment that could not forget the way Castro handled the Batista officer corps.[30]

A combination of police repression, poor organization, and a weak and confusing land reform act pushed some of those involved in the peasants' organizations into guerrilla warfare. Early guerrilla attempts, in 1962-63, had been easily handled by the police and did not require military intervention. Apparently the guerrillas learned their lesson, and after widespread notice they went into operation in June 1965. This time, however, the rural constabulary was no match for them. Fairly well equipped and organized, they acted ruthlessly in their operations, wiped out entire patrols of the civil guard and forced the military to take on themselves the responsibility of handling the situation.[31]

Some of Belaunde Terry's advisers were reluctant to publicly acknowledge the existence of guerrillas, since acknowledgement of their presence would indicate a widespread dissatisfaction with the administration, particularly in the rural areas. The Aprista and Odriista opposition, on the other hand, attempted to diminish the administration's popularity and damage the president's image by exaggerating the threat posed by the guerrilla bands. Those newspapers that articulated the views of the traditional upper class also exaggerated the significance of the bands, hoping to enroll the military establishment in a comprehensive clean-up operation that would eliminate the peasant organizations as well as the guerrillas. Senator Martinelli Tizon, who represented one of the departments of the Sierra region, stated, "Let the 'rangers,' the army, and the air force go after the guerrillas! We shall back them, because we cannot allow the constitutional regime to suffer sabotage, subversion; we cannot allow it to fall into the hands of the reds. Half-measures are out of place."[32]

Even pro-Belaunde publications felt the pressure of the events and advanced the idea that the guerrillas were "a challenge to the efficiency of the armed forces," and that "if they were not bloodily repressed by the Peruvian Army—the revolt may provoke in the long-run an ominous intervention of the United States armed forces."[33] The military soon began to see it that way too and, as Francois Bourricaud put it, "made the liquidation of the guerrillas a point of honour."[34] In July 1965, the joint general staff presented an ultimatum to the Belaunde government, demanding that all constitutional guarantees be suspended and that they be put in charge of the repression with authorization to do whatever they considered necessary. At the same time, General Oscar Benavides, Jr., was put in charge of the intelligence service and mentioned in military circles as Belaunde Terry's replacement, if a change was considered necessary.

These emergency measures were happily approved by the APRA-UNO congressional majority and reluctantly signed by the president. Antiguerrilla units, reportedly advised by members of the U.S. Special Forces,* went into action and after a few months of fighting badly mauled the guerrillas and killed or captured practically all their leaders. The effectiveness of the military was underwritten by the traditional

---

*The information received by the writer indicates that the relations between the Peruvian forces and their American advisers were not always cordial. The Peruvian officers often refused to follow the advice and the Americans, in turn, refused to provide certain types of ordnance.

upper class, which rapidly bought 200 million soles (approximately $8 million) of government bonds especially authorized by the congress at the end of August to finance counterguerrilla operations. Pedro Beltran, owner of the newspaper La Prensa, contributed 1 million soles ($40,000), the commercial banks 60 million soles, the National Fishing Society 20 million, and so on. By early 1966 the guerrillas had been almost completely wiped out, although a few groups had not been accounted for in the military communiques. Probably for this reason an armed forces report closed with the warning, "the struggle is not over. The danger remains."[35]

The appearance of guerrillas, who constituted a threat to the established order and whose objective was to bring about a Peruvian version of the Cuban revolution, suggested that a new link between the traditional upper class and the military establishment had been provided. The alliance that developed in 1965-66 was, however, highly unstable because the traditional upper class wanted to keep both its understanding with APRA and its community of interest with the military. However, while it is true that all members shared their opposition to communism and Castroism, and that the Apristas had been strong backers of the military's antiguerrilla operations (providing them with a certain measure of popular support), it is evident that the military neither made gestures indicating acceptance of Aprista support nor implied that they were ready to forget the "Trujillo massacre." The instability of the situation has been reflected in reports which indicate that the Peruvian military leadership "lump with the same sharp repugnance the largest party, Accion Popular; its weak ally, the Christian Democrats (now divided); and certainly the right wing forces: Haya de la Torre's APRA and former dictator Odria's UNO."[36] The end product was the overthrow of the Belaúnde Terry administration in October 1968.

THE UNFOLDING OF THE 1968 COUP D'ETAT

Vague threats and rumors of forthcoming coups d'etat had been widespread in Peru since 1965, when the guerrilla bands went into action. They intensified both in number and in credibility during 1967 and 1968. Most of the rumors centered on the army and, within it, on the intermediate officer ranks. Besides the political preferences of the colonels and their view of the Belaunde Terry regime, two factors seem to have annoyed them. Firstly, military promotions were subject to some congressional control, thus forcing military officers to deal with legislators and particularly with Apristas. It is no accident that Colonel Gonzalo Briceno, who led the takeover of the presidential palace in the 1962 coup d'etat, was still a colonel when he led a remarkably similar operation on October 3, 1968.

A second contributing factor, as so many times before, was the military share of the national budget, or, more accurately, the distribution of the military budget among the three services. In total the armed forces were receiving approximately 23 percent of total governmental expenditures, but that 23 percent was divided as follows: the army (with more than 70 percent of all men in uniform) received 9 percent; the air force received the same percentage; and the navy was allocated 5 percent.[37] This distribution was obviously considered detrimental by most army officers, while air force and navy personnel felt satisfied and, as it will be shown, were unwilling to act against the Belaunde Terry administration. The satisfaction felt by the navy and air force may also have been because the percentage of top-rank officers went up significantly in these two services but did not change in the army, as Table 14.1 shows.

The plotting was reported to have been conducted by an unidentified group of colonels who, early in the morning of October 3, met at Lima's international airport to settle the final details. A few hours later they pulled Belaúnde Terry out of bed, took him to the headquarters of the tank division and then to the airport. There he was put aboard a Peruvian Airline jet commandeered during the colonels' previous visit to the airport. These events have led to widespread speculation that the coup was engineered and spearheaded by the dissatisfied army colonels with the passive acceptance of the senior officers. If this version is correct the senior army officers actively joined the coup and took over leadership of the government when it became evident that they could not prevent the coup.

On the other hand, it is clear that such pressure was not present within the air force and navy. Neither service participated in the over-

TABLE 14.1

Top-Rank Officers as a Percentage of
All Officers in Active Service,
1960-68

Year	Army	Navy	Air Force
1960	1.2	2.9	2.8
1968	1.2	3.6	6.2

Source: Victor Villanueva, Nueva Mentalidad Militar en el Peru? (Buenos Aires, Editorial Replanteo, 1969), p. 251.

throw. On the contrary, General Gagliardi, the air force minister, joined the other members of the last cabinet named by Belaúnde Terry in a show of defiance after the civilian government's overthrow. The navy minister, Vice-Admiral Luna Ferrecio, was reported to have joined "the naval forces which were loyal to the Belaúnde government."[38] The existence of disagreements between the army and the other two services became apparent when the military cabinet was announced. The army received the presidency and five ministries, including the premiership, the navy was awarded two seats, and the air force three. The new ministries, created almost two months after the coup, added two more navy representatives and another army officer. This distribution is substantially different from that which took place after the 1962 coup, in which the three services shared the presidency. It has also been widely reported that the swearing-in ceremony, held approximately 15 hours after Belaunde Terry was overthrown, was attended almost exclusively by army officers, with only two or three navy and air force officers present. It is extremely likely that,

> Only at noon Wednesday, the high commands of the navy and the air force joined the coup, after tense deliberations. A number of high air force officers are said to have backed the constitutionalist attitude of the Air Force Minister Jose Gagliardi. And in the navy, where a cordial feeling toward Belaunde was always visible, agreement was obtained after some hours of debate.[39]

These disputes between the services have not ceased. The navy chief of staff was ignored in the appointment of the new service minister despite that fact that (according to the proclamation of the leaders of the revolt) he was entitled to that position. Two days later it was announced that he had resigned, without indicating his reasons. Another unexplained resignation made public shortly after the new government took office was that of the army chief of staff, who at the end of October flew to Spain to take up the position of military attaché. Again no reasons were given although his son-in-law acknowledged the existence of disagreements.[40] Still another significant change occurred three weeks after the military government was installed: the chief of staff of the air force, who also occupied that service's ministry, resigned without explanation and was temporarily replaced by another air force officer already serving as minister of public health. Three other officers of higher rank in active service were thereby ignored.[41] The new military leadership seems to be willing to pay a relatively high price to achieve the consensus so easily developed in the "institutional" coup of 1962.

THE POLICIES AND PERFORMANCE OF THE 1968
MILITARY REGIME

If the researcher remembers that he is dealing here with a coup d'etat inspired and executed by the army; if he also remembers that in a survey of 36 army generals 29 rejected the previous agreement reached with the International Petroleum Company; then it is not surprising that one important action of the military government would concern the IPC. Furthermore, the new government was faced with the opposition of most political parties and almost total apathy on the part of the populace. It needed an issue that could rally the support of most Peruvians. For a long time the question of the La Brea and Parinas oil fields had been such an issue, deeply felt not only by the middle and lower classes but by the nationalist military officers as well. Consequently, within a week of the coup, its leader and the new president of Peru, General Juan Velasco Alvarado, announced the military takeover of the oil fields in question and of the Talara refinery, while army troops occupied the facilities. The government also cancelled the agreement reached by the Belaunde Terry administration two months earlier. Two sympathetic observers put it quite well:

> With the full revindication of La Brea and Parinas, with the authentic recuperation of our Talara oil, the overthrow of a government which did not know how to respond to the requirements of its historic moment is thus justified. [42]
> And the starting point of the great embrace between the People and the Armed Forces, united in an exalted nationalistic and revolutionary ideal, has been the expropriation of the oil wealth which, against all reason, in violation of our sovereignty and in outrage to our national dignity, was held by rapacious foreign enterprises. [43]

The desired effect was achieved. After the spectacular takeover it was difficult to find Peruvians willing to express reservations regarding this action. Approval came from such contradictory sources as Cardinal Landazurri and Peru's National Liberation Front. In consequence it was not difficult for the military government to convert support for the takeover into a short-term legitimation of its existence. Riding on the popularity gained by the swift action it closed newspapers, magazines, and radio stations that had been critical of it. [44] The new government suddenly enjoyed at least the qualified approval of nearly every political party in Peru.

In reality the original takeover, though spectacular, was limited. It did not include other oil fields exploited by the IPC or its distributional services, although they were taken over later. It was also announced that all concessions granted, both to extract oil and to refine it, would be respected. The first reaction of the company and of the U.S. government could be considered mild. The former did not sabotage the takeover and asked its staff to continue working, which they did. The latter recognized the military government within a short time and made only mild representations regarding adequate compensation. It would appear that the La Brea and Parinas takeover had been considered by all interested parties domestically as a necessary move to strengthen and popularize the new regime. In view of the association that many observers saw between the Peruvian military leaders and their Argentine counterparts, who took over the government in 1966, it may be that this was originally an attempt to create a nationalistic facade for domestic consumption, without essentially altering American penetration under the protection of just such a facade.

The military's attitude toward land reform was initially cautious and unclear. The new minister of agriculture, General Oscar Benavides, Jr., stated,

> It is understandable that the difficulties met in the process
> of agrarian reform be natural and explainable owing to
> the complexity of the matter and the limited experience in
> it. In accordance with reality based on the fiscal possi-
> bilities, it is the intention of the Revolutionary Government
> to define the actions which it is going to carry out in the
> process of agrarian reform, in order to clear up the
> uncertainty of those affected and benefited by it, and to
> dedicate the greatest effort of the Public Agrarian Sector
> to the technical and economic assistance of the small
> farmers. In spite of the restrictions imposed by the
> scarcity of financial resources, the government wishes
> to make the agrarian reform process more agile.[45]

When Benavides, the most conservative officer in the cabinet, resigned in mid-June 1969 he was replaced by General Jorge Barandiaran Pagador, a student and later a faculty member of CAEM. At the end of June the revamped government announced a new Agrarian Reform Act and ordered the occupation of some large landholdings, particularly those located in the coastal region and owned by foreigners. Without entering into details of this important law (a task that exceeds this chapter), it can be said that it tends to neutralize land ownership as a source of political power but offers what appears to be fair

compensation to the owners. In view of the corruption that exists
in most Latin American countries it is possible to assume that the
cash payments for cattle and land improvements can be stretched to
cover the real value of the properties subject to agrarian reform.
The payment in bonds for the land itself and for industrial installations
could be profit; former landowners willing to become industrialists
are promised cash for the bonds if they constitute 50 percent of new
investment in an "approved industry." Thus the political objective
of the Agrarian Reform Act is to transform the traditional upper
class into an industrial upper class. The law seems to have increased
the military's popularity, at least in the northern part of the country.[46]

In the area of taxation, also essential to structural change,
the military regime announced that in view of the economic situation
it faced the government was forced to utilize existing taxes. Thus,
badly needed reforms appear to have been postponed. In fact, in outlining the government's priorities it was stated that its efforts would
be directed toward refinancing Peru's foreign debt, guaranteeing the
existing foreign exchange system, and balancing the budget.[47] To
negotiate the refinancing of the foreign debt, the military selected
Fernando Berckemeyer, one of the most distinguished members of
the traditional upper class. The choice was lauded in international
financial circles, although not among Peruvian nationalists. Berckemeyer appears to have been successful in his mission: a month after
his appointment, the International Monetary Fund approved the stand-
by credit arrangement badly needed by the new regime.[48] Finally,
the Industrial Reform Act was announced in mid-1970 but cannot yet
be properly assessed. It gives the workers a share of the profits
but its actual operation is far from clear. The reaction of management has been generally negative; the workers appear to have taken
a "wait and see" attitude.

Little seems to have changed in the treatment of peasants who
engage in disputes with landlords, regardless of the much-publicized
new Land Reform Act. Prior to the new legislation an attempt to invade
a landholding in the Sierra region was prevented by the police and
the landlord, who killed 7 peasants and injured 15 more. According
to the peasants the landlord also burned 50 of their huts. As a magazine relatively friendly to the military regime pointed out, "the government reported the event repeating the same impassive, cold, insensitive arguments used by all the previous governments."[49] This episode
gave some substance to reports of increasingly closer contacts between
certain members of the military government and elements of the
traditional upper class.[50] The appointment of followers of former
dictator Odria and persons close to Pedro Beltran to important positions
also appeared to confirm these bits of political gossip. These events
may explain the original attitude of La Prensa which, after indicating

its disagreement with the route taken by the army officers, quoted from its own editorial commenting on the 1962 coup d'etat, and went on to subscribe to most of the objectives made public by the military leaders.[51] Attempts at social co-option, however, do not seem to have been successful, although it is too soon to be definitive about them.

It is also interesting to point out that such reliable (from the point of view of the traditional upper class) sources as Odria and some of the interest groups that initially supported his regime came out in favor of the military takeover. Furthermore, the list of requests presented by the secretary general of the Confederation of Peruvian Workers two days after Belaunde Terry was replaced received no reply from the new regime. The petitioner was called in by the colonel in charge of the city of Lima a few days after he made the presentation, and was told in no uncertain terms that nothing would be done in the immediate future. It is not surprising that three days after the coup La Prensa editorialists began considering Belaunde Terry responsible for his own overthrow and three weeks later the same newspaper applauded the economic and fiscal policy announced by the minister of commerce and finance, General Angel Valdivia Morriberon.[52] Even those originally favoring the coup d'etat were prompt to point out the presence of representatives of the traditional upper class in the presidential palace; the existence of pressures that were blunting the reformist zeal of the new authorities; the close ties between individuals close to former President Prado and some members of the government; and the lack of direct reference to the problem of the distribution of wealth.[53]

Finally, the "moralizing campaign," which promised to denounce and prosecute those who had profited illegally while holding public office, bogged down in a general denunciation of legislators for taking junkets at public expense and putting relatives on the government's payroll. The findings of a committee that had investigated smuggling were not fully utilized when it became evident that some high-ranking military officers could be involved; reference to this campaign was made when opposition newspapers, radios, and magazines were closed and the action was justified under this label.[54]

THE ROLE OF THE MILITARY IN PERUVIAN SOCIETY

Once again since October 1968 the Peruvian armed forces have formally taken over their country's government. This time they have presented themselves as Peru's developmental elite, implying that no civilian group was qualified for the task. It is too early to assess their performance in the new role but it seems useful to analyze the previous roles the military elite has played or tried to play in Peruvian politics.

It is becoming apparent that although the military were happy to show their ability and fighting spirit in defeating the guerrillas, as well as to save the nation from communism and to protect the survival of their institution in the process, they are not looking forward to further demonstrations of this kind. The self-image developed by the Peruvian officer corps is that of a traditional military establishment responsible for the safety of national boundaries. It is clear that the armed forces have accepted responsibility for internal security, but they are not looking forward to intervening every time a group of individuals decides to go outside "normal channels" in their search for political power. Politically, the military would like to be recognized as the arbiter of political disputes, and to a certain extent it is justified by article 213 of the Peruvian constitution, which entrusts the armed forces with "the protection of the rights of the Republic, the enforce- ment of the Constitution and the laws and the maintenance of public order." What is perhaps more important, if this role of the military has not been recognized as something that ought to be it has certainly been recognized as something that is; and in the attitude of many as the only way it can be. Consequently only a handful of those who participate actively in politics question the principle of the military as referees of political disputes. What different people do question, at different times, is the choice the military makes. But by the same token there are always political figures (not necessarily the same ones) who benefit from the military's involvement and therefore praise it. Belaunde Terry followed this course; APRA, UNO, and the traditional upper class cheered the military in 1965-66; the left-wing faction of the Popular Action party welcomed the 1968 coup.

On the other hand, although the armed forces would like to arbitrate disputes only when there is total agreement within, it is difficult to see how they would go about keeping national controversies from taking hold inside the military. While unquestionably a communist would not be able to remain in the officer corps (control is quite strict, with at least one representative of the intelligence service in every unit), the fact is that even at the height of the military hatred for the Apristas, in the period 1930-50, there were seven attempted revolts by military units tied to Aprista elements. The replacement of General Perez Godoy on the military junta in early 1963 shows that not even the 1962 coup d'etat constituted a perfect compromise of the different political philosophies within the military. At any rate, the temporary agreement within the military which made the overthrow of the Prado regime possible broke down soon after, and the different positions reflected the cleavages existing in the country at large and particularly between the different groups of Peru's middle class. As already indicated, even deeper cleavages appeared after Belaunde Terry's overthrow.[55]

Thus the current political role of the Peruvian armed forces does not fit any of the traditional patterns outlined by most scholars. In a country with deep political cleavages the military seems to have set itself apart from (and, from their point of view, on top of) the domestic political struggle. With an overwhelming superiority in the management of violence which they do not hesitate to employ in the political arena, they have been in a position to lend their support to the changing groups trying to influence national policy. Successful political involvements by the military have had the backing of different sectors at different times, i.e. the coastal sector of the traditional upper class in 1948, most Belaunde Terry partisans in 1962, and the termocefalos (left-wing Popular Action) in 1968. This "adaptability" of the military establishment has not been overlooked by any political group. Often, in fact, those temporarily victimized by military involvement in politics are reluctant to criticize the armed forces publicly, in the hope of benefiting the next time around. Even Apristas and communists, who would be expected to have lost all hopes along these lines, have not been consistently critical of the military. The truth is that at one time or another and with varying success almost all politically active groups have "knocked at the door of the military" and asked them to replace the government of the day. Peruvians tend to distinguish between the action of certain military officers in the political realm (when they disapprove) and the military institution (which is always blameless).

Furthermore, the military officers of the more important South American military establishments tend to think of themselves as members of an organization capable of carrying out the duties traditionally assigned to the military, namely, defense of the national territory against external aggression. While they recognize the necessity of engaging in counterinsurgency when guerrilla movements threaten the established order they tend to look down upon that aspect of their responsibility, which used to be within the realm of the police or of paramilitary units. The Peruvian military officers now in power are no exception. Many were involved in the operations against the guerrillas in 1965. Some of them seem to feel that under different conditions and with better leadership and equipment the fight might have turned out differently, and they cannot fail to remember what happened to the officer corps after the Castro movement triumphed in Cuba. Therefore many of these officers believe that it is in the interest of the military establishment to effect basic social, economic, and political changes which will diminish the likelihood of future guerrilla movements or at least will ensure their isolation from the population at large. Such a policy would make it unnecessary for the military to engage in new counterinsurgency efforts and would transfer whatever popular support the reforms may produce to the armed forces themselves.

Since the officer corps of the Peruvian armed forces see themselves as regular members of the military profession, they cannot fail to be unhappy about their dependency on foreign weapons. At the same time they recognize that national sources can only appear as a by-product of a widespread industrialization program which, they feel, only they are in a position to lead. But industrial development is closely tied to basic structural changes which previous Peruvian governments have been unwilling or unable to make. Therefore, if the Peruvian military establishment is to acquire a greater degree of independence from outside sources its officers will have to lead the country on its road toward industrialization.

The political role played by the Peruvian military appears to have been tacitly legitimated, at least in political circles, and probably by default. Obviously, this role is heavily influenced by the interests of the military establishment itself, as defined and identified by its leadership. To what extent the identification of those interests is the product of inputs from the lower levels or the consequence of forcible consensus backed by strict military discipline is something quite difficult to ascertain accurately because of security regulations. In any case, it probably changes with time. Regardless of the type of decision-making process in existence within the armed forces, they continue to be the most influential political party, the most effective labor union, and probably the key power elite in Peruvian politics. Nothing within the political system offers a realistic possibility of altering that fact. In spite of doubts and contradictions, they may be on their way to becoming their country's developmental elite. If this is so, they may very well alter radically their role and, by their example, that of other Latin American military establishments.

15

INSTITUTIONAL STRATEGY
AND ECONOMIC PERFORMANCE
IN REVOLUTIONARY CUBA
Arch R. M. Ritter

> We copied with exaggerated exactitude the techniques
> of planification of a brother country.
>
> Ernesto ("Che") Guevara[1]

> Our population has increased, and yet, in some items,
> production is no higher; in fact, it's lower. . . . What
> is this bottomless pit that swallows up this country's
> human resources . . . the country's wealth, the mate-
> rial goods that we need so badly? It's nothing but in-
> efficiency, non-productivity, and low productivity. . . .
> Everybody, every branch of the economy, and practi-
> cally every work center, is guilty of the same crime.
>
> Fidel Castro[2]

The year 1971 was officially designated as the Year of Productivity in Cuba, while 1972 was labelled the Year of Socialist Emu-
lation. The function of this nomenclature has been to spotlight the
low productivity which has probably been the most serious economic
problem confronting Cuba in recent years.*

---

*"The name [Year of Socialist Emulation] points the revolutionary
way to continue the battle for increased productivity and production;
greater quality; rational and most efficient utilization of available
material and human resources; strengthening of labor discipline and
the ideological, technological and cultural education of our workers,
students and people in general."[3]

Primarily because of low productivity, the phenomenal investment effort of the latter 1960s and the large-scale mobilization of the
populace for the economic tasks of the revolution have not resulted in
the desired growth impulse. Despite gross investment rates of possibly
31.0 percent of gross material product (GMP) by 1968, and despite
the alleged elimination of unemployment, and the massive deployment
of labor in agriculture, the overall growth record for the latter half
of the 1960s is not what it could or should have been.[4] Though there
have been successes in some sectors (poultry, fishing, rice, citrus
fruits, and beef and dairy cattle) the remaining sectors of the economy
have not fared as well as they might have. Cuban estimates indicate
that in absolute terms (constant 1965 prices) GMP was lower in 1967
than 1962, and per capita GMP in 1967 was only 87.0 percent of per
capita GMP in 1962. Investment rates, however, were higher in the
latter 1960s. Despite the high priority given to export sectors under
the second growth strategy (1964-70), Cuba became even more dependent on economic assistance from the Soviet Union than under the
first growth strategy (1961-63). (See Tables 15.1 to 15.4 below for
statistical verification of these generalizations.)

A large part of the productivity problem can be explained in
terms of the organization of the economy. It is the thesis of this
chapter that inherent in Cuba's economic administration are certain
structural features which have given rise to ubiquitous micro-inefficiencies, to low productivity, and to excessively stagnant production
levels in too many sectors of the economy. These characteristics
of the administrative structure stem first from the adoption of an
institutional model insufficiently suited to Cuba's resource endowment and stated objectives.

A second important part of an explanation of the problem of
low productivity lies in the nature of the system of incentives. This
aspect of the problem has been examined in some detail elsewhere.[5]
It will be considered here only to the extent to which the structure
of incentives has been affected by the nature of the economic administration, and especially by the so-called budgetary system of finance.

The institutional organization of the Cuban economy has facilitated the achievement of other objectives, however, particularly
income redistribution and the reduction of overt unemployment (and
the harmful social consequences thereof). From the standpoint of
these two objectives, the institutional strategy of the revolutionary
regime has probably been successful.

Higher productivity and thence improved economic performance
in the decade of the 1970s requires some change in Cuba's institutional
structure. There are a number of possible directions in which institutional modification could move: toward more orthodox Russian-
style patterns, or toward greater decentralization, and ultimately to

workers' management under markets as in Yugoslavia. Though movement toward the second alternative has some distinct advantages for
Cuba, it appears that Cuba in fact has been moving since mid-1970
toward the former. Some interesting probes toward workers' management and decentralization have also occurred since 1970, however.

It must be emphasized, from the beginning, that the concentration
in this chapter on some economic problems of Cuba is in no way intended to detract from the very real accomplishments of the revolutionary regime in the areas of income redistribution, employment
creation, education, public health, and athletic endeavor.

INSTITUTIONAL STRATEGY:
ORIGINS AND NATURE

The institutional model installed in early 1961 was essentially
the Czech variant of the Russian economic administration before
the reforms of the early 1960s, adapted only slightly to Cuban circumstances.[6]

It would have been impossible to predict in January 1959 which
of the alternative institutional strategies would ultimately be adopted.
One widely held though poorly articulated strategy advocated "business
as usual" plus incorrupt constitutional government. Castro's History
Will Absolve Me statement envisaged selective nationalizations and
an active governmental role in bringing about structural change and
economic development.[7] The most comprehensive blueprint for the
new economic order, the Pazos-Boti Tésis del Movimento Revolucionario 26 de Julio, envisaged democratic "planification" and
"Cubanization and nationalization" of some firms.[8] Finally, the
Moscow-oriented Partido Socialista Popular, together with some
non-PSP Marxists including Guevara, very likely took the classical
"Soviet" economic administrative model for granted.

In retrospect, it is not surprising that a Soviet institutional
model was adopted in 1960-61. In the first place, the breaking of
relations with the United States and the realignment with Russia
and Eastern Europe meant that the Soviet model was the natural
alternative to the previous capitalist system of "colonial dependency,"
which could be construed without much difficulty as the source of
the major economic problems of Cuba. In view of the administrative
difficulties of 1960, it appeared to be advantageous to borrow from
the institutional experiences of the centrally-planned economies,
which had performed well in the decade of the 1950s.

Second, some features of the Soviet model had strong appeal
to the impatient revolutionary leaders. Centralized administrative
control of the economy gave promise of enabling large-scale mobilization of resources for the achievement of both rapid industrialization

and increased social consumption. The model seemed well suited
to Cuba in that (a) it apparently economized on the scarcest resource—
decision-making ability—which was to be concentrated at the top
of the planning hierarchy; (b) industrial and agricultural organization
had been relatively centralized before 1959; and (c) Cuba was a small
country with well-developed communications systems so that centralized physical administration of the economy could, it was thought,
be easily instituted. The Soviet institutional model also gave promise
of reducing if not eliminating unemployment and of permitting a further
redistribution of income in favor of the lower-income groups (and
against the former owners of natural and capital resources).

Third, it came to be regarded as necessary to eliminate markets
as well as private ownership of the means of production, so that direct
controls could be used to allocate resources without the "chaos" and
"anarchy" which, it was thought, were characteristic of market
allocation. The process of nationalizing and demarketing the economy
also acquired a certain momentum of its own. With the original bias
against the "anarchy" of the market system, the problems arising
from each state intervention in the economy gave rise to further
demarketizing interventions. Finally, the new economic administration came to be desired by the revolutionary leadership because it
was thought that it would eliminate the "petty bourgeois" individualism
and selfishness engendered by private ownership, the "alienation of
man from his work," the "exploitation of man by man," and the maldistribution of income in favor of the owners of natural and capital
resources.

The institutional strategy of the Cuban revolution thus became
to eradicate private ownership of the means of production and to
demarketize the economic administration by setting up a system of
comprehensive and direct central management. By the end of 1961,
roughly 85 percent of industrial production, 35 percent of farm lands,
and most of the transportation, communication, and construction
sectors had been nationalized. The state agricultural sector included
70 percent of farm land after the Second Agrarian Reform in 1963.
Following the nationalizations of the "Revolutionary Offensive" in
1968, the state sector encompassed 100 percent of industry, the
service sector, and of course utilities and mineral extraction. The
current policy toward the small private farmers is gradual uncoercive
elimination through voluntary incorporation into cooperatives, material
incentives to the small farmers to join the state sector, and education
and relocation of the children of the small farmers so that they will
have neither the interest nor the appropriate skills for taking over
the family farm when the parents die.

The "institutional strategy" was but one component part of the
overall Cuban "developmental strategy" or "Grand Design" for

construction of the good society. A second important component was
the "growth strategy": import substituting, 'balanced' industrialization
of "big push" dimensions (aborted in 1963), and the subsequent heroic
sugar-centered, export-oriented strategy from 1964 to 1970. The
third component substrategy in the Grand Design was human resource
mobilization by moral exhortation—appeals to conciencia, heroic
guerrilla self-sacrifice, altruism, and patriotism—for the task of
economic development. The "New Man," while he was the major
objective of the revolution, was also the major means to the ultimate
communist society. Only by hard selfless work and acceptance of
consumer austerity could investment be increased sufficiently to make
possible production of the 10 million tons of sugar by 1970. And
only with intensive exhortative appeals and the contrivance of a climate
of crisis could the self-interestedness and lethargy of the economic
bureaucracy be sufficiently shaken to permit nonroutine, prodevelopmental decision making.

THE ECONOMIC ADMINISTRATION:
STRUCTURE AND PROBLEMS

While there have been many minor changes in the economic
administration since it was installed in 1961 and activated in 1962,
its essence and its functioning have changed very little since then.
In this section, a brief outline of the institutional structure of the Cuban
economy is presented, followed by an examination of some of the
major problems involved in its operation.[9]
The economic administration of Cuba has been very highly
centralized, formally, particularly after the period of mild experimentation and debate from about 1962 to 1966. At the apex of the
organizational pyramid has been the revolutionary leadership, particularly Premier Castro (through the Economic Committee of the
Communist Party of Cuba). Under this small group, has been the
Junta Central de Planificación (Juceplan), the function of which is
to formulate and implement short- and long-term plans in accordance
with the politico-economic directives articulated by the leadership.[10]
The second tier of the planning hierarchy consists of the ministries
which are composed of third-tier consolidated enterprises or "trusts"
under which are fourth-tier productive enterprises. Cutting across
these vertical relationships, however, are geographically oriented
administrative bodies such as the National Physical Planning Institute,
some regional planning organizations, and municipal planning bodies
(initially Juntas de Cooperacion, Execucion y Inspeccion, later Poder
Local, designed to coordinate plans and initiate projects at the local
level). Cutting into and across the vertical planning hierarchy are

the party and the military bureaucracies, both of which have been of great and increasing significance in management and plan-implementation since the mid-1960s. One additional and rather unique feature of Cuban economic organization is the existence of vertically integrated "combines" which unite a number of cultivation and production stages, storage, distribution, and perhaps export (e.g., Cuban tobacco and poultry combines). Finally, in the latter years of the 1960s a myriad of "Special Plans" (sometimes labelled "Fidel Plans") were set up to deal with specific problems as they emerged. These plans, operating outside the jurisdiction of the Central Plan, have complicated the general process of planning in that the administrators of, and the priority allocation of resources to, these programs are outside Juceplan. The Special Plans do add a degree of flexibility to the planning process, however.

The essential feature of the new economic administration is the substitution for anonymous horizontal information transmission through the price mechanism by bureaucratized flows of information and directives through the planning hierarchy. In the new system coordination of the activities of productive enterprises was to be achieved ultimately by centralized economic control. The major method for the coordination and subordination of all economic activities to the key plan objectives was physical planning by "material balances."[11] Originally in 1962 this method was used to balance the total supplies of and uses for some 640 intermediate and final (generic) products—100 items by Juceplan and another 550 by the ministries—accounting for 95 percent of the total products produced and consumed.[12] The physical outputs and inputs for all productive enterprises were then allocated by the relevant ministries and consolidated enterprises. This was done in physical terms, with financial considerations playing a passive, enabling role.

Control over the operations of individual enterprises was exerted in large part through the so-called budgetary system of finance. In this system, the financial accounts of all productive enterprises are consolidated into one single national set of accounts.[13] All the funds for payment of productive inputs including capital equipment come from central funds while all revenues go to the state. The allocation of funds to enterprises is based not on their productivity or profitability but on the directives emanating from the planning authority. There has been little if any connection between the income or revenues of an enterprise and its expenditures or costs. Firms running budget deficits (or surpluses) have these cancelled (or absorbed) into the overall budget. Indeed, enterprises are unlikely even to be aware of what their costs and revenues are because no payments are made for the use of natural or capital resources. Moreover, it appears that from about 1968 to 1970 many productive enterprises ceased keeping financial records so that little or no financial control on the actions of individual firms existed. Under this system enterprises have lacked financial autonomy and responsibility.

There was some experimentation with alternate financial systems from 1963 to 1965, especially in agriculture. The uniquely Cuban type of "self-financing" system gave enterprises greater authority and responsibility in that a direct connection between a firm's revenues and costs was established, the objective of the enterprise becoming "profit" maximization (instead of budget maximization). Enterprises were also granted some authority to supplement centrally planned and financed investments with lesser investments of their own. This system seems to have been relatively short-lived, however, with "budgetary finance" becoming predominant after 1965. Indeed, one author has argued that as practiced in Cuba the system of self-management turned out to be a "disguised budgetary finance system," with little substantive difference from the latter.[14]

There are a number of distinctly advantageous features of this new administrative system—strengths of the system correctly perceived by the revolutionary leadership in 1960-61.

The chief strength of this type of command administration is macro-flexibility—the capability to rapidly mobilize and shift natural, capital, and human resources on a large scale for purposes of economic development. The ability of such a system to quickly divert resources from the importation and (or) production of luxury commodities to productive investment, for example, is clearly advantageous to economic growth.

The new economic administration has also been quite successful in improving income distribution and reducing unemployment, as discussed in the next section.

Unfortunately, there have been serious transitional difficulties in installing the new economic administration. Moreover the new economic administration as it has operated in Cuba seems to have had certain inherent weaknesses. Most serious of these in Cuba's case have been (1) the lack of economically rational prices to guide resource allocation; (2) burocratismo; (3) excessive politicization of the economic administration; (4) insufficient negative feedback to the higher echelons of the planning hierarchy; (5) the "campaign" technique of blueprint implementation; and (6) the consequences of the perennial disequilibrium between aggregate income generated and the value of commodities and services produced.

Transitional Difficulties

The transitional costs of rapidly reorganizing the structure of the economy from a market-oriented to a centrally planned system

along the lines of the Russian model were severe. In general, demarketization was imposed on the economy before the planning bureaucracy had the ability to effectively replace the markets destroyed.
An early example of this was the abolition of the "old market" in
Havana before the ministry of internal commerce had even begun to
work on a new system to replace it.[15] As Guevara put it:

> The Ministry of Internal Commerce had had the grave
> defect of being excessively optimistic regarding its
> capabilities. To take this distribution organization
> already functioning, changing and distorting it entirely,
> and sometimes to create serious disturbances. [sic][16]

A second example of premature demarketization was the establishment of a state monopoly, el Acopio, for the collection and purchase of agricultural crops from farmers and for the wholesaling
of foodstuffs to the state and private retail networks. This monop-
sonistic monopoly was designed to "plan all the activity of supply"
and to "substitute for the thousands of private businesses which acted
independently guided only by their personal interests . . . in an anarchic way."[17] Having destroyed a food collection and distribution
network which had evolved over many decades, it was found that there
were not a sufficient number of qualified personnel to run the Acopio
bureaucracy and to perform the tasks previously performed spontaneously (if imperfectly) under the market mechanism.

> For all of this, a small group of well-intentioned com-
> rades was relied upon; but none of them were experi-
> enced and almost all of them lacked the political and
> economic knowledge necessary to organize the supply
> apparatus in the form demanded by the mercantile re-
> lations which were being developed in the new society.[18]

Perhaps the most serious result of the establishment of the
Acopio monopoly was the replacement of pricing through markets
by decree pricing. How prices were set in 1961-63 is not clear.
There were some cases in these years, however, of serious production distortions wrought by poor pricing policies. One source
of such distortions was the setting of commodity prices without consideration of the quality of the commodities concerned. In Pinar del
Rio, the major tobacco producing area, for example, a "mistaken
egalitarian concept" led to the elimination of price differentials based
on the quality of the tobacco produced.[19] With this reduction in the
incentive to produce fine tobacco, "quality tended to adjust to the
minimum acceptable level." This error apparently was rectified

by 1964. Another source of production distortion was the tendency, until October 1963, of raising the prices of final foodstuffs under pressure from the Asociacíon Nacional de Agricultores Pequeños, ANAP, (National Association of Small Farmers) while holding the prices of crops requiring further industrial processing constant (such as corn, coffee, and cocoa) under pressure from the Ministerio de Industrias (Min Ind). The subsequent reduction of small farmers' production of the fixed-price crops and expansion of higher-priced crops is hardly surprising.[20] A third source of such distortion was the irrational constellation of prices, for some crop prices were set at levels permitting very high profits, which naturally encouraged their production, while other products (pineapple and malanga) were seriously underpriced.[21] Finally, no attempt was made to structure prices according to the seasonality of the harvest of many crops. These types of pricing problems were undoubtedly pervasive in agriculture and were counterproductive, though any quantitative judgment on their impact on production is impossible.

More serious, perhaps, than the inefficiency of the state agricultural purchasing monopoly was the inadequacy of the INRA and ANAP organizations in the distribution of production inputs to the small and medium-size private farmers. (The private sector continued to provide over 50 percent of all agricultural crops—excepting only beef, sugarcane, cotton, rice and chickens and eggs in 1963.)[22] The middle-size farmers were largely ignored until their nationalization in 1963. The small farmers, though not officially ignored, experienced great difficulty in obtaining production inputs. In fact, no organism existed at least until late 1963 for the planning and distribution of inputs to the small farmers, "because the Department of Supplies of ANAP did not plan, but simply calculated the [input] needs and presented them to the corresponding department of INRA."[23] Concerning the coffee farmers of the mountainous areas one writer lamented the lack of production inputs. "Without cement and nails for the construction and reparation of dryers and shelters, there is no coffee; each spring the roads in the mountains must be rebuilt; for transportation there must be replacement parts and maintenance facilities."[24] The maladministration of inputs of all kinds to the small tobacco farmers received repeated emphasis. Undoubtedly this problem affected almost the whole of the small-farm sector. This was to be expected given the difficulties of reconstructing a complete distribution system for farm inputs by means of a state bureaucracy rather than using a more decentralized marketized arrangement.

A more recent example of premature demarketization was the nationalization of some 56,000 small servicing, repairing, retailing, and handicraft private businesses in the heat of the revolutionary offensive (March 1968).[25] The stated objectives of this move were to completely eradicate the individualism and selfishness engendered by private ownership, to eliminate alienation and exploitation, to destroy the

consumption privileges obtained by the private operators, and to provide improved and more sanitary services. Unfortunately the administration was unable to completely replace the operations it eliminated,
especially the informal food collection and distribution networks in
urban areas. The result of this was reduced commodity production and
supply, worsened material levels of living, longer queues for many
products, and a larger disequilibrium between the total income and
total peso value of goods and services per unit of time.

Examples of this sort could be multiplied in other areas of
industry, internal commerce, and agriculture. The essential problem
was the attempt to move too rapidly to a Russian-style centralized
planning apparatus which required large numbers of skilled personnel
(accountants, satisticians, and capable managers) which were in
scarcest supply in Cuba at the time.

The Lack of a Rational Configuration of Prices

Under the budgetary system of finance the prices of many commodities are ostensibly based on "costs" of production, but the cost
elements themselves are of course determined by input prices set by
the planners. Thus all prices except for internationally traded commodity prices and black market prices are determined ultimately by
the planning apparatus with little regard for market forces. The
lack of economic rationality in the structure of prices has very
likely been increasing over time because such price structures are
inherently rigid, due to the complexity of simultaneously changing
the whole interrelated matrix of prices and physical allocations, and
it has been explicit policy to hold such prices fixed for long periods.[26]
Furthermore, interest and rental payments (not to mention profits)
do not exist, so that there is little likelihood that prices reflect true
"scarcity values" or opportunity costs.

Bureaucratization

Accompanying the demarketization of Cuban economic organization was the spread of burocratismo which manifested itself
in forms well known to students of Downs or Parkinson.[27] In the
economic administration, middle- and lower-level officials appear
to have behaved less for the benefit of the whole nation than in their
own self-interest, following "conserving strategies" to maximize
the security of their current levels of power, income, and prestige.
Guevara attributed this phenomenon to "lack of inner motivation"
rooted in "lack of revolutionary consciencia" as well as to lack of

organization and "knowledge".[28] The overall result of this was that
bureaucracies took on lives and purposes of their own and lost sight
of their original purposes. "Red tape," "passing the buck," "empire
building," and reunionismo* gave rise to general inertia of the bu-
reaus. An editorial in Granma Weekly Review described it as follows:

> Bureaucratism deforms methods of revolutionary labor,
> converting collective decision-making into a means
> with which to avoid individual responsibility. . . . The
> bureaucrat drowns himself among little plans, mem-
> orandums . . . [and] orientations . . . substituting dis-
> cussion for action. . . . He forgets the problem which
> affects the people and concentrates his attention upon
> papers, plans, discussions, and the proper channels
> which supposedly exist to resolve the problem.[30]

Another manifestation of bureaucratism was the inflation of the
number of bureaucrats throughout the public service and planning
apparatus. So serious did this megalocephalia of the bureaucracy
become that in 1964 "Commissions for the Battle Against Bureaucracy" were established to reduce the number of employees in the
central organizations, consolidated enterprises, and work centers.
By March 1966 some 5,000 work centers and 80 central organizations
had been "rationalized" with "savings" of some 29,483 employees.[31]
To prevent bureaucratic "reinflation" the commissions were granted
the function of authorizing the hiring of new employees by all state
establishments. Apparently these measures did not do the job. On
February 29, 1967, Premier Castro declared, "Burocratismo [is] in
full offensive, in full counterattack: the Commissions for the Battle
against Bureaucracy [have themselves become] bureaucratized."[32]
Bureaucratism came to be seen as a phenomenon which "causes us
much more damage than imperialism itself."[33] Increased efforts
have been made in recent years to cut out bureaucratic deadwood and
to divert school dropouts to "productive work," mainly in agriculture.
Perhaps the "ultimate solution" to the problem of "bureaucratic
inflation" was the abolition of financial accountancy in many sectors
of the economy in 1968 and the reassignment of such bureaucrats
to physical production positions.

---

*"Meetingism:" the tendency to refer decisions to endless series
of special meetings until the problem is shelved, works itself out,
or forces acceptance of "any solution, no matter how unsuitable."[29]

With the centralization of much of the decision-making functions to the planning apparatus, the managers of firms became in effect foremen or lower-level bureaucrats. Their more important managerial functions (pricing, allocating inputs, distributing outputs, and undertaking investment) were absorbed by the planning authorities. The main "success indicators" throughout the economy were no longer profits but quantitative output targets or the size of the ministerial or enterprise budgets, with little emphasis upon costs. Because managers have not had to be overly concerned about the saleability or the ultimate usefulness of their products (due to excessive purchasing power and general commodity shortages as well as the nature of the "success indicators"), there has been great concern with quantity, at the expense of quality. Deterioration of product quality has been a very serious problem from 1961 to the present.[34]

There has also been a tendency for managers to hoard raw materials, equipment, and personnel despite greater needs for the same inputs in other sectors of the economy.[35] By overordering and holding productive inputs, managers attempt to reduce the risks of plan underfulfillment in an environment of unsteady and uncertain input flows and in the absence of costs for holding inventories.

Politicization of the Administration

The recruitment and promotion of personnel in the economic administration more on the basis of political reliability than of competence has been a problem in that such selection lowers the caliber of the administration. The involuntary as well as voluntary replacement of first the Batistianos from the civil service and then many of the administrators and executive employees of the private businesses is understandable, given the evolving political nature of the regime. Clearly, politically acceptable but technically unqualified military personnel, revolutionary students, or workers from the ranks could not be expected to administer the farms or factories of which they had acquired control as well as did the careerist professional managers they replaced.

What was surprising was the tendency, evident in 1965, for the political party to merge with the governmental administration.[36] This contrasted sharply with previous custom and with current East European practice, in which the party and administrative bureaucracies are kept separate. This tendency—reversed by 1970[37]—undoubtedly intensified the preference within the system for political loyalty over competence as the main criterion for selection of administrators. While a politicized administration is advantageous in that it is more susceptible to mobilization "campaigns" it is disadvantageous in that its capacity to scale-down ill-advised "campaigns" is

lowered, and in that its general capability is impaired vis-à-vis a
professionally oriented administration.[38]

The effectiveness of the military officer corps which was relied
upon heavily in 1969-70 for managerial services in the economy is
not known.

Insufficiency of Negative Feedback

The absence of media through which negative feedback or information flows could rise up the planning hierarchy to appropriate
decision makers has also impeded efficient economic performance.

In the first place, the communications media, especially from
1968 to July 1970, have been excessively dedicated to exhortation
from above. While in Russia muckraking economic journalism
scrutinizes middle-level managerial behavior, the Cuban press, particularly since the demise of such journals as Cuba Socialista from
1965 to 1967, has not performed this function. Such a function is of
very great importance if the behavior of middle-level managers
concerning the screening and distorting of information flowing upward
and the selective execution of directives from above is to be minimized.

Second, there has been a greater tendency for some of the mass
organizations, notably ANAP and the Centrál de Trabajadores de Cuba
(CTC), until November 1970, to serve as "arms of the state" and to
hand down directives from above than to articulate the felt needs of
the small farmers and workers. This tendency, though now perhaps
partly rectified in the unions, prevented valuable information and
criticism from percolating upward.

Third, the party does not seem to have fulfilled its function
of passing information and criticism upward as well as passing
directives and exhortation downward. This is not surprising, because
promotion in the party, and thus power, status, and consumption
perquisites have largely been determined by the evaluation of party
superiors. Party members are under strong incentive to please and
impress their superiors and are thus understandably loath to criticize
their directives. This phenomenon undoubtedly operates at very high
levels as well. Both Premier Castro and his ministers have been
less likely to have their current proposals subjected to criticism
from below in both the party and planning bureaucracies, for the
critic would risk demotion or worse. Thus Premier Castro has
tended to be surrounded by "yes men" if not sycophants.

Premier Castro tried to short-circuit the schlerotic information
channels in the economic administration by communicating directly
with the workers and listening to their views and criticisms. This
direct communication technique has served to check the inefficiencies
in flows of information up the hierarchies.[39]

A by-product of Castro's continuous leapfrogging of bureaucratic channels, however, has been serious disruption of economic
planning and organization. By continuously creating "Special Plans"
and by contravening plans at the micro-level, the rational implementation of plans has sometimes been obstructed.

The Campaign Technique of Plan Implementation

The nature of Cuba's economic administration perhaps has
required that all-out political "campaigns" be waged to achieve
various targets or objectives.[40] Because realistic incentive structures were not designed to elicit prodevelopmental action from
either managers or workers, it has been necessary to concentrate
regional attention on a particular target (such as the 10 million tons,
the Havana greenbelt project, bureaucracy, or absenteeism), to
contrive crisis (or to use the semantics of crisis), and to set over-
ambitious goals. Political or moral appeals have been necessary
to overcome the lethargy and the inertia of the planning and party
bureaucracies. Such campaigns may be necessary also to mobilize
additional concern and effort from a labor force which has grown
increasingly hardened to saturation advertising for previous campaigns and which has not been confronted with a realistic incentive
structure.

The main danger of reliance upon contrived crisis and campaign
techniques of plan implementation is that because national attention
can be fixed fully upon not many more than one target at any one time,
no sooner will one bottleneck sector or problem have received attention than other sectors may have fallen further behind.

One additional purpose of plan implementation via all-out
campaigns is of course to expose other bottlenecks in the economy
and thus to facilitate, stimulate, and indeed necessitate the making
of the appropriate decision by the planning bureaucrats. Again,
however, there is the persistent danger that the "planners' tensions"
created through the campaign technique become lethal, for if the
targets are patently unrealistic and if the rigidities in the system
seriously obstruct creative response, the planner, manager, or worker
may give up any serious attempt to meet the target.

The essential logic of the campaign technique as well as its
dangers can be observed during the drive for the 10 million tons.
From 1964 to 1967, the linkages to all activities associated with the
sugar sector were carefully spelled out. Expected bottlenecks and
emerging problems elicited action as well as verbal responses from
the economic administration. But after 1968, when the campaign for
the 10 million tons became the paramount preoccupation, the sacrifices

imposed on other sectors increased seriously, to overcome bottle-necks in the sugar sector. The systematic creation of imbalances to provide clear signals and strong incentives to the economic admin-istrators seems by mid-1969 to have been replaced by a sucro-maniacal obsession.

The Inflationary Disequilibrium

Under the centralized "budgetary system of finance," as it has operated in Cuba, there seems to be a tendency for too many productive enterprises to incur costs greater than the value of the output produced. The aggregate effect is a surplus of money incomes generated over the value of consumer and investment goods and services produced. In Cuba, this inflationary disequilibrium has been severe since 1961. Price increases do not occur, for prices have been fixed for social welfare reasons and the inflation is suppressed through rationing and queuing. Black market prices, however, have risen to very high levels.

Suppressed inflation—or too much money chasing too few rationed goods—has had an adverse impact on labor mobilization. First, Cuban workers have absented themselves from their work in order to queue up for rationed goods and services. Many women, for instance, permanently abandoned their jobs in 1969 to 1970 in part because of the large amount of time they had to spend queuing for their families' food supplies and other rationed products.[41] Second, many workers have been able to earn enough money to buy the month's rations with perhaps three weeks' work, so that there is little material inducement to work all month long.

The result of this has been high absenteeism and low on-the-job productivity. For example, during May, June, and July, 1969, "work attendance did not go above 65 percent" for the permanent agricultural workers in the province of Camaguay. Also, from Novem-ber 30, 1968, to November 30, 1969, "under-utilization" of the work day reached a level of 19.3 percent for Cuban industries.[42] Indeed, absenteeism has been so serious that penal sanctions against it were promulgated in March 1971. An example of the fall in labor productivity was the 30.8% decline in average tonnage handled by each port worker from 1967 to 1969.[43]

One final weakness of such highly centralized large-scale decision making is that the scope for possible economic error is greatly magnified. Moreover, the system risks susceptibility to unrealistic idées fixes on the part of the decision makers—witness Khruschev's virgin-lands policy, the Chinese "Great Leap Forward", the 10 million tons, and the Havana greenbelt coffee program (the

latter being the partly ill-fated program for the planting of huge
areas around Havana in coffee).

THE ECONOMIC ADMINISTRATION AND
ECONOMIC PERFORMANCE

Revolutionary Cuba has pursued a variety of economic developmental objectives since 1959. The most important of these have been
economic growth, income redistribution, reduced unemployment,
and reduced external "dependence." The emphasis that has been
placed on different objectives has changed since 1959. At first, the
emphasis was on income redistribution and the reduction of unemployment. Following this, economic growth became the overriding
objective (from 1963 to 1970). The reduction of external dependence
has been virtually abandoned as an objective in recent years.

The institutional strategy requires an evaluation from the
standpoint of each of the four criteria mentioned above, as well as of
other primarily political or sociological objectives such as democratization, the creation of the "New Man" or the reduction of "alienation." This section, however, focusses primarily on the impact of
the new administrative system on economic growth—the primordial
objective for most of the revolutionary period. The effects of the
new system on income redistribution, unemployment, and external
dependence are also discussed, though with greater brevity. In this
section, however, primarily political and sociological criteria are
not used to evaluate the administrative system.

Economic Growth

It is most difficult to isolate and disentangle the effects of the
new economic administration on economic growth from the effects
of other factors such as the embargo, the emigration, and poor
plan implementation.

The American embargo on trade with Cuba caused severe
economic disruption for Cuba because the machinery used in industry,
agriculture, and transportation was largely American in origin, requiring replacement parts and in some cases raw materials or components of American (and nonmetric) specifications. The economic
costs of the embargo have been high though accurate measurement
of these is impossible. The real consumption of the capital stock
must have been large due to lack of replacement parts; the inappro-
priateness of some imported raw materials or semifinished imports

designed to Soviet and metric system specifications; some cannibal-
ization of machinery and equipment; and inadequacies in the maintenance of machinery.

The large-scale net emigration, totalling at least 568,000 persons by January 1, 1971, exacerbated the existing shortage of high
and middle management and technical personnel.[44] While Cuba had
been short of managerial and technical personnel before 1959, even
more such cadres were required to man the new planning apparatus.
The improvisation of new managerial staffs for the Juceplan, the
ministries, the consolidated enterprises, and the work centers undoubtedly made the administrative restructuring unnecessarily
clumsy.[45]

The mode of implementation of the two growth strategies also
had a negative impact on economic performance. The first import-
substituting industrialization strategy was in its broad outline fairly
sound. As the detail of the plan was worked out and implemented,
however, disastrous results occurred because sugar was in fact
neglected; the new industries were not intelligently selected; and
administrative, technical, foreign exchange, and savings constraints
were insufficiently understood. The second, sugar-centered, export-
oriented strategy was probably an optimal growth strategy, for 1964
to 1970. Extremist implementation of the strategy in 1968-70, however, purchased relative success in sugar production at the expense
of most other sectors of the economy.

The transitional difficulties of installing the new economic
system, together with weaknesses inherent in the new system in
general, reduced productivity, thereby impairing production and
growth. The previous section outlined the ways in which the new
system—its installation and operation—affected productivity. Data
scarcity, however, prevents a close analysis of how the various
weaknesses actually affected production in an accurate quantitative
as opposed to qualitative sense.

Cuban economic performance in terms of growth was good
in 1959 and 1960 because the effects of the institutional restructuring
as well as the embargo and emigration did not occur until 1961.
Increases in gross output of from 5 to 10 percent in 1959 and 1960
were made possible by income redistributive reforms which "widened
the market" especially for Cuban-produced nonluxury commodities;
the existence of some excess capacity in industry and agriculture;
and some disinvestment in the form of reductions of raw material
and goods-in-process inventories and of foreign exchange reserves.[46]
Growth in agricultural production in these years before the dis-
ruptions of the embargo and the imposition of central planning was
remarkable. (See Table 15.1.)

The growth performance of the Cuban economy from 1961 to
1963 was unsatisfactory, though public health and education were
expanded in these years. Agricultural production fell disastrously
in this period (roughly 30 percent, see Table 15.1). Real gross
material product in absolute and per capita terms fell sharply from
1961 to 1963 as well. (See Table 15.2.) A balance of trade crisis
also occurred, because exports fell while imports continued to rise.
The trade deficit with Russia (297 million pesos in 1963 or 41 pesos
per capita) can be considered as pure financial assistance because it
is not likely that Cuba will be able to repay this, if required to do
so, for perhaps a decade (see Table 15.3).

The aggregate growth record under the second, sugar-centered,
export-oriented growth strategy appears to have improved in 1964
and 1965 but worsened seriously in 1966 and 1967, the last years
for which data are available (see Table 15.2). Per cápita real gross
material product fell by 13 percent from 1962 to 1967. Russian
economic assistance to Cuba decreased in 1964 and 1965 but then
increased in 1966 and 1967 (see Table 15.3). Gross investment
increased greatly from 1962 to 1967, from about 18 percent to 27
percent of gross material product. Furthermore, the proportion
of investment devoted to "directly productive" activities (as opposed
to "nonproductive" sectors, that is, education, public health, etc.)
increased from 51.5 percent to over 81.1 percent from 1961 to 1966
(see Table 15.4).

In the absence of aggregate and detailed data after 1967 and
1968, accurate judgments on performance are difficult to make.
While some sectors, notably fisheries, rice cultivation, agriculture,
dairy farming, nickel extraction, and fertilizer production have proceeded very well, other sectors such as light industry, food processing, and construction have shown little dynamism. The campaign for the 10 million tons did serious damage to nonsugar sectors
of the economy, since labor, investable resources, production inputs,
transport capacity, and national attention were diverted to sugar
at the expense of other sectors.[47] It is not clear whether the very
large sugar harvest of 1970 (8.5 million tons) overwhelmed the losses
in other sectors of the economy in that year. It is clear that Russian
financial assistance in 1968 and 1969 surpassed the aid provided in
any previous year, reaching approximately 50 pesos per capita in
1969. Russian aid fell sharply in 1970, however, owing to the large
volume of sugar exports to Russia (See Table 15.3).

It is important to emphasize here that the lack of greater
economic success is not due to any lack of public effort or political
commitment to development. Indeed, as measured by marginal savings
rates, investment rates, consumption austerity, and voluntary hours
worked, the Cuban developmental effort has been heroic and almost

TABLE 15.1

Cuban Total Agricultural and Food Production Indexes, 1957-69, and
Sugar Production, 1957-70

	1957	1958	1959	1960	1961	1962	1963	1964	1965	1966	1967	1968	1969	1970
Total agricultural production	108	107	112	114	122	100	86	93	112	94	116	106	99	*
Total food production	108	108	112	113	122	98	85	93	114	93	116	107	99	*
Per capita agricultural production	101	98	101	101	106	85	72	75	89	72	88	79	73	*
Per capita food production	101	99	101	100	106	83	71	75	90	72	88	80	73	*
Sugar production (millions of metric tons)	5.7	5.8	5.9	5.9	6.8	4.8	3.8	4.4	6.1	4.5	6.1	5.1	4.3	8.5

*Not available.
Note: 1952-56 = 100.

Source: UN Food and Agricultural Organization (FAO), Production Yearbook 1969, Vol. 23. UN FAO, The State of Food and Agriculture (Rome, 1970).

TABLE 15.2

Selected Cuban Aggregate Economic Indicators, 1962-68

	1962	1963	1964	1965	1966	1967	1968
Aggregates (millions of pesos):							
Gross material product (Producto bruto)	3,698.2	3,736.7	4,074.6	4,136.5	3,985.5	3,612.5	4,000
Net Material Product (Ingreso nacional) GMP less depreciation	3,509.5	3,544.2	3,856.6	3,888.2	3,727.4	a	a
Gross investment (state sector)	607.6	716.8	794.9	827.1	909.8	979.0	1,240
Net investment (state sector)	418.9	524.3	576.9	578.8	651.7	a	a
Aid (trade deficit with Russia)	190.9	296.9	135.0	106.0	247.4	214.6	376.8
Consumption Total	2,908.2	3,049.5	3,269.0	3,361.6	3,245.9	a	a
Personal	2,491.1	2,653.0	2,780.5	2,887.3	2,772.3	a	a
Per capita (pesos):							
Gross material product	523.2	516.4	548.1	542.1	511.1	455.1	a
Aid (trade deficit with Russia)	27.0	41.0	18.2	13.9	31.7	27.0	46.0
Personal consumption	352.0	367.0	374.0	378.0	355.0	a	a
Indexes:							
Gross material product	100.0	101.0	110.2	111.9	107.8	97.7	a
Net investment (state sector)	100.0	125.1	137.7	138.1	155.5	161.3	a
Personal consumption per capita	100.0	104.3	106.3	107.3	100.9	a	a
Gross material product per capita	100.0	98.7	104.8	103.6	97.7	87.0	a

a = Not available.
b = Projections.
Note: All numbers except index numbers are in pesos; all pesos are in terms of constant 1965 prices.

Sources: Juceplan, Boletin Estadístico, 1968; and Fidel Castro, Speech of March 13, 1968, Granma Weekly Review, March 15, 1968.

TABLE 15.3

Cuban International and Bilateral Russian Trade, 1959-69

	1959	1960	1961	1962	1963	1964	1965	1966	1967	1968	1969	1970
Exports:												
Total	637.7	618.2	624.7	520.7	543.8	713.8	685.0	592.5	710.8	649.9		
To Russia	12.9	103.5	300.9	220.5	164.0	274.9	322.4	273.8	367.3	289.6		
Imports:												
Total	673.2	579.9	638.7	759.3	867.3	1018.8	866.2	925.5	997.8	1094.8		
From Russia	0.0	80.2	262.6	411.4	460.9	409.9	428.4	521.2	581.9	666.4		
Balance of Trade:												
Total	-35.5	38.3	-14.0	-238.6	-323.5	-305.0	-180.7	-333.0	-287.0	-444.9		
Bilateral with Russia[a]	12.9	23.3	38.3	-190.9	-296.9	-135.0	-106.0	-247.4	-214.6	-376.8	-418. [b]	
Bilateral with Russia[c]	n.a.	32.7	35.6	-131.5	-232.9	-77.2	-32.9	89.1	-188.1	-343.9	-388.4	-126.5
Trade deficit per capita (pesos)[a]	-	-	-	-27.0	-41.0	-18.2	-13.9	-31.7	-27.0	-46.0	-50.9[b]	
Trade deficit per capita (pesos)[c]	-	-	-	-18.6	-32.2	-10.4	-4.2	-24.2	-23.7	-42.0	-47.3	-15.4

[a]Russian figures.
[b]Estimated.
[c]Cuban figures.

Note: All figures are in pesos. 1 peso = U.S. $1 at pre-U.S. $ devaluation official exchange rates.

Sources: Juceplan, Boletin Estadístico, 1966, pp. 124-125, for 1961 to 1966; and Mincex, Comercio Exterior, Vol. II, No. 2, April-June 1964, for 1959-60. U.S.S.R., Foreign Trade (annual), 1961 to 1970, for Russian figures on "bilateral with Russia"

TABLE 15.4

Cuban Planned and Actual Investment by Sector and in Aggregate, 1961-68

	1961	1962		1963		1964		1965	1966	1967	1968
	Actual	Plan	Actual	Plan	Actual	Plan	Actual	Actual	Actual	Actual	Projected
Productive sectors:	51.5%	66.7%	55.9%	78.6%	70.4%	67.0%	79.1%	81.9%	81.1%		
Agriculture	16.8	—	23.9	24.6	25.6	22.0	30.5	40.4	40.3		
Industry	15.7	—	18.7	32.6	24.3	26.0	29.1	18.1	16.7		
Communications	3.5	—	2.8	1.5	1.2	2.0	1.4	0.9	1.0		
Transportation	11.2	—	8.4	6.5	8.4	8.0	7.6	10.8	13.3		
Commerce	1.2	—	2.4	4.3	3.5	4.0	3.5	4.6	3.2		
Construction	3.1	—	3.7	5.3	5.3	3.0	4.6	3.8	2.2		
Other	—	—	—	1.8	2.1	2.0	2.4	3.2	4.3		
"Nonproductive" sectors	48.5%	33.3%	44.1%	21.4%	29.6%	33.0%	20.9%	18.1%	18.9%		
Total investment (millions of pesos)	489.0	—	534.0	738.4	581.0	—	794.9	827.1	909.8	979.0	1,240.0
Investment as % of gross material product	17.9%	27.0%	17.8%	—	17.9%	17.0	19.5%	20.0%	22.8%	27.1%	31.0%

Sources: UN Economic Commission for Latin America, Economic Survey of Latin America, 1963, p. 288 (for first, third, and fifth columns). R. Bóti, "El Plan de Desarollo Económico de 1962", Cuba Socialista, No. 4, December (for second column). R. Bóti, "Plan para 1963", Cuba Socialista, No. 20, April 1963 (for fourth column). Juceplan, Boletin Estadístico, 1962, 1966 (for seventh, eighth, and ninth columns). A. Martinez, "El Plan de la Economía nacional para 1964", Cuba Socialista (for sixth column). Fidel Castro, "Speech of March 13, 1968", Granma Weekly Review, March 15, 1968, pp. 5-6 (for tenth and eleventh columns).

250

without parallel. It is unfortunate that, due in part to ubiquitous mal-organization and micro-efficiency, productivity and growth have not been higher. However, due to long investment gestation periods in public health, education, administration, and in some agricultural and industrial projects, it is to be hoped that the massive investment effort will bear greater fruit in coming years.

Income Distribution

The institutional strategy has been quite successful from the standpoint of achieving a more equitable distribution of income. Un-fortunately, statistical verification of this is impossible because data on income distribution in the 1950s and the later 1960s appear to be nonexistent. Certain institutional changes, however, had the effect of drastically reducing the incomes of the higher-income groups and increasing the real incomes of lower-income groups.

In the first place a series of reforms were implemented in 1959-60 that considerably redistributed income in favor of lower-income groups. Among these reforms were reduction of rural electricity rates and telephone charges; a 30 to 50 percent reduction in urban rents; elimination of rents for tenant farmers under the first agrarian reform; and raising of the minimum salary for governmental employees. In the first four months of 1959 most labor contracts were renegotiated, thereby increasing wages and salaries by 15 to 25 percent. As a result of the wage increases and redistributional reforms, the share of wages and salaries in the national income rose from approximately 65 percent to 78 percent while the money supply rose by 30 percent from June-July 1958 to the same months in 1960. Surprisingly perhaps, this expansion of monetary demand did not lead immediately to price inflation, but instead elicited increases in real output. Because the gainers from the redistribution were largely the lower-income groups (who generally consumed more unsophisticated, domestically produced commodities than did the upper-income groups, who consumed many imported commodities) the monetary expansion increased the demand for local commodities the supply of which could be increased owing to underutilized capacity.

Secondly, the nationalization of industry and commerce in 1960-61, of agriculture under the first and second agrarian reforms; and of all the remaining nonfarm enterprises in 1968—with little or no compensation—eliminated the returns to the owners of natural and capital resources and to entrepreneurship.

Thirdly, the expansion of the educational and public health delivery systems and free access to these by users has increased the real incomes of lower-income groups.

Fourthly, the suppression of inflation through the rationing of virtually everything means that everyone can afford to purchase the rationed commodities on the minimum incomes which are in effect guaranteed because employment of some sort is guaranteed. The purchasing power of money incomes above those required to purchase rationed commodities has been severely limited due to very high prices for the few consumer durables available, for food in state restaurants, and for black market commodities. Because of this comprehensive rationing, the distribution of real income has been considerably more equitable than the distribution of money incomes, as wide differentials have existed in the latter.

The equity of income distribution was marred at least in the latter part of the 1960s by the allocation of private transport (cars), some housing, foreign travel, and access to dining facilities according to political criteria.[48]

Employment

A positive result of Cuba's institutional strategy has been the elimination of overt unemployment and the social costs imposed on those overtly unemployed. While the Third World in general and the Latin American countries in particular face serious problems of employment creation in the decade of the 1970s, Cuba has ostensibly experienced an acute labor shortage since 1961.

The employment-unemployment situation in revolutionary Cuba is more complex, however, for it appears that to a considerable extent overt unemployment has been transformed into covert unemployment (or "underemployment") particularly in the state bureaucracies. From 1960 to 1964, employment in the service sector of the Cuban economy expanded extremely rapidly, from 25.2 to 33.2 percent of total employment, while employment in both industry and agriculture fell, from 56.1 to 48.4 percent. (See Table 15.5.) The great expansion in the service sector reflected the expansion of the health and educational systems to some extent, accounting for an estimated 40,000 out of the 260,000 increase in the sector. A large proportion of the remainder in the service sector were employed in the rapidly expanding planning bureaucracies, discussed in the previous section.

Indeed the focus on low productivity in 1971 and 1972 is implicit recognition that a sizeable proportion of the labor force is "unemployed-while-on-the-job," that is, covertly unemployed. The institutional strategy—together with other factors—has been successful in ameliorating the social costs of overt unemployment to the unemployed, but has transformed this overt unemployment to covert unemployment.

TABLE 15.5

Distribution of Cuban Labor Force by Sector

	1958–59 (millions)	(%)	1960–61 (millions)	(%)	1964 (millions)	(%)
Agriculture	813.0	37.0	826.0	38.0	838.0	33.4
Industry & Mining	378.5	17.2	411.8	18.1	375.7	15.0
Construction	82.8	3.8	71.7	3.2	119.0	4.7
Transport	80.6	3.7	86.5	3.8	89.7	3.6
Commerce	284.3	12.9	265.5	11.7	252.9	10.1
Services & Others	558.3	25.4	572.2	25.2	832.0	33.2
Total	2,197.5	100%	2,270.2	100%	2,508.0	100%

Sources: B.A. Pollitt, Employment Plans, Performance and
Future Prospects in Cuba. (University of Cambridge, 1971), p. 21.

Dependence

Cuba's institutional strategy was designed in part to reduce
"dependence" on foreign-owned enterprises. Nationalization of all
such enterprises eliminated their micro-economic control of the
economy. Nationalization could not reduce Cuba's need for imported
financial capital, technology, and technical expertise, all of which
are currently imported from the Soviet Union.

The weaknesses of the new institutional structure and the problems arising from its installation have exacerbated Cuba's economic
problems in general and the trade balance in particular. Impaired
export performance due to institutional difficulties has necessitated
immense volumes of Russian financial assistance. Russia in effect
has underwritten the Cuban economy and the revolutionary leadership as well. The magnitude of Russian aid undoubtedly creates a
very powerful type of dependence.

The institutional strategy has had only peripheral effects on
other facets of Cuban external dependence. Continued concentration
on sugar production and exportation and heavy reliance on Russia
as the major export market, import source, and aid provider stems
only in a very small part from the nature of the new economic administration. The fact that Cuba initially adopted (and is currently

moving toward) the Russian model is not unrelated to Cuba's great
economic dependence on Russia.

ALTERNATIVE INSTITUTIONAL STRATEGIES

There are a number of types of institutional modification that
Cuba could introduce to improve her economic growth performance.
The only directions in which it is ideologically feasible for Cuba to
move, however, would be toward current Soviet orthodoxy, toward
a publicly owned and democratized market economy (of which Yugoslavia is the stereotypical case), or toward some unique hybrid of
these types. Needless to say, reestablishment of a privately owned
market economy is not within the realm of possibility.

Democratized, Publicly Owned, Market Model

There may be some distinct advantages as well as disadvantages
to Cuba in an institutional structure which combines public ownership of the means of production, resource allocation through the
market mechanism (where this would operate effectively), and self-
management of enterprises by the workers therein. This is not to
suggest that the experiences of any particular country or any national
"model" should be imposed on the Cuban economy, because such
an imposition would create serious transitional costs similar to
those of installing the Czech variant of the Soviet model on Cuba
in 1960-61. However, Cuba can learn from the experiences of
other countries. Yugoslavia, Hungary, Peru, Guyana, and Chile all
bear watching.
Worker management of productive enterprises operating
autonomously under the "discipline" of the market and activated
by income maximization and cooperative income sharing should reduce, if not eliminate, absenteeism and should increase on-the-job
labor and capital productivity, perhaps immensely. Indeed, workers'
management would seem to be ideal as a means of harnessing the
creativity of workers and of reducing the in-plant micro-inefficiencies
which workers are in a unique position to recognize and remedy.
Furthermore, a meaningful workers management is an end in itself
in that it is an attempt to achieve economic democracy on the production side. Worker management should also help prevent in-plant
managerial bureaucracies from using their latent power to appropriate
usufruct benefits for themselves.
Marketization, that is, the decentralized allocation of resources
and final commodities through markets in those sectors where effective

competition is a feasible instrument for the social control of economic activities, should greatly improve the efficiency of resource
allocation, and thus productivity and growth. Competition, where
operable, is likely a more efficient technique of controlling economic
activities than incorporating them into monolithic and monopolistic
planning bureaucracies. Marketization, where possible, would compel
producers to respond with greater sensitivity to the demands of
consumers and would efficiently allocate factors of production within
and between industries and productive enterprises. Moreover marketization would permit the reduction of personnel in the planning
apparatus and the diversion of redundant bureaucrats to more important tasks. Finally, if economic democracy on the consumption
side (from the standpoint of consumers determining what is produced)
is to operate, then it is necessary that markets exist to transmit
consumer demand to productive enterprises.

    Public ownership of the means of production, the establishment
of a capital market, and the permanent imposition of interest charges
on capital loaned to firms would yield revenues for the financing of
public expenditures; would maintain some income equality between
workers in capital-intensive and labor-intensive industries; would
maintain distributional equity (through public ownership), and together
with regional developmental policies and indicative planning should
improve the efficiency of investment allocation.

    This type of system has a number of disadvantages, however.
As the system has operated in Yugoslavia it has been unable to
absorb the large volumes of labor entering the job market and
migrating from agriculture. Consequently both emigration and unemployment have remained at fairly high levels. Inflation has continued to be a serious problem. It is also the case that there are
considerable income differentials between enterprises and regions
because workers' incomes are tied to the success of their enterprises.

    In any transition toward a participatory marketized economy
some difficulties would be faced. First, there would be economic
disruption and some real economic costs to be incurred. After a
decade of demarketization the economic costs of transition to a
participatory market system are greater now than they might have
been in 1960. Many inefficient firms would come under extreme
pressure when forced to compete in markets. Penalization of the
workers in such firms by low incomes would have to be mitigated.
Second, there are strong vested interests in the planning bureaucracies
which would of course resist their possible replacement by markets.
Decentralization of economic decision making may also reduce the
concentration of economic power at the center. Third, it may be
argued that profit sharing by workers would destroy the attempt to
build the "New Man" by replacing moral incentives with blatant

material incentives. It should be noted, however, that materialistic activators exist already, for consumer durables such as appliances and watches are allocated at work centers to workers partly on the basis of their work records. The penal sanctions of the 1971 anti-loafing law also contain a large materialistic component. In any case, the ideal of the "New Man" may be more easily achieved after the achievement of abundance than before.

A Return to Soviet Economic Orthodoxy?

It appears that since the difficulties during the latter years of the drive for the 10 million ton sugar harvest (1968-70) Cuba has been moving toward Soviet economic orthodoxy. Originally, after the 1970 Zafra, however, Premier Castro did make a number of statements suggesting that the revolutionary leadership was considering some innovative moves.

Castro discussed a variant of workers' management in his speech of July 26, 1970. He proposed that instead of an appointed manager being "absolutely in charge," a collective body in each plant should be formed consisting of the appointed manager, heading the body, and representatives of the vanguard workers' movement, the party, the Young Communist League, and the Women's Front. This body, as envisaged by Castro, would allocate housing and some consumer durables, though no other functions were specified. It is questionable how much this scheme would democratize plant management. The makeup of the collective body suggests that the established insiders would merely be better coordinated. The lack of real management functions for the "collective body"—i.e., controlling product type and price, disposition of plant profits, allocation of inputs or distribution of outputs—suggests that the body would merely share foreman functions under the command system. At any rate, there has been no subsequent discussion of workers' representation in plant management.

On other occasion Premier Castro proposed an interesting technique for assuring managerial responsiveness to consumer demands.[49] Under this technique, which might be called "confrontational consumer sovereignty," the citizens directly affected by poor performance and low product quality at a production "minicenter" would confront the managers and insist that improvements be made. For example, the managers of an underperforming bakeshop would be confronted by those who bought bread there and compelled to improve quality and quantity of bread production, to improve hygiene standards, and to reduce absenteeism, privilege, and "lack of feeling."

There seems, however, to have been little discussion of the appropriateness of existing managerial success indicators, nor, of course, of any possible debureaucratization or marketization.

One change which has in fact been implemented was the holding of elections in the labor unions. Many observers, including L. Huberman and P. Sweezy have commented on the lack of democracy in the unions before 1970.[50] This was also implied in Premier Castro's statement in September 1970, in which he announced the elections.

> We are going to trust our workers and hold elections in
> all locals . . . right away. They will be absolutely free
> and the workers can choose the candidates. . . . If the
> worker has really been elected by a majority vote of all
> his comrades, he will have authority; he won't be a
> nobody who has been placed there by decree. If a social-
> ist society doesn't have the support of the masses, it will
> fail. And to have the support of the masses it must be
> as democratic as possible and eliminate administrative
> methods altogether.[51]

Elections in the unions were held by April 1971. It is difficult to know how "democratic" these in fact were, and of what significance they have been.[52]

Certain other changes imply that the Cuban institutional framework of the late 1960s is being modified toward current Soviet practices.

The reintroduction of work norms and salary scales throughout the economy indicates that moral incentives are being deemphasized in favor of material incentives. (This system of salary scales and work norms turns out to be a piece-rate wage system which is highly "materialistic.") This new system should also permit a more rational micro-allocation of labor.

It also appears that some form of accounting at the enterprise level was reintroduced in July 1971—possibly on the advice of Baibakov, the head of the Soviet Gosplan who visited Cuba in the first half of 1971. This type of accounting will undoubtedly be similar to the system of enterprise self-financing used in Russia in the latter part of the 1960s.

Finally, productive enterprises were granted increased though still severely limited autonomy in early 1971.[53] Small investment decision, the hiring of transport services, and the disposal of machinery were functions allocated to the managers of industrial and agricultural enterprises.

CONCLUSION

In the early 1960s the Cuban economy was fitted into what was in essence a Soviet institutional framework of 1950s vintage. In the latter half of the decade there was a general move toward "voluntarism" in the belief that correct "New Man" motivation on the part of managers and workers could overcome institutional inadequacies as well as an anarchic proliferation of special plans operating outside the formal planning structure.

Installation of this demarketized command system was accompanied by very high transitional costs due to the inability of the planning bureaucracy to effectively perform the functions previously performed by markets as rapidly as the markets were destroyed. Moreover some serious weaknesses were inherent in the new system as it operated in Cuba. Most severe of these have been the lack of a rational configuration of prices, bureaucratism, insufficient negative feedback up the planning hierarchy, excessive reliance on the campaign technique of plan implementation, and excessive politicization of the economic administration. These difficulties have resulted in persuasive micro-inefficiencies and mal-organization, in low productivity and high absenteeism, and in an excessively slow rate of growth. Thus, despite high political commitment and a Herculean public effort, the growth performance of the Cuban economy in the 1960s was unsatisfactory.

The institutional strategy of the Cuban revolution has facilitated the achievement of both a high degree of equality in the distribution of real income and an eradication of overt unemployment (though it appears that this has merely been transformed into covert unemployment). While nationalization of the economy eliminated dependence on foreign-owned enterprises (but not foreign technology, personnel, or investment capital), the institutional difficulties of the 1960s impaired general economic performance and resulted in very great dependence on foreign (Russian) aid.

It appears that Cuba is now moving toward current Soviet institutional orthodoxy to reduce some of the especially severe organizational problems of the late 1960s. Despite some innovative proposals by Premier Castro, movement in the direction of a marketized, worker-managed, and publicly owned institutional model is most unlikely.

In any event, the massive investment in elementary and higher education and the emphasis on training engineers, technicians, mechanics, and scientists during the 1960s should bear fruit in the 1970s. The improvements in public health and in general dietary levels also should begin to pay off. Similarly the experience acquired by the economic administration in the last decade of central planning should improve administrative performance in the next decade even if no organizational changes are introduced. Thus if Cuba can maintain the gains made in the 1960s regarding income distribution and the reduction of unemployment, and if improved economic administration permits more rapid economic growth, one can optimistically estimate that Cuban economic performance in general should be better in the decade of the 1970s than in that of the 1960s.

16

**MONTANA SETTLEMENT
AS A PARTIAL SOLUTION
TO PERU'S ECONOMIC
AND DEMOGRAPHIC PROBLEMS**
Rolf J. Wesche

The objective of this chapter is to demonstrate the vital role
that massive settlement of the montaña* must play in a successful
Peruvian development program, and to examine the potential for such
action under the auspices of the present "revolutionary" military
government. It is argued that the integration of the montana into the
national economy would represent a breakthrough more incisive and
far-reaching in its consequences for the country's future than any of
the comprehensive socioeconomic reforms initiated in Peru since 1968.

THE MONTAÑA IN THE CONTEXT OF PERU'S
OVERALL DEVELOPMENT PROSPECTS

For centuries the montana was utterly neglected as an area both
inaccessible and apparently unfit for civilized settlement. After a short-
lived quinine boom in the 1870s and rubber boom at the turn of the
nineteenth century it reverted to relative oblivion. This situation has
gradually changed since the 1930s with the advent of trans-Andean dirt
roads of which a dozen presently reach into the western montana. Only
a minute fraction of montana land resources has however been developed
thus far in the hinterlands of these dead-end penetration arteries.

A Canadian Council grant which supported four months of research in eastern Peru is gratefully acknowledged.

*The montaña, in its broad definition used for the purpose of
this article, encompasses the rain forest areas of eastern Peru below
1,800 meters elevation and covers 63 percent of the nation's territory.

Peru's commitment to large-scale montana development began under the government of Belaunde Terry (1963-68) with his scheme of the Carretera Marginal de la Selva. This was a highway to traverse the eastern foothills and intermontane valleys of the Andes from the boundary with Ecuador to that with Bolivia, designed to serve as the backbone of a future transportation network of the western montana and to open some of the most promising agricultural lands of this area.

The willingness of Belaunde to tax the country's financial resources to their limits in pursuit of this project quickly brought his government into conflict with large sectors of the nation's economic elite, who saw their own interests in the traditional centers of development and to whom the Carretera appeared as an extravaganza leading from nowhere to nowhere. This conflict of interests helped contribute to the downfall of the Belaunde government in 1968. Nevertheless Belaunde was able to demonstrate to all concerned the viability of large-scale, government-supported montana settlement, and to increase mass awareness that a promising frontier was beckoning in the east. At the same time accumulated experience and accelerated experimentation with colonization and agricultural techniques, under his administration, were beginning to outline modern approaches to montana resource use. Thus the stage for a new era of montana development was set.

The current government, much less dependent on elite support than its predecessor, is vigorously advancing construction of the Carretera. It has thus far been difficult to establish clearly whether this represents a major commitment to montana development or is rather the continuation of one development project which already has absorbed too many funds to be discontinued.

A number of considerations favor the argument that the military government has both the capability and favorable disposition to undertake montana development on an unprecedented scale. The government appears so firmly established that its continuation in power throughout most or all of the 1970s can hardly be doubted. It will thus be in condition to assure continuity of developmental programs and—at least temporarily—to disregard public opposition from the increasingly urban-oriented society. Furthermore the technocrat army, which forms the basis of support of the government, suscribes increasingly to desarrollismo which would find its most challenging outlet on the frontiers of the montana, where impressive developmental achievements can be wrested from an untamed environment. Several army engineer and colonization units have a tradition of involvement in montana development. The prominence of the Brazilian and Bolivian armies in the conquest of the Amazonic frontiers of their respective countries provides a stimulating and competitive example.

THE PRINCIPAL BENEFITS AND COSTS

Desarrollismo is closely linked to the current policy of economic nationalism, which seeks total development of national resources and expansion of the internal markets. The montana cannot be neglected in this context. It would appear to be destined for a particularly important role as regards agricultural production, in view of the modest output increases realized in the traditional agricultural areas and the growing food deficit which must be covered by imports. Limitations of water, terrain, and climate restrict possible intensification of land use or expansion of the cultivated surface in the sierra and on the coast. The capital investment required to achieve major production increases in these areas is significantly higher than that necessary to obtain similar production increases in the montana.

Constituting another important factor favoring montana development are strategic considerations which guide the present government to a much larger extent than its civilian predecessors. Among these, considerable importance is attached to Ecuadorian claims to territories annexed by Peru in 1942, and particularly to Brazil's ambitious road-building and settlement program in the Amazon, which will bring this conservative and potentially imperialistic neighbor to the eastern doorstep of Peru before the end of the decade. To counter such perceived threats, the military government is inclined to seek effective incorporation of the eastern territories. This, as a basic element of the national defense policy, contributes to the government's ability to justify a rather sizeable military establishment. Finally the government's laissez-faire approach to Peru's dramatic population growth, at least in part motivated by its thinking in terms of the strategic population balance with neighboring countries, is closely linked to the need for development of new settlement frontiers.

Demographic considerations provide probably the strongest argument for montana settlement. Peru's population, presently exploding at a rate of 3.2 percent per year, is expected to grow from an estimated 13,586,300 in 1970 to at least 18,587,000 in 1980, 25,142,300 in 1990, and 33,491,000 in 2000.[1] A very high proportion of this growing population will annually enter the labor force due to the predominance of the lower age groups,[2] creating unprecedented problems of potential unemployment and underemployment. The process of rapid urbanization has aggravated rather than ameliorated the employment crisis. At the end of the last decade, 37 percent of Lima's labor force and an average of over 40 percent of the labor force in nine other urban centers did not have adequate employment[3] and it is unrealistic to expect improvement of this situation in the near future.

Since the revolutionary government has taken no noticeable steps in the direction of a welfare state and since its economic reform legislation primarily benefits—to a degree which remains the subject of discussion and criticism—the labor force of those larger enterprises which are most strongly affected, it is evident that participation in economic growth and, indeed, the very survival of the masses depends on their access to gainful employment.

Thus far there has been considerable optimism that economic growth per se, measured in per capita GNP and based predominantly in the modern urban sectors of the economy, would ultimately trickle down to the totality or near-totality of the population, raising their standards of living. If however one understands economic advancement of the individual as linked to employment and considers the statistics of deteriorating employment conditions in the major urban centers, it is difficult to share such optimism.

The underlying problem, with no indication of an upcoming solution, is that Peru pursues modern capital-intensive industrialization in an attempt to bypass the traditional stage of labor-intensive manufacturing. Capitalistic operating principles are safeguarded and encouraged by the "revolutionary" industrial reform law. Under these conditions it is inconceivable that an approximation of full employment can be attained in the major urban centers, should rural-urban migration continue unabated, even if potential investment sources were to be fully exploited.

It is not only difficult but futile to project the possible nature of mounting problems connected with an increasing urbanization which generates a growing number of unemployed. In any case one must envisage a rising response of government to the demands of the population aggregating in the large urban centers, and expenditure of an ever-larger proportion of public resources toward their satisfaction. The possibility of hinterland development will be accordingly reduced. Vital natural resources and settlement opportunities will remain unexploited unless viable alternatives to excessive urbanization are firmly established in the near future.

The most promising alternative is a major expansion of the agricultural sector, where relatively labor-intensive practices are feasible and reasonably competitive and where subsistence production and supply of urban markets can be combined. Resulting secondary and tertiary activities in the rural areas and their immediate service and manufacturing centers would also be more labor-intensive than those of the large urban areas.

The obvious beneficiaries of the expansion of the agricultural sector and related activities would be the rural Indian masses, whose integration into the modern national society and economic mainstream is receiving unprecedented attention from the military government.

The rural Indian is in general unprepared to function effectively in
the urban context but willing to continue farming if provided with economic incentives and assured of moderate improvements in his living
standard. According to a 1965 survey of the Instituto Nacional de
Planificación, possibilities for expansion of agricultural settlement
were "nonexistent" in the sierra, at that time already burdened with
an excess rural population of 1,531,600. They were seen as feasible
at high cost on the coast, where an additional 833,700 rural dwellers
could be accommodated, and "quite promising" in the montana, which
was considered capable of increasing its rural population by 8,186,700.[4]

Several other studies, investigating the nearer future, confirm
the possibility for significant expansion of agricultural settlement in
the montana. A. Maas has demonstrated that assured national demand
for agricultural products from the montana would provide a livelihood
for an additional farm-based population of at least 250,000 in the decade
1965-75.[5] The study by the Joint Commission of Bolivia, Colombia,
Ecuador, and Peru proposes the settlement of 500,000 persons on the
strip of land opened by the Carretera Marginal.[6] R. C. Eidt illustrates
the magnitude of conceivable agricultural settlement with an example
from the Pachitea valley, in which a rural work force of 78,000 could
be employed according to his estimates.[7]

None of these studies gives detailed consideration to settlers
dependent on secondary and tertiary activities, which an Organization
of American States study projects as 50 percent of the agricultural
population[8] and which according to the author's estimates vary between 20 percent and 100 percent of the agricultural population in
eight established settlement zones of the western montana, depending
largely on the extent of their domination by sierran and coastal
centers. If the montana were to develop a higher degree of regional
self-dependence, reducing its present exclusive function as primary
resource hinterland of these centers, a much greater proportion of
nonagricultural settlers could be expected.

Investment in montana development can be highly productive in
terms of generating employment, if one considers that large areas
in the eastern border valleys of the Andes, the Andean piedmont and
the lowland floodplains permit intensive forms of land use without
any significant land improvement or reclamation effort.

The abundance of free land will encourage settlement even if
only the most basic infrastructure and services are provided. Meanwhile, even costly and comprehensive land reclamation will extend
the agricultural surface and employment opportunities in the traditional
area to only a limited extent, and further sizeable expenditures on
infrastructure and services would be required to permit the modern
intensive land use which could justify the cost of such land reclamation. The relationship between capital investment and employment
generated is even less favorable in the modern industrial sector.

The thorough agrarian reform program of the "revolutionary" government which has swept through coast and sierra may be expected to improve the livelihood of a certain portion of the rural population but does little to solve employment problems in these areas. The emphasis on conversion of large properties to cooperative ownership has rather tended to restrict continued participation of seasonal labor and other elements of the rural work force that were not firmly attached to expropriated estates. On several coastal estates newly established cooperatives have been critical of governmental efforts to add unemployed resident labor to their membership. Experience with agrarian reform efforts in other countries indicates that spatial mobility of rural populations in reform-affected areas increases under conditions of land shortage. Thus no agrarian reform program in Peru can be complete without the opening of new settlement frontiers.

The arguments that have been advanced in favor of montaña development are based on the assumption that large numbers of Peruvians, particularly rural Indians, can be induced to settle in this area. This premise, while increasingly supported by specialists, is still not widely accepted by the coast-oriented elite and has critics even among the large landowners in the montaña. In the past, Indian montaña settlement on a significant scale was not considered feasible, due to Indian traditionalism as well as lack of cultural and physical adaptability to rain forest conditions.[9]

A number of facts seemed to give credence to this pessimistic assessment. The vast majority of highland Indians, in spite of deteriorating living conditions, have never attempted montana settlement. Those who did appear in the montana were generally engaged in seasonal labor rather than permanent settlement. Whether seasonal migrants or permanent settlers, they have shown a marked preference for the cooler western fringes of the montana and locations close enough to their areas of origin to permit continuing contact with them. Even permanent settlers are widely convinced that environmental conditions in the montana are extremely unhealthy. Few Indian settlers have accumulated significant wealth.

On the other hand, Indian montaña settlement has rapidly increased in recent years as highland living conditions deteriorated. Indian settlers are distributed throughout the accessible portions of the eastern border valleys and are encountered in growing numbers in the piedmont. Generally their economic condition has improved over that to which they are accustomed. Furthermore one can observe large numbers of Indians in search of a livelihood wherever land transportation arteries make access possible.

It is time to deemphasize cultural factors, which admittedly hamper the progress of the Indians in the montaña, as they do in any other Peruvian environment, and to seek other explanations for the

Indian's inability to avail himself to a larger extent and with more success of montana opportunities.

In the past, montana colonization has proceeded in narrow bands along a few existing penetration roads and their trail, river, and occasional feeder-road extensions. Once the frontage on these transportation arteries was occupied, access to the interior became difficult and could be effectively blocked by frontage lot owners intending to retain control over land reserves.

Mestizo and white landowners were quick to monopolize choice land in the more promising and better serviced colonization zones of the central and northern montana. The Indians, unable to compete and lacking governmental support, generally sought seasonal or long-term employment on the haciendas rather than venturing into the less attractive terrain which remained unoccupied. It must also be noted that the central and northern sierra have effective road links to the major coastal cities and plantation areas and contain the principal sierran mining zones, thus offering convenient alternate migration targets to the area's Indian population.

Much more active Indian montana colonization has taken place in the south, where the most populous and overpopulated sierran zone faces a portion of the montana which (due to poor-quality penetration roads, relative absence of services, and inadequate access to major markets) has attracted few whites and mestizos and even fewer large entrepreneurs. Here alternate migration targets are remote and relatively inaccessible and economic aspirations are more limited. As a result a veritable flood of Indian migrants has poured down the eastern slopes of the Andes in recent years. These migrants were able to establish homogeneous Indian settlements in which accustomed forms of life and social ties could be maintained to a large extent, providing security and stability.

Their approach to permanent settlement has been cautious. Migrants generally maintain properties and residences until their lowland clearings reach significant production, and await improvements in infrastructure and services before making a final commitment to the montana. Some highly intelligent adaptations to local conditions have been developed, particularly in the eastern valleys of Puno department, where poor access and rugged terrain limit commercial production to coffee. Here seasonally complementary highland cropping and montana coffee cultivation are combined in a fashion that assures maximum income and use of family labor while permitting a flexible response to the vagaries of the coffee market.[10]

The foregoing are rational approaches rather than indicators of a basic reluctance toward montana settlement on the part of the Indian. It must also be noted that there has been no shortage of Indian applications for lots in the three major government-organized colonization schemes, which provide an unusual range of services, and that Indian lot-recipients have been more stable settlers than their mestizo counterparts. One may assume that access to suitable land and availability of adequate services and governmental assistance would ensure massive Indian participation in montana development.

PREREQUISITES FOR SUCCESS

To conclude the argument in favor of extensive montana settlement as an essential part of Peru's developmental program one must reflect at least briefly on the prerequisites for its success.

In the past it was assumed a priori that the scope and spatial distribution of possible montana development is determined almost entirely by access to existing markets. Since the sierran market is quite limited and coastal centers can be reached only at high cost (due to the unique transportation barrier presented by the Andes), it was accepted that only small fractions of the western montana have developmental potential for the time being. This concept, while correct in the context of an uncontrolled capitalistic economic system, is no longer acceptable in view of the increasing imbalance between population growth and resource use.

If large-scale montana development is to take place, as it must, it has to be based to a considerable extent on regional self-dependence and internal complementarity. Planned primary resource development must be coordinated with the establishment of regional service and manufacturing centers that provide the full range of required services, urban employment alternatives, and the basis for a continuous internal urbanization process. The future geography of the country is envisaged as comprising a highly advanced coastal zone, a relatively under-developed sierran sector that continues to function as a major transportation barrier, and a dynamic montana that maintains economic ties with both western Peru and countries to the east that are accessible via the Amazon and Atlantic.

Maximum return on montana infrastructure investments can be assured only under a master plan that efficiently coordinates the establishment of a road-river transportation network with orderly land occupation. Further extension of trans-Andean penetration roads should be deemphasized in favor of a balanced system of main arteries and feeder roads with the dual purpose of providing access to existing trans-Andean roads and serving as means of internal communication. In the initial stages the quality of such roads is of less importance than the quantity of agricultural land made accessible. The prospect of land ownership in accessible locations is sufficient to motivate immigration, while gradual improvement of road quality can proceed as production increases in newly opened areas.

An appropriate land tenure policy would reserve areas of greatest accessibility and agricultural potential for controlled high density settlement by small farmers, cooperatives, and communes while adopting a liberal attitude toward the development of less attractive land on a large scale by capitalistic entrepreneurs, who can be encouraged to establish local feeder roads serving their purposes. This approach would not only permit accomodation of the greatest possible number of settlers at least cost but would also minimize expenditure for essential services.

While economic opportunity is the principal factor that induces settlement, the availability of a number of basic services determines stability of settlement and productivity of land use.

Few migrants are willing to transfer their families to the montana unless at least primary educational and elementary health care facilities are accessible from their places of residence. Economic success and the settler's outlook concerning his future in the montana depend on the availability of credit and agricultural extension services. All this is particularly relevant during the initial stages when the migrant's financial resources have been eroded by the expense of relocation, when he is faced with the cost of forest clearing, house construction, and the purchase of essential production inputs, when he has to confront an alien environment, and when there is a considerable time lag between his arrival and the commencement of significant production.

Provision of the above and a number of less important services, otherwise entirely dependent on the limited capabilities of the government, can be facilitated in the context of cooperatives and communes. These are furthermore an essential tool for the promotion of settlement stability, adaption, mutual assistance, and economies of scale, in an environment which limits the progress potential of the individual left to his own resources.

The massive montana development effort suggested in this chapter is clearly a task which would strain national planning and investment capability to its limits for a considerable period of time. As a result it may not be acceptable, though preconditions for such an undertaking are more favorable under the "revolutionary" military government than ever before.

The current socioeconomic reforms, conveniently advertised as a "revolutionary transformation," are by their very nature directed to existing areas of settlement. They represent temporary and partial solutions, unable by themselves to arrest a deterioration of living conditions with truly revolutionary potential. To avoid a permanent threat of revolutions, none of which would solve the problems associated with continuing population growth, a new balance must be established between man and the available resource base. More than half the country lies unused east of the Andes, awaiting a new Peruvian departure into a more stable future based on such a balance.

17

DEVELOPMENT PROSPECTS
IN THE COMMONWEALTH
CARIBBEAN IN THE 1970s
Vincent A. E. Richards

The countries of the Commonwealth Caribbean are at varying stages of development. With respect to their political character, Trinidad-Tobago, Jamaica, and Barbados are independent members of the British Commonwealth; Guyana is a republic within the Commonwealth; Antigua, St. Kitts, Grenada, St. Lucia, Dominica, and St. Vincent are associated states of Great Britain, a constitutional arrangement that gives each country complete control over its internal affairs and leaves the handling of external affairs and defense to the British government;[1] Montserrat is still a colony of Great Britain, while British Honduras (Belize) has a measure of internal self-government similar to that of the associated states.

SOME ECONOMIC CHARACTERISTICS OF
THE COMMONWEALTH CARIBBEAN

With respect to economic development also there are significant variations. First, the land area of the Commonwealth Caribbean states ranges from a mere 32 square miles in the case of Montserrat to 83,000 square miles in Guyana's case. Second, on the basis of preliminary 1970 census estimates, the crude population density ranges from 9 persons per square mile in Guyana to 1,434 per square mile in Barbados. Third, the per capita gross domestic product, a very rough index of the level of economic development, ranged from U.S. $181.5 in St. Vincent to U.S. $776.3 in Trinidad-Tobago in 1969.[2]

Given this diversity of political character and level of economic development, any attempt at predicting what the 1970s hold for the Commonwealth Caribbean is bound to be a difficult task. In this chapter, predictions are made only about the economic future of the

region. This is not to say that political development is an unimportant
aspect of the overall transformation of Commonwealth Caribbean
society. On the contrary, political development will be a crucial factor
in determining how successfully the countries increase their pace of
economic development. To illustrate, in all countries the government
plays a large role in the developmental process in terms of the number
of people it employs, the magnitude of its expenditure, the relative
size of the national income generated by the governmental sector,
and the variety of activities with which it is directly concerned. Of
future importance is the development of an efficient and competent
public administrative machinery geared toward producing change and
transformation of the various economies. The inherited colonial
administrative setup has attempted to maintain the iniquitous status
quo.[3] Also, if the developmental process is not to be hampered
government must have the support of the populace. This calls for the
opening up and the maintenance of channels of communication between
the governed and those who govern so that there will be a national
commitment to the developmental effort. In short, the citizens must
have confidence in the political machinery. Absence of confidence
can only thwart the success of any economic developmental program.*

Still, the economic future of the region will influence all these
political developments. The Commonwealth Caribbean countries all
suffer from high levels of unemployment, the estimates ranging
between 12 and 20 percent, and are highly dependent on foreign trade.
The central problem in their economic development is that of over-
coming the limitations resulting from an unfavorable ratio of a dense
population to a narrow natural resources base.[4] Faced with this
problem, which has been compounded by the rising expectations of the
population, Commonwealth Caribbean governments have adopted the
strategy of regional economic integration as a leading apparatus for
rapid economic development of the region. It is within this framework
that prospects for the 1970s will be mainly discussed.

The two major manifestations of the regional approach to economic
development are the Caribbean Free Trade Association (CARIFTA)

---

*A case in point is the situation in Trinidad and Tobago over
the past couple of years. Among the events that have taken place—and
which can be attributed partly to a loss of confidence in the political
machinery—are: a mutiny of army officers; several declarations of
a state of emergency; a call by the major opposition political groups
for a national boycott of the last general elections, a call that was
successful since less than one third of the eligible voters turned out
at the polls.

and the Caribbean Development Bank. These two regional institutions will be examined and their potential role in development during the 1970s will be assessed.

The extent of the economic interrelation between the Commonwealth Caribbean states that have formed CARIFTA may be judged in terms of their complementarity and competitiveness. If these countries produce a different range of commodities, they are said to be complementary. Removal of tariffs will lead to trade diversion if the lowest-cost country—for a particular product—is not a member. This is because tariff elimination for members and the maintenance of tariffs for nonmembers can price the lowest-cost nonparticipating country out of the regional market. Therefore, in a case where the degree of complementarity is great, potential trade diversion is strong, and the increase in intraregional trade will be considerable. In terms of static welfare criteria such an occurence is unfavorable, since a high-cost supplier will replace a lower-cost supplier. But from an economic developmental, and hence a dynamic standpoint, this may be a beneficial occurrence if the trade diversion brings into the productive process resources that were previously idle. Competitiveness refers to the degree of overlapping in the range of protected industries that the member countries possess before the economic union is formed. If there is considerable overlapping, the removal of tariffs will lead to a more efficient allocation of resources, and the greater the differences in production costs, the greater will be the gains.

How competitive and how complementary are the economies of the Commonwealth Caribbean? A recent study of West Indian economic integration answers the question as follows:

> Although opportunities do exist for expanding trade in some agricultural and industrial commodities by a system of free trade, it is evident that the possible quantity and range of trade which could take place at present are limited by the structure of our own demand and by the existing narrow production-capacity of West Indian economies. The range of goods within which trade creation is possible is limited immediately by the fact that the area over which internal competition can prevail is minute. The constituent members' production is geared almost entirely to external demand. And similarly, their structure of demand is geared almost entirely to external production. In effect then, West Indian economies are neither competitive nor complementary.[5]

The pattern of trade of the Caribbean countries reflects this almost complete reliance on the metropolitan markets of the United

States, the United Kingdom, and Canada. Of the total domestic exports of the Caribbean countries, excluding Belize, of E.C. $1,430.3 million* (U.S. $725.2 million) in 1967, the three industrial countries accounted for 65.7 percent (U.S. 35.1 percent; U.K. 21.6 percent; Canada 9.0 percent), while intra-Caribbean trade accounted for only 5.7 percent. This has been the pattern for decades. The import picture is not very much different. The same three metropolitan countries provided 54.3 percent of total imports, (U.S. $920 million), while intra-Caribbean imports were 4.7 percent. This trade pattern is one indication of the relatively minor economic intercourse that takes place between the Commonwealth Caribbean economies. But let us now turn to the efforts at economic integration in the region.

CARIFTA: ITS ORIGIN AND EVOLUTION

The Caribbean Free Trade Association emerged from the desire of the governments of Antigua, Barbados, and Guyana to foster the economic development of their respective countries. The view that a free trade area could accelerate the development of the members is in large part due to the demonstration effect. The industrial countries of Europe had placed themselves into regional economic blocs—the European Economic Community (EEC) and the European Free Trade Area (EFTA)—and the success of the EEC suggested that regional economic integration was one way in which growth and development might be fostered. In addition, the developing countries of Latin and Central America were forming several economic unions among themselves.[6] Then, too, developmental economists were arguing that economic unions can accelerate the pace of economic development of a region and its constituent parts. The arguments for this contention are now fairly well known; essentially they are that the establishment of a free trade area (or other form of economic union) can foster economic development by increasing the gains from trade, by facilitating efficiency of production in existing industries, and by offering a better climate for the setting up of new industries. Market expansion and the realization of large-scale economies are said to result from the formation of such a union.[7]

After a series of negotiations, the governments of the three countries signed an agreement in 1965 which saw the birth of CARIFTA. Several difficulties were encountered after the signing and a supplementary agreement was made in 1966 to amend and clarify articles

---

*East Caribbean dollars.

of the original agreement. The agreements expressed the signatories' desire to see other Commonwealth Caribbean countries join the union. The other countries, with the exception of British Honduras, joined the union in 1968, at which time a second supplementary agreement was signed. In May 1971 British Honduras became a member of the free trade area, which went into force on May 1, 1968.

The objectives of CARIFTA as set out in the principal agreement are:

(a) to promote the expansion and diversification of trade in the area of the Association;
(b) to secure that trade between Member Territories takes place in conditions of fair competition;
(c) to encourage the progressive development of the economies of the Area;
(d) to foster the harmonious development of Caribbean trade and its liberalization by the removal of barriers to it.

With respect to the first objective, it should be noted that those products which could offer expansion of trade coupled with specialization, although covered in the agreement, are subject to special arrangements.

These are placed in the so-called reserve list, and the complete elimination of tariffs on them will in some cases take up to 10 years. For example, the "effective protective element"* in revenue duties on beer (including stout and ale), gin, vodka, whiskey, and petroleum products will be removed over a 5-year period; for rum, such protection is to be removed over a 5-year period by the more developed members (Barbados, Guyana, Jamaica, Trinidad, and Tobago), while the remaining members, the less-developed ones, are given a 10-year period for such elimination. In addition, a similar 5-year period for the more-developed members and a 10-year period for the less-developed ones are given for the complete removal of import duties on some 13 products.** Several of the CARIFTA members are producers of these products. It was pointed out above that only a small

---

*The "effective protective element" in revenue duty is defined as the difference between the charge on the imported product and the charge on the comparable domestic product.

**The products are: preserved fruits and preparations, unmanufactured tobacco, manufactured tobacco, prepared paints, detergents, crates and wooden containers, radio and television sets, batteries, wood and metal furniture, mattresses, underwear and shirts, leather slippers, and leather footwear.

part of the productive capacity of the economies caters to regional demand. This fact coupled with the nature of the tariff-elimination plan suggests that improvements in productive efficiency as a result of increased competition are, in the short run, virtually ruled out in those industries where it would seem to be greatest. There is little promise of expansion of the market for special-status products as a result of the formation of a free trade area until the 5-or 10-year period has elapsed. Consequently, there is no reason to expect further expansion of trade in these products because of the existence of CARIFTA.

With respect to the second objective, the various CARIFTA documents attempt to ensure nondiscrimination in trade. Freedom of transit of area-origin products is allowed within the area; "fiscal charges" which comprise customs duties and internal taxes are to be the same for domestic goods and goods from any other member; export drawbacks, which refer to the refunding of import duties applied on imported materials used by export industries, are prohibited; governmental aid to export industries is not permissible; restrictive business practices that will lead to "restriction or distortion of competition within the Area" are to be outlawed or controlled; nationals of all countries are to be given equal treatment in the setting up of economic enterprises; and the council, which is responsible for executing the agreement, is advised to make recommendations toward coordination of the various countries' investment concessions to foreign capitalists.

The big question, however, is whether the council, together with the Commonwealth Caribbean regional secretariat, the principal administrative organ of the association, will be able to ensure that the above rules of the game are observed.

The CARIFTA pact is loaded with numerous exceptions to the general provisions for the liberalization of intraregional trade and these are presumably to fulfill the third objective, namely, the progressive development of the economies. A country that is having "an appreciable rise in unemployment in a particular sector of industry or region . . . caused by a substantial decrease in internal demand for a domestic product" because of trade creation is allowed by article 22 to seek solace in a reimposition of quantitative restrictions. Such a solution, however temporary, will only tend to maintain the inefficient allocation of regional resources. One can only hope that the council will offer alternate solutions to such problems when they arise! Surely more meaningful policies can be devised to ensure that all the constituent parts of the union experience economic growth.

The provisions for fair competition in trade outlined with reference to the second objective, together with other safeguards, seem to provide the basis for attaining objective (d), a harmonious

expansion and liberalization of intraregional trade. Compensatory
action is allowed for in the case of dumped or subsidized imports
into a member from another member; and a member encountering
balance of payments difficulties is temporarily excused from some of
its obligations until such difficulties are overcome. Here again, one
would hope that these allowances will not lead to more restrictive
trade policies when temporary cases of external imbalance appear.

In considering CARIFTA's prospects, the distinction between
"area-origin" and "nonarea-origin" commodities is an important one,
for the removal of trade restrictions applies only to the former. The
CARIFTA pact defines area-origin products as those that fall under
one of the following:

(a) that they have been wholly produced within the area;
(b) that they fall within a description of goods listed in a
    Process List* to be established by decision of the
    Council and have been produced within the Area by the
    appropriate qualifying process described in that List;
(c) that they have been produced within the Area and that
    the value of any materials imported from outside the
    Area or of undetermined origin which have been used
    at any stage of the production of the goods does not
    exceed 50% of the export price of the Goods.[8]

In addition, the agreement provides for a "basic materials list."
Most of the products in this list are not produced in the area, but will
be considered of "area origin." The list reflects the developmental
objective of the signatories, for it contains the primary products
which are considered to be essential for the establishment and expansion of a manufacturing sector. The effect of this list will be to allow
many manufactures of the area to meet the percentage criterion of
area-origin products. At the same time, it will encourage foreign
capitalists to invest in the area in industries that use materials in this
list as inputs in order to take advantage of this preferential treatment.
The benefits of this provision could therefore be considerable in the
long run if manufacturing industries based on the transformation of
these materials are established. As such, the list enhances the
dynamic potential of the agreement.

As a companion to the CARIFTA pact, there is an Agricultural
Marketing Protocol, which is to supervise intraregional trade in some

---

*Three years have elapsed since CARIFTA began operations;
yet to date, the members have been unable to agree on a Process
List.

agricultural products.* Import requirements and export availability
of each country will be estimated and the secretariat will allocate the
regional market for these products among the members on the basis
of these projections.

The Agricultural Marketing Protocol can play a significant role
in increasing intra-Caribbean agricultural trade. G. L. Beckford and
M. H. Guscott[9] cite several cases in which the job of balancing surpluses
and shortages can go a long way toward the expansion of agricultural
trade. And H. Brewster and C. Y. Thomas have explored dynamic
potentialities of agriculture, were it viewed in a regional framework.[10]
In tomatoes, Montserrat produces a surplus, while the other islands
experience shortages; in carrots, the same island has a surplus from
March to July, while there is a shortage in Guyana; Dominica has a
surplus in cabbages, while Guyana experiences an all-year shortage;
and in Antigua, there is a great demand for fresh fruits and vegetables
especially during the tourist season. Possibilities of regional import-
substitution on an efficient basis exist for many more agricultural
products.[11] One study has found that "many Caribbean countries are
in a position to supply fruits and vegetables and the products thereof
in good quality and competitive prices, and at the same time in sufficiently large quantities."[12] It is clear that the unwarranted amount
of food imports to the region can hardly be justified on grounds of
comparative disadvantage.

As the CARIFTA arrangement presently stands, it offers a
distinct possibility for the fusion of the product markets of the countries
for those goods that qualify as "area origin." Whether this will
materialize will depend upon the quality and cost of regional transportation, a question that will be discussed presently. CARIFTA does
not, however, permit the integration of the resource base of the region,
and as such falls far short of an encompassing regional integration
scheme. Moreover, the complete removal of all tariffs and quantitative
restrictions on intraregional trade in area-origin products will not
occur until 1978, when the full impact of the agreement, limited in
scope though it be, will be allowed to operate. In its present form,
therefore, CARIFTA does not seem to hold out any great prospects
of a favorable character for regional economic development in the
1970s. This, I hasten to add, is not an argument against the existence

---

*The products are: carrots, peanuts, tomatoes, red kidney beans,
black pepper, sweet pepper, garlic, onions, potatoes (sweet and Irish),
string beans, cinnamon, cloves, cabbages, plantains, pork and pork
products, poultry products, eggs, okra, oranges, pineapples, and
pigeon peas.

of CARIFTA. Indeed, given the extreme smallness, in terms of both population and gross domestic products, of even the largest member,* the only meaningful developmental strategy for the Commonwealth Caribbean is one that gives regional economic integration a predominant role to play. CARIFTA is the first serious attempt along these lines and as such is a step in the right direction. The challenge for Commonwealth Caribbean governments in this decade is to transform the loose form of economic integration that presently exists in the form of CARIFTA into one in which the resource base and the factor markets of the region become integrated, thereby expanding not only product markets but factor markets as well. The prospects, I would think, of a successful resolution of such a challenge within the next 10 years are not very bright.

CARIFTA, as we have just noted, offers a distinct possibility for the fusion of the island product markets of area-origin goods into a regional market for these products, but whether this in fact takes place will depend on how much regional infrastructure in transportation improves.

Transportation facilities within the area are quite inadequate. Sea transportation infrastructure within the region has been very poor, and continues to be so in some of the islands. Facilities at the sea ports have now improved, with several of the islands acquiring modern berthing facilities. But the number of ships plying the trade between islands is still very small, so much so that it is a simple matter to get suitable shipping space from the islands to Canada and the United Kingdom, whereas acquiring suitable shipping space from Jamaica to Trinidad or Barbados can entail quite a few problems. The West Indies Shipping Service operates two ships in the region, but the service offered is not satisfactory and transport costs are high. Several Jamaican firms engaged in food processing, when questioned as to why they failed to acquire export markets in the Commonwealth Caribbean, listed the inadequacy of transport facilities and high transport costs as major reasons.[13] We seem to have here something of a vicious circle where poor transport facilities result in very little trade, and the small volume of trade is to account for the poor transport overhead.

---

*The total population of CARIFTA countries including Belize is given as 4.4 million from preliminary 1970 census figures. The largest member, Jamaica, has a population of 1.9 million. In 1969, the GDP at current factor cost was approximately U.S. $2.3 billion, with Jamaica accounting for close to U.S. $1.0 billion and Trinidad and Tobago for some U.S. $0.8 billion.

The air transport situation is not very different from that of sea transport.[14] Many of the countries have modern international airports, but because of demand considerations these deal in the trade with metropolitan centers rather than with each other. And the smaller islands, with the important exceptions of Antigua and St. Lucia, lack proper airport facilities. Here again, we find, a vicious circle. Air cargo rates between the member countries are high because the volume of trade is small. This bottleneck could seriously retard expansion of intraregional trade, especially in fresh fruits and vegetables, even with CARIFTA. If a fusion of the product markets in area-origin products of the countries is to materialize, and if CARIFTA is to lead to any significant increase in intraregional trade, the transport bottleneck must be broken and regional transportation infrastructure will have to show a marked improvement.

The question of telecommunications is of interest also. A few examples will suffice to illustrate the gravity of the problem. It is much easier to telephone London from Trinidad, or Jamaica from London, than it is to telephone Port-of-Spain from Kingston.[15] A similar statement may be made with respect to Montserrat, Barbados, and Miami. No wonder that with such a depressing state of market intelligence the volume of intraregional trade is very small.

THE CARIBBEAN DEVELOPMENT BANK

This is an appropriate juncture to look at the Caribbean Development Bank, for it has a crucial role to play in helping to solve the regional transportation and communication problem. Another important function that it must fulfill is that of reducing the economic polarization tendencies which are likely to occur with the operation of CARIFTA. As pointed out above, there is considerable disparity in the level of economic development among the Commonwealth Caribbean countries. In an economic integration scheme among countries exhibiting such varying developmental levels, the adverse "backwash" effects emanating from the more-developed members are generally of high order. "Backwash" effects are movement of capital and skilled labor from the less-developed to the more-developed members, changes in the location of industries detrimental to the less-developed countries, and the disproportionate allocation of new private investment from abroad favoring the more-developed countries of the union. If regional economic integration is to be attractive to all of the member countries, the economic development flowing from the integration scheme should be "harmonistic," that is, the disparity in levels of economic development should not increase and if feasible should be decreased. In underdeveloped countries, where capital and labor markets are generally fragmented, the price system fulfills its allocative function less satisfactorily than it does in developed countries; left by itself, it will tend to produce economic polarization. It will be the bank's function to prevent this occurrence and ensure "harmonistic" economic development in the region.

The main objective underlying the establishment of the Caribbean Development Bank, which began operations in 1970, is to provide the Caribbean area with an institution that can contribute to the harmonious economic growth and development of the member countries of the region and will promote closer economic cooperation and a greater degree of economic integration among them, with special and urgent regard to the needs of the less-developed members. The functions of the bank are:

1. To assist regional members in the coordination of their developmental plans, with a view to promoting international trade and particularly intraregional trade.

2. To mobilize within and outside the area additional financial resources for regional development.

3. To finance projects and programs contributing to the development of the region or any of the regional members.

4. To provide appropriate technical assistance to its regional members.

5. To promote public and private investment in developmental projects.

6. To cooperate and assist in efforts designed to promote regional and locally controlled financial institutions and a regional market for credit savings and to encourage the development of capital markets within the region.

The bank has an authorized share capital of U.S. $50 million, of which Canada and the United Kingdom have each contributed U.S. $10 million. The remainder is contributed by the regional members. Colombia has recently applied for membership in the bank, and if and when her application is approved it is expected that the authorized capital will increase to U.S. $60 million, Colombia's contribution being U.S. $10 million. In addition to these financial resources, the bank will be able to draw upon a soft loan fund which is to be set up.[16] The bank has decided to give priority in its lending operations to productive enterprises and closely related infrastructure. Its loans will be concentrated on investment projects in agriculture, livestock, fisheries, manufacture, mining, tourism, and transportation.[17]

What can we expect from the Caribbean Development Bank in the 1970s? We should not look for any spectacular achievements. The tasks the regional governments have assigned to it are quite formidable, and 10 years is, after all, a short period in terms of economic development. A marked improvement in infrastructure in the less-developed members can be expected, and there is a high probability that by the end of the decade the regional transportation problem will be close to a satisfactory solution. With proper regional transportation the CARIFTA pact will then be allowed to exert its full influence, thereby increasing intraregional trade. The Caribbean Development Bank and CARIFTA should therefore be regarded as complementary tools working toward regional economic integration. They will undoubtedly have some positive effect on economic development in this decade, yet their developmental impact is most likely to be felt in the decade of the 1980s, when both institutions will have been firmly established and their activities will have achieved a reasonable degree of coordination.

Mention should be made of plans to establish a customs union among the less-developed members—the associated states and Montserrat—within the larger CARIFTA framework. Present plans envisage the putting into effect of a common external tariff by April 1972. This arrangement, together with the conscious efforts of the bank, is expected to prevent the economic polarization tendencies alluded to above. These, then, are the major concrete efforts at regional economic integration, but they are by no means the only ones. The subject of the establishment of a regional air carrier is presently being studied, as are the questions of an appropriate regional policy toward foreign investment and the harmonization of company law throughout the region. Taken together, we may say that the attempts at regional economic integration will offer modest assistance to economic development in the Commonwealth Caribbean in the 1970s.

At the same time that emphasis is placed on the strategy of economic integration, importance must also be placed on export expansion to nonregional countries. Accelerated economic development requires increasingly complex capital goods; since these goods are not produced by the members and are unlikely to be produced by them in the near future, they must be imported. This implies that exports to nonmember countries must also expand.

THE EXPORT OUTLOOK

What are the prospects for Commonwealth Caribbean exports in the 1970s? As noted above, the range of production in the Commonwealth Caribbean economies is small and this limited production pattern is reflected in their export trade, which essentially consists of a few primary products. Sugar is still a dominant agricultural export product in Jamaica, Guyana, Trinidad-Tobago, British Honduras, and Barbados. The industry depends predominantly on guaranteed external markets at preferential prices: of the United Kingdom under

the Commonwealth Sugar Agreement, of the United States under the
U.S.-West Indies sugar quota, and of Canada. Of the three markets,
the United Kingdom is by far the most important. Market prospects
appear to be good until at least 1974, when the present Commonwealth
Sugar Agreement expires. Market prospects from 1975 onward will
depend on the results of the British government's efforts to obtain
special arrangements for Commonwealth Caribbean sugar in her
present negotiations for entry into the European Economic Community.
With respect to production prospects, recent performance in the
current largest Commonwealth Caribbean producer, Guyana, suggests
that prospects of a rising trend for the 1970s are good. The output
of sugar in 1969 in that country reached a record level of 364,000 tons,
a 15 percent increase over the previous year, and the target level for
1970 was set at 375,000 tons. In Trinidad-Tobago, sugar holds a predominant position in the agricultural sector of the economy. Sugar
production averaged 222,922 tons for 1960-63, and 221,188 tons for
1964-67. On the basis of this recent performance, one may argue that
production prospects for the 1970s are not particularly good in Trinidad-
Tobago.

In Jamaica, sugar production has showed an absolute downward
trend since 1965. Production in that year was 506,000 tons, and by
1969 it was down to 360,000 tons, the five-year average annual output
being 452,000 tons.[18] These figures would suggest that prospects in
this area are not bright.

Yet, viewing prospects as being bright when there are signs of
an upward trend in sugar output and as poor when production trends
follow the opposite pattern is valid only in terms of a partial analysis,
specifically the foreign exchange aspect. While an increase in sugar
output is favorable from the foreign exchange standpoint, there can
be no question that such a development would hinder rather than be
conducive to the proper development of the agricultural sector of the
regional economies. An expansion of sugar production might mean
that the region's agricultural resources were being devoted more to
the production of sugar, while the domestic agricultural sector which
is engaged in the production of food and livestock products for the
regional market might not have enough of the agricultural resources
allocated to it. Moreover, it has been established that were it not
for the special marketing arrangements that Commonwealth Caribbean
sugar receives in the United Kingdom and the United States, the industry in its present structure would not survive for long. This therefore
means that the favorable label attached to the upward trend in regional
sugar output is valid only for the short run. In the long run what is
needed is a transformation of agriculture in the region; a more
diversified sector geared to regional demand and engaged in products
which the region can produce at competitive cost. Sugar may not be

one of these. Viewed in this long-run perspective, the trends in
Jamaica are indeed encouraging if they are accompanied by an expansion of the nonexport-oriented areas of the agricultural sector. The
development of areas of agriculture adapted to regional demand would
have the effect of reducing the excessively high import bill for foods
of the CARIFTA countries and thus releasing the foreign exchange
earned from the present levels of the traditional exports for other
purposes, such as the purchasing of capital equipment from abroad.

The question might be posed as to what the Commonwealth
Caribbean governments are doing to transform the agricultural sector
of the economies. The response to such a query is that the various
developmental plans envisage a policy of agricultural diversification,
but unfortunately there is at present no policy as to how agriculture
may be rationalized at the regional level. Given the small size of
these economies, it is clear that diversification on an individual
country basis has serious limitations. It is to be hoped, therefore,
that the recent decision of the Commonwealth Caribbean regional
secretariat to study the mechanisms and approaches that may lead to
a rationalized and diversified regional agricultural sector will give
results that can and will be implemented in the next few years. But
let us return to the question of export expansion to non-CARIFTA
countries.

Guyana and Jamaica are major world producers of bauxite. In
Guyana, the output of dried bauxite was 2.1 million tons in 1969, a 14
percent increase over the previous year. Output of calcined bauxite
rose by close to 10 percent, to 644,000 tons, while alumina production
increased by 12 percent, to 298,000 tons, between 1968 and 1969.
Export earnings were up from $102 million to $120 million, a 17.6
percent increase. Projected production in 1970 suggested a 10 percent
increase in dried and calcined bauxite as well as in alumina. Prospects
for the 1970s are good in this area. The contribution of bauxite-alumina
to Guyana's gross domestic product (GDP) has been increasing over
the past decade, averaging 13 percent for 1962-64 and 18 percent for
1967-69. As in the case of Guyana, recent performance of the bauxite-
alumina industry in Jamaica suggests a favorable outlook for economic
growth in this area. Production of bauxite in 1969 rose by 23.1 percent
over the previous year, to 10.3 million tons; production of alumina
showed a similar spectacular performance, increasing by 25.1 percent
over 1968, to 1.1 million tons. Current plans envisage a tripling of
the 1968 level by 1973. The industry's contribution to GDP has averaged
9.5 percent for 1963-68.[19]

The spectacular growth of the industry in Guyana and Jamaica
fails to underscore what is perhaps the most important feature of
the industry from an economic developmental standpoint—its organization. The production of bauxite-alumina in the Caribbean has been

in the hands of four international corporations. There is a large degree
of vertical integration in the activities of these companies; each
company is engaged in each stage of the production process from
mining to semifabricating. Such a form of industrial organization
may not be conducive to a maximization of benefits by the local, that
is to say Caribbean, economies. First, only the mining, drying, and
to a smaller extent the beneficiation stages are carried out in the
Caribbean, and these are the stages in which the value added is comparatively small. It has been estimated that in the production of one
ton of aluminium, the value added by the mining and drying (of bauxite)
stages is E.C. $37.69, by beneficiation stage (with output alumina)
E.C. $104.01, by the smelting stage (with output aluminium) E.C.
$333.74, and at the semifabrication stage E.C. $655.68. That is, the
domestic income derived from the production of one ton of semi-
fabricated aluminium is more than 17 times the domestic income
generated by the mining and drying of the 4.9 tons of bauxite that is
needed for the ton of aluminium. And the present organization of the
industry is such that the Caribbean economies do not participate in
the later production stages, though this may be economically feasible.[20]
     Second, with the present organizational structure, corporate
transfer pricing can be used not only to concentrate corporate profits
in the country where the corporate tax structure is most favorable
but also to circumvent a government's controls on capital transfers
and foreign exchange.[21] Such power of the corporations can easily
result in Caribbean countries not reaping as many benefits as they
could.
     In short, the question of ownership and control is a vital part
of the analysis that attempts to assess the economic developmental
impact of the bauxite-alumina industry in the Commonwealth Caribbean. Two recent developments are worth mentioning. The first is
the government of Guyana's nationalization of Demerara Bauxite, a
wholly-owned subsidiary of Alcan of Canada. Such a change in ownership, it is anticipated, will lead more quickly to the location of some
of the later processing stages in the region. The second development
is the expansion of the beneficiation process in both Jamaica and
Guyana. From the figures given above, it will be noticed that the value
added at this stage is more than twice the value added by the mining
and drying stages combined. The effect of this development will be
to increase the linkages in the Caribbean economies. So, while the
growth performance of the industry in terms of output and exports
is important, the change in ownership and relative shift in stages of
processing undertaken locally are likely to be more significant for
the long-run economic transformation of the Commonwealth Caribbean.
     For Trinidad-Tobago, petroleum and petroleum products occupy
an important position. These products accounted for 80 percent of

gross export receipts in 1967. The Third Development Plan, for the
years 1969-73, envisages a structural shift in the economy away from
almost complete dominance by the oil industry to greater diversification
in total production, but moderate growth in this industry can still be
expected during the 1970s.

The field of tourist development as an earner of foreign exchange
offers great prospects for the Commonwealth Caribbean. In Barbados,
Antigua, Trinidad-Tobago, and Jamaica tourism is already of great
importance. In 1967 the estimated gross expenditures of tourists was
$32.94 million, $17.8 million, and $30.81 million (in East Caribbean
dollars) respectively, in the first three countries mentioned. Even
with these large expenditures, however, there is much scope for
expansion. Commonwealth Caribbean governments have realized this
and are expected to pay particular attention to this aspect of regional
economic development. Growth prospects in this area are exceptionally
good in the less-developed members once the regional transportation
situation can be improved.

Yet the net contribution of the tourist industry in its present
structure to the economic development of the Commonwealth Caribbean
countries can be questioned on several grounds. First, although it is
a major earner of foreign exchange, because of a large import content
of tourist expenditures its capacity as a net foreign exchange earner
is considerably reduced. Second, the pattern of ownership of the
industry is such that the main beneficiaries are not likely to be nationals.
Third, in its present form, it perpetuates an undesirable feature that
in the past has been associated with the sugar industry. This is the
seasonal nature of employment in the industry. Fourth, the present
structure of the industry, geared as it is mainly for the North American
tourist, is very susceptible to the vagaries of possible frequent changes
in foreign demand which can lead to instability of the regional economies
—a characteristic of the economies that economic development is
attempting to reduce. In addition, the economic developmental process
must be viewed within the overall context of the development of
Commonwealth Caribbean society. In such a case the harmful social
and political consequences and the effects on workers' psychology of
a large group of visitors lolling on the beaches cannot be easily down-
played. Consequently, although there is much scope for expansion
the proper long-run economic development of the region may dictate
that caution be exercised in this field if Commonwealth Caribbean
society is not to be overwhelmed by the undesirable features of
tourism.

As pointed out earlier, the central developmental problem in
the Commonwealth Caribbean revolves around an unfavorable popula-
tion-to-natural resources ratio. It follows that one approach toward
a solution is to reduce the rate of population growth. In the Commonwealth Caribbean recent information on the rate of population growth

indicates that it is not as high as was earlier thought. In Guyana, for example, the rate was estimated at 2.90 percent annually for 1960-69, but the preliminary census figures show a rate of 2.45 percent annually for the 1960-70 period. Similarly, the estimate for Trinidad-Tobago for 1960-69 was 2.50 percent annually, but the census estimate is a very low 1.33 percent. Indeed, the estimated growth rate for the CARIFTA countries, including Belize which has an annual rate of 2.83 percent, is 1.52 percent for 1960-70. This comparatively low rate of population growth is no doubt due to the success of family planning programs, especially in Barbados and Jamaica. Their population growth rates were 0.26 percent and 1.46 percent respectively per annum for the period 1960-70. Intensification of a commitment to family planning as evidenced in the Jamaican government's acquisition of a $2 million loan from the World Bank to expand its program will probably lower the growth rate, but hardly very much lower. Clearly then, a reduction of the population growth rate taken by itself can hardly be considered an appropriate solution under the given circumstances. The regional economic integration strategy will have to do most of the work. Also, some economic planning, which will hopefully alter the organization of industry, and the ownership and control of regional resources will have to be relied upon.

One major economic problem that is likely to be no closer to a solution by the end of this decade is that of unemployment. Estimates of the extent of the problem in the Commonwealth Caribbean as mentioned at the outset of this chapter indicate that the rate of unemployment ranges between 12 and 20 percent. To improve this situation to any marked degree requires the creation of jobs far in excess of the number of school dropouts entering the labor force. Great priority has been given to this problem, especially in Trinidad-Tobago, but the magnitude of the problem should caution us against expecting any significant breakthrough.

CONCLUSION: THE STRATEGY OF
REGIONAL INTEGRATION FOR THE 1970s

In sum, therefore, the strategy of economic development taken by Commonwealth Caribbean governments, that of regional economic integration, seems to be the appropriate one for these countries. The concrete manifestations of such a strategy have not yet had time to gain firm footing. This should be accomplished in the 1970s. One should therefore not expect spectacular progress in the next 10 years, simply because of the existence of CARIFTA and the Caribbean Development Bank. Modest improvements are perhaps the most that can be expected; with a process as complex as economic development, shortcuts are not easy to find. But this very fact of the slowness of the developmental process poses a serious dilemma for the governments of the region. National unemployment around 20 percent (with unemployment among the younger members of the labor force much higher) with no signs of a reasonably quick resolution to the problem is the type of situation on which social unrest thrives. Already in Trinidad and Tobago such a situation (among other things) has led to social and political upheaval and various revolutionary activities. The declaration of a state of emergency to handle such a situation can at best be only a temporary solution. The effective long-run solution to such social and political disorders is removal of the root causes. This is the formidable task facing Commonwealth Caribbean governments in the decade of the 1970s.

18

**DIRECT FOREIGN INVESTMENT
AND INDUSTRIAL
ENTREPRENEURSHIP
IN CENTRAL AMERICA**
L. N. Willmore

It is now generally recognized that direct foreign investment is
more than a financial transaction, for the foreign investor provides
entrepreneurial services in the form of modern technology, management, and the ability to successfully market a product. Indeed, the
international corporation prides itself on supplying these services,
and it is the components other than plant and equipment which justify
the high rate of return for equity investments compared with investments in the form of bonds.[1] But the introduction of these entrepreneurial inputs into a developing economy can have a negative impact on human resources, even though the investment itself adds to
the productive capacity of the region. By supplying management and
technology and by refusing to sell shares in the local operation, the
international investor may well retard the development of local institutions that could perform these functions. In the words of Felipe
Pazos, "the main weakness of direct investment as a development
agent is a consequence of the complete character of its contribution."[2]

The Central American Common Market (CACM), which includes
Guatemala, El Salvador, Honduras, Nicaragua, and Costa Rica,
provides an excellent opportunity to study the simultaneous emergence
of native entrepreneurs and subsidiaries of international corporations
in the manufacturing sector of a developing economy. Factories began
to replace artisan methods of production during the 1940s, when the
governments of the region adopted protective tariffs and offered industrial incentives to encourage import-substitution. The removal
of artificial barriers to trade between the five countries, which began
in the late 1950s and was completed for the manufacturing sector by
1965, has stimulated the domestic production of manufactures and
has attracted a considerable amount of direct investment from abroad.

The emerging Central American industrialist feels threatened
by competition from the subsidiaries of foreign corporations, and for

this reason has appealed for measures to restrict direct foreign investment in existing industries. The purpose of this chapter is to examine the merits of this appeal and the overall impact of direct foreign investment on industrial entrepreneurship in the region. In particular, the study considers the change in the pattern of foreign investment which resulted from import-substitution and economic integration, the reaction of the local industrialist to this changed pattern of investment, and the policy measures which have been implemented in the CACM as a result.

Before he proceeds, the reader is asked to bear two points in mind. First, following A. H. Cole,[3] the function of entrepreneurship can be viewed as innovation, management, and adjustment to external conditions. But management alone, however essential it may be for the success of a business enterprise, is not synonymous with entrepreneurship. For the purposes of this chapter a "manager" is assumed to function as an entrepreneur only to the extent that he is given the authority—the decision-making power—to innovate and adjust to changes in the business environment. Second, there has been little research in Central American industries at the level of the firm, so many of the points in this chapter that relate to the structure of Central American enterprises must be regarded as tentative hypotheses which may be confirmed (or rejected) by subsequent empirical investigation.

THE PATTERN OF FOREIGN INVESTMENT

Direct foreign investments have a long history in Central America. In 1897 the book value of equity investments held by foreigners was calculated at about $12 million and was concentrated in the banana-growing countries of Costa Rica, Guatemala, and Honduras.[4] In recent years foreign investments have penetrated all five countries, and in a way far different from that of the "Banana Republic" type of investment.

Since the Central American countries record capital flows but not direct foreign investment in the region, a study of the pattern of foreign investment must be restricted to direct investments of U.S. firms. The task of compiling statistical evidence is made more difficult because prior to 1968 the U.S. data treated Central America not as a unit but rather as a balancing entry ("other Central American and West Indies") following Mexico and Panama.

Nonetheless, from the data published periodically by the U.S. Department of Commerce it can be estimated that the book value of U.S. investments in manufacturing increased sixfold from the time the General Treaty establishing the CACM was signed (December 1960) to the end of 1968. U.S. investments in agriculture and services have remained largely unchanged over the same period. The increased investment in "other" activities (mostly the export sector of agriculture) shown in Table 18.1 is most likely due to the purchase of sugar plantations in the Dominican Republic following the 1965 intervention, for there is no evidence that U.S. fruit companies have increased their holdings in Central America.

Japanese, German, and Mexican companies have established manufacturing plants in Central America,[5] but the United States still accounts for most of the direct foreign investment in the region. As U.S. enterprises operating public services are nationalized,[6] other companies, including United Fruit and W. R. Grace, are diversifying and investing an increasing amount in the manufacturing sector of the economy. Firms that formerly exported their products to Central America have opened plants in the region to cross the tariff barrier and retain their share of the local market.[7] The available evidence seems to support the observation made frequently in the press that the formation of the CACM has encouraged large international companies to produce consumer goods in the region, in competition with smaller Central American enterprises.* Central America thus appears to have entered a "new stage of foreign intervention"[9] which is very different from that which the region experienced in the past.

THE INTERNATIONAL FIRM AND
NATIONAL ENTREPRENEURSHIP

By encouraging import substitution in the postwar period the Central American governments have fostered the emergence of a new type of entrepreneur, one who manufactures commodities for the domestic market. At the same time, foreign investment has been diverted from the export and service sectors and toward the manufacturing sector of the economy. Economic integration has accelerated this process by making production for a regional market more

---

*A Guatemalan columnist, expressing a point of view which is frequently encountered in the Central American press, suggests that "the common market is nothing more than an expansion of the productive zones of the United States of America—and to a lesser extent of Japan, Germany and other countries which have incorporated some of their industries in the integration plans. And to our greater dismay, there have even been cases of prosperous industries, built by Central American entrepreneurs, which have been sold to wealthy foreign companies."[8]

TABLE 18.1

Book Value of U.S. Direct Investment in Central
America and West Indies,* 1960, 1964, and 1968
(millions of U.S. dollars)

	Total	Mining and Smelting	Petroleum	Manu- fact- ures	Utili- ties	Trade	Other
1960	464	20	71	19	132	18	204
1964	589	31	139	46	142	26	205
1968	725	33	198	121	147	45	251

*Exclusive of Cuba, Panama, and Caribbean dependencies.

Note: The five Central American countries account for approximately three-fourths of the total values shown.

Source: U.S. Department of Commerce, Survey of Current
Business, various issues.

TABLE 18.2

Book Value of U.S. Direct Investment in the Central
American Common Market, 1968, 1969, and 1970
(millions of U.S. dollars)

	Total	Mining and Smelting	Petroleum	Manufactures	Other
1968	596	6	151	104	335
1969	630	8	154	113	335
1970*	624	10	160	73	381

*Preliminary.

Source: U.S. Department of Commerce, Survey of Current
Business, various issues.

attractive to both the Central American industrialist and the large
international firm. As a result of policies that protect local industry
but not the local industrialist, foreign capital is increasingly competitive with local capital and a conflict has developed between the
Central American industrialist and his foreign counterpart.

The Central American industrialist typically employs his local
manufacturers' association as a pressure group to oppose what he
considers to be "unfair" competition from abroad. A case in Honduras
provides an excellent example of this type of activity. In May 1968
the Honduras Association of Timber Producers published an open
letter to President Oswaldo Lopez Arelleno in which they expressed
their opposition to the establishment of a large pulp and paper mill.
The proposed company, Industria Papelera Centroamericana, was to
be a "joint venture" with International Paper (a U.S. firm) controlling
51 percent of the stock and Standard Fruit and United Fruit an additional 15 percent each. The remaining minority shares were to be
purchased by the Central American Bank of Economic Integration
(BCIE), the government-owned National Development Bank, and the
Luxemburg-based Adela Investment Company. The local producers
argued that the proposed ten-year tax exemption and the creation of
unemployment in existing mills would outweigh any benefits which
might accrue to the Honduran economy. [10] In this instance the government was more interested in increasing exports to the rest of Central
America than in protecting the national entrepreneurs, so the company was granted a charter as planned in February 1969. [11] Were it
not for the fact that Honduras has a serious balance of payments
problem, the local producers might have been more successful in
influencing governmental policy.

Thus far, the industrialist has had more effect on foreign investment policy at the regional level than he has at the national level.
In an important public statement published in March 1965 the Central
American Federation of Chambers of Industry (FECAICA) proposed
that a total of eight restrictions be imposed on foreign direct investment in the region. The most important of these proposals were: (1)
certain areas of the economy should be reserved exclusively for
Central American investment, (2) "joint ventures" of domestic and
foreign capital should be encouraged, (3) foreign firms should employ
Central American administrators and managers, (4) no fiscal incentives should be granted to foreign investors who "threaten the
stability of established firms," and (5) regional and state financial institutions should give preference to Central American investors,
since "foreign investors are in a better position to provide their own
financing." [12]

The FECAICA declaration was apparently quite effective, for
less than three months later the ministers of economics of the five

CACM countries issued a policy statement that echoed the FECAICA proposals. In their joint declaration, the ministers urged that local resources be developed whenever possible, that joint industrial ventures be encouraged when a high level of technology requires foreign participation, and that in all other cases priority be given to Central American investors.[13] This declaration is not, however, binding on the individual governments, as is evident from the case of the pulp and paper mill in Honduras.

The industrialist pressure groups are, of course, motivated by self-interest and self-preservation. A governmental or regional developmental agency that is interested in the long-run development of human resources must consider the net impact of foreign direct investment on the formation of national entrepreneurs. And foreign direct investment does have a stimulating as well as a stifling effect on the development of entrepreneurship.

Direct investment from abroad can strengthen local entrepreneurship in three distinct ways. First, the manufacture of final demand goods creates opportunities for local entrepreneurs through the effects of what Hirschman calls "backward linkages," i.e., the purchase of intermediate goods in the domestic economy. Second, international firms train national managers who may become independent entrepreneurs in the future. Third, local industrialists become more efficient as a result of competition with and imitation of foreign-owned enterprises. The relevant question is then to what extent do these positive stimuli offset the negative impact of foreign direct investment on the development of industrial entrepreneurs in Central America.

At the present stage of industrial development in Central America, the industrialist has not become a supplier to the subsidiaries of international firms and, with the exception of plants that process agricultural products, backward linkages have not formed as a result of the establishment of new factories in the region. The present pattern of industrialization has resulted in a proliferation of plants that do little more than assemble imported component parts, plants that—to paraphrase a Guatemalan economist—package imported commodities in imported containers and add the label "Producto Centroamericano."[14] Costa Rica, for example, has four automobile assembly plants that import all component parts and a number of television and radio assembly plants that operate under similar conditions.[15] In Nicaragua, to cite another example, the chemical, cosmetics, and soap industries are composed primarily of plants that handle the final blending and bottling of imported products. These industries import 86 percent of their inputs from abroad, with the result that the value added by Nicaraguan blending, packaging, and distribution amounts to only 36 percent of the final retail price.[16]

The proponents of this indiscriminate type of industrialization argue that backward linkages will form in time. This may be true for some industries, but there is always a natural resistance on the part of the manufacturer of the final product to allow these linkages to form. If the manufacturer is an international firm, the only reason for establishing an assembly plant in Central America may be to escape the high duties on final consumer goods by exporting parts rather than the finished products. In other words, the parent company may continue to regard the small Central American economy as an export market, even though it has a "manufacturing" subsidiary in the region. In addition, the manufacturer may regard a domestically produced input as an inferior and more costly substitute for the imported good.

Albert Hirschman has suggested that this resistance to backward linkages is not a serious problem when one considers that the manufacturers of final demand goods can expand vertically and thus become their own suppliers.

> The resistance is almost wholly premised on the supposition that manufacturing in the higher stages of production is going to be undertaken by entrepreneurs other than the already established industrialists (or other than members of his immediate family). For if he himself undertakes it, most of the listed objections to the expansion of manufacturing via backward linkage fall to the ground. Thus, the fear of unreliability and poor quality of the domestic article should abate and the fear of domination by a monopoly supplier will disappear entirely.[17]

But what happens when the manufacturer is an international corporation? On the one hand, the corporation is predisposed to supply its Central American subsidiary with inputs produced by the parent company or a low-cost producer abroad.[18] On the other hand, if the host country stimulates the formation of backward linkages by collecting a higher duty on imported inputs, the subsidiary will expand through vertical integration rather than purchase intermediate goods from local entrepreneurs. In either event, the prospect of promoting national entrepreneurship through the effects of backward linkages is not very promising.

A second way in which a subsidiary of an international firm can increase the supply of local entrepreneurs is by training managerial personnel. In the case of Central America this impact is likely to be insignificant for two reasons. First, in many cases the parent company has simply substituted the export of component parts for the export of assembled units, with the result that the scope for innovation

within the subsidiary operation is probably quite limited.* Second,
even if a local employee should learn the requisite skills for successful entrepreneurship, he will find it difficult to obtain financial support
for an industrial venture, given the present state of the Central
American capital market.˙ The prospective entrepreneur may seek
employment in a firm that allows him greater scope for his entrepreneurial talents, but this solution presupposes that such enterprises
exist in the region.

     For a complete picture of the development of human resources
in industry, one must bear in mind that the native manufacturer is no
more willing to entrust his employees with decision-making power
than is his foreign rival. With few exceptions, the Central American
firm is a family affair, and outsiders generally are not permitted to
participate in decision making at any level. Thomas Cochran reports
that in the case of the Puerto Rican firm, the owner-manager was
very reluctant to delegate authority or provide information to non-
relatives.

>   The fear of delegating authority helped to prevent the rise
>   of a middle management group. Managers could not be
>   found by advertising in the newspapers or consulting an
>   agency. Sales managers or chief accountants had to be
>   trained from the ranks, and unless they were relatives, the
>   senior partner was unlikely to consult them on policy.[20]

This situation persisted in Puerto Rico in the mid-1950s, and in my
opinion is characteristic of most Central American firms today.[21]
The existing firms in Central America are probably not making a
significant contribution to the formation of entrepreneurs, and the
introduction of the international corporation into this environment is
not likely to alter the picture from the standpoint of human resource
development.

     The third way in which direct foreign investment can stimulate
local entrepreneurship is by forcing existing firms to improve the
efficiency of their operations as a result of competition and demonstration effects. There is no doubt that foreign direct investment has, in

---

     *This point—like many others in this chapter—is a tentative
judgment subject to empirical investigation. But Litvak and Maule,
in their study of U.S. subsidiaries in Canada, have concluded that
"potential Canadian creativity is often not encouraged and in fact may
be obstructed." A priori one would assume that the delegated authority
to local personnel in an underdeveloped and small economy like Central
America would allow even less scope for individual initiative.[19]

this sense, had an effect on the Central American industrialist. As Paul Rosenstein-Rodan has noted, "the stimulating effect is undoubtedly strong, perhaps so strong that the problem is that the patient should not be weakened (or killed) by overstimulation."[22]

The Central American industrialist has been unable to respond quickly to the stimulus of competition with the international firm, and many of his difficulties stem from the formation of the common market itself. The program of economic integration, which has given considerable impetus to Central American industrialization, is paradoxically contributing to the decline of the Central American industrialist. The industrial entrepreneur, who was accustomed to produce for the market of his own country, suddenly found himself operating in a larger regional market in the mid-1960s. Although the industries of each country were able to survive the competition of intraregional imports,[23] the industrialist has not been as successful in meeting the competition of the international enterprise.

The local entrepreneur needs time to adapt his finances, production, and marketing to the changed business environment.[24] Regional marketing requires an expanded sales organization and promotional advertising on a scale to which the national enterprise is usually not accustomed. The industrialist may also find it necessary to adapt his product line, alter his production techniques by purchasing modern equipment, or, at the very least, increase his inventory to meet the needs of a larger and more geographically dispersed market. Credit is generally available for additions to fixed plant and equipment, although the local entrepreneur may lack the technological information required for efficiency in planning capital expenditures. The major financial problem is the need for working capital to finance an enlarged inventory and sales promotion, and the small firm has little hope of obtaining credit for such purposes.

The international firm has an advantage over the local industrialist in marketing, technology, and finance. The parent company has exported its products to all five countries in the past, so it has a marketing and sales organization that encompasses the entire region. The international firm is not only aware of but is most likely an innovator with respect to technology. And financially, the international enterprise can more easily incur the expenses of initiating regional production and marketing, for it has access to both the retained earnings of the parent company and the international money market.

In short, a program of protection and encouragement of national entrepreneurship is not without merit from the standpoint of human resource development in Central America. Throughout the postwar period the five countries have made every effort to protect their "infant" industries and stimulate the process of industrialization. They are now beginning to implement measures to protect their

"infant" industrialists and encourage the development of national
entrepreneurship.

REGIONAL INDUSTRIAL POLICY

Although Central America does not yet have a comprehensive
program of "infant" industrialist protection, the five countries have
utilized the common market framework to institute a number of
policy measures in favor of national entrepreneurship. These measures
fall roughly into two categories: positive attempts to improve the competitive position of the local industrialist, and attempts to restrict the
activity of the international firm so as to favor domestic over foreign
investment.

The positive measures to improve local entrepreneurship are
directed at marketing, technology, and finance—three respects in
which the international firm has a distinct advantage over the local
industrialist. Three new regional institutions have been created to
deal with these problems. The Central American Institute of Business
Administration (INCAE), which was founded under the auspices of
Harvard University, is training potential independent entrepreneurs
and increasing the pool of management personnel that is available to
local firms. In addition, the universities in the region have added
courses in business organization, marketing, and finance to the
traditional accounting courses in the commerce curriculum. The
Central American Institute of Research and Industrial Technology
(ICAITI) provides technical advice and carries out feasibility studies
for private enterprise in all five countries. This institute has no
doubt improved the efficiency of existing enterprises and it provides
useful information to those entrepreneurs who consider investing in
a new industry. The Central American Bank for Economic Integration
(BCIE) has improved somewhat the availability of credit to the industrialist. But the bulk of the funds of the bank have been received
as a part of the foreign aid programs of the industrial countries, and
these funds are often tied to the exports of the country that has
extended the credit to Central America. Thus bank credit is restricted
largely to expenditures on capital goods and does not aid the businessman who seeks to increase his inventory and extend his marketing
operations.

The inability of the Central American industrialist to finance
his expansion into a regional market undoubtedly accounts for much
of the weakness of domestically owned enterprises. In this respect
it is significant that in El Salvador, where some industrialists have
been quick to seize the opportunities of the CACM, many of the local
manufacturers have extensive interests in financial institutions.[25]

In general, however, the absence of a capital market of any importance in the region means that there is no mechanism by which savings
are allocated to entrepreneurs who have investment opportunities. As
a result, a considerable amount of savings is invested abroad or held
by Central Americans as liquid assets in financial institutions outside
the region.[26]

To strengthen the local capital market, a Costa Rican economist
has suggested that the CACM form a "public investment corporation"
which, in the manner of a mutual fund, could channel private savings
to local industry.[27] But this increase in the demand for equity shares
would have little effect on the level of investment unless an increased
supply of industrial shares is forthcoming. At the present time
neither the international corporation nor the family-owned firm is
eager to sell equity shares in the local market. The international
firm generally avoids issuing any significant number of shares in a
subsidiary company, for there may be a conflict between maximization
of global profits and maximization of profits in any single region, or
there may be a conflict of interest, with the local shareholder pre-
ferring to maximize short-run profits and the parent company long-
run profits.* The family firm, like the international enterprise, is
adverse to issuing shares out of fear of losing some control of the
company. Thus most domestically owned firms prefer to expand
gradually through debt financing and reinvested earnings rather than
seek outside shareholders who are willing to hold equity in the firm.[28]

Even with an effort to develop a strong Central American capital
market, improve the technology of existing plants, and train business
managers, the Central American industrialist needs time to adapt to
his changed environment, and this requires governmental action to
restrict direct foreign investment and protect the "infant" industrialist.
No single country in the region is able to impose meaningful restrictions on foreign investment for fear that the international enterprise
will simply move its subsidiary to another CACM country. At the
same time, the national governments are reluctant to delegate to a
regional body the authority to make decisions with respect to industrial
investments, decisions which are of vital importance to any national
economy. After several years of negotiations, the Central American
governments have agreed to harmonize their fiscal incentives to industrial development, but an international firm can still "play off"
one country against another to obtain a right to majority ownership
and effective control of a subsidiary company. The CACM councils

---

*Sears Roebuck is a notable exception, but it is not an industrial
corporation.

can suggest guidelines but cannot, in most cases, make these guide-lines binding on the member states.

The Central American Economic Council, which is made up of the five ministers of economics and is responsible for the overall direction of the CACM, is prepared to use its persuasive powers on behalf of the local industrialist. On the occasion of the visit of Governor Nelson Rockefeller in the spring of 1969, for example, the council emphasized that "direct foreign investment cannot be regarded as a substitute for international transfers destined to finance develop-ment projects in the public sector" and urged that direct investment be "channelled to priority sectors of the economy in such a way as to strengthen Central American entrepreneurship." [29]

Under the terms of the General Treaty of Economic Integration and the various protocols to that treaty, the Economic Council can do little more than encourage governments to favor domestic investors. The body can advise, but cannot decree, the composition of investment capital in almost all cases—with one important exception. This excep-tion occurs when a company seeks to be declared an "integration in-dustry" and thus obtain a privileged and protected position within the CACM for a period of ten years or more. [30]

When the ministers of economics drafted the 1963 protocol which designated the first two "integration industries," they were careful to restrict foreign participation in the enterprises. [31] The first "integra-tion" enterprise—the GINSA tire and tube plant in Guatemala—had been established in 1957 with predominantly (94.2 percent) Central American capital. [32] The General Tire Company of Akron, Ohio, supplies techni-cal assistance in exchange for minority participation and a contractual fee. As a condition of "integration" status, GINSA is required to issue a majority of any new shares to Central Americans. Similarly, a minimum of 40 percent Central American participation was required in the second "integration industry"—a new caustic soda and insecticide plant in Nicaragua.

The Economic Council's desire to protect Central American entrepreneurship was most evident during a dispute that developed between GINSA and the Firestone Tire and Rubber Company. GINSA was successful in substituting its own brand for some of the imports, and requested an increase in the tariff in the hope of supplying virtually all of the Central American demand for tires and tubes. [33] In reaction to the competition of GINSA in the regional market, Firestone decided to cross the tariff barrier and establish an "integra-tion" plant in Costa Rica. This was legally permissible, for the 1963 protocol (Article 27) allows the executive council of the CACM to designate, by majority vote, additional "integration" plants for tires provided that 60 percent of the capital stock is offered to Central Americans and that at least 30 percent is actually purchased by them.

Firestone, however, was willing to sell a maximum of 25 percent of
the initial shares in the local market, so Costa Rica's application for
a second "integration" tire plant was referred to the Economic
Council in February 1965. The council ruled that foreign participation
could not exceed 30 percent—far less than the 75 percent requested
by Firestone—and that the tires produced by the plant would have to
carry a Central American brand name rather than the well-known
Firestone insignia.[34]

Firestone could not accept the conditions imposed by the Economic
Council, so built a plant without "integration" status in order to supply
the Costa Rican and (by special arrangement) Panamanian markets.
Under the terms of the Regime of Integration Industries, the tariff in
the other four countries will be reduced by 10 percent each year, with
free trade in tires at the end of ten years. Costa Rica cannot protect
her industry from Guatemalan imports, so Firestone will undoubtedly
incur losses during this transitional period. It is alleged, however,
that Firestone intended to retain its share of the Central American
market and was therefore not concerned with the fact that the plant
would not be a profitable investment.[35]

The Central American tire and tube industry should provide an
interesting case study of duopolistic competition during the present
decade. If economies of scale are important in the industry, GINSA,
which has three times the installed capacity of the Firestone plant,
should have substantially lower costs per unit of output. However,
competition between the two companies will most likely take the form
of increased expenditures on advertising, and in this nonprice competition Firestone has the initial advantage of a well-established
brand name. When Firestone began production in 1967, GINSA conducted an extensive advertising campaign to make Costa Ricans aware
that GINSA, unlike Firestone, is a Central American company with a
large number of shareholders throughout the isthmus. For several
months the Costa Rican press and radio carried announcements of a
promotional contest in which the prizes were shares of GINSA stock.
As tariff barriers are removed for Firestone tires this type of
advertising will undoubtedly increase throughout Central America.
Ultimately the two companies will have to reach some type of tacit
agreement regarding division of the market, or continue to face
expensive outlays for promotional purposes.[36]

The inability of the Economic Council to prevent Firestone
from investing in one of the CACM countries on its own terms is a
direct consequence of the lack of a clearly defined agreement on
foreign direct investment in the region. Nor does there exist a
comprehensive policy on foreign ownership at the national level. The
ministers of economics, acting jointly, have suggested some policy
guidelines; but the party (or military junta) in power in each country

has failed to formulate a similar statement of policy. Cabinet ministers are appointed by the president in each country, so one might conclude that silence on the issue is a weak approval of the ministerial statements. But in considering any particular case the national governments invariably ignore the appeals of local industrialists and accept foreign investment of any type so as to improve the balance of payments and stimulate the process of industrialization.

CONCLUSION

Economic integration and the substitution of imports in Central America has encouraged the development of the modern indigenous industrialist and, at the same time, threatens his existence. Direct foreign investment in the manufacturing sector is often competitive with the existing enterprises of local entrepreneurs. For this reason the Central American industrialist, through FECAICA and other pressure groups, is attempting to restrict foreign investment to areas that are not competitive with his own activities.

Thus far, the Central American industrialist has not been able to restrict the penetration of the international firm, which has an advantage in marketing, technology, and finance, and sufficient mobility to bargain with five independent republics. If Central America is to protect and favor national entrepreneurship, there must be an increased effort to improve the competitive position of domestically owned enterprises and there must be a common foreign investmental policy throughout the region.

Economists now generally accept the concept of an "infant" industry, and are beginning to admit the need for protection of national ("infant") entrepreneurship in a developing economy. It is very likely that Central America, like Mexico[37] and Peru[38], will begin to restrict direct foreign investment and promote national entrepreneurship.

Native industrialists, intellectuals, and common market officials increasingly share the opinion that most of the benefits of integration are accruing to "certain migratory birds,"[39] to international corporations rather than to local entrepreneurs. If the members of the Central American Common Market do not agree to a uniform policy with respect to foreign investment, individual governments may well find themselves under pressure to adopt more radical measures, such as the nationalization of foreign-owned subsidiaries.

LATIN AMERICAN PROSPECTS FOR THE 1970s:
WHAT KINDS OF REVOLUTIONS?

Program of the Conference Held at
Carleton University, Ottawa

Friday, November 13, 1971
OPENING REMARKS - Professor P. E. Uren, Acting Director, School
of International Affairs, Carleton University
PUBLIC ADDRESS, "Latin America at Crossroads: Diagnosis and
Prognosis."
- P. N. Rosenstein-Rodan, Professor of Econom-
ics, Massachusetts Institute of Technology

SEMINARS (2:30 to 3:50 p.m.)
NO. 1.   "The Pearson and Prebisch Reports: The Crucial Issue
of Unemployment"
- D. H. Pollock, UN Economic Commission for Latin
America; Visiting Professor, School of International
Affairs, Carleton University
NO. 2.   "The Church in Latin America"
- C. A. Astiz, Graduate School of Public Affairs, State
University of New York
Discussants: L'Abbe Dionne, Canadian Catholic Office for
Latin America; B. Tyson, School of International Service,
American University; T. C. Bruneau, Political Science,
McGill University
NO. 3.   "Changes in Class Attitudes in the Military and Bougeoisie
in Peru and Cuba"
- G. DeGré, Sociology, University of Waterloo
NO. 4.   "Economic Integration in Latin America: The Allocation
of Industrial Capacity Among Members"
- J. Ahmad, Economics, Sir George Williams University
NO. 5.   "The Future of Agrarian Peoples in Central America"
- D. Holden, Sociology, Queen's University
NO. 6.   Contemporary Military Elites in South America - A Com-
parative Analysis"
- J. Harbron, Associate Editor, Toronto Telegram
Discussant: H. Massey, Political Science, York University

SEMINARS (4:00 to 5:30 p.m.)

NO. 7.   "Planning: Alternative Institutional Forms"
          - E. Iglesias, Inter-American Development Bank; Chairman
          of the Board of the Latin American Institute for Economic
          and Social Planning
          Discussant: M. Chassudovsky, Economics, University of
          Ottawa

NO. 8.   "The Constraints of Agricultural Organization"
          - P. Y. Denis, Institut de Geographie, Université Laval

NO. 9.   "Social Structure, Power, and Development"
          - L. Ratinoff, Inter-American Development Bank
          Discussant: R. Melaffe, Visiting Professor of History,
          University of Toronto

NO. 10.   "Latin American Indian Prospects for the 1970s"
          - J. P. Rona, Linguistics and Modern Languages, University
          of Ottawa

NO. 11.   "Ecology and Prospective Latin American Development"
          - M. Chapman, School of International Affairs, Carleton
          University
          Discussant: M. Frankman, Economics, McGill University

NO. 12.   "Guerrillas"
          - J. C. M. Ogelsby, History, University of Western Ontario
          "Guerrilla Movements: Their Essential Ingredients for
          Success"
          - P. Mars, Political Science, Carleton University

PUBLIC ADDRESS, "Latin America's Alternative Futures"
                - K. Silvert

Saturday, November 14, 1971

SEMINARS (9:00 to 10:30 a.m.)

NO. 13.   "Foreign Investment Policy and the Multinational Firm"
          - P. N. Rosenstein-Rodan

NO. 14.   "The Role of the Latin American Military Today as Military
          Managers"
          - B. Tyson

NO. 15.   "Planning"
          - M. Chassudovsky
          "Development Through Social Planning"
          - H. A. Wood, Geography, McMaster University
          "Obstacles to Development in Latin America: An Evaluation
          of the Planning Process" - H. A. Wood

NO. 16.   "The Diplomat as Hostage: Revolution in the Context of
          Latin American Foreign Relations"

- G. S. Smith, History, Queen's University
NO. 17.   "Literature and Social Change in Latin America"
- R. Glickman, Hispanic Studies, University of Toronto
- M. Martinez, Linguistiques et Langues Modernes, Univer-
sité d'Ottawa
Discussant: E. Glickman, Humanities, York University
NO. 18.   "Urbanization"
- M. Frankman

SEMINARS (10:30 a.m. to 12 noon)
NO. 19.   "Brazil"
- M. Pone, Economics, Algoma College, Sault Ste. Marie
Discussants: P. S. Smith, History, Waterloo; H. Makler,
Sociology, University of Toronto
NO. 20.   "Central America"
- L. N. Willmore, Economics, Carleton University; D.
Holden; E. Laberge, Institut de Cooperation Internationale,
University of Ottawa
NO. 21.   Peru - "Peruvian Migration to the Montana, A Partial
Solution to Economic and Demographic Problems"
- R. Wesche, Geography, University of Ottawa
NO. 22.   Uruguay
- E. Iglesias
Discussant: J. P. Rona
NO. 23.   "The Caribbean: A Stumbling Block or Stepping-Stone
Towards a Canadian Latin American Policy"
- M. Morris, School of International Affairs, Carleton
University
Discussant: C. H. Grant, Political Science, University of
Waterloo
NO. 24.   "Aspects of Cuba in the Context of Latin America"
- J. A. Hechavarria.
NO. 25.   Haiti and Santo Domingo
- J. C. M. Ogelsby

SEMINARS (1:00 to 2:20 p.m.)
NO. 26.   "Peru: The Revolutionary Potential of the Military Regime"
- C. A. Astiz
NO. 27.   Chile
- L. Escobar, Executive Director, International Monetary
Fund
Discussant: R. Melaffe, History, University of Toronto
NO. 28.   Argentina
- P. Y. Denis
NO. 29.   "Development Prospects in the Commonwealth Caribbean
During the 1970s"

               - V. Richards, Economics, Carleton University
               Discussant: C. H. Grant

NO. 30.   "Bolivia in the 1970s: What Kind of Revolution?"
               - B. Wood, Parliamentary Center, Ottawa

NO. 31.   Cuba
               "Development Strategies and Economic Performance: Past, Present and Prospective"
               - A. R. M. Ritter, Economics, Carleton University
               "Aspects of the Cuban Approach to Socialism"
               - F. Park, Montreal

SEMINARS (2:30 to 3:50 p.m.)

NO. 32.   "The Military as National Modernizers in Latin America: The Cases of Brazil and Peru"
               - B. Tyson
               Discussant: T. C. Brunneau, Political Science, McGill University

NO. 33.   "Revolution Mexican Style"
               - I. Bar-Lewaw, Foreign Literature, York University

NO. 34.   "Changing Patterns in Intra-Caribbean Relations"
               - J. Sokol, Canadian Institute of International Affairs.

NO. 35.   "Chile: What Role in Marxist Hemispheric Doctrine?"
               - J. Harbron
               Discussant: R. Melaffe

NO. 36.   "An Evaluation of Castro's Contribution to the Cuban Revolution"
               - I. Lumsden, Political Science, York University

NO. 37.   "Colombia: The Crucial Years, 1971-74"
               - H. Cleveland, former Canadian Ambassador to Colombia
               Discussant: G. S. Mount, History, Laurentian University

PANEL DISCUSSIONS (4:00 to 6:00 p.m.)

A.   Canadian Relations with Latin America and the Caribbean
     Panel Members:
     D. Madden, Latin American Section, Canadian International Development Agency (CIDA); H. Massey; M. Morris; J. C. M. Ogelsby (Chairman); J. Pearson, Latin American Studies, University of Toronto; C. Sanger, author, CIDA; B. Wood

B.   Alternative Paths to Modernization and Democracy in Latin America
     Panel Members:
     C. A. Astiz; J. Harbron; D. H. Pollock (Chairman); L. Ratinoff; P. N. Rosenstein-Rodan; B. Tyson

PUBLIC ADDRESS - I. Illich, Centro de Documentacion Inter-cultural
(CIDOC), Cuernavaca, Mexico
Introduced by: A. D. Dunton, President, Carleton University

CHAPTER 1

1. P. Calvert, Revolution (London: MacMillan, 1970), p. 15. According to Calvert, coups and "palace revolts" that successfully alter the personages of the ruling group qualify for the label "revolution", even though no social or economic change may accompany the new regime. Unsuccessful use of physical force for such purposes would be labelled a rebellion, insurrection, or uprising.

2. Merle Kling, "Violence and Politics in Latin America," in U. L. Horowitz, et al., eds., Latin American Radicalism (New York: Random House, 1969).

3. From a panel on "Alternative Paths to Modernization and Democracy in Latin America," at the Conference, "Latin American Prospects for the 1970s: What Kinds of Revolutions?

4. C.f. P. Baran, The Political Economy of Growth (New York: Marzani and Munsell, 1960); A. G. Frank, Capitalism and Underdevelopment in Latin America (New York: Monthly Review Press, 1967); and A. G. Frank, Underdevelopment or Revolution (New York: Monthly Review Press, 1969), for a persuasive presentation.

5. Regis Debray, The Chilean Revolution: Conversations with Allende (New York: Random House, 1971), p. 52.

6. UN Economic Commission for Latin America (ECLA), Social Change and Social Development Policy in Latin America (New York, 1970), p. 88.

7. In absolute terms, however, the real incomes of the lowest-income receivers (the bottom four deciles) increased by 1.95 percent per year according to the estimates of I.M. Navarrette, "La Distribución de ingreso en Mexico: Tendencias y Perspectivas," in V. Urquidi, ed., El Perfil de Mexico en 1980 (Mexico: Siglo XXI Editores, 1970).

8. UN ECLA, Recent Events in the Latin American Free Trade Association (ALALC: Associación Latinamericana de Libre Comercio) April-May 1971, p. 22.

9. See chaps. 5 and 6 in this volume for discussion of policies aimed at reducing unemployment.

10. See International Labor Office, Towards Full Employment: A Programme for Colombia (Geneva, 1970), and K. Marsden, "Progressive Technologies for Developing Countries," International Labour Review (May 1971).

11. Frank, Capitalism.

12. E.g., O. Sunkel, "National Development Policy and External Dependence in Latin America," Journal of Development Studies (Summer 1971) and "Big Business and Dependencia," Foreign Affairs (April 1972).

13. J. Gerassi asserts without substantiation that per capita incomes in Latin America have actually declined: "Latin America today is poorer and more suffering than it was ten years ago, ten years before that, and so on back through the ages," in Horowitz, et al., ed., Latin American Radicalism p. 493.

14. Frank, Capitalism, pp. 6-8.

15. Frank, Underdevelopment or Revolution, p. 6. Pablo Gonzales-Casanova presents a more complete and most eloquent variant of this type of argument. Cf. "Internal Colonialism and National Development," in Horowitz, et al., eds., Latin American Radicalism, pp. 118-140.

16. Frank, Capitalism, p. 120.

17. Ibid., pp. 3, 115-120.

18. Fidel Castro, Ediciones el Orientador Revolucionario, No. 6, (Havana, 1967), p. 17.

19. For a more articulate if less polemic examination of the constraints imposed by asymmetric interdependence, see Sunkel, "National Development Policy."

20. "This liaison of labour radicalism and populist revolt painted on the wall the imminent danger of a social revolution. . . . The rise of socialist radicalism, and in particular the Bolshevik Revolution, tended to drive all more or less privileged, more or less well-to-do elements in the society into one 'counter-revolutionary coalition,'" P.A. Baran, "On the Political Economy of Backwardness," The Manchester School (January 1952).

CHAPTER 3

1. UN Economic Commission for Latin America (ECLA), Notas sobre la Economía y el Desarrollo de América Latina #40 (1970).

2. A. B. Rofman, "Efectos de la Integración Latinoamericano en el Esquema de Localización Industrial," América en el Año 2000; La Integración y el Desarrollo (Mexico D.F., Mexico; Sociedad Interamericana de Planificación, 1970), pp. 232, 234.

3. ECLA, Notas, #7 (1968).

4. At the Tenth Latin American Free Trade Association (LAFTA) Conference, in Montevideo in 1970, "an intense, acrimonious debate [was] transcribed in the Minutes of Negotiation. Since it was evidently considered unseemly for the transcript to appear in full, the delegations agreed that hereafter the minutes would only contain 'the results obtained in negotiation and the additional decisions adopted by the Contracting Parties for their execution.'" Comercio Exterior de México, January 1971, p. 9.

5. For example, Brazil is outraged by Argentina's restoration of duties on a number of items which Brazil had been supplying. Paraguay is complaining loudly that Argentina is creating obstacles to trade which prevent her smaller neighbor from benefiting from concessions which were awarded. Uruguay is threatening to withdraw from the association because of its alarming trade deficits with LAFTA countries. The Uruguayan minister of economy and finance, speaking on May 12, 1971, stated, "A number of factors indicate that the free trade movement which the LAFTA is supposed to be is really turning into an organization wherein each country seeks its own advantage rather than reciprocal benefits." Comercio Exterior de México, January and July, 1971.

In the Central American Common Market, tensions exacerbated by the integration process led to the still-unresolved hostilities between El Salvador and Honduras. The Pan-American highway through Honduras is closed to goods from El Salvador, which can now reach Nicaragua and Costa Rica only by water. Decree #97, passed by the Honduran government on December 31, 1970, states in its introduction, "the Central American Economic Integration Program has not fulfilled the objectives for which it was created, by failing to obey its original precepts and guidelines." Comercio Exterior de México, February 1971, p. 12.

6. Chile's Ambassador Pedro Daza Valanzuela spoke for much of Latin America when he told the Tenth LAFTA Conference, "In order to achieve their national objectives, affirm their own personality and be able to take an active role in the construction of an international society based on justice, the countries of Latin America must make a great internal effort, as well as perfect a system of Latin American cooperation. The guidelines and forms of this effort are a matter to be determined by each of our countries; the choice of road is a sovereign decision to be arrived at freely by each people." Comercio Exterior de México, February 1971, p. 19.

7. A. Kaplan, "Aspectos Políticos de la Planificación en América Latina," Revista de la Sociedad Interamericana de Planificación, September 1970.

8. BOLSA Review, July 1971, p. 392

9. H. A. Wood, "Technology and Productivity; Examples from Mexico and Central America," The Professional Geographer, May 1970, pp. 147-151.

10. The literature on regional planning is vast, but two references may be selected for special mention: W. B. Stohr, "Regional Planning as a Necessary Tool for the Comprehensive Development of a Country," paper presented at the United Nations Inter-Regional Symposium on Training of Planners for Comprehensive Regional Development, held in Warsaw, Poland, June 14-28, 1971; and

J. Chi-Yi Chen, Estrategia del Desarrollo Regional: Caso de Venezuela, (Caracas, 1967).

11. Helio Jaguaribe, "Dependencia y Autonomía en América Latina," América en el Año 2000; la Integracion y el Desarrollo (Mexico D.F., Mexico: Sociedad Interamericana de Planificación, 1969).

CHAPTER 4

1. UN, Multinational Economic Cooperation in Latin America, I: Texts and Documents (New York, 1962).

2. Edward G. Cale, Latin American Free Trade Association-Progress, Problems, Prospects, a report prepared under contract for the Office of External Research, Department of State (Washington, D.C., May, 1969).

3. The Economist Intelligence Unit, Ltd., London, 1968.

4. M.S. Wionczek, (ed.) Latin American Economic Integration: Experiences and Prospects (New York, 1966); Victor L. Urguidi, "LAFTA and the Economic Integration of Latin America," Quarterly Review of the Bank of London (July, 1966).

5. UN Economic Commission for Latin America (ECLA), A Contribution to Economic Integration Policy in Latin America, E/CN. 12/728 (New York, 1965).

6. J. Bhagwati, "Trade Liberalization among LDCS, Trade Theory and Gatt Rules," in J. N. Wolfe, ed., Value, Capital and Growth (Edinburgh University Press, 1968).

7. S. Dell, A Latin American Common Market? (London, 1963).

8. H. Brewster, Methods and Procedures for Regional Development and Trade Expansion (Geneva: UN Conference on Trade and Development, 1970).

9. Ibid.

10. R.G. Lipsey, "The Theory of Customs Unions: A General Survey," "Economic Journal (September 1960); J.E. Meade, The Theory of Customs Union (Amsterdam, 1955).

11. Tibor Scitovsky and Petrus Johannes Verctoorn, Economic Theory and Western European Integration (London, 1958).

12. H. G. Johnson, "The Gains from Freer Trade with Europe," Manchester School (September 1958).

13. Edward F. Denison, Why Growth Rates Differ (London: Brookings Institution 1958).

14. A. Harberger, "Using the Resources at Hand More Effectively," American Economic Review: Papers and Proceedings (May 1959).

15. Paul G. Clark and R. Weisskoff, "Import Demand and Import Policies in Brazil" (Williamstown, Mass: Center for Development Economics, Williams College, October 1966).

16. Scitovsky, Economic Theory.
17. Bela Balassa, Economic Development and Integration (Mexico: Centro de Estudios Monetarios Latinoamercanos, 1965); Allan S. Manne, Key Sectors of the Mexican Economy, 1962-1972 (Stanford, Calif.: Research Center in Economic Growth, 1965).
18. Thomas Victorisz and Alan S. Manne, "Chemical Processes, Plant Location and Economies of Scale," in A.S. Manne and H. Markowitz, eds., Studies in Process Analysis (New York, 1963).
19. UN ECLA, A Study of the Iron and Steel Industry in Latin America (New York, 1962).
20. Manne, Key Sectors.
21. Goran Ohlin, "Trade in a Non-Laissez-Faire World," International Economic Relations, Proceedings of the Third Congress of the International Economic Association (New York: St. Martins Press 1969).
22. Bhagwati, "Trade Liberalization."
23. Balassa, Economic Development.
24. Bhagwati, "Trade Liberalization."
25. B. Hansen, Long-and Short-Term Planning in Underdeveloped Countries (Amsterdam, 1967).
26. H.B. Chenery, "Structural Imbalance and Future Development in Latin America," paper presented at Cornell University Conference on the Next Decade of Latin American Economic Development (Ithaca, New York April, 1966).
27. R. Prebisch, Change and Development—Latin America's Great Task, (Washington, D.C., Inter-American Development Bank 1970).
28. Osvaldo Sunkel, "Structural Background of Development Problems in Latin America," Weltwirtschaftiches Archiv (September 1966).
29. Paul N. Rosenstein-Rodan, "Multinational Investment in the Framework of Latin American Integration", in Inter-American Development Bank, Multinational Investment in the Economic Development and Integration of Latin America (Bogota, 1968).
30. C.A. Cooper and B.F. Massell, "Towards a General Theory of Customs Union for Developing Countries," Journal of Political Economy (1965).
31. David A. Kendrick, "Investment Planning and Economic Integration," Economics of Planning, VII, 1 (1967).
32. J.R. Boudeville, Problems of Regional Economic Planning (Edinburgh, 1966).

CHAPTER 5

1. D. H. Pollock, "Pearson and UNCTAD: A Comparison," International Development Review, XII, 4, (December, 1970).

2. An excellent amplification of this point will be found in R. E.
Asher, "Development Assistance in DD II: Recommendations of
Perkins, Pearson, Peterson, Prebisch and Others," International
Organization, Winter 1970.

CHAPTER 6

1. The Italian Development Plan, 1970-80 ("Progetto Ottanta,"
Feltrinelli, Milan, 1969) has excellent data on how a 1 percent
increase in value added in different sectors creates an increase
in employment varying from 0.16 to 0.28.

2. See I.M.D. Little, "The Real Cost of Labour and the Choice
Between Consumption and Investment," Quarterly Journal of
Economics (February 1961), pp. 1-15.

3. "Program of Investment in the South of Italy," Rome,
SVIMEZ, 1951.

4. See I.M.D. Little, article in Quarterly Journal of Economics,
1958-59, and other papers in the India project of Massachusetts
Institute of Technology (M.I.T.).

5. For details, see Paul N. Rosenstein-Rodan, "How to Indus-
trialize a Non-Industrial Area," M.I.T., and "Remarks on Regional
Development," Milan, 1962.

CHAPTER 8

1. The best survey of this literature is still Lyle McAllister,
"Recent Research and Writings on the Role of the Military in Latin
America," Latin American Research Review, II, 1 (Fall 1966),
5-36. Examples of the first attempts to deal with the new type of
military leader largely using old categories would be: Gino Germani
and Kalman Silvert, "Politics and Military Intervention in Latin
America," in Jason Finkle and Richard Gable, eds., Political
Development and Social Change (New York: John Wiley and Sons,
1966), pp. 397-402; Edwin Lieuwen, Generals versus Presidents:
Neo-Militarism in Latin America (New York: Praeger Publishers,
1964). On the other hand, Victor Alba had early correctly perceived
and described the military technocrat. See his "The Stages of
Militarism in Latin America" (especially pages 172-176), in John
Johnson, (ed.), The Role of the Military in Underdeveloped Countries
(Princeton University Press, 1962—note date).

2. See, for example, Julio Cotler, "Crisis Política y Populismo
Militar en el Perú," Estudios Internacionales (Santiago), No. 12
(January-March 1970).

3. Two recent books have provided an extensive amount of
historical and sociological data, as well as careful interpretations
and conceptual schemes. I wish to thank the two authors for the
opportunity to read both books in manuscript before they were

published. They are: Ronald Schneider, The Political System of Brazil: Emergence of a "Modernizing" Authoritarian Regime, 1964-70 (New York: Columbia University Press, 1971); and Alfred Stepan, The Military in Politics: Changing Patterns in Brazil (Princeton, N.J.: Princeton University Press, 1971). An interesting article on the same subject is Frank D. McCann, "The Military and Change in Brazil," in Merrill Rippy, ed., Cultural Change in Brazil (Papers from the Midwest Association for Latin American Studies) (Muncie, Indiana: Ball State University Press, 1970).

4. This article is in many ways an attempt to build on ideas suggested by Alfred Stepan in "The 'New Professionalism' of Internal Warfare and Military Role-Expansion," a paper originally given at a Workshop on Brazilian Development Since 1964, at Yale University, April 23 and 24, 1971, quoted by permission. Even though Victor Alba (note 1, above) and other writers have described what Stepan calls "the new professional," Stepan has given it what is to this author's knowledge the clearest description and interpretation. When Morris Janowitz wrote in the mid-1950s that "The consequences of the new tasks of military management imply that the professional soldier is required more and more to acquire skills and orientations common to civilian administrators and even political leaders," he was certainly anticipating Stepan's work. Morris Janowitz, "Military Elites and the Study of War," Journal of Conflict Resolution, No. 1, 1957.

5. See Philippe C. Schmitter, "The Portugalization of Brazil?" A paper given at the same conference as Stepan's (note 4 above). Like Stepan's, it may well be a "landmark" article in the understanding of the nature of the present Brazilian government. Both Schmitter and Stepan as well as the author of this article freely acknowledge their great debt to the work and interpretation of Juan Linz. See especially Linz's article, "An Authoritarian Regime: Spain," in E. Allardt and S. Rokkan, eds., Mass Politics (New York: Free Press, 1970), pp. 251-283.

6. See Thomas E. Skidmore, "Politics and Economic Policy-Making in Authoritarian Brazil" another paper delivered at the workshop at Yale (see note 4 above). Along with Stepan's and Schmitter's papers, it will be published by Yale University Press in 1972. In his paper Skidmore compares the corporatism of Vargas with the present Brazilian political system, and finds that the military has in good part followed the model of the Estado Nôvo. He compares Brazil today with modern Portugal and Spain, finding them essentially similar in basic political structure. The articles by both Skidmore and Schmitter open up many new and stimulating questions for the scholar.

7. President Juan Velasco Alvarado has actually called it an "Independent International Policy." For an exposition of this policy see his speech, "Naturaleza y Objetivos de la Revolución; Mensaje a la Nación (28 de julio de 1969). Estrategia (Buenos Aires), No. 2 (July-August 1969), pp. 78-97.

8. Skidmore, "Politics," p. 51.

9. See Stepan, "The 'New Professionalism,'" pp. 6,7.

10. Skidmore, "Politics," p. 17.

11. Ibid.

12. This is a famous remark attributed to Getulio Vargas. Apocryphal or not, it expresses the genius of Getulio, and the system of the Estado Nôvo. As Schmitter ("Portugalization," p. 26) has written about the "authoritarian response to modernization," "These regimes seek not so much to arrest change—in fact, they often promote it—as they seek to control its consequences from above."

13. Stepan, "The 'New Professionalism,'" pp. 21-23.

14. Cotler, "Crisis Política," p. 449.

15. Velasco Alvarado, "Naturaleza y Objetivos," p. 89.

16. Ibid, p. 79.

17. Stepan, "The 'New Professionalism,'" p. 21.

18. I am indebted to Paulo Freire for the basic scheme here expanded, especially as he sets it forth in his book, Educacão como Prática de Liberdade, (Rio de Janeiro, 1965). He outlines three competing forms of education: (1) education as transmission of traditional values (conservative), (2) education as training of technicians for a more efficient national and corporate structure (modernization), and, (3) education as self- and group-realization (liberation).

19. For a description of these two contrasting mentalities in the church, see Brady Tyson, "Dom Helder Câmara, Symbolic Man," in Catholic World (July and August 1971), or in IDOC International (North American ed.), March 27, 1971.

20. See Schmitter, "Portugalization," pp. 39-41, for a description of the political-religious instruction that has been imposed by the present Brazilian government to inculcate the proper "civic and moral attitudes."

21. See Ibid., pp.8-9). Schmitter writes about "an elective affinity between certain structural and behavioural attributes of 'delayed-dependent' development and permanent authoritarian rule."

22. James Petras and Nelson Rimensnyder, "Los Militares y la Modernización del Perú," Estudios Internacionales (Santiago), IV, 13 (April-June 1970), p. 113.

23. Luigi R. Einaudi, "The Peruvian Military: A Summary Political Analysis" (Santa Monica, Calif.: Rand Corporation, 1969). Einaudi refers to "CAEM's doctrinal tendency to statism," p. 18.

24. Cotler ("Crisis Política," pp. 484, 488) argues that the emergence of the middle sectors offset the power of the established oligarchy in Peru, thus giving the army an autonomy of action hitherto denied it. Einaudi ("The Peruvian Military," writes: "No single group, domestic or foreign, can any longer intimidate the military."

25. J. L. Klaiber, "New Militarism in Peru" America, CXX, March 29, 1969), p. 367.

26. For such studies of the sociological backgrounds of the officer corps, and some interpretations of the influence on the thought and behavior, see the book by Stepan, Military in Politics, the article by Valdez Pallete (op. cit.), the study by Einaudi, "Peruvian Military," and Luigi R. Einaudi and Alfred C. Stepan, "Latin American Institutional Development: Changing Military Perspectives in Peru and Brazil" (Santa Monica, Calif.: Rand Corporation, 1971).

27. But see the forthcoming article by Frederick Nunn, "Influence of European Military Missions Upon the Latin American Military."

28. The story of the "developmentalist ideology" of ISEB (Institute Superior de Estudos Brasileiros, Advanced Institute of Brazilian Studies) has been well told by Frank Bonilla.

29. I am grateful, throughout this whole chapter, to the work of Juan Linz ("Authoritarian Regime") in pointing out the distinction between authoritarian states and totalitarian systems.

30. Testimony before the Subcommittee on National Security Policy and Scientific Developments of the Committee on Foreign Affairs, House of Representatives, 91st Cong., 2d sess., October 6-8, December 8 and 15, 1970 (Washington, D.C., 1970), p. 107.

33. Both Stepan and Einaudi have worked on this. Petras and Rimensnyder also summarize the data concerning the Peruvian officer corps, "Los Militares," pp. 96-98, and pp. 119-120.

34. Enrique Alonso, "Fuerzas Armadas y Revolución Nacional en Bolivia y Perú," Estrategia (Buenos Aires), No. 9 (September-December 1970, January-February 1971), p. 17.

35. Ibid., p. 22.

36. McCann, 12.

37. Victor Alba, "New Alignments in Latin America: Trends Toward Technocratic Paternalism," Dissent (July-August 1970), p. 367.

CHAPTER 9

1. References to these incidents can be found in Journal do Brasil, October 31, 1969, p. 9; Evangelist, May 1, 1969, p. 1-A; Excélsior (Mexico), November 30, 1969, p. 4-A, respectively.

2. According to a member of the Peruvian clergy, the post-independence period was better for the Catholic church of Peru than the years prior to independence; see Luis Lituma P., "La Iglesia Peruana en el Siglo XX," in Jose Pareja Paz-Soldan, ed., Visión del Perú en el Siglo XX (Lima: Ediciones Librería Studium, 1963), Vol. 2, p. 478.

3. These topics have been treated at length in Carlos A. Astiz, Pressure Groups and Power Elites in Peruvian Politics (Ithaca, N.Y.: Cornell University Press, 1969) particularly chap. 8, and in "La Iglesia Católica como Factor de Poder Político: El Caso Peruano," Revista Mexicana de Ciencia Política, Vol. 15 (October-December 1969), pp. 453-478.

4. Gonzalo Torrente Ballester, Off-Side (Barcelona: Ediciones Destino, 1969), p. 180.

5. Victor Villanueva, Hugo Blanco y la Rebelión Campesina (Lima: Librería-Editorial Juan Mejia Baca, 1967), p. 29.

6. Carta Pastoral de Pedro Pascual Farfan con Motivo de la Próxima Festividad de Santa Rosa de Lima (Lima: n.pub., 1937).

7. F. M. Arriola Grande, Discurso a la Nación Peruana (Buenos Aires: Editorial Pueblo Continente, 1959), p. 237. Events of this type are also described by Luis Alberto Sanchez, Aprismo y Religión (Lima: Editorial Cooperativa Aprista Atahualpa, 1933), passim, and Harry Kantor, El Movimiento Aprista Peruana (Buenos Aires: Ediciónes Pleamar, 1964), pp. 168-173.

8. Villanueva, Hugo Blanco, p. 149; a similar report is made by Hugo Neira, Cuzco: Tierra y Muerte (Lima: Problemas de Hoy, 1964), p. 89.

9. Lituma P., "La Iglesia Peruana," pp. 476, 485, 486.

10. Christian J. L. Bertholet and others, Puno Rural (Lima: CISEPA, 1969), p. 129.

11. The following year the extreme left received 15 percent of the vote in the Lima municipal elections. The electoral data can be found in Astiz, Pressure Groups, chaps. 4 and 6.

12. Salomon Bolo Hidalgo, Cartas de Mi Refugio (Lima: Imprenta Gráfica T. Scheuch, 1963), p. 114.

13. See ibid, pp. 136, 137.

14. See some of his numerous letters to the editor, published in Oiga, August 15, 1969, p.3; June 27, 1969, p. 3; September 3, 1969, p. 4; April 17, 1970, pp. 3, 42; July 2, 1971, p. 4; and July 23, 1971, pp. 45, 50. It would seem that by doing this and by supporting specific measures of the military government he is making himself and the National Liberation Front acceptable to the armed forces. However, he has occasionally been critical of specific measures of the present administration.

15. Bolo Hidalgo, Cartas, pp. 139-140.

16. The book being discussed here is Romeo Luna Victoria, Ciencia y Práctica de la Revolución (Lima: Editorial Studium, 1966). The author's views cannot be completely understood without reading his previous work, El Problema Indígena y la Tenencia de Tierras en el Perú (Trujillo, Peru: Cosmos, 1964), and his numerous articles in the nationalist reformist magazine Oiga.

17. Luna Victoria, Ciencia y Práctica, p. 280.

18. Ibid., pp. 190-203. The definition of "elastic property" is not quite clear, but Luna Victoria accepts confiscation of certain types of property.

19. Ibid., p. 26.

20. The statements are reprinted in Rogger Mercado, Las Guerrillas del Peru—El MIR: De la Predica Ideológica a la Acción Armada (Lima: Fondo de Cultura Popular, 1967), pp. 140-145 and 183, respectively.

21. Ibid., p. 143.

22. Gustavo Gutierrez, in his introduction to Signos de Renovación (Lima: Comisión Episcopal de Acción Social, 1969), pp. 7, 12. Father Gutierrez, a member of the faculty of the Catholic University of Peru, was involved in the exchange with the papal nuncio and is a member of ONIS. For a more recent statement of his views, see Gustavo Gutierrez, "Liberation and Development," Cross Currents, Vol. 21 (Summer 1971), pp. 243-56.

23. Gutierrez, Signos, pp. 11 and 13.

24. Of course some reformist priests, e.g., Don Helder Camara and Valdir Calheiros, have addressed themselves to the more essential political issues of their country. But it should be emphasized that they did not have to involve themselves in the larger socio-economic question to oppose the government.

25. For the author's preliminary assessment of the degree of reformism existing in the present Peruvian Military regime, see Chapter 13 in this volume.

26. The declaration was reproduced in Oiga (Lima), June 27, 1969, pp. 20-4; the quote is from p. 22.

27. Oiga, October 10, 1969, pp. 22, 23.

28. Oiga, November 21, 1969, p. 11; January 9, 1970, pp. 42, 43; and January 30, 1970, pp. 35, 36. The military had no compunction about granting themselves a 30 percent pay raise; see Caretas, May 23-June 12, 1969, p. 13.

29. Oiga, July 11, 1969, p. 34.

30. La Prensa (Lima), October 11, 1968, p. 2, and Caretas, May 23-June 12, 1969, p. 15.

31. Oiga, March 7, 1969, p. 10; and November 14, 1969, pp. 12, 33.

32. Caretas, May 23-June 12, 1969, p. 15; and July 10-23, 1969, p. 32.

33. News and commentaries of this episode were in the front pages of all Peruvian newspapers. The account is based on the information published in Oiga, May 14, 1971, pp. 10-12, 15, 16, and 38; and El Peruano (official newspaper of the Peruvian government), May 13, 1971, pp. 1, 3, and May 14, 1971, pp. 1, 3. The quote is from this last issue of El Peruano, p. 3.

34. Both articles in La Prensa, June 17, 1969, p. 8.

35. Oiga, October 10, 1969, p. 23.

36. Oiga, July 18, 1969, p. 41; and La Prensa, June 11, 1969, p. 7.

37. See Centro de Estudios y Publicaciónes, "Movimiento Sacerdotal ONIS: Declaraciones" (mimeo., Lima, June, 1970), pp. 38-44; and the 3-page release, "Propiedad Privada y Nueva Sociedad" (mimeo., Lima, August 15, 1970).

38. Noticias (weekly newsletter of the Catholic Information Center of Lima), May 10, 1971, p. 1.

39. Elias Condal, "El Vaticano y el Tercer Mundo," in Bernardo Castro Villagrana et al., La Iglesia, el Subdesarrollo y la Revolución (Mexico: Editorial Nuestro Tiempo, 1968), p. 196.

CHAPTER 10

1. Martin S. Stabb, In Quest of Identity (Chapel Hill: University of North Carolina Press, 1967), pp. 12-33.

2. Alberto Zum Felde, El problema de la cultura americana (Buenos Aires: Editorial Losada, 1943), pp. 114-118.

3. Mariano Picón Salas, Intuicion de Chile (Santiago de Chile: Biblioteca América, 1935), pp. 107-112.

4. My source of inspiration for this term is the Inca Huayna-Cápac, as depicted by José Joaquín de Olmedo in "La victoria de Junín. Canto a Bolívar."

5. Arcesio Aragón, "Valencia, cifra de un pueblo," Revista de las Indias, No. 54 (June 1943), p. 355; Rafael Maya, Alabanzas del hombre y de la tierra (Bogota: Editorial Santafé, 1934, p. 70; Jose Domingo Rojas, "Cómo recita Valencia," Revista Javeriana, XV, 72 (March 1941), 102-103.

6. Sonja Karsen, Guillermo Valencia: Colombian Poet (New York: Hispanic Institute in the United States, 1951), p. 49.

7. Esteban Echeverria, "Literatura mashorquera," Obras completas de D. Esteban Echeverria (Buenos Aires: Imprenta y Librerías de Mayo, 1874), Vol. V, p. 141.

8. José Enrique Rodó, Ariel (Montevideo: Imprenta de Dornaleche y Reyes, 1900), pp. 30-31.

9. Manuel González Prada, "Discurso en el Politeama," Pájinas libres (Paris: Tipografía de Paul Dupont, 1894), pp. 69-70.

10. Rubén Darío, "Palabras liminares," Prosas profanas y otros poemas (Buenos Aires: Imprenta de Pablo E. Coni e Hijos, 1896), pp. viii-ix.

11. "América y el disparate," p. 107.

12. José Antonio Portuondo, "El rasgo predominante de la novela hispanoamericana," in La novela iberoamericana: Memoria del Quinto Congreso del Instituto Internacional de Literatura Ibero-americana (Albuquerque: University of New Mexico Press, 1952), p. 84.

13. Angel Rama, "Diez problemas para el novelista latino-americano," Casa de las Américas, IV, 26 (October-November 1964), reported in Juan Loveluck, ed., La novela hispanoamericana (Santiago de Chile: Editorial Universitaria, 1969), p. 290. It should be noted that the population of Mexico has risen substantially since Rama's article was written.

14. Mario Vargas Llosa, "La literatura es fuego," Mundo Nuevo, Vol. XVII (November 1967), p. 94, as reproduced by Roberto Escamilla Molina in Julio Cortázar: Visión de conjunto (Mexico: Organización Editorial Novaro, 1970), pp. 14, 15.

CHAPTER 11

1. Norman Gall, "The Legacy of Che Guevara", Commentary, Vol. XLIV (December, 1967), p. 38. I may in fact be a little hard on Guevara when I suggest this. Neill Macauley, a veteran of the Escambray struggle during the Cuban revolution, thinks so, and he knew Che. However, I prefer to let it stand as a point of view and an impression. There is, of course, a wealth of material on Che and by Che. See Robert J. Scàuzillo, "Ernesto 'Che' Guevara: A Research Bibliography," Latin American Research Review, Vol. V (Summer 1970), pp. 53-82.

2. Che Guevara, Guerrilla Warfare (New York, 1961), p. 16.

3. Ibid., p. 17.

4. See George I. Blanksten, "Fidel Castro and Latin America," in Robert Tomasek, ed., Latin American Politics, 24 Studies of the Contemporary Scene (New York, 1966), p. 358.

5. Regis Debray, "Revolution in the Revolution, Armed Struggle and Political Struggle in Latin America," Monthly Review, XIX, 3 (July-August 1967), 119.

6. For an account of Guevara's role as a symbol see Lewis H. Diuguid's Washington Post report, January 15, 1968.

7. For a recent statement to this effect see Ramon Eduardo Ruiz, Cuba, The Making of a Revolution (New York, 1970), pp. 168, 169.

8. Teresa Casuso, Cuba and Castro (New York, 1961), pp. 101-105.

9. Andres Suarez, Cuba: Castroism and Communism, 1959-
1966 (Cambridge, Mass., 1967), pp. 30-34.

10. Neill Macauley, The Sandino Affair (Chicago, 1967),
describes the Nicaragua guerrilla activity against the U.S. Marines
between 1927 and 1933. For an account of the Peruvian movement
see Luis F. de la Puente Uceda, "The Peruvian Revolution: Concepts
and Perspectives," Monthly Review, Vol. XVII (November 1965),
pp. 12-28.

11. Time (Canada), Vol. XCVI (November 2, 1970), p. 23.

12. Vincent L. Padgett and Enrique Low Murtra, "Colombia,"
in Ben G. Burnett and Kenneth F. Johnson, eds., Political Forces
in Latin America (Belmont, Calif., 1968), pp. 239, 240.

13. There is a substantial number of studies on Indian communi-
ties and the attitudes of the Indians themselves. The following are
useful introductions: Charles Wagley and Marvin Harris, Minorities
in the New World (New York, 1958), pp. 48-86; Nathan L. Whetten,
Guatemala, The Land and the People (New Haven, 1961); Richard
W. Patch, "A Note on Bolivia and Peru," American Universities
Field Service Reports, West Coast South America Series, Vol. XII,
No. 2. December, 1966. See also the novels of Miguel Angel
Asturias, Guatemala's 1967 Nobel Prize winner, particularly
Hombres de Maíz (Buenos Aires, 1957). For a study of more
recent peasant movement in the Andes see Anibal Quijano Obregon,
"Contemporary Peasant Movements," in Seymour Martin Lipset
and Aldo Solari, eds., Elites in Latin America (New York, 1967),
pp. 301-340.

14. A. P. Short, "Conversations with the Guatemalan Delegates
in Cuba," Monthly Review, XVIII, 9 (February 1967), 33.

15. Latin American Digest, V (October 1970), p. 3.

16. John D. Martz, "Venezuela," in Burnett and Johnson, eds.,
Political Forces, pp. 216-217; Irving Louis Horowitz, "The Military
Elites," in Lipset and Solari, eds., Elites, pp. 183-184.

17. John Bartlow Martin, Overtaken by Events (New York, 1966),
pp. 381, 382.

18. Debray, "Revolution in the Revolution," p. 90. The military
are, of course very active in government these days! In Brazil
and Argentina they are the Right kind; in Peru and Bolivia they
appear to be of the Left. I say "appear to be" because it is too
early, I think, to decide that these governments are revolutionary.
Only time will tell whether or not the military leaders in Peru
and Bolivia can retain their social consciousness against the
pressures of the more traditional elitist values. I am not optimistic
on this score. See Carlos A. Astiz, Pressure Groups and Power
Elites in Peruvian Politics (Ithaca, N.Y., 1969).

CHAPTER 12

1. See, for example, Edmund Stillman and William Pfaff, Power and Impotence: The Failure of America's Foreign Policy (New York, 1966); and Ronald Steel, Pax Americana (New York, 1967).

2. Ramon Eduardo Ruiz, "The Impact of the Cuban Revolution," in Neal D. Houghton, ed., Struggle Against History: U.S. Foreign Policy in an Age of Revolution (New York, 1968), p. 149.

3. Exponents of this "consensus" interpretation include Richard Hofstadter, The American Political Tradition and the Men Who Made It (New York, 1948); Louis Hartz, The Liberal Tradition in America: An Interpretation of American Political Thought Since the Revolution (New York, 1955); and Daniel Boorstin, The Genius of American Politics (Chicago, 1953).

4. On this point see Richard Hofstadter and Michael Wallace, eds., American Violence: A Documentary History (New York, 1970).

5. Merle Kling, "Violence and Politics in Latin America," in Irving L. Horowitz, et al., eds., Latin American Radicalism: A Documentary Report on Left and Nationalist Movements (New York, 1969), pp. 190-192.

6. Edwin Lieuwen, Arms and Politics in Latin America (rev. ed., New York, 1961), p. 21; Lee B. Valentine, "A Comparative Study of Successful Revolutions in Latin America, 1941-1950," unpublished doctoral dissertation, Stanford University, 1952, pp. 246, 247.

7. Kalman H. Silvert, The Conflict Society: Reaction and Revolution in Latin America (rev. ed., New York, 1966), pp. 19-24.

8. Kling, "Violence and Politics," p. 193.

9. Harry Eckstein, "On the Etiology of Internal Wars," History and Theory, IV (1965), pp. 150-151.

10. On Latin American violence generally, see Daniel Goldrich, "Toward an Estimate of the Probability of Social Revolutions in Latin America: Some Orienting Concepts and a Case Study," Centennial Review, Vol. VI (1962), pp. 394-408; Irving L. Horowitz, "Political Legitimacy and the Institutionalization of Crisis in Latin America," Comparative Political Studies, Vol. I (1968), pp. 45-69; Irving L. Horowitz, "The Norm of Illegitimacy: The Political Sociology of Latin America," in Horowitz, et al., eds., Latin American Radicalism, pp. 3-28; Raymond Tantner and Manus Midlarsky, "A Theory of Revolution," Journal of Conflict Resolution Vol. XI (1967), pp. 264-280; Carl Leiden and Karl Schmitt, The Politics of Violence: Revolution in the Modern World (Englewood Cliffs, N.J., Prentice Hall: 1968); and Frank Moreno and Barbara Mitrani, eds., Conflict and Violence: Cultural and Psychological Factors in Latin American Politics (New York, 1971).

11. Victor Alba, The Latin Americans (New York, 1969), p. 45n.

12. On modernization, see Cyril E. Black, The Dynamics of Modernization: A Study in Comparative History (New York, 1966).

13. Victor Alba, Nationalists Without Nations: The Oligarchy vs. the People in Latin America (New York, 1968), p. 56.

14. An excellent biography is Peter Geismar, Fanon (New York, 1970).

15. Hannah Arendt, On Violence (New York, 1970), p. 20.

16. The writer's analysis is based upon Victor Perrera, "Guatemala: Always La Violencia," New York Times Magazine (June 13, 1971), p. 13+; and Eduardo Galeano, "With the Guerrillas in Guatemala," in James Petras and Maurice Zeitlin, eds., Latin America: Reform or Revolution? (New York, 1968), pp. 370-380.

17. Perrera, "Guatemala," p. 13.

18. Ibid., p. 50.

19. See Joseph A. Page, "The Little Priest who Stands up to Brazil's Generals," New York Times Magazine, May 23, 1971, pp. 26-27.

20. Le Monde (Paris), March 8, 9, 1970.

21. "Terror in Brazil: A Dossier," (April, 1970), a pamphlet in possession of the writer.

22. New York Times, July 19, 1970; January 17, 1971.

23. This discussion is based upon source readings in Benjamin Keen, ed., Readings in Latin-American Civilization, 1492 to the Present (Boston, 1955), pp. 172-178.

24. Reliable material discussing the Tupamaros is difficult to obtain. The discussion here rests upon reportage in the New York Times, Time, and Newsweek, and two publications by Alphonse Max, "Tupamaros: A Pattern for Urban Guerrilla Warfare in Latin America," and "Guerrillas in Latin America." The former document was published in February 1970, the latter in June 1971, both by INTERDOC in The Hague.

25. Norman R. Humphrey, "Ethnic Images and Stereotypes of Mexicans and Americans," American Journal of Economics and Sociology, Vol. XIV (1955), p. 309, quoted in Kling, "Violence and Politics," p. 203. See also, Alba, Latin Americans, p. 45; Evelyn P. Stevens, "Mexican Machismo: Politics and Value Orientation," Western Political Quarterly, Vol. XVIII (1965), pp. 848-857.

26. Octavio Paz, The Labyrinth of Solitude (New York, 1961), pp. 57-58. See also portions of Leopoldo Zea's stimulating The Latin-American Mind, trans. by James H. Abbott and Lowell Durham (Norman, Okla., 1963).

27. Kling, "Violence and Politics," p. 204.

CHAPTER 13

1. See for example J. Hamilton-Paterson, "Brazil under the Colonels," New Statesman, June 26, 1970; Tito Alencar Lima, Look, July 14, 1970; T. Quigley, "Repression in Brazil: Protest vs. Protocol," Commonweal, January 15, 1971; "How One Pleasant, Scholarly Young Man from Brazil Became a Kidnapping, Gun-Toting, Bombing Revolutionary," New York Times Magazine, November 15, 1970; H. J. Steiner and D. M. Trubek, "Brazil—All Power to the Generals," Foreign Affairs, April 1971.

2. There is fair agreement on this point. See for example W. Baer, Industrialization and Economic Development of Brazil (Homewood, Ill.: Richard D. Irwin, 1965); Joel Bergsman, Brazil: Industrialization and Trade Policies (Oxford University Press, 1970), p. 58; Celso Furtado, Economic Growth of Brazil (Berkeley and Los Angeles: University of California Press), 1968, chap. 35.

3. The effect inflation has on the real growth rate is the subject of much debate. For an exposition of the issues see Dudley Seers, "A Theory of Inflation and Growth in Under-developed Countries Based on the Experience of Latin America," Oxford Economic Papers, June 1963, and W. Baer, "The Inflation Controversy in Latin America: A Survey," Latin American Research Review, Winter 1967.

4. See Werner Baer, Isaac Kerstenetzky, and Mario H. Simonsen, "Transportation and Inflation: A Study of Irrational Policy-Making in Brazil", Economic Development and Cultural Change, Vol. XIII, No. 2 (January 1965); and Alan Abouchar, "Inflation and Transportation Policy in Brazil," Economic Development and Cultural Change, Vol. XVIII, No. 1 (October 1969).

5. Data are from Bergsman, Brazil, p. 76.

6. See N. H. Leff, "Export Stagnation and Autarkic Development In Brazil, 1947-1962," Quarterly Journal of Economics, LXXXI, 2 (May 1967), 256-301.

7. This interpretation for the decline of Brazilian growth rate has been advanced by N. H. Leff, particularly in his "Import Constraints and Development: Causes of the Recent Decline of Brazilian Economic Growth," Review of Economics and Statistics, November 1967, pp. 494-501. As A. E. Blair has pointed out in his "Import Bottlenecks and Inflation: The Case of Brazil," Oxford Economic Papers, July 1967, pp. 235-244, import capacity, at least until 1961, did not diminish, however, because of falling import prices and Brazil's ability to secure compensatory financing, despite sluggish export performance.

8. There is a substantial body of literature on the causes and consequences of the political crisis in Brazil. It includes at least one bibliography ("Bibliografia sôbre a Revolução de 31 de Marco,"

Boletim da Bibliotéca da Câmara dos Deputados, XIII, 2 (1964), 499-514).

9. For details on the resignation of Quadros see Helio Juaguaribe, "A Renúncia de Jânio Quadros e a Crise Política Brasileira," Revista Brasileira de Ciências Sociais, Vol. I, No. 1 (November 1961).

10. Celso Furtado, Economic Development of Latin America (Cambridge: Cambridge University Press, 1970), p. 147.

11. For a fuller treatment of problems and policies of this period see Alexandre Kafka, "The Brazilian Stabilization Program, 1964-66," The Journal of Political Economy, Vol. LXXV (August 1967), pp. 596-631; and Samuel A. Morley, "Inflation and Stagnation in Brazil," Economic Development and Cultural Change, XIX, 2 (January 1971), 184-203. Both authors point to the pivotal role of a government that is strong enough to resist the political temptation of too quickly abandoning a stabilization policy.

CHAPTER 14

1. The role of the armed forces as a power factor is only now being discussed in the literature of Latin American politics; until recently they were lumped together with institutions such as labor unions or chambers of commerce. For a discussion of the military in the Peruvian political system and its interplay with other elites, see Carlos A. Astiz, Pressure Groups and Power Elites in Peruvian Politics (Ithaca, N.Y.: Cornell University Press, 1969).

2. Victor Villanueva, El Militarismo en el Perú (Lima, 1962), Chapter I; Liisa North, Civil-Military Relations in Argentina, Chile and Peru (Berkeley: University of California, 1966), p. 19.

3. On this point, see Francois Bourricaud, "Remarques sur l'Oligarchie Peruvienne," Revue Francaise de Science Politique, Vol. XIV, (Octubre, 1965), pp. 694-695. Also see North, Civil-Military Relations, p. 9.

4. Jose Urdanivia Gines, Una Revolución Modelo del Ejército Peruano (Lima: Editorial Castrillón Silva, 1954), p. 17. The author was one of the leaders of the 1914 revolt.

5. Villanueva, El Militarismo en el Perú, p. 45.

6. Urdanivia Gines, Una Revolución Modelo del Ejército Peruano, p. 65.

7. Villanueva, El Militarismo en el Peru, p. 66.

8. See Pedro Ugarteche, Sánchez Cerro; Papeles y Recuerdos de un Presidente del Perú, 2 vols. (Lima: Editorial Universitaria, 1969), Vol. 1, pp. 208-216.

9. The revolts of this period are described by Leonidas Castro Bastos, Golpismo (Lima: Editorial Libreria e Imprenta "D. Miranda," 1962), pt. I; Villanueva, El Militarismo en el Peru,

chaps. II, III, IV, and V; and Jorge Basadre, Historia de la República del Perú (Lima: Ediciones "Historia," 1961-64), Vols. 8 and 9.

10. For further details on the 1945-48 political maneuvering, see Oscar Bueno Tovar, Las Fuerzas Armadas y el Apra (Lima: I.M.P., 1963) passim; Villanueva, El Militarismo en el Perú, chaps. V and VI; Victor Villanueva, La Tragedia de un Pueblo y un Partido (Santiago de Chile: Ediciones Renovación, 1954), passim.

11. El Comercio, October, 29, 1948, p. 1.

12. Enrique Chirinos Soto, Cuenta y Balance de las Elecciónes de 1962 (Lima: Ediciones Perú, 1962), pp. 75-86; Villanueva, El Militarismo en el Perú, pp. 121-129.

13. The faculty included one member, Gregorio Garayar, who was considered to be communist. This point was made by an Aprista leader, Andres Townsend Excurra in his article, "Frente a la Ley, los Tanques," Panoramas (March-April 1963), p. 59.

14. Liisa North, op. cit., p. 53. Also see Villanueva, El Militarismo en el Perú, pp. 174-189. For specific examples of military writing in this field, see Jose R. Calderon M., "El Comandante y la Comunidad," Revista Militar del Perú (May-June 1962), pp. 33-35; and Lisandro Mejia Zagastrizabal, "Acción Cívica en el Campo Laboral," Revista Militar del Perú (January-February 1964), pp. 100-111.

15. Reported by William F. Whyte, La Mano de Obra de Alto Nivel en el Perú (Lima: Editorial Senati, 1964), pp. 51-52.

16. Richard Patch, "The Peruvian Elections of 1962 and Their Annulment," American Universities Field Staff Service Reports, West Coast of South American Series, IX, 2 (September 1962), 16.

17. The data have been published in Victor Villanueva, Nueva Mentalidad Militar en el Perú? (Buenos Aires: Editorial Replanteo, 1969), p. 92. These figures ratify the pattern discerned by the writer in his contacts with military officers, mostly of middle ranks; a profile of dependent middle class background appears, with more than proportional representation from the Sierra regions; most of the officers contacted would be classified as mestizos. These findings were confirmed by President Velazco, who was quoted as saying that the military officers were part of the middle class, and claimed that they were at the time trying to articulate its interests. El Comercio, October 29, 1968, p. 4.

18. This argument is corroborated by a survey of the occupational preferences of high school students throughout Peru (Whyte, La Mano de Obra de Alto Nivel en el Peru, p. 56).

19. This oversimplified interpretation of Marx can be found in S. E. Finer, The Man on Horseback (New York: Frederick A. Praeger, 1962), p. 40. For a documented criticism of this abusive use of social background data, see J. Edinger and D. D. Searing,

"Social Background in Elite Analysis: A Methodological Inquiry," The American Political Science Review, Vol. LXI (June 1967), pp. 428-45.

20. This point is also made, in reference to other Latin American countries, by Jose Nun, "A Latin American Phenomenon: The Middle Class Military Coup," in Institute of International Studies, Trends in Social Science Research in Latin American Studies: A Conference Report, p. 86.

21. Jacques Lambert, América Latina: Estructuras Sociales e Instituciones Políticas, p. 359.

22. There are numerous accounts of these events such as: Humberto Ugolotti Dansay, Las Elecciónes de 1963 y la Lección del 62 (Lima: Tipografía Peruana, 1963); Enrique Chirinos Soto, Cuenta y Balance de las Elecciónes de 1962 (Lima: Ediciones Perú, 1962); M. Guillermo Ramirez y Berrios, Examen Espectral de las Elecciónes del 9 de Junio de 1963 (Lima [n. pub] 1963).

23. Chirinos Soto, Cuenta e Balance, p. 77.

24. Ibid., pp. 63, 64.

25. On this question, see James L. Payne, Labour and Politics in Peru: the System of Political Bargaining (New Haven, Conn.: Yale University Press, 1965), chaps. 6 and 8; also, Astiz, Pressure Groups, chaps. 5 and 9.

26. The writer has seen some of the files, which are also mentioned by Justo Piernes, "Democracia Directa," Leoplán (August 15, 1962), pp. 12-15. Piernes even warned his readers that "Nasserites" had taken over a Latin American country.

27. Almost every day, from July 19, 1962, on, La Prensa had something to say on these subjects. On the "communist menace" see particularly the editorials and the first-page news in the period December 21-29, 1962, just before the dragnet.

28. Cf. Victor Villanueva, Un Año bajo el Sable, chaps. 6 and 7; and Genaro Ledesma Izquieta, Complot (Lima: Talleres Tipográficos Editorial "Thesis," 1964), passim.

29. For a discussion of electoral arithmetic in Peruvian congressional elections, see Astiz, Pressure Groups.

30. Good reports on the matter of land invasions can be found in Hugo Neira, Cuzco: Tierra y Muerte (Lima: Problemas de Hoy, 1964) and Victor Villanueva, Hugo Blanco y la Rebelión Campesina (Lima: Libreria-Editorial Juan Mejia Baca, 1967). Regarding the peasant organizations, see Anibal Quijano O., "El Movimiento Campesino del Perú y sus Líderes," América Latina, Vol. VIII (October-December 1965), pp. 43-64.

31. Accounts of the guerrilla operations can be found in Hector Bejar, Perú 1965: Apuntes sobre una Experiencia Guerrillera (Lima: Campodonico Ediciónes, 1969); Rogger Mercado, Las

Guerrillas del Perú; el MIR: De la Prédica Ideológica a la Acción Armada (Lima: Fondo de Cultura Popular, 1967); Gonzalo Ani Castillo, *Historia Secreta de las Guerrillas* (Lima: Ediciones "Más Allá," 1967); and Americo Pumaruna, "Perú: Revolución; Insurrección; Guerrillas," *Cuadernos de Ruedo Ibérico* (April-May 1966), pp. 62-86.

32. Quoted in Pumaruna, *ibid.,* p. 73.

33. *Oiga,* July 9, 1965, pp. 1, 8.

34. Francois Bourricaud, "Les Régles du Jeu en Situation d'Anomie: Le Cas Peruvien," *Sociologie du Travail,* Vol. IX (July-September 1967), p. 348. Also see Villanueva, *Nueva Mentalidad Militar en el Perú?* pp. 45-57.

35. *Confirmado,* November 17, 1966, p. 40.

36. *Primera Plana,* August 1, 1967, p. 32.

37. The percentage of men in the Peruvian army comes from Irving Louis Horowitz, "The Military Elites," in Seymour Martin Lipset and Aldo Solari, eds., *Elites in Latin America* (New York: Oxford University Press, 1967), p. 154. The budgetary breakdown, which refers to the 1968 budget, appeared in *La Prensa* (Lima), October 29, 1968, p. 2. The matter of promotions is mentioned in *Oiga,* October 25, 1968, p. 8.

38. *Siete Días del Perú y del Mundo,* supplement of *La Prensa* (Lima), October 6, 1968, p. 14. The events and role of the colonels have been described in *Oiga,* October 4, 1968, pp. 4-6; *La Prensa,* October 3, 1968, pp. 1-4, and October 4, 1968, pp. 1-5; *Primera Plana* October 8, 1968, pp. 25-27; and *El Comercio,* October 3, 1968, p. 1, and October 4, 1968, p. 1.

39. *Siete Días del Perú y del Mundo,* October 6, 1968, p. 5.

40. See *La Prensa,* October 31, 1968, p. 2.

41. See *La Prensa,* October 27, 1968, p. 1; and *Primera Plana,* October 29, 1968, p. 28.

42. Francisco Igartua in *Oiga,* October 11, 1968, p. 3.

43. Francisco Bendezu in *ibid.,* p. 8.

44. See, *Oiga,* November 4, 1968, pp. 8-10 and 36; and *La Prensa,* November 1, 1968, pp. 1, 2.

45. *La Prensa,* November 4, 1968, p. 4.

46. Evidence of this support can be found in *Caretas,* October 15-24, 1969, pp. 8-10C.

47. See "Junta Communiqué," No. 10, reproduced by *La Prensa,* October 6, 1968, p. 1.

48. International Monetary Fund press release No. 708, dated November 8, 1968, and reproduced in *International Financial News Survey,* Vol. XX (November 15, 1968), p. 381.

49. *Oiga,* November 4, 1968, p. 36. The events are also reported by *La Prensa,* October 31, 1968, p. 1.

50. An example of this type of contact was reported in El Mundo (Lima), June 2, 1969, pp. 16-19.

51. La Prensa, October 4, 1968, p. 11.

52. La Prensa, October 6, 1968, p. 15, and October 27, 1968, p. 13.

53. Oiga, October 11, 1968, p. 6, October 18, 1968, p. 6, October 25, 1968, p. 16, and November 19, 1968, p. 9.

54. See section 3 of "Junta Communiqué," No. 14, reproduced by La Prensa, November 1, 1968, p. 1.

55. Along the lines suggested by Jose Nun, "A Latin American Phenomenon: The Middle Class Military Coup," pp. 55-99.

CHAPTER 15

1. Ernesto ("Che") Guevara, "On the Cuban Experience," in John Gerassi, ed., Venceremos! (New York: MacMillan, 1968), p. 260.

2. Fidel Castro, "En la clausura de la Plenaria Nacional de Justicia Laboral," Granma Weekly Review, August 17, 1969, pp. 3, 4, cited by C. Mesa-Lago, "Employment, Unemployment and Underemployment in Cuba: 1899 to 1970" (unpublished manuscript), p. 64.

3. Granma Weekly Review, January 9, 1972, p. 12.

4. Fidel Castro, Speech of March 13, 1968, Granma Weekly Review, March 15, 1968, pp. 5, 6; "Dos Anos de Desarrollo Agropecuario Cubano, 1968-1970," Economia y Desarrollo, No. 4 (October-December 1970), p. 29.

5. See, for example, C. Mesa-Lago, "Cuba: Teoría y Práctica de los Incentruos," Latin American Studies Occasional Paper, No. 7 (Center for Latin American Studies, University of Pittsburgh, June, 1971); and R. Bernardo, The Economics Of Moral Incentives in Cuba (University of Alabama Press, 1971).

6. Cf. D. Boorstein, The Economic Transformation of Cuba. (Monthly Review Press, 1968), pp. 151-8 for an inside description of the installation of the new planning apparatus; and R. Boti, "El Plan de Desarrollo Económico para 1962," Cuba Socialista, No. 4 (December 1961).

7. Fidel Castro, History Will Absolve Me (Havana, May 1960), pp. 35-43.

8. R. Boti and F. Pazos, "Algunos Aspectos del Desarrollo Económico de Cuba: Tesis del Movimento Revolucionario 26 de Julio," Revista Bimestre Cubano (July-December 1958), pp. 249-283.

9. For a detailed and recent outline of central planning in Cuba, see C. Mesa-Lago, ed., Revolutionary Change in Cuba (University of Pittsburgh Press, 1971), chaps. 7 and 8.

10. Junta Central de Planificatíon (Juceplan), "Economic Planning in Cuba," in UN, Economic Commission for Latin America (ECLA), Documents from a Symposium (Santiago, Chile, February 1968), p. 123. The description of the planning system draws on: ibid.; UN, ECLA, Economic Survey of Latin America for 1963, pp. 259-269; and R. Boti, "El Plan de Desarrollo Económico de 1962," Cuba Socialista (December 1961).

11. UN, ECLA, Economic Survey of Latin America for 1963 pp. 259-260.

12. Boti, "El Plan de Desarrollo Económico de 1962," p. 26.

13. Juceplan, "Economic Planning in Cuba," pp. 125-127.

14. R. M. Bernardo, "Financing and Managing the Firm," in Mesa-Lago, ed., Revolutionary Change in Cuba, pp. 195-204.

15. Boorstein, "The Economic Transformation of Cuba," p. 110.

16. E. Guevara, "Informe . . . ," Obra Revolucionaria, No. 30 (August 29, 1961), p. 128.

17. O. Duyos, "Los Problemas Actuales del Acopio, y los Precios de Compra de los Productos Agrícolas," Cuba Socialista, No. 33 (May 1964), p. 76.

18. Ibid., p. 74.

19. "Notas Economicas: Problemas de la Producción Tobacalera," Cuba Socialista, No. 43 (March 1965), p. 124.

20. Duyos, "Los Problemas Actuales," p. 75.

21. "Notas Economicas: Hacia la Sistematizacion de los Precios de Acopio de Productos Agricolas," Cuba Socialista, No. 48 (August 1965), p. 123.

22. Boletin Estadístico, 1967 (Havana 1966), pp. 35-43, 58-59.

23. "Notas Economicas: Algunas Experiencias de la Zafra Cafetalera," Cuba Socialista, No. 42, (February 1965).

24. "Notas Economicas: Problemas de la Producción Tabacalera," p. 126; A. Martin. "La Produccion Tabacolera y los Pequenos Agricultores," Cuba Socialista, No. 67 (February 1967), pp. 66-72.

25. "Nations Private Sector Now Almost Completely Nationalized, Granma Weekly Review, April 7, 1968, p. 3.

26. UN, ECLA, Economic Survey of Latin America for 1963 p. 262.

27. A. Downs, Inside Bureaucracy (Boston: Little Brown, 1967); C.N. Parkinson, The Law and the Profits (Boston: Houghton Mifflin, 1960).

28. Ernesto Guevara, "Against Bureaucratism," in Gerassi, ed., Venceremos! pp. 221-224.

29. Ibid., p. 222.

30. Ediciones El Orientador Revolucionario, No. 6 (1967), pp. 16-17.

31. "La Racionalización del Personal Administrativo: Arma Efectiva Contra el Burocratísmo," Cuba Socialista, No. 58 (June 1966).

32. Fidel Castro, "Speech of February 20, 1967," Ediciones el Orientador Revolucionario, No. 5 (1967), p. 14.

33. Ediciones el Orientador Revolucionario, No. 6 (1967), p. 17; cf. also Ediciones el Orientador Revolucionario, No. 6, (1966), pp. 21, 22.

34. Cf. Guevara, "Informe," and F. Castro, "26th of July Speech, 1970" Granma Weekly Review, 1970, for commentaries upon problems with declines in qualities of commodities.

35. Fidel Castro, "Speech Given to the Central Organization of the Cuban Trade Unions (CTC)," Granma Weekly Review, September 20, 1970, p. 4.

36. A. Lataste, Cuba: Hacia una Nueva Economia Politica del Socialismo? (Santiago: Editorial Universitaria, S.A.), 1968.

37. Fidel Castro, "26th of July Speech, 1970."

38. Cf. Juceplan, "Economic Planning in Cuba," pp. 127-140, for comments on the administrative role of the party.

39. The recent round of meetings with the workers in different sectors of the economy seems to have been quite effective in performing this function. Cf., for example, "Meeting of the Central Organization of Cuban Trade Unions," Granma Weekly Review, September 20, 1970, pp. 7-12.

40. See A. Nove, The Soviet Economy (New York: Praeger, 1961), chap. 12, for a discussion of Soviet experience of plan implementation through "campaigns."

41. Jorge Risquet, labor minister, ". . . Problemas de Trabajo y Productividad . . .," Granma Weekly Review, August 1, 1970, p. 2.

42. Cf. Granma Weekly Review, October 19, 1969, p. 4 and Risquet, Ibid.

43. Ibid.

44. Juceplan, "Economic Planning in Cuba," p. 12.

45. Cf. Guevara, "Informe."

46. F. Pazos, "Comentarios a Dos Articulos sobre la Revolución Cubana," El Trimestre Economico, Mexico, XXXXX, 13 (January-March 1962), 1-13.

47. See Castro, "26th of July Speech, 1970", and Fidel Castro, "Speech to the CTC."

48. Cf. R. Dumont, Cuba Est-il Socialiste (Paris: Editions du Seuil, 1969), and Le Monde, Paris, March 20, 1971, p. 6.

49. Fidel Castro, "Speech of September 28, 1970," Granma Weekly Review, October 4, 1970.

330   LATIN AMERICAN PROSPECTS FOR THE 1970s

50. L. Huberman and P. Sweezy, Socialism in Cuba; New York: Monthly Review Press, 1969, pp. 219-220.

51. Fidel Castro, "Speech of September 2, 1970," Granma Weekly Review, September 20, 1970, pp. 3-4.

52. N. Valdes New Politics (Fall 1970) holds that it is incorrect to consider what happened in the unions as a democratic process. See also Le Monde, ibid.

53. Le Monde, ibid.

CHAPTER 16

1. These figures represent the moderate-growth hypothesis of the Oficina Nacional de Estadísticas y Censos. A high-growth hypothesis of the Centro de Estúdios de Población y Desarrollo projects 19,847,000 inhabitants in 1980, 28,476,000 in 1990, and 40,015,000 in 2000.

2. According to the last census (1961), 53 percent of the population was in the 0-19 age group, a percentage which since has certainly increased.

3. These are results of four surveys conducted between 1967 and 1970 by the Servicio del Empléo y Recursos Humanos in Lima, Arequipa, Chiclayo, Cuzco, Huancayo, Iquitos, Juliaca, Piura, Puno, and Trujillo.

4. Perú, Instituto Nacional de Planificación, Bases para un Programa de Desarrollo Nacional a Largo Plazo (Lima, 1969), pp. 135, 151-52. Potential rural population estimates are based on the assumption of full employment under the most intensive use of all suitable land with current technology. Market requirements are not considered.

5. A. Maas, Entwicklung und Perpektiven der wirtschatlichen Erschliessung des tropischen Waldlandes von Peru, Unter besonderer Berücksichtigung der verkehrsgeographischen Problematik (Tübingen: Selbstverlag des geographischen Instituts der Universität Tübingen, 1969), pp. 230-231.

6. Comisión Conjunta de Bolivia, Colombia, Ecuador y Perú, La Carretera Marginal de la Selva: Estudio Preliminar (Lima, 1965).

7. R.C. Eidt, "Economic Features of Land Opening in the Peruvian Montana", The Professional Geographer, XVIII, 3 (May 1966), 148-149.

8. Organización de los Estados Americanos, Unión Panamericana, Integración Económica y Social del Perú Central (Washington, D.C., 1961).

9. C.M. Medrano, Acclimatization in the Andes (New York: American Geographical Society, 1948).

NOTES   331

10. This system is described in greater detail in H. Martínez, Las Migraciones Altiplánicas y la Colonización del Tambopata (Lima: Ministerio de Trabajo y Asuntos Indígenas, 1961); and R. Wesche, "Recent Migration to the Peruvian Montana," Cahiers de Géographie de Québec, Quinzième année, 35, (September 1971), pp. 258-259.

CHAPTER 18

1. In underdeveloped countries as a whole, equity investment now forms 90 percent of private international investment, with a 10 to 15 percent return after taxes, compared with a 5 to 6 percent rate of return for bond credit. Paul N. Rosenstein-Rodan, "Multinational Investment in the Framework of Latin American Integration," in Inter-American Development Bank, Multinational Investment in the Economic Development and Integration of Latin America (Bogota, Colombia, 1968), pp. 54-55.

2. "The Role of International Movements of Private Capital in Promoting Development," in John H. Alder, ed., Capital Movements and Economic Development (London: Macmillan, 1967), p. 196. Quoted in A.O. Hirschman, "How to Divest in Latin America, and Why," Princeton Essays in International Finance, No. 76 (November 1969).

3. Arthur H. Cole, "An Approach to the Study of Entrepreneurship," Journal of Economic History, Vol. VI (Supplement, 1946), pp. 1-15.

4. Cleona Lewis, America's Stake in International Investments (Washington, D.C.: Brookings Institute, 1938). Cited in UN Economic Commission for Latin America (ECLA), External Financing in Latin America, E/CN.12/649/Rev.1 (New York, 1965), p. 15.

5. Mexican direct investment is usually in the form of a "joint venture." One recent project involving both Mexican and Costa Rican businessmen is a dehydrating plant for fruits and vegetables. See La Republica (San Jose), June 11, 1971, pp. 1, 17.

6. The process of nationalization of public utilities and railroads is still continuing in Central America. "Costa Rica Completa Nacionalizacion de Energia Electrica," Secretariado de Integracion Economico Centro American (SIECA), Carta Informativa, Vol. LXXXV (November 1968), p. 14; "Guatemala Declara Caducidad de la Concesion a Ferrocarriles Internacionales de Centroamerica," SIECA, Carta Informativa, 87 (January 1969), pp. 6-8.

7. See "Central Americans Lift Trade by Tariff Cuts; Arrow Shirt, Other Firms Rush In," Wall Street Journal, March 10, 1965, p. 1; Sheldon L. Schreiberg, "The United States Private Investor and the Central American Common Market," in U.S. Congress, Joint Economic Committee, Latin American Development and

Western Hemisphere Trade, Hearings (Washington, D.C., 1965), pp. 260-285.

8. Alvaro Contreras Velez in Prense Libre, 1965. Quoted by Francisco Villagran Kramer in Integración Económica Centroamericana: Aspectos Sociales y Políticos (Guatemala: Universidad de San Carlos, 1967), p. 235. My translation.

9. This phrase is borrowed from Eduardo Lizano F., "El Problema de las Inversiones Extranjeras en Centroamérica," Revista del Banco Central de Costa Rica, 67 (September 1966), p. 59.

10. "Honduras: the 78 Million Dollar Question," Latin America (London), May 31, 1968, pp. 170, 172.

11. SIECA, Carta Informativa, 89 (March 1969), pp. 22, 23.

12. "Pronunciamiento de la FECAICA en Relación a las Inversiones Extranjeras en el Área Centroamericano," March 25, 1965, in Villagran Kramer, Integración Económica Centroamericana, pp. 237-239.

13. "Declaration of the Ministers of Economy of Central America," June, 21 1965, in Inter-American Economic and Social Council, The Role of Foreign Private Investment in the Development of Latin America (Washington, D.C.: Pan American Union, 1969), pp. 168, 169.

14. Raul Sierra Franco, "La Industrialización en Centroamérica," in Seminario de Historia Contemporánea de Centroamérica (San Salvador: Editorial Universitaria, 1964), p. 25.

15. Roger D. Hansen, Central America: Regional Integration and Economic Development (Washington, D.C.: National Planning Association, 1967), pp. 87-89. (The 1969 ECLA Survey of Latin America notes that "several projects for the assembly of motor vehicles" have been initiated in Guatemala.)

16. Ibid., pp. 48-49.

17. Albert O. Hirschman, "The Political Economy of Import-Substituting Industrialization in Latin America," Quarterly Journal of Economics, Vol. LXXXII (February 1968), p. 21.

18. See Judd Polk, "U.S. Exports in Relation to U.S. Production Abroad," in Bela Balassa, ed., Changing Patterns in Foreign Trade and Payments (rev. ed., New York: Norton, 1970), pp. 61-71.

19. See I.A. Litvak and C.J. Maule, "Canadian Entrepreneurship and Human Resource Development: The Effect of Direct Foreign Investment," Business Quarterly, Spring 1972.

20. Thomas C. Cochran, The Puerto Rican Businessman: A Study in Cultural Change (Philadelphia: University of Pennsylvania Press, 1959), p. 86.

21. Warren Dean in The Industrialization of Sao Paulo (Austin: University of Texas Press, 1969), pp. 176-178, reports that

Brazilian industrialists, whether immigrant or native, "demonstrated almost no interest in the technical training of their manpower pool." He notes that "it was true in a narrow sense that
importing technicians was cheaper than training them, and yet of
how little use to Brazil was an industrial system that condemned
its citizens to unskilled labour." Very often criticisms of the
international corporation apply with equal force to the family firm
in Latin America.

22. Rosenstein-Rodan, "Multinational Investment," p. 64.

23. See L. N. Willmore, "Free Trade in Manufactures among
Developing Countries: The Central American Experience," Eco-
nomic Development and Cultural Change, (Chicago: University of
Chicago Press, July, 1972).

24. This argument and the discussion which follows draws
heavily on Lizano F., "El Problema de las Inversiones Extranjeras
en Centroamerica," pp. 57-58.

25. Robert T. Aubbey, "Entrepreneurial Formation in El
Salvador," Explorations in Entrepreneurial History, Vol. VI (Spring
1969), pp. 268-285.

26. The "Comision ad hoc para el Estudio del Mercado de
Valores en Centroamerica" reports that liquid Central American
assets held by the United States totalled U.S. $45.4 million in 1963,
and U.S.$50.5 million in 1964. Banco Centroamericano de Integra-
ción Economica (BCIE), Un Mercado de Capitales Centroamericano:
Dos Estudios (Mexico: Centro de Estudios Monetarios Latinoameri-
canos, 1967), p. 12.

27. Lizano F., " El Problema de las Inversiones Extranjeras
en Centroamerica," p. 61.

28. This is apparently true even for El Salvador, whose entrepreneurs are reputedly the most progressive of the isthmus. See
Guillermo Atilio Lopez Z., "Problemas de Desarrollo Industrial
en El Salvador," Bacen, Vol. V (May 1966), pp. 19-23.

29. "Exposición del Consejo Económico al Gobernador Nelson
A. Rockefeller," SIECA, Carta Informativa, 92 (June 1969), pp.
4-7.

30. See "Convenio sobre el Régimen de Industrias Centroamericanas de Integración" in Escuela Superior de Administración
Pública (ESAPAC), Los Instrumentos del Mercado Común Centroamericano (San Jose, 1965), pp. 111-116. An English translation
of the agreement is in Joseph Pincus, The Central American Common Market (Mexico: U.S. Agency for International Development,
1962), pp. 171-176.

31. "Protocolo al Convenio sobre el Régimen de Industrias
Centroamericanas de Integración," in ESAPAC, op. cit., pp. 117-
131.

32. GINSA is an atypical firm in that its ownership is widely dispersed throughout the five Central American countries. David E. Ramsett, Regional Industrial Development in Central America: A Case Study of the Integration Industries Scheme (New York: Praeger, 1969), p. 46.

33. GINSA has an installed capacity of 300,000 tires, but its annual production was less than 180,000 in the mid-1960s. The company thus requested the CACM to increase the tariff on standard tires from U.S.$0.90 specific and ten percent ad valorem to U.S. $2.00 specific and ten percent ad valorem. Ibid., pp. 60-73.

34. Consejo Económico, Cuarta Reunión Ordinaria, San Salvador, February 5-9, 1965. Cited in Ramsett, Regional Industrial Development, p. 51.

35. Conversation with Manuel Noriega Morales, Director of the Central American Institute of Research and Industrial Technology (ICAITI), July 14, 1970.

36. Ramsett, who has made an extensive investigation of GINSA, suggests that "the most probable occurrence would seem to be a [geographic] splitting of the market between the two firms." In his Regional Industrial Development, p. 74.

37. For an assessment of Mexico's policy on foreign investment, see I.A. Litvak and C. J. Maule, "Foreign Investment in Mexico: Some Lessons for Canada," Behind the Headlines, Vol. XXX (July 1971).

38. Peru's current industrial policy is discussed in L.N. Willmore, "Estrategia Peruana de Desarrollo Económico," Problemas del Desarrollo, Universidád Nacionál Autonomo de México (U.N.A.M.), 9 (October-December 1971), pp. 97-109.

39. Celso Gamboa, "Ante Imperdonables Fallas del Congreso Jurídico Sobre la Integración Economica Centroamericana," La Nación (San José), November 27 and 28, 1964. Quoted in Lizano F., "El Problema de las Inversiones Extranjeras en Centroamerica," p. 61.

ABOUT THE AUTHORS

DAVID H. POLLOCK, originally of Kinistino, Saskatchewan, Canada, served in the Royal Canadian Air Force during the Second World War. He worked in the IBRD (1949-50), ECLA (1951-63), and UNCTAD (1964-67, as Special Assistant to the Secretary General). Since 1968 he has been Director of the UN Joint ECLA/S Institute Washington Office and a Visiting Professor for the School of International Affairs, Carleton University, Canada. He has contributed to many UN reports and has published separately in Chile, Mexico, U.S.A., and Canada. He has been a member of United Nations delegations to numerous international conferences.

ARCH R. M. RITTER, originally of Sudbury and Kingston, Ontario, Canada, is currently Assistant Professor of Economics and International Affairs, Carleton University, Canada. He was the organizer of the conference entitled "Latin American Prospects for the 1970's: What Kinds of Revolutions?" held under the auspices of the School of International Affairs and the Canadian Institute of International Affairs, from which the articles in this volume were generated.

JEROME LEVINSON, a graduate of Harvard Law School and a Fulbright Scholar, is currently Special Adviser to the President of the Inter-American Development Bank. He is also a lecturer at Georgetown University and co-author, with Juan de Onis, of The Alliance That Lost Its Way (New York: Quadrangle Books, 1970).

JALEEL AHMAD is Associate Professor Economics, Sir George Williams University, Montreal, Canada, and is author of Natural Resources in Low Income Countries (University of Pittsburgh Press, 1960).

CARLOS ALBERTO ASTIZ, currently Associate Professor of Political Science, State University of New York at Albany, has recently published Pressure Groups and Power Elites in Peruvian Politics (Ithaca, N.Y.: Cornell University Press, 1969) and Latin American International Politics; Ambitions, Capabilities and the National Interest of Argentina, Brazil, and Mexico (Notre Dame, Ind.: University of Notre Dame Press, 1969).

ROBERT JAY GLICKMAN, author of Manual for the Printing of Literary Texts and Concordances by Computer, as well as of The Poetry of Julian del Casal: A Critical Edition (forthcoming), is Associate Professor of Hispanic Studies, University of Toronto.

IVAN ILLICH, founder of the Centro Intercultural de Documentacion at Guernavaca, Mexico, is well known, particularly in Canada, for his views on education.

J. C. M. OGELSBY, Associate Professor of History, University of Western Ontario, is currently completing a study of Canadian-Latin American relations since 1867 and is author of some 50 articles and reviews on Latin America.

MARIS PONE is Assistant Professor of Economics, Algonna College, Sault Ste. Marie, Canada, and has previously been engaged as a financial analyst for Ford of Canada, and with the Export Development Corporation, Ottawa, Canada.

VINCENT A. E. RICHARDS, from Antigua, West Indies, is currently a Doctoral Candidate in Economics at Cornell University.

PAUL M. ROSENSTEIN-RODAN, Professor of Economics at M.I.T. and the University of Texas has had a long and distinguished career as adviser to a number of governments including India and Chile as well as the Grupo Andino. He is author of one of the seminal works in the economics of development, "Problems of Industrialization in Eastern and South-Eastern Europe," Economic Journal, 1943, and numerous articles and books since.

G. S. SMITH is Assistant Professor of History, Queen's University, Kingston, Canada, and is author of an article on the War of the Pacific in Hispanic American Historical Review, 1969.

BRADY TYSON is Associate Professor of Political Science, Graduate School of International Service, American University, Washington, D.C.

ROLF JURGEN WESCHE is Assistant Professor and Acting Chairman, Department of Geography, University of Ottawa, Canada.

L. N. WILLMORE is a Doctoral Candidate in Economics, Carleton University, Ottawa, Canada, and recently published, "Free Trade in Manufactures among Developing Countries: The Central American Experience", Economic Development and Cultural Change, July 1972.

HAROLD ARTHUR WOOD is Professor of Geography, McMaster University, Canada. He is author of many articles and books on Latin America including The United States and Latin America (Toronto: Copp-Clark Publishing, 1962) and Northern Haiti: Land, Land Use and Settlement (Toronto: University of Toronto Press, 1963).